The Politics of Unpaid Labour

The Politics of Unpaid Labour

How the Study of Unpaid Labour Can Help Address Inequality in Precarious Work

Valeria Pulignano
Markieta Domecka

OXFORD
UNIVERSITY PRESS

OXFORD
UNIVERSITY PRESS

Great Clarendon Street, Oxford, OX2 6DP,
United Kingdom

Oxford University Press is a department of the University of Oxford.
It furthers the University's objective of excellence in research, scholarship,
and education by publishing worldwide. Oxford is a registered trade mark of
Oxford University Press in the UK and in certain other countries

Published in the United States of America by Oxford University Press
198 Madison Avenue, New York, NY 10016, United States of America

British Library Cataloguing in Publication Data

Data available

Library of Congress Control Number: 2024942157

ISBN 9780198888130

DOI: 10.1093/oso/9780198888130.001.0001

Printed and bound by
CPI Group (UK) Ltd, Croydon, CR0 4YY

Preface and Acknowledgements

This book draws heavily on the intensive and fruitful five-year collaboration of an international and interdisciplinary team of senior and junior scholars, including in alphabetical order, Ladin Bayurgil, Markieta Domecka, Milena Franke, Juliane Imbusch, Claudia Mará, Bart Meuleman, Karol Muszyński, Ella Petrini, Me-Linh Riemann, Hyojin Seo, Lander Vermeerbergen, drawn from a wide range of disciplines to examine precarity at the continuum between paid and unpaid labour. The research for this book was made possible by an Advanced Grant from the European Research Council (ERC) called ResPecTMe under the European Union's Horizon 2020 Research and Innovation programme (grant agreement number 833577), with myself as principal investigator. I am indebted to Miriam Glucksmann, Arne Kalleberg, Rudi Laermans, Jill Rubery, Steve Vallas for their valuable support, guidance, and generous time spent discussing the book's contents, and for providing constructive critical feedback which helped further shape the thinking upon which this book is based. The Centre for Sociological Research (CESO) within the Faculty of Social Science at Katholieke Universitet (KU) Leuven where I am currently based, and the Industrial Relations Research Unit (IRRU) at Warwick University where I was formerly employed as Lecturer and am now a Senior Research Fellow, both provided an intellectually rich and stimulating environment for the gestation of the ideas upon which this book is based. At both, I discussed and received feedback on my earliest papers and articles published over the course of my almost twenty years as a researcher from several colleagues, including Rudi Laermans, Wim van Oorschot, Jos Bergmann, Jacques Billiet, Glenn Morgan, Paul Marginson, Gregor Murray, Tony Elger, Paul Edwards, Guglielmo Meardi, Mike Terry, Linda Dickens, Richard Hyman, James Arrowsmith, Colin Crouch, Tony Edwards. This feedback greatly helped in shaping my career as a comparative labour scholar.

Broadly speaking, the principal motivation behind ResPecTMe is to develop a novel understanding of precarious work and a tool for measuring it which break with the orthodox dichotomy of considering work as either paid (productive or waged) or unpaid (reproductive or unwaged). As historian Van der Linden argues, the traditional view of paid labour is a simple 'artefact' of the post-war era in developed economies as, for most of human history, work has occurred under unstable conditions, with little legal regulation and little expectation of long-term continuity. My intention with ResPecTMe is thus to contribute to an encompassing and relational understanding of work, and especially of precarious work. ResPecTMe is underpinned by a macro-micro and micro-macro approach interlinking different levels of analysis via a (mixed) method combination of qualitative and quantitative research.

Early studies in sociology, social critical philosophy, and economics have discussed unpaid labour in different forms. For example, Ivan Illich talked about 'shadow work', while Arlene Daniels introduced the concept of 'invisible work' to shed light on the 'value' of labour irrespective of whether paid or unpaid. Within the field of economic and labour sociology, Jonathan Gershuny and Miriam Glucksmann have brilliantly acknowledged the need to establish 'dynamic interdependencies' and 'relational interactions' between different socio-economic modes and forms of work, such as paid employment and socially reproductive labour. These interdependencies are at the core of ongoing sociological and economic debates on 'sustainable work' under ecological and digital transformations (see Bénédicte Zimmermann's speech at a webinar on *Transforming Work towards Social-Ecological Sustainability: A Capability Perspective* on 22 February 2024, https://hd-ca.org/event/webinar-talk-on-sustainable-work-by-benedicte-zimmermann). However, to date no serious attempt has been made, by the different critical social science disciplines on work, to explore the various aspects of unpaid labour and to examine how they are integrated into different national institutions and socio-economic contexts. As Paolo Virno (2004) stated in *A Grammar of the Multitude*, subtle forms of exploitation by 'cognitive' and 'immaterial' labour reveal a pressing need for research to encompass different forms of paid and unpaid work.

Differentiating between paid and unpaid labour has contributed to marginalizing unpaid labour in studies on paid employment, especially when conceptualizing precarity in both research and policy. I consider this problematic for two reasons. First, it neglects many forms of unpaid labour within the market, whether performed 'voluntarily' in adherence to a dominant work ethos (i.e., for the sake of a non-monetary higher value) or 'involuntarily' in the form of supplementary tasks outside the defined work scope and thus constituting 'wage theft' among employees or 'income theft' among freelancers. Second, it neglects unpaid labour performed outside the market (e.g., socially reproductive labour) but increasingly necessary to support work—especially when such work is precarious—within the market.

Moved by these critical considerations, ResPecTMe was conceptualized. It took off in October 2019, a few months before the outbreak of the Covid-19 pandemic and its potential negative impact on the project. Despite this challenge, the team of motivated young PhDs and post-doctoral researchers collected a wide and rich array of empirical data around the meanings and motivations of unpaid labour, why people perform it, and how it affects their work and life. The empirical focus is on the biographical narratives of workers and their work audio diaries within three distinctive areas of work in service-based sectors: creative (i.e., dance, TV/film, voice over, theatre operators), social care, and platform work, in a selection of European countries (Sweden, the Netherlands, Germany, the United Kingdom, Italy, Poland, France, and Belgium). Of the more than 400 biographical interviews and around ninety audio work diaries collected within the scope of ResPecTMe, 129 interviews and thirty-eight diaries were selected to inform this book. The diaries reported both the time spent and the typology of each work activity (i.e., tasks) undertaken within a period of ten working days. Unfortunately, only eight diaries were collected for creative dance (ballet) as dancers stopped work due to the pandemic. Similarly, only seven diaries were collected in residential care because of the dramatic consequences of Covid-19. Interviews and diaries were collected in 2020–2.

Based on this rich data the book develops a theory of the politics of unpaid labour to explain how class-based inequality in precarious work unfolds. The focus on inequality in precarity is an unexpected outcome of the inductive qualitative analysis underpinning this study. It started out trying to understand how and to what extent unpaid labour—understood as unpaid labour *time* spent to undertake tasks pertaining to a distinct job description—accounts for precarious work, and ended up revealing the unequal conditions underpinning precarity for those undertaking unpaid, underpaid and poorly paid labour.

Focusing on unpaid labour across different employment statuses (i.e., 'waged' and 'non-waged' labour) allowed us to uncover the contradictions and paradoxes surrounding both emerging (e.g., online platform work) and traditional (e.g., care and creative work) areas of work characterized by endemic unpaid labour *time*. We found that unpaid labour can be a resource which someone can use to mitigate the objectively precarious conditions of their jobs. Yet we also found that this is not always the case, with the disparity explainable by linking precarity to class-based inequality. In the search for a relevant theory to understand and analyse the findings presented in this book, we draw on a critical sociological tradition explaining inequality by social class, with 'class' defined as material inequality in capitalist society structured by both income and identity, such as gender, age, or race. Income and identity indicate two analytically different forms of inequality, however, these forms interact. Findings presented in the book reveal this interaction by illustrating how these 'classes' relate to the possession of resources which can be individual—such as income or socially reproductive labour—or collective, such as social benefits and welfare, as well as those linked to employment such as collective bargaining and workers' voice.

I am delighted to present this book which offers a theoretical framework and research programme for the analysis of inequality in precarity by focusing on unpaid labour. To the best of my knowledge, this is the first book presenting a theory of the politics of unpaid labour which explains why and how its study is important for addressing inequality in precarious work. The book focuses on the class divisions of unpaid labour, the role played by unpaid labour in the distribution and exchange of both economic and symbolic resources, and various forms of capital. It reveals the interconnectedness and 'relationality' of various forms of work across various spaces and domains by presenting evidence of class-based inequality based on the individual and collective resources available to sustain unpaid labour within various sectors and occupational practices, such as creative dance, residential care, and online platform work. Differentiating between employees and freelancers, how people work unpaid in these different work areas reflect the social and economic benefits of socially reproductive labour, individual income and pay, property, and employment-related social benefits which provide the invisible 'scaffolding' supporting their unpaid labour.

As is to be expected, I am indebted to many people alongside those already mentioned. Together with my team, I would like to thank all workers who participated in the research project by giving up their time to be interviewed, facilitated access to individuals and other workers, or otherwise allowed us to observe their working lives. I am also extremely thankful to policymakers, experts, and researchers, such as Niels van Dorn, Martijn Arets, Uma Rani (International Labour Organization (ILO)), Michael Thye (ILO), Janine Berg (ILO), Jonathan Potter (Organisation for Economic Co-operation and Development (OECD)), David Halabiski (OECD), Agnès Parent-Thirion (European Foundation for the Improvement of Living and Working Conditions (Eurofound)), Isabella Biletta, Koen Frenken, all of whom willingly talked to us. Particular thanks are extended to the ResPecTMe team of junior and senior researchers as indicated above, and also to our administrative support, Greet Louw, Marina Franckx, and Martine Parton at the CESO. We are deeply grateful for the invaluable contributions and unwavering dedication of Marina Franckx, whose presence in our administrative team will be profoundly missed. Her legacy will forever be remembered with gratitude and respect.

The evidence presented in this book is only part of the output delivered by ResPecTMe over the last few years. I have co-authored articles and papers based on the project findings with my team and several colleagues to whom I owe particular thanks: Glenn Morgan, Damian Grimshaw, Deborah Dean, Stefan Kirchner, Stefania Marino, Matthew Johnson, Matie Tapia, Rebecca Taylor, Paul Stewart, Carol Stephenson, David Mangan, Annalisa Murgia, Joseph Choonara, and Adam Mrozowski. I also extend my thanks to my colleague and friend Bart Meuleman, with whom we shared the bad and good sides of ResPecTMe, and the Advisory Board, including Arne Kalleberg, Steve Vallas, Jill Rubery, Valerio De Stefano, Agnieszka Piasna (ETUI), Uma Rani and Janine Berg (ILO), Damian Grimshaw, Isabella Biletta, Agnès Parent-Thirion (Eurofound), Bernard Gazier, Kea Tijdens and Paulien Osse (Wage Indicator). I also thank Warwick mates, Jane Parker and Deborah Dean, for being always ready to provide comfort and moral support. I am greatly indebted to Steve Vallas, Knut Laaser, Chris Tilly, and Miguel Martinez Lucio who have carefully read a draft version of this book and provided generous comments. I am immensely thankful to Wolfgang Streeck for the gracious invitation to the Max Planck Institute, where our exchange of ideas and rich conversations have been incredibly enlightening. I have gained invaluable insights from our discussions, and it has been an honour to learn from such a distinguished scholar. I am deeply grateful and eagerly anticipate the opportunity to spend time visiting both the Max Planck Institute, courtesy of the invitation from the current Director Lucio Baccaro, and the Weizenbaum-Institut für die vernetzte Gesellschaft and WZB Berlin Social Science Center, the latter invitation extended by Martin Krzywdzinski.

At the various international workshops and conferences where I was invited to deliver keynote speeches, I was able to present the papers upon which this book is based. These opportunities provided valuable and generous feedback. In this respect, I would like to extend insightful thanks to the organizers of the Manchester Institute for Inequality conference held in Manchester; the Italian Society of Economic Sociology and its Società Italiana di Sociologia Economica (SISEC) conference held in Brescia; the Leeds University and Monash University co-organizers of the international conference on digital transformations held in Prato; the organizers of the Bristol University seminar series; the organizers of the WORKS 2023 international conference at Turku University, where I have also been Visiting Fellow; the organizers of the Industrial Relations Association Conference (IREC) in Durham; the Centre de recherche interuniversitaire sur la mondialisation du travail (CRIMT) Centre for Globalization and Work; the organizers of the workshop on algorithm control at the Max Planck Institute; the Centre for the Study of the International and Comparative Labour Law (ADAPT); the organizers of Research Network 44 (RN44) on Labour Movement at the International Sociological Association conference; the organizers of the AI (Artificial Intelligence) and Work conference, Oxford Internet Institute and the Institute for Ethics in AI, University of Oxford; the Social Boundaries of Work Conference in Uniwersytet Wrocławski; the Centro Studi Marco Biagi in Modena, Eurostat and ILO for the generous invitation to the Global Conference Measuring New Forms of Employment. I extend particular thanks to all participants at these international conferences and events, including the sessions organized during 2024 at several international conferences, such as the International Labour Process Conference at Göttingen: and the World Conference on Employment and Industrial Relations, ILERA/LERA in New York, discussing the findings of the book with prominent scholars in the field of work, employment, and labour markets. In particular I thank Jill Rubery, Antony Rafferty, Stephen Mustchin, Miguel Martinez Lucio, Mark Stuart, Greg Bamber, Gregor Murray, Lucy Taksa, Michele Tiraboschi, Francesco Seghezzi, Edoardo Ales, Luigi Burroni, Steve Vallas, Lisa Dorigatti, Ekatarina Hertog, Kathleen Griesbach, Wolfgang Streeck, Lucio Baccaro, Arianna Tassinari, Alex Wood, Chris Tilly, Mathew Johnson, Martin Kuhlmann, Vera Trappmann, Knut Laaser, Gregor Murray, Isabelle Ferreras, Tom Barnes, Adam Mrozowicki, Anne Kovalainen, Bernd Brandl, and Barbara Becher. In particular, my research unit for comparative research into precarity and labour and for employment relations and labour market research at CESO owes much to the discussions and workshops organized by international research institutes and partnerships. Participating in the CRIMT network gave me the opportunity to develop and test my ideas. A particularly important collaboration started thereafter with Virginia Doellgast and Nathan Lillie within the scope of a book project entitled *Reconstructing Solidarity* (Doellgast, Lillie, Pulignano, 2018) and with Glenn Morgan with whom I had the pleasure of co-authoring several publications (two book chapters and two articles) around the topic of precarious work, unpaid and socially reproductive labour, and solidarity. I owe much to the intense discussions and debates with Glenn which become important milestones in developing the ideas on which this book is based (see Chapter 2). I enjoyed the intellectually challenging and constructive experience with Steve Vallas with whom I co-organized a session on precarious work and the gig economy at the International Labour Process Conference in 2020 and the interesting experience with a community of young and senior researchers—some at ResPecTMe—including Karol

Muszyński, Markieta Domecka, Me-Linh Riemann, Elena Ayala-Hurtado, and Adam Mrozowicki with whom we organized a mini-conference at The Society for the Advancement of Socio-Economics (SASE) in 2021.

I am particularly indebted to Michèle Lamont, Steve Vallas, Rebecca Taylor, and Melinda Cooper for engaging in insightful discussions with us while presenting their research at the ResPecTMe ERC Lecture Series held in May–June 2023. I extend heartfelt gratitude to Ruth Yeoman for her lecture on 'Instituting Meaningfulness (Work and Life) in Democratic Systems', organized as part of the ERC ResPecTMe initiative in May 2024. Insightful and rich, the excellent contributions from these scholars provided a great opportunity to foster debates around the main themes of this book. I am thankful to David Mangan and Karol Muszyński for their valuable contribution and intense discussion around the implications of ResPecTMe for legal studies. I am similarly grateful to the Dean of the Faculty of Economics, Social and Political Science and Communication at Université Catholique de Louvaine (UCLouvain), Professor Olivier Servais, for honouring me with the prestigious Jacques Leclerq Chair, allowing me to share with colleagues and students at UCLouvain the fruit of my work and analyses on the various forms of precarious work and my experience of international comparisons. I thank Marc Zune and Isabelle Ferreras for their support in bridging the gap between the Flemish- and French-speaking parts of our Catholic University. I am also extremely grateful to the Francqui Stichting for allowing me to dedicate so much time to the main theme of the research on which this book is based by awarding me the prestigious Francqui Research Professorship while I was writing this volume. Huge thanks to KU Leuven, the Faculty of Social Science, and its Dean, Steven Eggermont, and all those who have believed in me and helped me make my dreams come true.

Other scholars have provided ongoing feedback on my work over several years along with inspiration, friendship, and emotional nourishment: Gregor Murray, Paul Thompson, Paul Edwards, Steve Vallas, Arne Kalleberg, Jill Rubery, Paul Stewart, Rick Delbridge, Mark Stuart, Miguel Martinez Lucio, Guglielmo Meardi, Marco Hauptmeier, Peter Turnbull, Roland Erne, Marteen Keune, Hajo Holst, Andrea Ciarini, Luisa De Vita, Patrick Cingolani, Stefania Marino, Matthew Johnson, Lucio Baccaro, Wolfgang Streeck, Lucy Taska, Chris Tilly, Adam Mrozowicki, Nadja Doerflinger, Christian Lévesque, Olga Tregaskis, Melanie Simms, Nick Hammer, Tod Rutherford, Vera Trappmann, Ian Greer, Virginia Doellgast, Nathan Lillie, Anna Ilsøe, and Rosemary Batt. Thanks also to Jacques Bélanger, who passed away before this book was conceptualized and whose intellectual inspiration was a source of incommensurable richness for me.

I would like also to thank my freelance proofreader Richard Lomax for being my language sentinel and vociferous watchdog for all aspects of freelancing—your patience and dedication have been an asset for this book. The theory, theoretical and analytical framework on which this book is based was developed by me as part of the ERC Advanced Grant (AdG) ResPecTMe, while the underlying empirics and data analysis were the result of a joint effort by myself and two post-doctoral scholars on the ResPecTMe, Markieta Domecka, mainly covering the three work areas, and Me-Linh Riemann, covering care. Milena Franke and Lander Vermeerbergen have supported the work of the post-doctoral scholars with great mastery. Karol Muszyński has co-authored with myself and Matie Tapia a paper on freelancing platform work, which informed Chapter 6 (See Pulignano et al. 2024). I would also like to thank Bernard Gazier for inspiring and co-writing the economic theory insights presented in Chapter 7 and Damian Grimshaw for writing the Conclusion.

Finally, my family. My lovely mother, Emirena, who passed away while this book was under development: *you have been the guiding light of my life, the unwavering source of belief and support that allowed me to become the person I am today. I dedicate this book to you, with eternal gratitude and love.*

Valeria Pulignano
Katholieke Universitet Leuven

Contents

This research was developed in the framework of the ResPecTMe European Research Council (ERC) project under the European Union's Horizon 2020 Research and Innovation programme (grant agreement number 833577).

Introduction

Why the Politics of Unpaid Labour?

The book's object is to address inequality in precarious work by an approach examining the 'politics' of unpaid labour, delving into the complex interplay of power dynamics and policies which influence how unpaid labour is valued, distributed, and recognized in society. Therefore, the 'politics' refers to the dynamics and policies surrounding its occurrence and the extent to which individuals sustain it: *who benefits from unpaid labour and who sustains it.* Our approach to unpaid labour is specific to paid work within labour markets, looking at the meanings and motivations people attribute to it. We also explore how unpaid labour is sustained, with socially reproductive labour as one important resource.

In a thought-provoking discourse, philosopher Paul Gomberg (2018: 559) compellingly contends that numerous individuals are subjected to 'unjust harm through their labour', pointing *inter alia* to inadequate compensation preventing workers from gaining a dignified livelihood. His assertion beckons us to delve deeper into the intricate fabric of circumstances shaping this phenomenon. In sociology and political and feminist studies, unpaid labour is traditionally understood as work performed outside the confines of the market, such as voluntary or community work, as observed by Tilly and Tilly (1994) and Taylor (2005); or socially reproductive work, as broadly explored by traditional class-based theories within feminist studies (e.g., Mitchel 1975; Crompton and Gubbay 1976; Crompton 1980, 1989; Leiulsfrud and Woodward 1987; Wright 1989) and recalled in Glucksmann's (1995) theory of the total organization of labour. Yet, theorists have started to expand its scope, pointing to its endemic nature as an integral component of paid employment within the market (Pulignano and Morgan 2022). Broadly speaking, studies have primarily revealed how the flexibilization of employment organization, the fissuring of production systems, and employers' use of short-term, on-demand, and insecure employment contracts have become potential determinants of unpaid in-market labour (Weil 2014; Rubery et al. 2018).

The Politics of Unpaid Labour. Valeria Pulignano and Markieta Domecka, Oxford University Press.
 DOI: 10.1093/oso/9780198888130.003.0001

Importantly, the spreading of job insecurity and unpredictability through capital resorting to unpaid labour means that workers are suffering the loss of 'value job features' and becoming subject to the strains of intensified work (Gallie 2017). This loss of 'value' influences both the social and political life of individuals as it includes pay, access to social benefits, and pensions, to mention just a few.

Also within the market, the concept of 'coerced labour' or 'waged unfree labour' as introduced by Strauss (2012), as well as the notion of 'free labour' introduced by Terrranova (2000) and 'wage theft' discussed by Clarke and D'Arcy (2016) and Judge and Cominetti (2019), have gained prominence. While the forms and underlying mechanisms may vary, in many cases workers engage in unpaid labour in response to employer demands (e.g., long hours or tight control over working times) (Massi and Longo 2023) and/or to advance their careers (e.g., internships) (Lee 2015). This implies that unpaid labour can be an important dimension of precarious work (Moore and Newsome 2018), and therefore inherent to the capitalist mode of production, with employers using unpaid labour as a 'value source' to realize profit through the extension and the intensification of the working day (Cole et al. 2022) while workers struggle to have their 'wage effort' compensated.

The 'unpaid labour' referred to in many of these studies is assumed to be performed within paid employment, i.e. for the benefit of a capitalistic employer. However, no explicit distinction is made between employment (under some form of employment contract) and self-employment. For instance, 'wage theft' cannot occur among freelancers because they do not receive a 'wage'. In this book, we make this differentiation, delving into the world of self-employment to arrive at a definition of unpaid labour encompassing both employment and self-employment. Our definition points to unpaid labour being similarly prevalent among certain groups of self-employed workers, albeit in a less discernible form. We then go on to ask why workers (whether employees or self-employed) in different sectors and countries perform unpaid labour, how it is sustained, and how it interlinks with precarious work.

Our empirical analysis reveals that workers may undertake unpaid labour with a view to adhering to an 'ideal worker' norm, wanting to avoid the stigmatization of being punished and hoping to be recognized for the work they do and rewarded in the future. In the words of Weeks (2011) in her brilliant analysis of *The Problem with Work*: 'to the extent that work acquires more meaning as an act of signification than as a production, there is something ritualistic about our adherence to its discipline' (Weeks 2011: 45). Thus, we theorize the link between unpaid labour and precarious work by contextualizing the individual motivations and meanings of unpaid labour within an understanding of the form of exploitation which triggers unpaid labour. Based on an inductive qualitative study covering three occupational fields (or work areas)—creative dance, residential care, and online platform work—our analysis shows in an original way that the exploitation triggering unpaid labour is embedded in class-based and intrinsically unequal power structures. Whether and how precarious work unfolds from unpaid labour therefore depends on an assessment of the social, economic, and institutional resources sustaining unpaid labour. Our analysis looks not only at precarious work *per* se, but also at inequality within precarious work, as reflected in differences in the availability of such resources. Moreover, the three work areas analysed are illustrative of the broad trend of transformation affecting work under neoliberalism, digitalization, and to a growing extent demographics, resulting in the reorganization of paid/unpaid work activities. For example, dancers are being induced to perform project work as independent contractors, freelancers working on online platforms are facing intensified competition *inter alia* from other freelancers working in low-wage countries, while privatization has disrupted the quality and stability of care work (see the Appendix for further explanation on sampling strategy).

While unpaid labour can mitigate or help people cope with situations of precarious work, it requires access to sufficient financial, institutional, and social resources to be sustained. Financial resources can come in the form of self-owned property or a partner's or other household income, while supplementary welfare benefits are an example of institutional resources. socially reproductive labour is an example of a social resource, with unpaid (domestic) work functioning to (re)produce and sustain paid work, as clearly evidenced in advanced industrial societies (Glucksmann 1995, 2005; Crompton 1998, 2006). Examining the economic and social underpinnings of unpaid labour from the perspective of the resources needed to sustain it can thus help address inequality within the context of precarious work by explaining the impact that unpaid labour has on the private lives and work of individuals and their families.

Precarious work is not just an economic condition but also a 'social process' (Alberti et al. 2018: 449; see also Kalleberg and Hewison 2013, on the concept of precarious work as a 'process') affecting both the public (paid employment) and private lives of individuals and their families (see also Choonara 2020; Pulignano and Morgan 2023). Examining precarious work as a process requires a wider political perspective addressing the economic and social dynamics surrounding work. In line with Agarwala (2013), what is needed is a relational definition of precarious work grounded in the social relations between labour, capital, and the state with regard to particular forms of work. Encompassing various forms of paid and unpaid labour inside (e.g., internships) and outside (e.g., care, volunteering, and certain forms of informal work) the labour market, work is a subject of political discourse, with its policy antecedents having important implications for inequality.

Contemporary debates on the sociology of work and employment have shown that precarious work has unfolded unevenly across economic sectors, the Global North, and the Global South, and across different social lines based on gender, race, and citizenship (e.g., Mosoetsa et al. 2016). This points to inequality in precarious work disrupting long-established hierarchies in ways that warrant careful analysis and further theorization (Kalleberg and Vallas 2018). As Bourdieu (1986: 17) has argued, 'agents are distributed in the overall social space ... according to the overall volume of capital they possess'. The uneven distribution of capital between agents reflects the structures underwriting a 'hoarding' of various kinds of opportunities for agents as the expression of power relationships (Tilly 1998). Accordingly, 'durable inequalities' (1998) are constructed within and through the distribution of resources—as economic and symbolic capital—by organizations and institutional fields. While theorists in cultural and labour sociology and employment relations studies have been quite vociferous and explicit in addressing the cultural, economic, and social resources shaping the effects of inequality—for example, in relation to stigmatization (e.g., Lamont et al. 2014; Lamont 2018, 2019; Sanchez et al. 2022); the role of a neoliberal state (e.g., Baccaro and Howell 2017; Howell 2021); and marketization (e.g., Greer and Doellgast 2017; Greer and Umney 2022)—they have been a lot less so in their endorsement of the role of such resources in how they relate to unpaid labour within the context of precarious work.

This book targets this gap in current research, arguing that understanding the politics of unpaid labour can help us to recognize and address the inequalities perpetuating the dynamics and policies surrounding the rise of precarious work under contemporary labour market reforms and societal and technological changes. The growing attention to inequality is tied to concerns about its increase within and among different countries, the deregulation of employment linked to neoliberal policy regimes, and the degradation of work for large groups of workers (Evans and Tilly 2016; Lee et al. 2020). At the same time, scholarly work has echoed the deleterious effects of inequality for democracy, democratic political systems, and society (Streeck 2016), highlighting not only its corrosive impact but also underscoring the rising challenge posed by populist political parties on the right, whose ideologies and actions further strain the fabric of democratic institutions and societal cohesion (Crouch 1999).

How then are we to think about unpaid labour enhancing our understanding of inequality in precarious work? At the core of the concept of 'sociological imagination' (Mills 1959) is the need for a more nuanced account of unpaid labour to advance understanding of inequality within the context of precarious work by forging the connection between the 'personal and the political'. This means establishing a relationship between the micro properties of the social system, such as the motivations and meanings individuals attribute to the unpaid labour they perform in a context where employment is increasingly precarious, and the macro-structural patterns of the system, such as the way in which individuals sustain unpaid labour by accessing resources within the social and economic private sphere of the family, as well as the regulatory arrangements at the level of the state and other social institutions such as labour markets or industrial relations systems. In other words, we explain the meanings of unpaid labour by combining accounts of the shifts in macro-level contexts associated with transformations in national labour markets and industries, examining the impact these shifts have on what is experienced at the individual level (Lefebvre 1974).

Barney and Felin (2013) refer to a 'double movement' to show that social interactions at a micro level create structures which in turn have a causal influence on agents and their social interactions, as they exert a potent influence on individual experiences of work arrangements (see also Marsden 1999; and broadly Coleman 1990). Hence, we argue that the way in which unpaid labour is embedded in shared systems of individual meanings more importantly reveals the unequal class-based structures of power relationships within broader societal and institutional fields. As we show, power dynamics can help theorize inequality in precarious work by accounting for the class-based power structures of exploitation triggering unpaid labour. These structures are underpinned by state and employment policy in labour markets. Thus, the politics of unpaid labour help address inequality in precarious work by reproducing and maintaining existing class structures through the unequal distribution of the resources required for it to be sustained. These resources intersect with socially reproductive labour and income support in the household sphere as they require social and financial support in the form of individual and family income. They also encompass the sphere of individual identities and other cultural resources (e.g., language, knowledge, skills, work ethos), and cover institutional support through labour markets' regulatory arrangements and social benefits.

Our approach to unravelling the politics of unpaid labour requires a theory able to explain how unpaid labour entails precarious work and how and to what extent precarious work unfolds from unpaid labour, based on theories and concepts of the 'ideal worker' norm and resilience as framed within power structures.

Our Argument in Brief

Discussing unpaid labour, precarious work, and inequality in capitalist society, this book offers a comprehensive exploration of the intersection between these three issues, while also examining the theorization necessary to address them. It suggests focusing on the political dimension (i.e., the 'politics') of unpaid labour as a potential way of addressing inequality within the context of precarious work. Such a focus spotlights the power relations and inequality structures produced, maintained, and reinforced by unpaid labour under certain conditions and which help reproduce these same conditions. The result is a compelling analysis of the social, economic, cultural, and institutional resources sustaining unpaid labour and thus is key to theorizing how and to what extent inequality in precarious work unfolds from unpaid labour. Importantly, our argument suggests a novel theoretical lens towards the study and research of precarious work.

Examining how the study of unpaid labour can help in addressing inequality in precarious work by revealing its economic and social underpinnings, we highlight the power dynamics and policies surrounding unpaid labour. Our look at the meanings and motivations people associate with it in turn enables us to understand its underlying structural and ideological conditions: generally speaking, when workers are lucky enough to have access to sufficient resources, unpaid labour can indeed create a 'narrative of hope' (Lamont 2019)—itself a resource against precarious work—in all other cases however, they may be doomed to precarity.

In a nutshell, our argument is that the underpinnings of unpaid labour, i.e. the structural and ideological conditions promoting and legitimizing it, encompass both the private (domestic) household sphere and the public paid employment sphere where regulatory arrangements provided through state policy and other institutions (e.g., welfare, collective bargaining) may help sustain it—although to different extents—within different national settings (see, e.g., Mosoetsa et al. 2016; Pulignano 2018). While a broad body of literature in the sociology of work and employment explores the changing social divisions of labour, with a focus on how socially reproductive labour supports paid employment (for a review of these debates, see, e.g., Pettinger et al. 2005), such research currently lacks analysis of the impact of the transformations occurring within national welfare and employment institutions on such divisions of labour. Given that socially reproductive labour now extends beyond the household realm and that the state increasingly considers it within the economic framework, we argue that it is beneficial to examine the evolving social divisions of labour by integrating a perspective combining public state policy and institutional analyses. This approach can provide valuable insights into how unpaid labour impacts the study of inequality, particularly in the context of precarious work. On the other hand, we contend that research in the institutionalist tradition of employment, industrial relations, and the political economy explaining how neoliberal politics and policies have harmed working conditions for workers by increasing capital discretion over labour needs to address the social and ideological processes driving all this.

Themes, Research Questions, and Contributions

The book explores two main themes. First, we look at the motivations and meanings people associate with unpaid labour. In the face of broadening forms of unpaid labour both inside and outside the market, we expect the motivations and meanings people associate with unpaid labour to change. Second, we examine the resources required to sustain unpaid labour. We thus interrogate the dynamics and structural conditions driving inequality in precarious work, exploring how it is supported in its different forms through economic, social, and institutional resources, across (and within) different jobs, sectors, and labour markets. Bringing these two themes together provides insights into the dynamics and processes contributing to inequality in precarious work by relating the *what*, *why*, and *how* issues of unpaid labour, here understood as the time and effort invested to enter *and sustain* employment socially and financially. These two themes are behind the following research questions at the core of the book:

Why does someone perform unpaid labour in paid employment? *What* are the motivations and meanings workers associate with unpaid labour?

How does unpaid labour articulate with precarious work. *How* do existing power structures of exploitation, which are class defined and therefore broadly unequal, contribute to producing, reproducing, and maintaining precarious work, while at the same time profiting from the unpaid labour?

How and *to what extent* are individuals able to access the resources needed to socially and economically sustain unpaid labour? Therefore, *how* and *to what extent* do state policy, framed within labour market practices, and other regulatory and policy arrangements support those performing unpaid labour? *What* are the implications of unpaid labour for income and wealth as well as for socially reproductive labour in families and households?

In short, this book makes four contributions:

First, we contribute to labour market research on unpaid labour by clearly establishing the characteristics differentiating employment from self-employment, and how these lead to a revised definition of unpaid labour.

Second, we contribute to employment relations research on precarious work by illustrating how unpaid labour can address inequality in precarious work which is class based. Importantly, we show that a nuanced analysis of the 'politics' of unpaid labour is necessary to appreciate inequality in precarious work by showing that unpaid labour is both shaped by class and serves to reproduce class interests. This implies that whether unpaid labour entails precarious work and whether precarious work automatically unfolds from unpaid labour depend on the social and economic underpinnings of unpaid labour, in turn revealing who performs unpaid labour, how they do it, and in what context. From the perspectives of the workers who perform unpaid labour, unpaid labour is driven by an 'ideal norm' which prioritizes work by disciplining workers through systems of punishment and reward underpinning shame and stigma.

Third, we contribute to the sociology of work and employment—and specifically the social division of labour and socially reproductive labour supporting all forms of paid employment—by illustrating that understanding unpaid labour in all its different facets helps explain how inequality in precarious work arises. This necessitates an in-depth analysis of the ongoing changes in welfare, employment, and state institutional policies. The underpinnings of unpaid labour—i.e., what we refer to as the 'politics of unpaid labour'—encompass power dynamics and policies surrounding its occurrence and how individuals sustain this unpaid labour. Resources at both the micro-individual level (e.g., family support, other sources of income, knowledge, and identity) and macro-regulatory level (e.g., employment and welfare policy) are key to sustain unpaid labour. These individual and collective resources enable individuals to build resilience to cope with unpaid labour.

Fourth, and directly linked to the third contribution, we add the collective dimension. This refers to labour market institutions and their promotion of what is known as the capability approach in socio-economic studies. We illustrate that whether unpaid labour fosters worker dignity and respect is influenced not only by personal resources and access to rights (Sen 1993), with wealthier and well-resourced individuals better able to perform unpaid labour due to better respective opportunity structures, but also by socially encompassing labour market institutions potentially providing the 'collective capabilities' necessary for social groups to build resilience *vis-à-vis* unpaid labour. The argument gains further depth when seen through Lamont's (2023) recent proposition. She urges us to embrace the diverse capacities of individuals to truly 'see others', arguing that: 'Once we reduce stigma, celebrate differences, and embrace the diversity of what humans are and can do, we can perhaps experience the promises of dignity for all' (2023: 15). This call prompts us to consider the necessity of constructing conducive conditions within the labour market. To genuinely honour the diversity of human abilities and actions, it becomes imperative to cultivate an environment within labour structures that allows for the manifestation of these diverse capabilities. Therefore, aligning with Lamont's call necessitates the establishment of labour market conditions facilitating and accommodating the varied ways in which individuals contribute, perform, and participate in unpaid labour, thereby affirming their dignity and diverse potential.

The Structure of the Book

The book is divided into three parts. Part I lays out the framework upon which our theory of the politics of unpaid labour is conceived. Our intention is for the theory to enhance our understanding of inequality in precarious work. It consists of three chapters presenting the argument and introducing the different concepts and theories of the 'ideal worker' norm, and the stigma and resilience which inform the theorization of the link between unpaid labour, precarious work, and inequality. Following the introduction of the book's main argument, themes, and research questions, Chapter 1 critically examines arguments of unpaid labour, precarious work, and inequality—all the while differentiating between employees in employment relationships and freelancers in service provision relationships—and introduces the theorization on the politics of unpaid labour. Chapter 2 develops the critique presented in Chapter 1 by examining arguments of unpaid labour and precarious work and discussing the implications for socially reproductive labour. It critically revises the common assumption that precarious work only refers to labour markets where the effects of organizational and institutional contexts on paid employment are clearly identifiable. Chapter 3 takes these arguments further, looking at how unpaid labour helps address inequality in precarious work by focusing on the class-based power structures of exploitation to explain how individuals experience the socio-economic activities surrounding work in their biographical histories in different ways. This approach requires a different kind of theorization specifically addressing inequality in precarious work. In particular, the theorization we suggest is based on the politics of unpaid labour and on understanding how and to what extent unpaid labour can be a resource to mitigate precarious work by building resilience through accessing resources of different kinds in order to sustain unpaid labour. In short, it reveals how unpaid labour is embedded in different ways in employment structures and practices, highlighting the structural inequalities through which opportunities and resources are circumscribed by class, including prestige, gender, and wealth. In so doing, we assess the extent to which precarious work can automatically unfold from unpaid labour, addressing the implications for inequality.

Consisting of Chapters 4, 5, and 6, Part II presents the empirical evidence from three work areas or occupational fields in the countries where we inductively based our theorization. We look at whether a binary or non-binary relationship exists between precarious work and the type of work in each work area, whereby the terms *binary* and *non-binary* indicate the strength of this relationship. Chapter 4 looks at creative dance in Sweden and the Netherlands. Belonging to what are known as the cultural and creative industries (CCI), creative dance (in our case ballet) is a field that has suffered from sweeping austerity-driven funding cuts, especially in the Netherlands. These cuts have led to a decline in permanent employment and a rise in freelancing in the form of project work. Young people, especially women, enter creative dance not for financial gain but *for the sake of art*. As much of the work is un- or underpaid in relation to the hours worked, survival in creative dance relies heavily on having access to financial and social resources provided by family support, such as networking opportunities. Consequently, the sector becomes class based, meaning that an individual's social position and opportunities within this field are strongly influenced by their inherited socio-economic status, leading to the perpetuation of prestige and advantage through family connections and resources. It is also a sector requiring subordination—often at the expense of a dancer's private life—and engendering the concomitant resilience.

Chapter 5 investigates residential care in the United Kingdom and Germany. As highlighted by the Covid-19 pandemic, residential care is an essential service provided by highly motivated caregivers. However, like most social occupations, it is underpaid. People—generally women from working-class backgrounds—enter the sector knowing that it is poorly paid. Unlike creative dance, the sector is easy to enter, as—especially in the UK—few formal qualifications are required. While caregivers often form emotional ties to residents, they are finding it increasingly impossible to 'live' these ties due to the intensification of work resulting from the marketization of the care sector. Driven by their desire to offer the best care to 'their' residents and thus working *for the sake of care*, they perform unpaid labour to accomplish schedules dictated by the stopwatch. This unpaid labour in turn impinges on their private lives, forcing them to decide whether to prioritize their low-paid but emotionally fulfilling work or family life. In several of our cases, carers resort to part-time or unconventional working hours in their pursuit of a satisfactory work-life balance. This comes at the cost of depleted financial resources engendering precarity and compromised social well-being and health.

Finally, Chapter 6 analyses online platform work in Belgium, the Netherlands, France, Italy, and Poland, looking at how translators, copywriters, information technology (IT) specialists, and other freelancers come to terms with platforms. We find two types of platforms: those where freelancers bid for work offered by clients, and those where clients seek the services of freelancers on the platform. While the first type of platform is very competitive and has little interest in either fostering freelancers' careers or building long-term client relationships, the latter type is the opposite, promoting freelancer portfolio building and long-term relationships with clients. Despite all freelancers striving to achieve the good reputation (*working for the sake of their reputation*) crucial for survival in the digital realm, the different platforms and structures within these digital landscapes can exacerbate existing class differences. Within this framework, economic necessity persists disparately among freelancers due to the varying platform models and structures. This situation highlights how class-based circumstances intersect with platform dynamics, influencing the economic realities experienced by freelancers.

The common thread running through Part II is the struggle experienced by workers in the three areas in coming to terms with low-paid, underpaid, and unpaid work, while developing the personal resilience needed to adhere to a self-given work ethos, the 'ideal worker norm'—*for the sake of art*, *for the sake of care*, or *for the sake of reputation*. This is more the case in the absence of strong encompassing social institutions.

Part III concludes the book, presenting an analysis of each work area and drawing comparative reflections across the different work areas by building on a capability approach in socio-economic studies (in Chapter 7 by Bernard Gazier and Valeria Pulignano) as well as some practical and policy implications with relevance for wage regulation and collective bargaining (in the Conclusion by Damian Grimshaw). The Appendix presents the epistemological approach, data analysis, and research design.

Background Information

The book is the product of an intensive five-year collaboration between a group of senior and junior scholars drawn from a wide range of disciplines to examine precarious work at the continuum between paid and unpaid work within the scope of an European Research Council (ERC) Advanced Grant called ResPecTMe. The empirical focus is on the narratives of employees and freelancers in three distinct areas of work: creative dance, residential care, and online platform work. Challenged by the Covid-19 pandemic, 129 biographical interviews were conducted, whereby thirty-eight respondents also recorded audio work diaries reporting the time spent and the typology of each work activity (i.e., tasks) undertaken within a period of ten working days. Diaries were collected in a homogeneous way from the different work areas. Creative dance and residential care turned out to be the exceptions, with only a few diaries collected due to people being forced to stop work because of the Covid-19 pandemic (dance) and the dramatic circumstances with which care workers were confronted because of the pandemic. Narratives and diaries were collected in 2020–2.

PART I
THEORIZING THE POLITICS OF UNPAID LABOUR

1
Unpaid Labour and Inequality in Precarious Work

Unpaid Labour, Power, and Class

What Is Unpaid Labour?

This book uses two all-encompassing perspectives to investigate unpaid labour within capitalist markets: the formal, legalistic aspect (*what* is unpaid labour?), and the informal—yet just as important—'work ethos' aspect or 'ascetic ideal' (see Weeks 2011: 46) making what would *prima facie* and formally be considered as free, voluntary, unpaid labour a 'must' or even a 'privilege' for those performing it (*why* is unpaid labour performed), thus an 'ethic's goal ... the supposed reward for this ethical practice' (2011: 46), and how this is intertwined with social considerations of power and class.

The following section starts by examining the formal aspect in order to arrive at a definition of unpaid labour taking account of different work relationships. These relationships are reflected in the three occupational fields or work areas covered in this book (i.e., creative dance, residential care, online platform work), whereby each features prevalent unpaid labour. Unpaid labour can be (or cannot be) a potential resource within each field, thereby reflecting Bourdieu's (1994) early analysis of a *social field* as a structural space organized around specific kinds of resources (capitals) or a combination thereof.

We spotlight the differences between employees and the self-employed, noting that employment relationships (ERs) dominate in the field of residential care, while service provision relationships (SPRs) (involving project workers or freelancers) dominate in dance and online platform work (see Appendix). In any discussion on unpaid labour performed within the context of paid work, it is essential to differentiate between that performed by an employee within an ER and that performed by a self-employed worker (aka freelancer) within an SPR. In the former, an employer pays for a specific amount of a worker's labour, whether for an unspecified period (an

The Politics of Unpaid Labour. Valeria Pulignano and Markieta Domecka, Oxford University Press.
 DOI: 10.1093/oso/9780198888130.003.0002

open-ended ER) or for a specific period (a fixed-term relationship). Similarly, the number of hours to be worked each day is contractually agreed: employees may work full-time, part-time, or for a demand-driven flexible number of hours. In the first two cases, any hours worked above the specified number count as overtime. Pay can take the form of hourly wages or a monthly salary determined by a collective agreement or an individual employment contract. In 90% of International Labour Organization (ILO) member states, a minimum wage applies. Minimum wages have been defined as the minimum amount of remuneration that an employer is required to pay wage earners for the work performed during a given period, which cannot be reduced by collective agreement or an individual contract (Berg 2015). This definition refers to the binding nature of minimum wages, regardless of the method of fixing them. Minimum wages can be set in two fundamentally different ways (Schulten 2006). Collective agreements between trade unions and employers can define the lowest possible wage grade in a certain company, sector, or national economy (Picot 2023: 235). Alternatively, the state can determine by law the lowest legal level of wages. Where force of law applies, any employer paying less than the minimum wage is liable to criminal charges for 'wage theft'. Conversely to minimum wages, a living wage is the amount an individual or family would need to make to avoid living in poverty. This amount is usually higher than the minimum wage and is not mandated by law. In addition to pay, workers receive statutory social protection in the form of health and unemployment insurance, contributions to a pension, paid leave, and possibly other fringe benefits. Moreover, job-related training and the equipment needed to perform the assigned work ('the tools of the trade') are generally paid for by the employer. Subject to employer approval, any work performed over and above the contractually agreed amount counts as overtime, paid either at an overtime rate or compensated by time off at a later date.

An SPR has nothing in common with an ER. The worker does not work as an employee for an employer but as a self-employed service provider ('freelancer') for a client, in competition with other service providers and thus is subject not to labour law but to competition law. As labour law does not apply, there are no restrictions on the number of hours worked per day or when work is performed. The guiding motto for any freelancer is to 'make hay while the sun shines', i.e. to work hard in periods where demand is high, in the knowledge that sufficient income has to be generated for periods when demand is low. For long-term assignments, a service contract specifying the work to be performed and the associated remuneration may be agreed between the freelancer and the client. Short-term assignments ('gigs') may be performed without a formal contract or purchase order, although in some cases service providers may have a framework contract (in many cases similar to a demand-driven zero-hour contract) binding them to a client and specifying pay rates for specific tasks (as commonly found among platform-based food delivery couriers). Such rates set by the client and accepted by the service provider are akin to 'piece rates'. This does not mean that there may not also be cases of self-employed contractors being paid on an hourly basis. For example, for undefined projects where the total amount of work is uncertain, hourly billing can be more practical. Whatever the form of contractual relationship, the rate should be high enough to provide an income allowing the freelancer to invest in training and the tools of his/her trade and to cover his/her basic needs, especially in periods without paid work or where demand for his/her services is low. In other words, remuneration should be a 'living rate' comparable to a 'living wage' in a standard ER and not *per se* condemning the freelancer to precarity. But even here, it should be remembered that it is the responsibility of the freelancer (and not of the organization avail itself of his/her services) to earn sufficient income (a living income). As in several countries (e.g., Germany, the Netherlands) a freelancer has no statutory social protection, so remuneration should also be high enough to provide the worker with access to an equivalent level of protection with respect to health and a basic pension. It should be remembered that there is no such thing as unemployment in the world of freelancing, and thus no general access to unemployment benefits (although a few national non-statutory schemes exist to cover periods of inactivity, for example among performing artists—see Pulignano et al. 2021). Remuneration should thus also be high enough to cover such periods of inactivity. Disability insurance to cover any periods where a freelancer is physically unable to work is advisable, but not always affordable. Periods where a freelancer has no work can be used to maintain and/or upgrade skills to improve attractiveness to clients (referred to here as 'personal investment work'), to search for new clients ('self-marketing' and 'branding'), or to 'enjoy life' (insofar as sufficient income has been previously gained) (see Table 1.1).

Given the imponderability inherent to freelancing, it would seem that an ER is always preferable to an SPR, especially seen from the perspective of job security. Nevertheless, many people enjoy freelancing on account of the autonomy it can provide, insofar as a modicum of success (expressed in earnings) is achieved. For many, an ER is regarded as too restrictive for their chosen personal lifestyle. However, there are also occupations where only few ERs are available. Such situations can occur when an employing organization's volume of work for the occupation in

Table 1.1 Comparison between an ER and an SPR

	Employment relationship	Service provision relationship
Worker classification	Employee	Service provider, aka freelancer
Relationship	Employee-employer	Service provider-client
Contract forms	Open-ended/fixed-term/part-time/zero-hour employment contract governed by national and EU employment legislation	For larger/longer assignments: service a provision contract or purchase order (but also a non-contractual 'gentleman's agreements') For short assignments (gigs): possibly a framework contract (similar to a zero-hour contract) or a non-contractual 'gentleman's agreement'
Work scope definition	Defined in the employment contract (number of hours, tasks to be performed, pay and other entitlements)	For project work: Defined in the service provision contract (tasks to be performed, fee, payment modalities) For gig work: None—the gig implicitly defines the work scope
Remuneration	Hourly wage (+ paid overtime) / monthly salary (possibly with paid overtime) set either individually or via a collective agreement	Fee for a completed assignment / rate per task (piece rate) or hourly rate paid
Other employment benefits	Paid leave, sick pay, possibly a company pension, bonuses	None
Statutory social security	Unemployment and health insurance and state pension contributions.	Possibly health insurance and state pension contributions (country-specific); basically no unemployment insurance
Income guarantees	Minimum wage (country–specific)	None
Working hours / statutory leave	Determined by national and EU legislation or collective agreements	None ('make hay while the sun shines')
Training and tools of the trade	Provided by the employer	Provided by the freelancer, whereby the cost thereof should be recoupable via the rates charged

Source: Author's elaboration.

question is too small or too volatile to warrant an employment contract. For example, whereas a small organization with merely a handful of translations a year will resort to freelancers (engaged either directly or via the intermediary of an agency or platform), a large international organization may have its own translation department. Moreover, there are occupations which typically target private households, and where there is thus no employer in the normal sense of the word. Typical occupations in this category include craftspeople or certain liberal professions like physicians or architects.

Another driver of freelancing is project work, as found in the field of creative and cultural industries (CCIs). As most potential CCI employers are subject to tight budgetary constraints and unable to plan more than a year in advance, they resort to freelancers. Whatever the circumstances, the dearth of ER opportunities can thus lead to 'involuntary freelancing' where a person desiring to work in a certain area (for instance, dancers or translators, as investigated in this book in the chapters on creative dance and online platform work) has no other option (i.e., involuntary) but to freelance. However, we make no attempt to assess whether the self-employment is 'real' or 'bogus', as this is outside the scope of this book.

Bearing in mind the distinction between an ER and an SPR, we now proceed to define unpaid labour. Looking first at the ER, at first sight unpaid labour is when an employee works overtime without being paid. However, a distinction has to be made here between whether or not the overtime is performed voluntarily, for instance in line with a self-defined work ethos or calling. When not performed voluntarily, it formally and legalistically constitutes 'wage theft'. In their reconceptualization of 'wage theft', Cole et al. (2022) criticize the existing concept of wage theft as a 'labour market violation' in the form of unpaid hours, unpaid annual leave, and unpaid overtime (see also Clarke and D'Arcy 2016; Judge and Cominetti 2019), contending that unpaid labour results primarily from exploitation by capital:

> Marx drew extensively on reports from the Factory Acts to explain how the extension and intensification of the working day enhances the valorisation process and generates profit for employers. In employers' own words: 'If you allow me ... [the capitalist] to work only ten minutes in the day over-time, you put one thousand a year in my pocket' (Reports, etc., 31 October 1856: 34, cited in Marx 1976: 352). Central to the valorisation process is the ability of employers to extract more labour time from workers than would be necessary to simply reproduce their labour-power. (Cole et al. 2022: 3)

The situation where overtime is performed voluntarily is trickier to define. From a purely formal perspective, an employer is under no compulsion to pay for such work, thus making it unpaid. However, as we will see in this book, employees may be guided by a certain work ethos, characterized by the norm of the 'ideal worker', to work longer hours than those specified in their employment contract in order to fulfil their own expectations of how the work should be done and when it can be considered completed. In cases of work intensification where work is increasingly divided into rigid employer-defined time slots, workers—for example in the care sector—may feel obliged to overrun the time slots in order to provide the service quality defined by their work ethos or calling. As this means that they are unable to complete their assigned work within their defined working hours, they end up performing the work unpaid. This cannot *per se* be defined as wage theft, as an employer can always argue that the work is doable within the assigned time, and that it is the personal decision of the worker to invest personal time. However, it becomes wage theft when an employer *opportunistically* takes advantage of (i.e., exploits) this, fully aware that overtime will be performed by the worker to conform to a certain work ethos and thereby helping upgrade the organization's reputation. This is likely to be the case within situations of professionalism. For example, Kelly and Moen's (2020) brilliant study on *Overload* illustrates how a large US electronics firm exploited software design professionals by paying them just a little bit more than the rate over which they were then exempt from overtime pay. For the purpose of this book, all wage theft and all work personally invested to conform with a certain work ethos are defined as unpaid labour.

Defining unpaid labour within an SPR is more difficult. From a formal perspective, there is no such thing as unpaid labour in an SPR, as freelancers themselves are responsible for managing their time and effort. Whether for instance a translation for which a freelance translator receives €100 is performed in one hour or ten hours, during the day or at night, on a weekday or at the weekend, is of no concern to the client. The latter pays solely for the completed assignment, irrespective of the hours worked or the tools used. At the end of the day, the time available to a freelancer to perform work is either paid for by a client or is invested by the freelancer to gain work ('personal investment work'). It is the responsibility of the freelancer to charge a 'living rate', i.e. a rate generating a living income and covering his/her expenses in work acquisition, training, and the tools of the trade. It can be expected that precarity will be incurred when the rates charged are insufficient to guarantee a living income.

Nevertheless, we contend that there are situations where work is unpaid, whereby we need to differentiate between short-term gigs and longer term project work. Looking first at gig work, our analysis of online platform work uncovers situations where chargeable rates are subject to downward pressure, for example through the (transnational) competition generated by bidding for gigs. As a result, some of the time and effort invested becomes unpaid, in the sense that it is not recoupable through a chargeable 'living' rate. A situation of 'income theft'—comparable to the possible 'wage theft' experienced in an ER—may even arise when a client *opportunistically* exploits a freelancer's position, for instance bending his/her arm to make him/her perform unpaid additional work within an assignment in return for a good rating.

Turning to longer term project work performed by freelancers, we again see situations where the rates chargeable are insufficient to provide a living income covering all expenses, including their personal investment work (see also Pulignano, Dean, et al. 2023). As seen in our analysis of dancers, a work area where labour supply exceeds demand, and online platform work, the resulting competition exerts downward pressure on rates, to the extent that they may not be sufficient to guarantee a living income. Moreover, freelancers may, through no fault of their own, be unable to charge a fee sufficiently high to guarantee a living income, for example when the client does not have sufficient financial leeway to pay a 'living fee' (as, for example, found among dance companies operating on a shoestring budget). In both cases, freelancers end up performing unpaid labour. However, should the client be able to pay for such extra work but refuse to do so, s/he may be accused of 'income theft'. Looked at from another perspective, a freelancer performing project work can be deemed to be performing unpaid labour when the total fee received from the client, divided by the hours required to perform the contracted work (including any personal investment work directly related to the assignment), results in an hourly remuneration below the minimum wage. In this case, the hours needing to be remunerated to attain the minimum wage are to be regarded as unpaid.

The term 'unpaid' implicitly suggests that the work should be paid. Notwithstanding the financial aspects of unpaid work discussed above, we contend that pay is not necessarily monetary, but can take the form of non-monetary recognition or reputation enhancement. As we will see later in this book, this is an important factor prompting workers to perform unpaid labour.

Concluding this section defining unpaid labour for both employees and freelancers, we overarchingly define unpaid labour as *the time and effort people invest to undertake tasks which relate to the work implicitly or explicitly assigned to them, but for which they are not paid.* Having defined unpaid labour, we go on to discuss the role of power and class in its emergence.

The Role of Power and Class in Unpaid Labour

Precarious work is defined by Kalleberg (2009: 2) as 'employment that is uncertain, unpredictable, and risky from the point of view of the worker', while ongoing discussion in the sociology of work and employment on precarious work has pointed to social class being an important analytical category (Kalleberg and Vallas 2018). For example, Standing (2011) has argued that the precariously employed constitute a heterogeneous 'class in the making', while Choonara (2020) has powerfully emphasized the central role of class distinctions in discussions on precarious work. Similarly, Pugh (2015) has pointed to marked class and gender differences when assessing how people cope with precarious conditions, while Witteveen (2018) has found variation in precarious conditions across different social classes, with women, racial-ethnic minorities, and lower class labour market entrants in the US more likely to encounter insecurity. Yet, Kalleberg and Vallas (2018) warn that there is still a need to theorize how to articulate social class as an analytical category adding inequality to precarious work.

Drawing on this important enquiry, this book introduces the politics of unpaid labour as a theoretical framework to explain the power dynamics and processes encompassing how unpaid labour can entail inequality in precarious work by reproducing class structures. Importantly, we start by examining whether and how unpaid labour can be a resource against precarious work. Whether this is the case depends on a person's accompanying social, financial, cultural, and institutional resources (or 'capitals'; see Savage et al. 2005), in reference to sociological theories of social resilience. As the availability and accessibility of these resources is to a large extent class based, inequalities reproducing social differences through social class are generated.

We go on to reveal the ideological and material processes framed by the power structures of exploitation which trigger unpaid labour—something we uncover by using theories and concepts of the 'ideal worker' norm and stigma. As we demonstrate, the social norms surrounding the 'ideal worker' and the processes of shaming and stigmatization associated with them significantly shape the motivations and meanings people associate with unpaid labour and the landscape of precarious work which subsequently unfolds. This is because the enforcement of the 'ideal worker' norm and stigmatization of those not conforming to it due to a scarcity of resources further solidify existing power dynamics and class-based structures and hierarchies. This in turn reinforces the unequal distribution of labour and resources, leading to the perpetuation of inequality within precarious work settings due to only those endowed with the requisite resources being able to perform the unpaid labour required by the 'ideal worker' norm. We conclude by stating that the social norms surrounding the 'ideal worker' and the processes of disciplining through stigmatization not only shape individual experiences of unpaid labour but also contribute to broader social and economic inequalities in precarious work. By highlighting the impact of these norms and processes, our work emphasizes the importance of understanding and challenging the underlying structures perpetuating inequality in precarious work. It calls for a critical examination of the material and social factors shaping the realities of labour under conditions of unpaid labour and calls for the unequal power dynamics perpetuating inequality in precarious conditions to be addressed.

The empirical section of the book (Chapters 4–6) focuses on the experiences of individuals, how they interpret and attribute meanings to the unpaid labour they perform, and how and to what extent they support it by drawing upon resources they access within their social, economic, and institutional constituencies. As we explain further below, this offers a novel perspective towards understanding how inequality in precarious work is created. While existing literature has focused on individual experiences of working conditions, we contend that a specific focus on how individuals experience unpaid labour within distinct social, economic, and institutional macro-level contexts complements contemporary studies on precarious work and inequality by offering a broader horizon able to inform our understanding of why, despite the bad (precarious) conditions of their jobs, people stay in these jobs and come to terms with their consequences.

Towards a Theory of the Politics of Unpaid Labour

Unpaid Labour, Inequality, and Precarious Work

Based on concepts and theories of resilience, which we interpret as resources around which the opportunity and capacity for power and agency are framed, and the 'ideal worker' norm underpinning stigmatization, this book attempts to define a theory of the politics of unpaid labour to explain how the study of unpaid labour helps address inequality in precarious work by revealing the dynamics surrounding the use and exploitation of labour that is not monetarily compensated and which therefore remains unpaid. We explain why it is worthwhile exploring the conditions of exploitation triggering unpaid labour in and/or in the run-up to paid employment in order to appreciate inequality in precarious work. Following the tradition of the critical political economy of work and employment in sociology, we connect the concepts of the 'ideal worker' norm and resilience to the structural histories of power as reflected in existing hierarchies at work, such as social class through prestige, gender, and employment status. In so doing, we employ novel avenues to theorize the way inequality in precarious work is addressed, paying attention to three main concepts and related sociological theories.

First, the concept of the 'ideal worker' norm (Williams et al. 2013) prioritizes work over private life and underpins stigmatization (Goffman 1963). We use this concept to theorize the link between unpaid labour and precarious work, investigating the motivations and meanings which workers associate with their unpaid labour. These meanings reflect fulfilment consistent with any 'identification with and systematic devotion to a "work ethic"' (Weeks 2011: 46). As we show, however, these meanings relate to a logic of discipline which underpins the politics of unpaid labour with punishments and rewards for the worker. In essence, we explain how and to what extent unpaid labour entails precarious outcomes, contextualizing these motivations, fulfilment, and meanings within an understanding of the form of exploitation triggering unpaid labour and which we found to be embedded in intrinsically unequal class-based power structures (Tyler 2018). In summary, we assert that considering the influence of ideology as 'hegemonic' (for further insights on 'ideological hegemony', see for example Weeks 2011; Fleming 2014) is crucial to understanding both labour control mechanisms and the experience of precarity, particularly in the context of unpaid labour.

Second, the concept of social resilience (Hall and Lamont 2013) is used to theorize the link between precarious work and unpaid labour, explaining that whether and how precarious work unfolds from unpaid labour depends on an assessment of the associated structural and ideological conditions. Defined by Hall and Lamont (2013), the term 'social resilience' has a dynamic nature as it refers to 'the capacity of people to sustain and advance their well-being in the face of challenges to it' (Hall and Lamont 2013: 2). Importantly, we illustrate that social resilience requires certain conditions to thrive. However, these are class-based and unequal as they pertain to the different capabilities of individuals to access the financial, social, cultural, and institutional resources needed to sustain unpaid labour (e.g., self-owned property and individual income and support from family members, knowledge and identity structures, social benefits, and social protections) within different jobs, service-based sectors, and labour market contexts.

Third, we conceptualize the link between unpaid labour, precarious work, and inequality. We explore the link between micro-power (i.e., class-based) and macro-dominant institutional and labour market dynamics driving inequality; for example, state policy mediating changes in different national labour markets and industry settings (Paton 2018). In other words, we use the social class-based power structures of exploitation to explain the precarity generated by unequal access to resources to sustain unpaid labour. Furthermore, we explain how and to what extent such power structures are produced and reflected in income, socially reproductive labour, and state policy, as well as through other institutional arrangements within industry and labour market contexts subject to ongoing structural transformations. As Laaser and Karlsson (2022) argue, individual experiences where meanings are framed emerge through the interplay of societal and individual relations, meaning that what people experience at agent level is shaped by wider dynamics at structural level.

In the following sections we substantiate the theory of the politics of unpaid labour by diving into existing theories and concepts of the 'ideal worker' norm, and stigma and resilience.

The 'Ideal Worker' and Stigma

Stigma has longstanding roots in sociology, social psychology, and social geography, all of which have contributed to generating a variegated definition of stigma. In sociology, stigma is at the core of Goffman's (1963) early theorization of 'social norms'. For him, society 'coheres' to the extent that members of a given society implicitly understand and share the norms in operation in a given social context. Goffman's understanding of stigma, therefore, relies on an appreciation of a 'social norm' as reflecting the social roles in place in a given setting and the role individuals are supposed to play therein. Goffman argues that 'there is some expectation on all sides that those in a given category should not only support a particular norm but also realise it' (1963: 2–7). Thus, the operation of a *norm* and the perceived 'lack of fit' thereof can induce shame and thus stigmatize an individual. In Goffman's understanding, the classically defined stigma conveys devalued stereotypes, i.e. the stigma arises (or is attributed) when an individual fails to realize a particular norm in a given social context. As such, a stigma is considered an 'attribute that is deeply discrediting' (Goffman 1963: 3) due to it revealing a 'lack of fit' between an 'ideal' (in Goffman's words a 'virtual identity') and an 'actual' identity.

This understanding of stigma is taken up in the early work of Lamont (2000) and her notion of the 'disciplined self', and in her subsequent insights into the centrality of the 'narratives of hope' in broadening the criteria of 'self-worth' (Lamont 2019). Key to understanding why someone takes on certain jobs and tasks, these criteria reveal the meanings and places of 'hope' in different contexts. However, explaining these meanings requires the application of a 'work devotion schema' (Blair-Loy 2003), i.e. the 'ideal worker' norm prioritizing work over private life (Williams et al. 2013).

Drawing on the theoretical frameworks of Weber and Marx, Kathy Weeks (2011) adeptly examines the 'ideological function' inherent in the 'work ethic', defining it not merely as an epistemological force, but as ontological effectiveness (Weeks 2011: 53). She conceptualizes the 'work ethic' as a discourse that individualizes labour while serving the ideological purpose of 'rationalizing exploitation and legitimizing inequality', thus making it a powerful justification for economic disparities (Weeks 2011: 53). We gain insight into the meanings and motivations of unpaid labour by drawing on the sociological perspective of the 'narratives of hope' (Lamont 2019) through the lens of the 'ideal worker' norm. This 'ideal' aligns with Kathy Weeks' perspective on the 'work ethic' (2011) as it refers to its 'ideological function'. In accordance with this, individuals conform to the norm, on the one hand to avoid a situation of individual shaming (Lamont 2019) in terms of being disrespected, discredited, and eventually isolated, and on the other hand in the hope of gaining a reward and remaining non-shamed (Lamont 2000). Weeks (2011: 52) also posits that the 'moral responsibility' to avoid shame lies squarely with the individual. For instance, she argues that poverty, traditionally associated with shame (see Walker 2014), is often morally questioned, implying that it stems from 'insufficient effort or lack of discipline in one's life' (Weeks 2011: 53). Here, however, we are less interested in how an individual creates a sense of self-worth to avoid shame and more in to what extent and under which conditions self-worth can be created. In short, we are interested in identifying *who* can do it, *what resources* are needed, and *why*.

One key aspect considered in the book is to assess how and to what extent unpaid labour enhances our understanding of inequality in precarious work with regard to the resources needed to sustain unpaid labour, while devoting specific attention to people's identification with their work. As Sayer clearly puts it when discussing people and inequality,

> Low income people are not disadvantaged primarily because others fail to value their identity and misrecognize and undervalue their cultural goods, or indeed because they are stigmatized, though all these things make their situation worse;

rather they are disadvantaged primarily because they lack the means to live in ways which they, as well as others, value. (Sayer 2005a: 947–8; see also Sayer 2005b)

Research on identity work in care, for example, has shown how the desire and 'hope' to give meaningful care services explains how workers are able to neutralize the negative effects of any stigma (Stacey 2011) by transforming ('reframing') the meaning of work through infusing it with positive values (Ashforth and Kreiner 2013). By the same token, and in relation to precarious work, similar studies have shown how the capacity to master certain jobs through intimate professional practices (e.g., the management of emotion) (Bolton 2005) may provide workers with the scope to navigate the uncertain and precarious conditions of such work (Brown and Korczynski 2017). However, a worker's capacity 'to retune a self-image' is deeply related to the distribution of opportunities within a context where workers have to mobilize support to sustain the precarious conditions they confront (Jamal and Lavie 2021).

The empirical evidence on jobs in creative dance, residential care, and online platform work presented in the second part of this book (Chapters 4, 5, and 6) illustrates how class-based histories of power to access resources explain the inequality effects generated through unpaid labour in precarious work. These histories unfold through practices of punishments and rewards underpinning stigma. We theoretically attend to the nature and consequences of stigma by adopting Link and Phelan's (2001) early conceptualization and definition of stigma as the co-occurrence of different components—i.e., labelling, stereotyping, separation, status loss, and discrimination—within a distinct power situation: 'for stigmatisation to occur, power must be exercised' (2001: 377). As such, we claim that stigma stems from someone being penalized and consequently not rewarded within a distinct power structure. We therefore propose considering punishments and rewards as a novel way to recast stigma, in turn helping us to theorize inequality in precarious work where unpaid labour is performed. In other words, we associate unpaid labour with stigma, recasting it as power wielded by punishments and rewards, rather than as a separate dimension.

In addition, as our evidence illustrates, the practices of punishments and rewards are implicit in forms of governance contributing to the political economy of 'shaming practices' by stigma (Tyler and Slater 2018), revealing how they are intimately linked to the institutional logic of capitalism (Smith 1996). With capitalist logic relating in particular to organizational business models and settings as well as regulatory institutions (Pulignano et al. 2022), the book forges a novel link between micro-level stigma and the macro-level policies and practices of the state and labour markets. As we illustrate, these policies and practices can equally contribute to intensifying the effects of stigmatization produced by the 'ideal' norm by making it more difficult for workers and their families to sustain unpaid labour at the micro level, for example by cutting back state support or shifting wealth from public to private funds at the macro level (Pulignano, Dean, et al. 2023). Importantly, we illustrate that the likelihood of stigmatization through non-compliance with the 'ideal worker' norm is relatively greater for those without sufficient resources to sustain unpaid labour, inducing them to perform unpaid labour by prioritizing work over private life. In this sense, the 'ideal worker' norm reflects deep cultural and structural assumptions that work demands and deserves a person's undivided and intensive allegiance.

Appreciating inequality in precarious work thus requires investigating the 'antinomy' between an 'ideal worker' and the 'reality of work' from the perspective of the challenges workers face, and which may eventually generate uncertainties for them. Importantly, this involves taking an ideological, political, and cultural stance as individuals often get trapped in unpaid labour while seeking self-realization by having their identities confirmed to counteract common stereotypes and misconceptions (Jones et al. 1984; McDonald et al. 2013). There is thus an *ideological* component to unpaid labour, i.e. the identity work built on the 'ideal worker' norm. Such identity work can induce class-based *real* effects (i.e., inequality in precarious work) determined by people's access to the resources needed to sustain unpaid labour.

As such, the book sheds light on the politics of unpaid labour as the dynamics and processes of power and inequality, forcing people into unpaid labour by engendering stigmatizing effects through the need to comply with the 'ideal worker' norm. It also assesses the different opportunities available to mitigate these effects through accessing resources to sustain unpaid labour. As such, unpaid labour can be rationalized as meaningful work; yet it is produced, maintained, and normalized as unrecognized, unrewarded, and undervalued through the class-based structure.

In sociology, stigma as shame is often associated to class (Skeggs 1997; Sayer 2005a). Our theorization builds upon a political economy perspective of stigma in sociology, framing stigma within class-based power structures between dominant and dominated classes. Accordingly, stigma is the 'exploitative apparatus ... a device for thinking more deeply how power etches itself into us' (Tyler 2020: 29). Stigma is thus not divorced from power—quite the contrary, 'it takes power to stigmatise ... stigma is dependent on power' (Link and Phelan 2001: 375–6) 'to keep people down, in and away' (Link and Phelan 2014: 30); 'stigma seeks to make it impossible to think of stigma separately from power'. (Tyler 2020: 16). Our appreciation of stigma therefore encompasses the structural relationships evolving from everyday social interactions, showing how these are structured through histories of power in well-established, class-based hierarchies at work. On the one hand, stigma serves class interests, as outward statuses, for example race and gender, shape hierarchies within small groups of unacquainted persons (e.g., men and white people are more likely to attain positions of power and prestige than women and black people) (e.g., Mullen et al. 1989). On the other hand, these interests resemble those of a broader political economy of neoliberal capital accumulation (see contributions in the special issue of *Sociological Review Monographs*, 2018) which, as we illustrate, intersects with institutional labour market arrangements and state employment policies.

We conclude that, whereas reframing or retuning a self-image by identity work may allow workers to define their jobs either as precarious and uncertain or as valued and fulfilling, such work may also exacerbate exploitative and insecure structural conditions. The existence of such conditions depends on the availability of opportunities to access the resources needed to neutralize them. Due to such access being based on social class (Scambler 2006), any capacity to build resilience to cope with the precarious and uncertain objective conditions of the job will likely be dependent on the extent to which a person can reframe or retune a 'self-image' of hope.

Resources for Resilience

Resilience refers to the capacity of a society as a whole to cope with various challenges by providing their members with the collective or individual resources essential to live a secure and meaningful life (Hall and Lamont 2013). Thus, resilience does not simply entail maintaining the *status quo*, but rather involves empowering people to utilize available resources effectively in the face of challenges (Hall and Lamont 2009). One such challenge is precarious work (Ayala-Hurtado 2021). Studies report that people either exit precarious work by disengaging from their work and seeking other forms of recognition (Kanter 1977), or carry on pursuing their goals despite the precarious conditions by actively coping with the pressures through resilience (Dardot and Laval 2013; Tyler 2020).

At the core of this book is an understanding of resilience as the availability and uptake of various resources, whether institutional (such as state policy and other regulatory arrangements in country- and sector-based settings), cultural and socio-economic (such as access to knowledge, skills, and work ethos), or financial (such as income support by family members and socially reproductive labour) as people prove themselves over and over again in all spheres of work and life (Rosa 2015). Our perspective thus emphasizes the agency of individuals to harness resources, possibly enabling unpaid labour to be recognized as a potential meaningful contribution within broader societal frameworks.

Within this perspective, for example, Smith (2010) considers that unpaid labour can be a mechanism for enhancing employability within the 'productive' market sphere of labour markets. As we explain in greater depth in Chapter 2, however, national labour market reforms have led to major transformations making paid work inside the 'productive' market sphere unstable, uncertain, and insecure due to cuts in welfare and social benefits, the weakening of employment protections following reforms in collective bargaining structures, and the decline in trade union membership, as well as the shifting of state-based funding to private funding. All this has opened societal fissures, with the recent wage inflation spirals highlighting the fragility and unsustainability of the current socio-economic system. The interplay between austerity measures, health crises such as the Covid-19 pandemic, social and economic challenges, and humanitarian tragedies such as wars and migration flows has laid bare the structural weaknesses within the 'productive' market sphere, amplifying the precariousness of paid work and widening societal disparities. At the same time, digital technologies and artificial intelligence (AI) are offered as the possible solution to these disparities and precariousness. Whether they can achieve this will likely depend on factors such as public ownership and control of technological infrastructure (Morozov 2015; Mazzucato 2017), reducing interdependencies, and introducing robust institutions and regulations (i.e., the 2023 proposal for an EU AI Act as recently approved by the European Parliament) that can pave the way for a more resilient and inclusive societal framework, diminishing the widening disparities exacerbated by existing market structures.

Moreover, short-term, unstable, poorly paid, unpredictable, and insecure work inside the market is increasingly putting pressure on socially reproductive labour, associated with the caring and domestic housework roles upon which a family depends (Pugh 2015). Thus, while a precarious worker prepares for work in the market sphere, what happens in the domestic sphere relates to how a family adapts to the insecurities and uncertainties manifested in the former. This means that 'changes in the distribution of work cannot readily be explained from within work but may be better appreciated by reference to their wider context, that is, the changing pattern of interconnectedness that results from (re)-structuring of the overall process and of the different stages of work activities' (Glucksmann 2005: 25).

Beckman and Mazmanian (2020) use the concept of 'scaffolding' to develop the idea that 'patterns emerge in how families distribute and manage precarious work, which correspond to different structures of support. Each structure relies on various forms and combinations of work to keep a household running' (Beckman and Mazmanian 2020: 132). Those with resources and fungible assets are able to build support ('scaffolding') to sustain family members in precarious work, while those without such resources and structures become increasingly impoverished and pressured. Relief is managed within families and households where efforts to erect 'scaffolding' to cope with the uncertainties of precarious work reflect the different socio-economic positions at the intersection of a person's status (e.g., class, race, gender) and that of the household and family (income).

People in precarious work increasingly rely on family support because they do not know whether they will be able to reap the reward of their (unpaid) investments. Workers become entrepreneurs of their own fate, doing everything to earn a living capable of giving them financial independence, building skills, and individual dispositions (i.e., *the (self)-entrepreneurial rhetoric*). In the heyday of the standard employment contract, there was to some extent a stable planning horizon for families in terms of a steady income, a fixed set of working hours, days, weeks, and even years, and a temporal and spatial firewall between home and work. Under conditions of precarious work this has all faded away. Individuals with an unstable income, variable work schedules, and requirements to qualify themselves for work by acquiring their own tools of the trade are rarely able to mitigate the financial and material consequences of unpaid labour alone. To build resilience, they need support and resources at both institutional and household level to sustain this unpaid labour, at least initially. As indicated, not everyone has access to the same (extent of) resources.

Overall, by advancing theory to address inequality in precarious work through pointing to the politics of unpaid labour in two interlinked ways (i.e., explaining the meanings and motivations someone associates with unpaid labour by using the concept of the 'ideal worker' norm and the concomitant concept of stigma), and addressing inequality in precarious work by assessing how and to what extent the unpaid labour reflected through the meanings is sustained by the availability of resilience-building resources, this book offers a novel perspective on precarious work.

Our Perspective on Precarious Work

Our perspective on precarious work with regard to the theory of the politics of unpaid labour presented in the previous section can be contrasted with influential perspectives emphasizing the psychological aspects of the subjective perceptions of insecurity and risk (e.g., the risk of losing one's job) alone. We are less interested in individual traits than in the power structures binding distinct frames of individual responsibility and freedom to contexts. Thus, we are sceptical about the efforts of certain governments, policymakers, and employers to seek solutions to social problems by upholding individual 'freedom'. As this book illustrates, social problems, such as inequality in precarious work, are nested in power structures, and therefore can be neither ignored nor institutionally resolved through a narrative of legitimation underpinning patterns of growth but not nested in common principles of equity and social justice (see Thompson 2018). In the following sections we frame our perspective on precarious work, with a focus on the context and reality of unpaid labour.

The Context and Reality of Unpaid Labour

The context of unpaid labour corresponds to the transformations occurring in different fields, such as labour markets and organizations (e.g., customer-centred business models) and the corresponding changes in the organization of work. These transformations include, though are not limited to, outsourcing. Digital technologies are helping drive the outsourcing of service provision, for example through online labour platforms organizing economic transactions between clients and workers. Fostering precarious work by establishing important contractual differences in employment status—i.e., dependent (flexible) employees and solo self-employed workers dependent on a single client—such technologies are helping remove 'unproductive' labour *time* from the remit of paid labour (Moore and Newsome 2018). Furthermore, in the online platform world, digital technologies based on AI are lowering the skills needed to perform certain forms of work, especially in the field of language processing (translating, copywriting, and even proofreading where DeepL has made significant inroads in recent years). This opens the door to lower skilled workers entering the market while at the same time reducing the amount of work available, as clients no longer need such services to be performed by workers, but can complete them themselves using digital tools. These two aspects are exerting downward pressure on freelancer rates, again fostering precarious work by reducing freelancers' capacity to recoup their investments in tools of the trade (Pulignano, Marino, et al. 2024). At the same time, the rise of flexible forms of employment contracts not providing a guaranteed minimum number of working hours (e.g., zero-hour contracts and work-on-demand) has created precarious work by individualizing the responsibility for earning sufficient income to make ends meet and pay for social protection (e.g., sickness, holiday, pensions). Both (solo) self-employed workers dependent on a single client and flexible (dependent) employees are responsible and accountable individuals (Dardot and Laval 2013) who spend time on performing tasks necessary to establish 'the value of their personal (*self*) entrepreneurial rhetoric' (Vallas and Cummins 2015).

The book takes a critical stand by arguing that the 'self-entrepreneurial rhetoric' retains the symbolic power to legitimize unpaid labour by binding workers to the contexts where unpaid labour is performed to make work meaningful. Mackenzie and MacKinlay (2020) have conceptualized unpaid labour as a potential resource where a worker invests in non-compensated labour time in the present in the 'hope' that future work may follow (referred to as 'personal investment work'). We broaden the conceptual relevance of 'hope' by relating it to precarious work, illustrating how unpaid labour shapes the expectations of someone towards a rewarding future. However, it can also serve as a punishment (i.e., *stigmatizing rhetoric*) for the individual by increasing the likelihood of being penalized in both the present and the future. As we argue, the realities of unpaid labour thus unfold from stigma due to a worker having to adhere to a *norm* (which usually resembles an 'ideal work' identity, see Lamont 1992) to not feel ashamed and eventually stigmatized.

As the empirical chapters in this book (Chapters 4, 5, and 6) illustrate, the meanings people associate with unpaid labour reveal the 'ideal' norm to which they in principle adhere. They also illustrate that the capacity of workers to build resilience by using resources in order to cope with the consequences of adhering to the 'ideal' norm accounts for the extent to which unpaid labour can be cast as 'hope', mitigating any class-based inequality effects. In essence, the way workers handle or adapt to societal norms influences how unpaid labour is viewed and how it drives inequality in different social classes.

Relating to the possession of resources, class describes levels of material (structured) inequalities in capitalist society. Critical sociology has widely represented these structured inequalities. For example, authors such as Bendix and Lipset (1967) have viewed the question of 'class action' stemming from structured inequality. Similarly, Tilly's (1998) concept of 'opportunity hoarding' and Wright's (1997) argument about the 'forms of inequality' point to the direct effects different levels of access to job opportunities may have on 'the acquisition of relevant resources' (1997: 122).

In summary, the book's primary thesis is that a full conceptualization of how unpaid labour contributes to understand inequality in precarious work is essential to assess whether and how unpaid labour is a dimension of precarious work. This implies placing the debate on precarious work on a stronger foundation:

First, to explain whether and how unpaid labour contributes to inequality in precarious work by revealing the meanings a person associates with unpaid labour. These meanings are contextualized within the class-based power structures of exploitation. The 'idealized' norm (i.e., the 'work ethic'—see Weeks 2011) which underpins the 'work ethos' prompts or induces unpaid labour by obscuring these structures. Importantly, workers undertake unpaid labour to adhere to an 'ideal worker' norm to avoid being punished in the present, for instance through disrespect, sidelining, discreditation, and/or shaming, and to maintain 'hope' for a reward in the future. Hence, stigma is a 'disciplining' device of unpaid labour which can entail inequality in precarious work by serving the interests of the disciplining class.

Second, to explain whether and how precarious work unfolds from unpaid labour by examining whether and how unpaid labour can become a resource for adhering to the 'ideal worker' norm. This involves exploring how and to what extent individuals have access to resources necessary to sustain unpaid labour and develop resilience. Determining whether precarity is experienced when undertaking unpaid labour, the extent of such class-based access is shaped by the political economy of a country and a sector, for example, the extent to which a state provides funding and/or access to social benefits, whether the state or collective bargaining institutions provide for minimum wages, and whether and to what extent public ownership and funding remain available. It is also shaped by the private sphere where gendered socially reproductive labour may or may not be available for sustaining unpaid labour.

We propose a three-pronged critique to underpin the above foundation.

A Critique

First, whereas precarious work may vary across different sectors and labour markets, there are certain commonalities related to the emergence of all sorts of work activities expected to be predominantly unpaid, unsupervised, and unorganized, yet which are an essential part of the work people undertake daily. We want to explain *how* individual responsibility (i.e., the 'entrepreneurial rhetoric of the self') is rationalized by explaining *why* people undertake these unpaid activities in the first place. Whereas paid employment can be precarious when it limits an individual's field of opportunity (Boltanski and Chiapello 2018), the opportunity to shape the conduct of a person's work (and life) under any contractual form of employment and under self-employment requires 'being healthy, educated and wealthy enough to develop higher human capabilities' (Rosa and Henning 2018: 5).

Second, unpaid labour under conditions of precarious work has implications for socially reproductive labour as the latter becomes dependent on the unpredictable and insecurely paid work within the 'productive' market sphere (Pugh 2015). For example, we illustrate that national governments' support for affordable childcare can be a resource used by individuals, workers, and their families to mitigate precarity. Importantly, it can be expected that wealthy households will be able to promote resilience among their members who undertake unpaid labour, whereas others will maintain their precarious conditions when other family members are unable to contribute to greater income sustainability (Pulignano and Morgan 2023). Hence, there is no automatism in precarious work unfolding from unpaid labour, as those with the highest resources, including in the socially reproductive sphere, are those best able to afford to perform such labour, while those without such resources are unable to do so. This finding thus underpins the emergence of inequality.

Third, and as a consequence, precarious work requires a focus to be put not just on an individual's employment position but also on how this precarity is socially (re)produced and sustained outside and inside the market, and on the consequences for employment and the individual life. This approach takes account of Judith Butler's (2012) important focus on the political decisions and social and cultural practices through which some lives are protected and others not. However, it also raises the question of *why*; in this book, we answer the *why* question by explaining how unpaid labour, stemming from the nature of the work in the three described work areas or occupational fields, for those with or without scarce resources can account for inequality in precarity, reproducing social class.

As we will explain in Chapter 2, this critique aims to revisit the traditional paid/unpaid dichotomy by positioning precarious work at the continuum between paid and unpaid labour.

Summary

In this chapter we have developed a critical examination delving into the discourse surrounding unpaid labour, precarious employment, and inequality. It distinctly differentiates between unpaid labour performed by employees engaged in formal employment arrangements and that performed by freelancers within SPRs. In the former case, unpaid labour may belong to the classical category of ‘wage theft’ while in the latter it may come under ‘income theft’. Although ‘wage theft’ and ‘income theft’ are similar in *what* they refer to, such as the unpaid nature associated with the *theft*, they also point to a distinction of the processes and to some extent the form of the unpaid labour. While ‘wage theft’ results primarily from exploitation by capital in a process of formalized economic dependency by labour as in the production process—such as the ER—‘income theft’ reflects a reduced space of autonomy and creativity—as the space where knowledge is created—of an independent contractor or freelancer which can result in economic and social alienation. On the one hand, ‘income theft’ deprives freelancers of the fruits of their labour, disrupting their financial stability, putting them in a position of economic vulnerability, and potentially creating feelings of powerlessness and economic isolation. On the other hand, freelancers may feel socially disconnected or marginalized, especially when reliant on that income for sustenance or when non-payment affects their ability to meet social obligations. It can lead to a sense of being excluded from certain social activities or experiences due to financial constraints. Repeated instances of income theft or non-payment can also damage their reputation and relationships within their professional network, possibly leading to a loss of trust and opportunities for future work and making them feel undervalued and disregarded, thereby impacting their self-worth and motivation.

Moreover, this chapter initiates the exploration of the theoretical framework concerning the politics inherent to unpaid labour—the core of the book. Presenting the intricate politics associated with unpaid labour, we discuss their potential in addressing the inherent inequalities prevalent in precarious work environments. This discussion strives to elucidate the rationale behind individuals’ experiences and the significance they ascribe to unpaid labour. As such, we introduce the concept and accompanying theories of the ‘ideal worker’ norm with its associated stigma, and resilience. While the ‘ideal worker’ norm is used to explain the meanings and motivations underpinning unpaid labour, the exploration of concepts and theories of resilience seek to understand the manner in which individuals access diverse resources to sustain their engagement in unpaid labour, and subsequently, the ramifications of these dynamics on the overall precariousness. Notably, these resources encompass a multifaceted spectrum of financial, institutional, and social resources, encompassing labour markets and public state-based initiatives, all of which profoundly influence the sustainability of unpaid labour and its impact on the realm of precarity. They also encompass the often-overlooked realm of socially reproductive labour, as illustrated and expanded on in Chapter 2.

2

The Paid/Unpaid Labour Dichotomy

The Theme

This chapter develops the critique already presented in Chapter 1 by examining arguments of unpaid labour and precarious work. These arguments relate unpaid labour to all sorts of work activities inside and outside the market that are predominantly unsupervised and unorganized but necessary to access and maintain paid work, and which therefore can potentially entail precarity. Under precarious work, unpaid labour inside the market can generate subtle yet significant costs for the intimate sphere of the home, i.e. socially reproductive labour outside the market. In short, this chapter argues in favour of a nuanced perspective of unpaid labour extending beyond the inside/outside market debate to develop a compelling analysis of precarious work and assess its consequences for class-based and possibly gendered inequality.

The rise of precarious work with highly flexible hours and reward systems has reassigned risks and functions previously covered by the standard employment contract and supported by the welfare state back to the individual and, in turn, to his/her household or family. The macro-structural changes in the collective institutions, operations, and outcomes of labour markets under neoliberalism have fostered a reconfiguration of the interdependencies between productive (paid) labour (undertaken within the public sphere) and socially reproductive (unpaid) labour (within the private household sphere). In other words, these interdependencies reflect a shift of risk from the employer to the state, and further to individuals and their families. Any attempt to mitigate this risk requires resources, including gendered labour, to be invested by workers and their households.

In Chapter 1, we define unpaid labour as '*the time and effort people invest to undertake tasks which relate to the work implicitly or explicitly assigned to them, but for which they are not paid*'. As we will see in the empirical section, many workers are increasingly finding it difficult to attain pay rates commensurate to the time spent on preparing for and performing tasks belonging to their job description. Indeed, many need to reorganize the often-limited

The Politics of Unpaid Labour. Valeria Pulignano and Markieta Domecka, Oxford University Press.
 DOI: 10.1093/oso/9780198888130.003.0003

resources available within a family and household to match the flexibilization of work in the public sphere of paid employment. Precarity, we suggest, is therefore not just a feature of work but an underlying aspect of everyday life (see also Kalleberg 2018) in both the private and public sphere for those trapped in this situation, and can perpetuate and even exacerbate stratified and potentially gendered inequality.

Moving 'Work' beyond the Inside/Outside Market Debate

Framed as a 'social process' (Alberti et al. 2018), precarious work requires a focus not just on an individual's employment position but also on how work is socially maintained and reproduced (Bá 2019; Choonara 2022; Pulignano and Morgan 2022). In her influential theory on the 'total social organisation of labour' (TSOL), Miriam Glucksmann suggests that 'changes in the distribution of work cannot readily be explained from within work but they may be better appreciated by reference to their wider context, that is, the changing pattern of interconnectedness that results from the restructuring of the overall process and of the different stages of work activities' (2005: 25). Considering precarious work as a social process, the TSOL approach requires appreciating how unpaid labour is performed both in the private (domestic) and in the public (paid employment) sphere. This involves looking at the interdependencies accounting for how unpaid labour is sustained. Indeed, whatever the scenario, unpaid labour has to be supported financially and socially, 'whether directly through a person's paid employment or through family wealth' (Taylor 2005: 135).

This chapter introduces the politics of unpaid labour (to be followed up in Chapter 3), guided by two aims. First, to position unpaid labour within existing studies in employment research on precarious work. In particular, we are interested in revisiting debates on the classic paid/unpaid labour dichotomy in order to reframe them in light of the changes characterizing contemporary labour markets where unpaid and underpaid labour are a distinct feature. As we explain, this has important implications, one of which is the necessity to explore how the conventional interdependencies generated by unpaid labour are becoming reconfigured, as unpaid labour needs to be socially and financially sustained. This in turn requires investigating different forms and domains of unpaid labour, including—but not limited to—socially reproductive (unpaid) labour. Second, to examine how and to what extent these interdependencies account for inequality in precarious work by blurring the boundaries of work while stratifying (possibly gendered) resources to sustain unpaid labour.

Precarious Work in Employment Research and Unpaid Labour

In employment research, precarious work is located in the processes undermining the standard employment contract (Rubery et al. 2018). We recognize that the speed, extent, and nature of such processes are fundamentally affected by different institutional configurations (Baccaro and Howell 2017; Doellgast et al. 2018) and relationships of power in the state (Howell 2021) and in the economy, alongside variations by sector and at the company level due to management strategies (Alberti et al. 2018). Highly flexible employment arrangements and precarious work are particularly prevalent in hospitality and retail services, personal and social care sectors, entertainment and creative industries, logistics and delivery, and platform work (Rubery et al. 2015; Umney and Krestos 2015; Moore and Newsome 2018; Wood et al. 2019; Pulignano, Grimshaw, et al. 2023) but also not absent in other sectors (Pulignano and Doerflinger 2018). These flexible arrangements have in common the manner in which they have undermined the standard employment contract to establish precarious work (Rubery et al. 2018). In particular, they have led to task fragmentation (by time and by function), poor-quality jobs, increasing unpredictability, and extreme variability in working hours and pay in the sectors concerned. Moreover, they provide little in the way of support through welfare and employment benefits, such as sick pay, pension rights, and unemployment protection, due to their marginal nature and fragmentated and limited contractual duration with regard to working hours.

Flexibilization is also associated with an increasing number of poorly paid independent contractors or self-employed freelancers outside the traditional realm of self-employment (a vast range of occupations from craftsmen, famers, translators, or photographers to medical doctors, architects, and lawyers). Among other examples (e.g., delivery drivers), one often-cited example is platform work. Research on the platform economy has illustrated how algorithms shape how work is assigned to platform workers, how their performance is monitored and evaluated, and what level of reward is available. Algorithms can be seen as non-bureaucratic means of control in the sense that workers are not told what to do by managers but by the algorithm. This is important because subjecting workers to bureaucratic control would damage a platform's claims that workers are independent contractors or self-employed, and therefore not eligible for the protections inherent to the employee status (Rahman 2020). Algorithms thus underpin a distinct form of precarious work characterized by a worker's lack of autonomy. Moreover, many of these new jobs are one-man shows, lacking opportunities for workers to share experiences and collectively organize (e.g., Cini et al. 2021; Bessa et al. 2022 Joyce et al. 2023; Mara' et al. 2023).

Many of those on flexible employment arrangements juggle multiple jobs and tasks while shouldering familial responsibilities for the care of children and the elderly. In other words, these flexible workers need support to cope with the low pay, unsocial working hours, and ever-present risk of dismissal inherent to such arrangements (Smith and McBride 2021). Such arrangements can also imply devoting an increasing amount of time to performing tasks which remain unpaid (Cole et al. 2022). Researchers have largely documented the occurrence of unpaid labour within care (e.g., Hochschild 1983), creative (e.g., Hesmondhalgh 2007) and platform work (e.g., Pulignano, Grimshaw, et al. 2023), associating it with income and job insecurity and therefore precarious work. This book draws on these examples as empirical cases to explore further the relationship between unpaid labour, precarious work, and inequality (see Chapters 4, 5, and 6 in Part II).

In our view, a key concept to appreciate how interdependencies caused by unpaid labour have historically contributed to inequality is the TSOL (Glucksmann 2005). For this reason, it is helpful to return to the early origins of this discussion, framing it along the lines of the gendered labour inequality form. As we explain in the following sections, these debates are framed within the traditional paid/unpaid labour dichotomy which we revisit to advance the study of precarious work and class-based and gendered labour inequality in the light of the changes characterizing contemporary labour markets.

The Recommodification of Labour

Unpaid labour within the political economy of work and employment in sociology relates to traditional debates around the distinction between 'productive' (inside) and 'unproductive' (outside the labour market) labour. Accordingly, the manner in which labour is employed specifies the concrete productive and unproductive content of labour, meaning that it is not the actual labour performed, but the nature of the relationship within which it occurs which determines its productive and unproductive nature. In chapter 1, volume 1, of *Capital*, Karl Marx argues that, for capitalist production, productive labour is that which individually or collectively produces surplus value, such as capital: 'That labourer alone is productive, who produces surplus-value for the capitalist, and thus works for the self-expansion of capital' (1976: 509). By contrast, Marx defines as unproductive any labour consumed not to produce surplus value, but to satisfy a concrete need. Therefore, as opposed to unproductive labour, productive workers are those whose labour power produces material commodities as an economically 'value-forming' *worktime* activity which enriches their employers (Marx 1939/1973: 328–9).

Further scholarly debates within the Marxist tradition have attempted to mitigate the productive-unproductive labour dichotomy by pointing to unproductive labour being a necessary component of capitalist production because it maintains capital value despite not accounting for surplus value (Gough 1972; Meiksins 1981). Furthermore, by discussing the concept of labour as a 'fictitious commodity' (Polanyi 1944/2001), Polanyi's concept suggests that labour transcends limitations, as it can be exchanged within market contexts just like any other commodity. This is for two reasons. First, labour has to be created and maintained outside the market, within the socially reproductive sphere of the family. Its appearance as a commodity is based on the unpaid labour provided within the family, a role primarily undertaken by women. Second, labour power has to be turned into actual labour within the workplace where the effort bargain is constantly adjusted between employers and employees in light of their respective powers in markets and in the state. As Polanyi argues, the history of capitalism can thus be read in terms of a 'dual movement' between markets as self-regulating and markets as socially embedded in various forms of institutions (Polanyi 1944/2001). Where employers are strong, they treat labour as a commodity subject solely to market conditions: when and for how long it is required, what is expected of a worker, and how much s/he is paid are determined by the employer. Unless employed, labour has no source of support for social reproduction other than what it can eke out through family, friendship, and social networks. As the history of industrialization in the advanced industrial societies of the Global North shows, this meant high levels of uncertainty for employees in terms of both their stability of employment and their wages and of broader conditions of social reproduction such as education, health, housing, and provision for old age.

Throughout the 19th and early 20th centuries, the extreme commodification of labour was tempered in various countries as employees organized into trade unions and secured some form of legal powers to engage in collective action, seeking to embed the market into society and to de-commodify labour. Crucial to this, however, was the development of a particular ideology of the domestic sphere and the family, associated with the traditional distinction between waged 'male breadwinner' (productive) labour and the unpaid socially reproductive labour provided by a household's women. This led to the creation of a coalition of middle-class reformers, male trade unionists, and Christians of various sorts, for whom the 'protection of women' (and children) could act as a twin justification for keeping women in the home (and therefore out of competing with men for jobs) and for wage campaigns based on the need to pay men as the main providers of money for the social reproduction of the family. The degree to which this was achieved in the industrialized economies prior to the era of welfare-state Keynesianism varied across countries, though as the 1930s' depression revealed, it was still possible for mass unemployment and deep levels of poverty to emerge and impact the survival of families and individuals. Large numbers of families were left to go hungry, homeless, uneducated, and diseased when employment ceased or when employers held wages down by coercion and their power over labour markets. Reproduction of the family under processes of industrialization could never be taken for granted; employment instability remained high; and the domestic sphere adapted in various ways to survive (Skinner 2011).

The situation began to change with the growth of income and employment security (labelled the standard employment relationship—SER) in the developed economies as a result of trade union and social democratic action during the 1950s and 1960s. Under the SER, labour de-commodification was embedded in collective institutions of wage bargaining and employment rights in labour markets which sought to minimize the focus on the specific characteristics of individual workers. A stable set of collective bargaining rules entrenched certain rights and responsibilities for employers, including relative security of employment and rewards essential to allowing the growth of personal consumption supported by Keynesian demand management and the expansion of credit facilities (Dörre 2015). Wages circulated into households, supplementing the domestic (traditionally unpaid or socially reproductive) labour of women and enabling adjustments in domestic labour as new technologies and new forms of consumption emerged. The income security of the SER emerged as a common feature based on full-time and relatively permanent male employment with stable reward systems deemed to constitute the 'family wage' (Land 1980), albeit controlled by the man in the household. Women generally entered the labour force in a part-time or temporary capacity, whereby women's work was not seen as necessary to the family wage but as so-called 'pin money' (Zeliser 2017), reflecting the substantial pay gap between women and men. State welfare benefits were generally secured through male full-time employment, reinforcing male power within a household and leaving women who exited (with their children) a male-dominated household reliant on poorly paid temporary work or means-tested benefits supplemented by charity.

This traditional and male-dominated setup became increasingly challenged from the 1970s onwards, as women's full-time and part-time employment across a range of occupations increased (particularly in the expanding state sector). This led to demands for equal pay and a gradual undermining of the 'family wage' discourse in favour of 'equal pay'. This was paralleled by debates relating to employment flexibility and domestic duties (e.g., the rise of the 'Wages for Housework' campaign; e.g., Federici 1975). Sociologists such as Rosemary Crompton asked 'how may sets of institutions moulded to the contours of the "male breadwinner" arrangement be reconstructed to new realities, how do families adjust to these changing circumstances' (Crompton 2006: 3) and provide support to the new flexible employment arrangements where unpaid labour dominates the work (and life) experiences of both men and women?

Indeed, at the core of these debates is the fact that non-standard, flexible, and on-demand work arrangements increasingly apply to both men and women in the labour markets, featuring unpredictable pay and working hours and often reduced social protection when compared to permanent employees. These workers are requested to work only when there is market demand. For example, research in Europe and the US indicates that many self-employed workers working for a single client may not be in search of flexibility and would prefer to work more hours but are somehow constrained from doing so (Mas and Pallais 2017; Boeri et al. 2020). This research also points to unpaid labour being 'wage theft' in that self-employment may be used by employers as a strategy to not pay the wages and benefits that their workers would otherwise be legally entitled to. For example, research into homecare has shown how self-employment contracts can strip so-called 'unproductive' labour from paid work, allowing employers to accommodate the national living wage (Moore and Hayes 2017).

Evidence on unpaid labour in the market illustrates that employers have succeeded in recommodifying labour in different ways: first, through offloading aspects of their responsibility for social reproduction back onto the individual and the family; and, second, through a tight focus on employing workers (both men and women) flexibly, i.e. only when and where there is market demand. In relation to the latter, workers have been forced to bear the cost of certain key aspects of equipping themselves for paid labour. Moreover, changing a worker's status to self-employed or subcontractor has gone hand in hand with a withdrawal of certain employment rights (e.g., Kalleberg 2009; Rubery et al. 2018).

These practices were massively extended by changes in labour markets and entire sectors increasingly dominated by individualized and flexible employment arrangements. Last but not least, the introduction of digital technologies has equipped employers with data to plan when they need labour. Importantly, these technologies provide employers with the ability—via algorithms rather than direct face-to-face contact—to allocate work as and when it arises to workers whose performance is constantly monitored and evaluated. Thus, what these studies illustrate is that understanding precarious work requires relating it to both the paid and unpaid labour dimension both inside and outside the market (Glucksmann 1995, 2005, 2009).

Precarious Work and the Paid/Unpaid Labour Debate

Miriam Glucksmann's important theory of the TSOL within the sociology of work and employment brings a novel relational perspective to work where 'each work activity has to be analysed in relation to each other' (Glucksmann 2005: 24–5). The TSOL approach (followed by the SEFL—i.e., the socio-economic formation of labour which includes the work of consumers as completing the division of labour, see Wheeler and Glucksmann 2015) emphasizes an appreciation of the unpaid labour performed in both the private (domestic) sphere and the public sphere as a form of work which may be voluntary (Taylor 2004). Importantly, TSOL builds on the traditional concept of social reproduction with its emphasis on the work necessarily undertaken within the private sphere to produce and sustain labour through and across generations. It considers the interconnections or relationships between the social reproduction of labour within the family, characterized by unpaid gendered labour, on the one hand, and the appearance of labour power on the market as a particular bundle of skills, capacities, and capabilities available to employers on the other hand.

However, these relationships change over time as new forms of work organization and business strategy emerge and as relations within the private sphere develop accordingly (Glucksmann 1995). Demographic changes, changing household structures, new ways of organizing work, new technologies, and the development of new subjective aspirations challenge the existing paradigm, setting the basis for a new social order. Under the influence of neoliberal capitalism and its expansive policies, employers have systematically eroded the bargaining power of labour in various ways. This includes the augmentation of managerial control over employment terms and conditions, as noted by Baccaro and Howell (2017). Paradoxically, while certain sectors foresee (skilled) labour shortages, which might potentially shift leverage back to workers, there is a simultaneous trend among employers of evading responsibility for these very conditions. This dual trajectory indicates a complex landscape where labour scarcity, instead of universally bolstering workers' bargaining power, coexists with employer strategies that circumvent accountability, creating intricate power dynamics within the labour market.

Some scholars have argued that one consequence of neoliberal practices is to turn the employment relationship back to a more 19th-century model of insecurity and uncertainty. In the pre-industrial era, before factories, uncertainty was reflected through the 'putting out' system where companies shipped materials to people to assemble items such as shoes, clothing, or firearms in their homes. More recently, and following the introduction of digital technology, we have witnessed how the digital 'putting out' system has generated unprecedented consequences for workers, with little control retained over the organization of the boundaries between 'work space' and 'home space' (Pulignano and Morgan 2023) and between 'working time' and 'free time' (Pulignano, Marino, et al. 2024). The former refers to workers needing to be reachable and available for work instantly when called up by an employer, regardless of whether this involves travelling between sites or having office space available at home or in a co-working space. The latter indicates the erosion of the standard linear time, with the introduction of flexible time schedules (i.e., 'flexitime') often accompanied by the introduction of self-employment arrangements to adapt labour market supply to employers' mapping of demand and convenience.

In the previous work of one of the authors of this book, Pulignano and Morgan (2023) have used the interconnected dimensions of temporality and spatiality to explain how a 'grey zone' of unpaid labour at the interface of work and home has resulted from these transformations, and how all this has consequently increased the likelihood of precarious work. At the core of the authors' explanation is the fact that individuals need to invest an increasing amount of unpaid labour to access even precariously paid work. Importantly, individuals with an unstable income, with variable work schedules, and with requirements to qualify themselves for work by possessing their own equipment and workspace are rarely able to mitigate the financial and material consequences of unpaid labour alone. Consequently, they look for ways of accessing extra resources to sustain it.

This perspective opens up important implications for research into the ideologies and legitimations of unpaid labour in paid employment and the intersectional gendered division of labour, as it calls for two issues to be resolved. First, it calls for extending the study of precarious work to the question of why people undertake unpaid labour and how they sustain it to mitigate the effects of precarity, or to avoid it altogether. Faced with precarious work, individuals and families manage their resources differently depending on their socio-economic position and class status, reflecting inequalities in economic, cultural, and social capital (Bourdieu 1986). Second, it raises the question of the impact of unpaid labour in paid employment for inequality based on social class and gender.

Unpaid Labour and the Gendered Division of Labour

Arguments related to the TSOL address unwaged forms of work found within the family and the household (see also Federici 1975, 2012; Molyneux 1979). Importantly, the discussion emphasizes the need to understand the unpaid labour performed mainly by women outside the market but necessary for capitalism due to its social reproduction purpose, i.e. allowing workers to regain energy on a daily basis, developing a new generation of workers through the rearing of children, meeting the needs of care for workers as they progress through a lifetime of labour and into old age.

As wages in the formal economy were insufficient for these social reproduction processes, domestic labour, predominantly performed by women, was necessary. This system was and still is integrally connected to the gendered division of labour in the household and the economy insofar as the family is considered the primary—though not the sole—unit for absorbing and sourcing the task of socially reproducing and sustaining labour, alongside institutional and income-based financial resources. Yet, this domestic labour is not deemed to be 'work' and is seen as lacking in skills despite its 'economic' contribution to maintaining the capitalist system by providing the labour necessary for the reproduction of labour power. It is important to recall here the contradiction at the core of the capitalist order as the expression of patriarchal (i.e., gendered), class-based relations of power. In accordance with Gramscian theories of class conflict, indeed, contradictions are internal (within) and external (between) the capitalist order and other fundamental orders, including the private space and the family where domestic and gendered work is performed.

Domestic labour was thus wrapped up in multiple layers of ideology emphasizing a woman's moral obligation to undertake this work (see McIntosh 1978), while a man's moral obligation was to support the family through paid work inside the market. As indicated, the idea of the 'family wage' was used to support the demands of male workers for a wage that reproduced labour on a day-to-day basis and over generations, under the assumption that women would be mainly responsible for the home and the tasks of reproduction, including childbirth and child rearing. Moral and religious justifications for the 'family wage' were influential in supporting working-class struggles for higher wages, forming the basis for a 'respectable' working class integrated into society through trade unions, cooperatives, friendly societies, religion, and social democratic mass parties.

Over the 19th and early 20th centuries, nation states, often prompted by war and the need to field a physically strong army instilled with a strong nationalist ideology, also took over or worked in conjunction with these institutions to support social reproduction through the provision of education, housing, unemployment and old age benefits, and health services (Mann 1993). If, as was often the case, women did enter the labour force, they could, by the same moral yardstick, be 'justifiably' paid lower wages on the basis that men were the main breadwinners. They could also be subjected to marriage bars requiring them to resign on marriage or on the birth of children. Having women working with limited expectations on pay, career, or employment rights was helpful for employers using large numbers of female workers to reduce costs, not just in some areas of manufacturing such as textiles, packaging, and food but also in the growing retail, health and social care, and secretarial sectors in the first half of the 20th century. The fact that many women were single or widowed, and therefore lacking any male 'breadwinner' support, was irrelevant to this framing.

State welfare structures tended to mirror these differences, with women primarily dependent on men for access to universal (as opposed to means-tested) benefits, though countries differed in the degree to which they encouraged women to enter the labour force and made institutional arrangements to ensure that this was possible (Esping-Andersen 1990). These debates, nevertheless, reflected a broader set of moral values which placed women primarily in the home with responsibility for the care of family members (Finch 1989). As the domestic labour and 'wages for housework' debate pointed out, work in the sense of the physical and mental effort involved in these tasks of social reproduction was made invisible and the skills necessary for undertaking them devalued and denigrated in comparison to 'real work' in the public sphere. The struggles of women and men to survive under these conditions were obvious in the late 19th and early 20th centuries when employment was unstable, wages were low, and state support was limited (Seccombe 1993). Nevertheless, in some form or other depending on the institutional context, the 'family wage' and all the gender power relations which underpinned it survived up to the 1970s. As noted by Wolfgang Streeck (2009), the economic security of the post-war era was premised on a tightly enforced sexual division of labour that relegated women to lower paid, precarious forms of employment and indexed the wage of the Fordist worker to the costs of maintaining a wife and children at home.

The notion of the appropriate 'family wage' was, in reality, determined by the relative bargaining position in the labour market of employees and their representatives as well as the role of the state in supporting women to prioritize motherhood roles and social reproduction (e.g., through pro-natalist policies keeping married women at home to have as many children as possible; see Skinner 2011) or alternatively encouraging them to enter the labour market (Fleckenstein and Seeleib-Kaiser 2011). Under the Fordist era of Keynesian macro-economic management, the requirement to boost production by growing consumption through rising living standards and new forms of credit, coupled with increased productivity in manufacturing and the rise of service sector employment, drew more women into the labour force. While there were various moral panics associated with this during the 1950s and 1960s (e.g., regarding declining fertility levels; see Seccombe 1993) and children going home to empty houses ('latchkey kids'), the limited and varied nature of state expansion into nursery education or after-school activities or into providing adequate care for the elderly meant that most of the pressure for change was exerted on women who had to be perfect housewives and consumers, managing the household economy albeit under the financial and physical power of the husband. The ubiquity of the standard employment contract based on the idea of the family wage, therefore, supported the clear distinction between the public world of work and the private sphere of the family intermediated by state institutions providing certain services for social reproduction under the Keynesian regime of accumulation.

However, other economic, political, and social changes in the 1960s and 1970s put a strain on this system and challenged the gendered division of labour in the economy and the household. These included the growing education and employment opportunities for women; declining opportunities for traditional male working-class jobs; feminist demands for greater equality; legislation on equal pay and equal opportunities; new patterns of household formation related to changes in reproductive technologies; the declining significance of marriage and the increasing frequency of divorce; and the availability under certain conditions of welfare and housing benefits to support single-parent households. Many of these tensions came about as political parties, driven by their electorates, demanded an increased role for the state in cushioning the impact of markets and for controlling and regulating market processes in the name of fairness and basic standards for all citizens (whether men or women). Though not eliminating the gender gap, the state—boosted by these processes—became a crucial labour market for many jobs associated with women's caring functions. As state services expanded and drew more women into the labour market, demands for greater equality in pay and employment opportunities grew, in turn prompting greater demand for state services, for example nurseries, schooling, and higher education, or expanded health and social services. Moreover, women were needed to perform the bureaucratic and operative roles associated with the expansion of the state (Crouch 1999). However, the turn towards neoliberalism from the 1970s onwards eroded all this.

Reconfiguring Interdependencies by Unpaid Labour under Neoliberalism

The rise of neoliberalism as a government policy paradigm from the 1970s onwards explicitly challenged aspects of the welfare regime by emphasizing the beneficial effects of free markets and the deleterious effects of government intervention. One consequence of this shift was the need for more family and individual responsibility for issues of social reproduction, potentially allowing a reduction in state expenditure and taxation rates. Melinda Cooper, for example, in her book *Family Values: Between Neoliberalism and the New Social Conservatism* argues that neoliberalism and social conservatism 'both agreed ... that the private family (rather than the state) should serve as the primary source of economic security' (Cooper 2017: 69). The continuous expansion of the state seen in most developed economies during the Keynesian era lost its legitimacy under this attack, even if it was more difficult for neoliberal governments to drastically prune services which by now had become part of the taken-for-granted institutional infrastructure of most societies.

The result has been a long-term ideological shift to the detriment of the welfare state and the social reproduction functions taken over from families during the Keynesian era, as reflected in different forms of state restructuring in advanced economies, such as variations in degrees of privatization, contracting out, retrenchment, and austerity over the last few decades (Hay and Wincott 2012; Hemerijck 2013; King and LeGales 2017). Neoliberal policies towards work have emphasized that social reproduction is best managed within the family household and that the services required to supplement this should be mainly provided through market mechanisms, with state involvement limited to areas of 'market failure' (Tronto 2013). State regulation of the labour market or entitlements to services and welfare benefits were to be reduced to different degrees across European societies (Häusermann and Palier 2008; Dolvik and Martin 2015).

With neoliberalism challenging the standard employment contract and pruning the welfare state, employers rely on families to fill the gaps. The state increasingly acts as a backstop, disciplining failing families through educational and social welfare services and developing mechanisms to control deviance. Those employed on part-time flexible contracts or performing relatively stable part-time work under an open-ended contract grounded in inegalitarian gender relations find it difficult to earn a wage sufficient to reliably support an adequate standard of living. They need to be supported during periods when they are not working or only earning small amounts. However, such periods are often out of their own control as a result of decisions taken by managers, clients, or—increasingly—algorithms. The unpredictability of when and where to work makes it difficult for support to be routinized. Therefore, family support is often called upon at short notice in the form of requests for urgent emergency aid. Yet, pre-existing inequalities mean that family resources are already pre-structured by the socio-economic conditions of class.

As Molyneux correctly noted, 'it is precisely where the value of labour power is lowest that the input of domestic labour is often most minimal' (1979: 11). Thus, those likely to be found in precarious jobs may have to accept lower standards of wage income while having less capacity to mitigate the impact thereof through the use of home-based resources, as family members may themselves be in relatively precarious employment or dependent on state benefits, with little slack to help each other either in financial terms or in terms of time and space. In particular, the author says:

> Single workers and migrants, whose labour power is usually reproduced on a daily basis without the benefit of female domestic labour, are invariably paid below-average wages. Even supposing that they were able and willing to afford the necessary appliances, such categories of workers live in conditions (slums, hostels, shanties) which make it difficult for them to perform their own domestic labour; as a consequence they tend to rely on services and food obtained on the market. (Molyneux 1979: 11)

In line with this analysis, Supiot calls for a closer tie to be established between work inside and outside the market as a way to provide social protection nowadays: 'The difficulty nowadays is to perceive the occupational status of persons as extending beyond the immediate contractual commitment to their work to cover the diverse forms of work experienced during one's life' (2001: 53). Importantly, and in contrast to the situation where, under the standard employment contract, wages flowed across the boundaries between formal paid work in the public sphere and work in the private home sphere, under these new conditions, new interdependencies between work inside and outside the market are created. This means that the private home sphere has to become much more active in supporting paid work (including its unpaid dimension), and therefore more oriented towards the marketability of its participants.

Summing up, precarious workers find themselves in a situation of having to continuously renegotiate with household members and alike (Brannen 2005) on two fronts. First, they must negotiate how a range of tasks associated with social reproduction *per se* (such as how to look after children and elderly members of the family; how to manage maternity leave; how to cope with illness; how to house the family adequately) can be managed against a backdrop of conditions of precarity and associated uncertainties over time (e.g., flexible work schedules) and location of work (Wood 2020). Second, they need to negotiate how they can survive in terms of being ready and available for unpaid labour; for example, this involves financial and social support for the tools of the trade, space, and training necessary to undertake unpaid labour inside the market.

To make this case, in the following sections we review the literature and discuss the implications raised by unpaid labour inside the market in terms of the boundaries of work and socially reproductive (unpaid) labour. Although there was a need to consider unpaid labour as domestic and reproductive work within the standard employment contract, we suggest that, under neoliberalism, paid time is being narrowed down by the precarious work form. This is novel insofar as it enables employers to snip away at the edges of the employment relationship, passing any uncovered costs and time back to the workers who, as we argue, in turn pass them back to families and households in the form of the socially reproductive work.

Unpaid Labour and the Boundaries of Work

Employers have been able to effectively push elements of paid work, which might in the past have been included in normal working hours and paid accordingly, into 'grey zones' of unpaid labour transcending the boundaries of work (Pulignano and Morgan 2023). This is because the 'grey zones' of unpaid labour extend the responsibilities of families and households when it comes to the preparation of labour in the form and type required for new precarious positions within the labour market.

Under conditions of precarious work, unpaid labour has gradually shifted away from being solely domestic towards a 'do-it-yourself' economy where it has become integrated in important ways in ideological discourses of accountability, *self*-responsibility, *self*-entrepreneurship, and *self*-reliance. These discourses are aligned with key aspects of employer and labour market practices and policies aimed at developing more flexible patterns of employment. Importantly, employers have been able to squeeze labour costs and the wage bill by circumventing regulatory labour market constraints, which in turn has led to precarious work. However, by pushing elements of work into unpaid labour, employers have generated important implications for domestic gendered socially reproductive labour. Thus, it is limiting to consider 'work today merely as a discrete activity carried out in exchange for remuneration and dependency' (Parry 2005: 10). Instead, a range of activities exist between the domestic private sphere (home) and the private one (work), transcending the (time and space) boundaries between work and non-work, and requiring unpaid labour to be sustained (Pulignano and Morgan 2023). Yet not all individuals and families have the resources necessary to sustain unpaid labour, meaning that precarious work is bound to produce unequal effects, depending on the resources available.

In principle, resources may be institutional, deriving from the way in which labour market settings are regulated and how state policy supports workers when either not employed or too poorly paid to be able to fully support themselves. However, under the neoliberal restructuring of the welfare state, access to state benefits has become more complex and has in fact led to new forms of semi-voluntary and compulsory unpaid work activities (i.e., internships, work experience, participating in training programmes, not to mention the considerable work required to fill in complex bureaucratic forms and provide appropriate documentation, a process which may particularly impact migrant communities and their families or second-generation families, as seen in the British Windrush scandal). Only by conforming to these requirements and engaging in these sorts of unpaid labour is it possible to maintain eligibility for benefits to cushion irregular, poorly paid work (Girardi et al. 2020). People thus have to engage in finding ways to train themselves by following online courses and to project their curriculum vitae and their *selves* to potential employers and customers (Greer et al. 2017). They have also to show the ability to be disciplined and accountable employees from the point of view of taking on responsibility, meeting specific obligations so that they can be relied upon to complete tasks in a responsible manner by turning up on time, regularly, and in a fit condition to work. Responsible and accountable individuals are also expected to be willing to take on jobs even when these do not provide sufficient income to live on. Taking on jobs whatever their quality is viewed as a sign of *self*-responsibility as it enhances *self*-reliance by reducing an individual's reliance on welfare benefits, which in turn often come with a feeling of shame and stigmatization (Tyler 2020). Labour market schemes and active labour market policies which rely on *self*-reliant and accountable individuals have thus succeeded in subsidizing low-paying employers and their policies for precarious work.

Resources may also come from cross-subsidization within the nuclear family and beyond. For instance, Schor (2020) describes individuals performing unpaid labour as a necessary requirement for accessing paid work as being trapped in economic dependency within the gig economy. Such work will in turn be dependent on hidden and unacknowledged support from others in the household (Joyce et al. 2020). For example, being available for paid work determined by market demand, the worker will endure indeterminate periods of time without pay and other benefits such as holiday pay, pension contributions, and sickness benefits. This unpaid time spent waiting for the opportunity to earn requires a household to manage its finances to deal with the irregular income of the precarious worker. This may take place through household members subsidizing each other in various ways, such as adult children living rent-free with their parents for much longer than previously because they do not have the income required to have their own accommodation. It could also include parents living with their adult children, because of the difficulties the latter face in providing care work when coping with flexible and precarious work patterns, including working unsocial hours during weekends and evenings. Hence, the result can be a change in family structures, featuring different approaches and capacities for domestic labour to supplement inadequate wage income. This is because 'precarious work needs labour' (Standing 2011). Indeed, precarious workers are found to be the ones struggling the most when attempting to reconcile their daily life with insecure jobs (Bá 2019).

This links into another important aspect of unpaid labour: the individual who accepts reduced expectations in relation to acceptable standards of living relative to prevailing norms. This is because those precarious workers required to spend time and money to be ready for work are likely to be the ones who then reorganize their home lives in the light of their expectations in terms of income and income stability (for a wide range of examples, see Pulignano and Morgan 2023). Whiting and Symon (2020), for example, discuss 'digi-housekeeping' which they relate to the unpaid work required to maintain the digital tools necessary to participate in the gig economy. Likewise, Amazon and Uber expect workers to equip themselves with cars and vans and to run them out of their own earnings. This often requires significant capital outlays from individuals and families if they are going to take part in delivery or taxi work (Alimahomed-Wilson and Reese 2020; Woodcock and Graham 2020).

Overall, we argue that it is not only work in the public sphere of paid employment that is becoming more precarious, but also families associated with household arrangements. Managing household finances under conditions of unpaid labour leads to multiple potential disruptions to families which have to be borne as a cost to the individual and the household. While middle-class families with resources may be able to supply this support, overall, we suggest that this process is deepening, intensifying, and reproducing inequalities between individuals and households. Importantly individuals without any household support, including income and domestic labour, are those who then may be pushed towards reliance on food banks and charities as well as facing homelessness and poverty. As we will illustrate in the following section, these arguments require a novel way of theorizing on how unpaid labour in precarious work increases the costs of reproductive labour by family members, with women in particular having to bear the costs of social reproduction in the first instance.

Socially Reproductive (Unpaid) Labour and Gender Equality

As above, Parry (2005: 10) has stated that it is limiting to consider 'work today merely as a discrete activity carried out in exchange for remuneration and dependency'. This statement opens a path for further reflections on the new ways in which socially reproductive labour within the home can supplement unpaid labour in precariously paid employment. One possibility is the reassertion of hegemonic structures of male dominance, reinforcing old disparities based on gender within the household. For example, this can happen by continuing to expose women to occupational segregation in flexible, devalued, and unpaid (or poorly paid) jobs because the sphere of domestic work (and with it primarily the activities undertaken by women in the home) is expanding again to cope with the increasingly precarious work situations of household members.

Traditional domestic labour debates about commodifying housework through the 'Wages for Housework' campaign went along with arguments for *de*-commodifying forms of socially necessary work, such as care and parenting work, by making them a state obligation. Neoliberalism, however, makes people work all the harder, persuading them that any loss of their lived time is adequately compensated by the freedom to enjoy more autonomy in the work process as well as more consumer goods for themselves and the family, thus encouraging families to adapt to the new context (Everingham 2002). By contrast, it can be argued that, by raising demands on the private sphere of home and the family, the unpaid element in paid precarious work fosters societal crisis precisely because of the pressures placed on families. Undertaking care responsibilities risks limiting the capacity of individuals and family members—particularly women—to take advantage of all the promise theoretically offered by the new freedoms under neoliberalism (Berg 2019).

Proposals based on women's assumed preferences for care—even via the 'dual-role' model based on the 'flexible family' (Streeck 2009)—have often made it unlikely for women to avoid being 'entrapped' by assuming responsibility for care work. The goal of gender equality is historically an ambitious one, with existing studies arguing that it is unlikely to be achieved unless something can be done about the nature of employment (Crompton 2006). Our discussion reinforces this statement by rejecting assumptions grounded in shaky theories about women's preferences or female essentialism.

Within a situation where paid workers are left having to continuously renegotiate their time with employers and with household members in order to engage in multiple and often diverse tasks in between the public and the private spheres of work (Brannen 2005), it is important to recognize that the commitment of the individual to undertake work for which s/he is indeed often not paid increases. This in turn enhances the costs for socially reproductive labour in terms of gender inequality, as most care work is still carried out within the household directly by women and/or supported by public funds.

However, even in the final instance, caregiver parity would unlikely result in income and gender equality in the division of domestic labour. As Fraser (1994) observes, for gender equality to occur, the shift should take place in the private sphere of home and the family. Conversely, as we argue in this chapter, contemporary neoliberal forces are nowadays curbing to a far greater extent the 'social bonds of care' (Fraser 2016) by squeezing social resources within families and households. Unpaid labour transcending the boundaries of work is a clear illustration thereof. Paradoxically, by presenting it as *self*-realization for individuals to be the 'boss' of their own fate, the neoliberal capitalist regime justifies unpaid labour as an extension of the freedom of the individual and the family to organize their lives as they see fit. However, as we have argued, neoliberalism refuses to recognize the value of socially reproductive work by piling more work into the blurred 'grey zone' of unpaid work (Pulignano and Morgan 2023). It does this by imposing flexible (unpaid) work schedules in terms of working hours, dictating how the allocation of such (mostly) unpaid work will occur. In so doing, it intensifies the difficulty for individuals to predict whether the choices they make will provide them with the income which they want (Kessler 2018; Acevedo 2020). However, individuals often find themselves ensnared in the performance of unpaid labour as they pursue both freedom and *self*-realization, seeking to have their identities validated. Hence, as we delve deeper into the subject, it becomes clear that unpaid labour carries a political message or dimension deeply intertwined with material and cultural or ideological factors perpetuating gendered inequality.

Summary

In this chapter we have argued that precarious work is a complex and constantly evolving process requiring sophisticated analyses of the increasing reliance of workers and individuals on unpaid labour inside and outside the market, including socially reproductive labour. In this light, we have illustrated that unpaid labour accounts for new interdependencies as it requires resources for it to be sustained. One such resource discussed in this chapter is socially reproductive (unpaid) and domestic labour. As access to such resources is dependent on individual and household circumstances, inequality may arise in the precarious conditions of individuals and households confronted with unpaid labour.

As we have argued, this appreciation requires relating the concepts of unpaid labour and precarious work to inequality by class and gender. More broadly, the risks for labour in precarious work involve substantial fluctuations or interruptions in income and benefits deriving from paid work, but also the emergence of significant unplannable and often unpaid tasks and activities which individuals (and/or their families) have to shoulder in order to gain and sustain access to work. This can involve having several jobs at once to both finance investments in unpaid activities and make ends meet, in turn producing disruptive effects, for example, on the care of children and the elderly, as well as on the running of the household sustaining an individual's ability to work. What is therefore being created as a result of the rise of unpaid labour inside the market is a reconfiguration of the TSOL (Glucksmann 2005) with a focus on the 'grey zone' transcending the boundaries of work and involving unpaid labour (Pulignano and Morgan 2023), with important implications for class-based gender equality. We extend this analysis to the institutional level, examining how neoliberal changes in institutional arrangements have affected the interdependencies between unpaid labour (both socially reproductive and otherwise) and precarious work, thereby expanding our understanding of the social and economic foundations of unpaid labour.

In Chapter 3 we delve into the politics of unpaid labour to explain how it can help address inequality in precarious work. Introducing the concept of the 'ideal worker' norm and stigma, we engage in a discussion of relevant sociological theories to explain the motivations and meanings individuals attribute to unpaid labour. We also introduce the concept and theories of resilience to appreciate whether and how individuals access resources to sustain unpaid labour, and how all this has an impact on precarity. As we will see, these resources include income and socially reproductive labour as well as financial, institutional, and social resources such as labour markets and public, state-based resources.

3
Establishing a Theory of the Politics of Unpaid Labour

The Theme

Drawing on 129 autobiographical narratives and thirty-eight audio diaries from the three areas of work or occupational fields (creative dance, residential care, and online platform work) presented in the empirical section (Part II), this chapter defines a theory of the politics of unpaid labour to explain inequality in precarious work. At the core of the theory is the political dimension of unpaid labour which impinges upon the motivations and meanings workers associate with it.

This chapter presents the foundations of the theory using concepts and sociological theories of the 'ideal worker' norm, stigma, and resilience. We recast the 'ideal worker' norm and stigma as power wielded via punishments and rewards to explain the motivations and meanings individuals associate with unpaid labour. As we illustrate in Part II (Chapters 4, 5, and 6) where the empirical findings are presented, respondents expressed positive attitudes when discussing the significance and meaning of unpaid labour, reflecting the importance and value they attach to the work they perform in the hope of gaining future recognition. This allows them to avoid feeling ashamed or stigmatized in the present for not engaging in unpaid labour. For the present task, recognition is defined as 'the affirmation of positive qualities of human subjects and groups' (Honneth 2014: 329, in Lamont 2018: 423), therefore referring to 'a social act by which an individual's or group's relative positive social worth is affirmed or acknowledged by others ... a growing consensus about the equal worth of individuals or social groups ... *with* stigmatization being a process that results in the mirror opposite of recognition' (2018: 423—italics added). Turning to the resources for collective resilience, we examine the effects of unpaid labour on inequality in precarious employment. Specifically, we look at the extent to which individuals are pushed into precarious situations when engaging in unpaid labour in the run-up to or during paid employment, a circumstance demanding resources to sustain it.

The Politics of Unpaid Labour. Valeria Pulignano and Markieta Domecka, Oxford University Press.
 DOI: 10.1093/oso/9780198888130.003.0004

As we demonstrate, these resources are distributed unevenly among different social classes, thereby limiting opportunities for certain social groups. The chapter ends with a general overview of the three areas of work or occupational fields where the theory will apply (see Chapter 4, 5, and 6, Part II).

The Political Dimension of Unpaid Labour

There is a political or ideological function of unpaid labour which can result in real outcomes, such as precarious work. Research has illustrated this by showing that, for example, under casual and flexible work arrangements in social care, which in many cases do not guarantee a minimum number of working hours, female care workers have a tendency to volunteer more (Taylor 2005), or generally to be more open to working longer hours to respond to their 'care duties' and 'moral ethos' as caregivers (Lewchuk et al. 2015). Likewise, many creative workers are freelance project workers, shifting from one project to the next without guaranteed social protection in their attempts to develop a portfolio of achievements, aka 'reputation', allowing them to be recognized as 'artists' (Hesmondhalgh and Baker 2011). Erin Duffy (2017) calls this work 'aspirational labour', i.e. the work someone performs to gain a reputation or to become known. In short, this research shows that, when individuals work under precarious conditions, it often leads to the formation of stereotypes and misconceptions about them (McDonald et al. 2013). However, individuals can counteract these stereotypes by engaging in unpaid labour. As a result, stereotypes reinforce the reality of precarious work, as individuals conform to an 'ideal work' identity (Lamont 1992) to avoid feelings of shame and potential stigmatization. To seek validation of their identity as *self*-responsible, *self*-reliant, and accountable individuals (Dardot and Laval 2013) they dedicate periods of unpaid labour in the run-up to or while performing paid tasks, thereby establishing the perceived value of their personal '*self*-entrepreneurial rhetoric' (Vallas and Cummins 2015: 4).

The analysis presented in this book supports the assertion that the '*self*-entrepreneurial rhetoric' serves as a binding force, connecting workers to unpaid labour by imbuing this labour with personal meanings. Consequently, those performing unpaid labour within paid jobs are less likely to face devaluing stereotypes arising from any inability to meet a specific 'ideal' norm. This norm underpins the 'idealized discourse' of a 'work ethic' (Weeks 2011) which people serve by acting as 'enterprising subjects' (MvNay 2009). In line with MacKenzie and McKinlay (2020), we thus agree that unpaid labour is often undertaken as an investment in the 'hope' of future work and *self*-realization. However, we also contend that sustaining unpaid labour socially and economically necessitates the availability of resources reducing the likelihood of stigmatization and feelings of shame in the present while striving towards a desired future. Hence, examining stigmatization sheds light on how an 'ideal' norm perpetuates unpaid labour by prioritizing individual *self*-realization over personal life commitments. Such an examination holds the potential to enhance our understanding of the individual motivations and meanings people associate with unpaid labour. Furthermore, this approach helps elucidate how unpaid labour in the run-up to or while performing paid work reflects the realities of precarious work, as it points to the political dimension of unpaid labour by assessing the exploitative power dynamics shaping individuals' ability to shield themselves from—or mitigate—the effects of stigma while engaging in unpaid labour to conform to the 'ideal' norm.

As we will show later in this chapter—and subsequently empirically illustrate in Part II—unpaid labour can be a driver (albeit not the sole one) of inequality in precarious work. Whether this is actually the case depends upon the resources available to sustain it. The practice of individuals engaging in unpaid labour, the interconnectedness of various work forms across different spaces and domains, the role of social reproductive labour, employment, and welfare structures collectively provide a supportive framework or 'scaffolding' for unpaid labour. The differing embedding of unpaid labour within family and institutional structures and practices underscores the presence of structural inequalities restricting opportunities and resources based on social class. Therefore, to understand the potential inequality generated by unpaid labour in precarious work, it is crucial to recognize the influential role of class-based power structures (Scambler 2006). As this book contends, this understanding is essential in explaining how individuals conform to the 'ideal' norm to avoid stigma and how they sustain unpaid labour, often by establishing interdependencies with social reproductive labour.

We locate stigmatization in Tilly's theoretical conceptualization of structured inequality as 'opportunity hoarding', a concept refined by Wright (1997: 31) who compares this to his own concept of 'non-exploitative economic oppression' where one group is advantaged at the expense of others. Tilly is clear that 'opportunity hoarding' is not necessarily an intentional strategy but can involve exploitation when 'the effort of a favored minority provides a resource-owning elite with the means to extract surplus from an essential but otherwise unavailable larger population' (1998: 154). Whereas the appearance of labour power inside the market relies on the social reproduction of labour within the family, characterized by unpaid and gendered labour

(Glucksmann 2005), Karl Marx's political economy of work considers unpaid labour as 'surplus labour (*time*)' in paid employment which is not compensated in terms of monetary payments, and which is therefore exploitative as it serves the institutional logic of capitalism.

As such, the political dimension of unpaid labour is revealed by such labour accounting for accumulation and valorization, in turn reflecting class-based inequality (Friedland and Alford 1991). Importantly, the emphasis here is on capitalism and class, as the institutional logic of capitalism can be seen as an element of an ideology and hegemony embedded in power capital and the labour relations of class (Vidal 2022). At the same time, the micro foundation of this institutional logic is an ideology rooted in the material practices of precarious work. Nonetheless, this ideology produces meanings for the worker, thereby contributing to motivate the individual choices to perform unpaid labour.

The Meanings of Unpaid Labour

Focusing on the individual meanings of unpaid labour, we take up the theoretical perspective of meaningful work in the sociology of work and employment as work which reveals pride and a sense of value and consequent attachment for the workers to the work they perform.

The term 'meaning' refers to 'the significance people assign to what they see, think, say or do' (Small and Calarco 2022: 27). Thus, when researchers seek to understand meanings, they are usually concerned with understanding the significance that a particular population assigns to a specific occurrence. In his *Economy and Society*, Max Weber describes a motive as 'a complex of subjective meaning which seems to the actor himself or to the observer an adequate ground for the conduct in question' (1922/1964: 98). Put differently, motivated actions are those an individual takes with a particular goal or outcome in mind. Since motives are themselves meaningful, understanding motivation involves understanding the meaning people give to their action, that is, how they interpret or account for what they have done. But it also involves understanding what people believe led them to act in particular ways (Weber 1922/1964). Although not all actions are motivated and intentional, they all need to be understood in the light of an individual's experiences and perceptions of specific circumstances. These circumstances thus shape the meanings individuals attribute to—and motivate—their action.

Sociological theory has highlighted the prevalent 'recognition gaps' exacerbated by the influence of neoliberalism and emphasized the imperative to bridge these gaps through the attribution of value and meanings, thereby combating stigmatization within society (Lamont 2018). This perspective offers a profound understanding of the intrinsic desires of workers in their pursuit of purpose and attachment to work, even in the face of mounting pressures and precarious conditions (Thompson 2018). This desire for acknowledgement necessitates recognition. Consequently, the meanings associated with unpaid labour amalgamate both the motivations that drive individuals as well as the necessary resources essential for sustaining their engagement in unpaid work.

We follow Laaser and Karlsson's (2022, 2023) approach to a sociology of meaningful work. The authors use a theoretical 'politics-of-working-life' perspective to illustrate that a view of the 'dynamics of the workplace as a contested terrain and workers' pursuit of scarce material resources' (Thompson and Vincent 1990, in Laaser and Karlsson 2022: 800) is essential to understanding workers' responses and their link to meaningful work. This implies that understanding meaningful work requires taking a 'human agency' approach to avoid conflation and to understand the interplay of 'structure with agency' (2022: 800). Workers' struggle for meaningful work is a fundamental condition of being human. From a human-centred perspective, delving into the philosophy of life, its origins, and subsequent implications proves to be a valuable pursuit. Existential philosophers and also psychologists have examined the distinctions between leading an authentic, intricate life versus a superficial, routine-driven existence labelled as 'everydayness' (e.g., May 1991; Frankl 1996; Schneider 2008) or existential apathy (Schnell 2008, 2009). Importantly, and in the context of work, this framework understands the search for meaningfulness as being driven by workers' desire to establish and defend spaces of autonomy at work, to be recognized for their efforts and treated with respect and dignity in the context of the social structures and necessities of the labour process and societal challenges at large (Ackroyd and Thompson 1999 in Laaser and Karlsson 2022).

In accordance with this conceptual understanding, we evaluate the meanings workers attribute to unpaid labour within the objective contextual conditions where inequality usually unfolds from the distribution of opportunities and resources to sustain unpaid labour among different social groups. As Chapter 2 has indicated, workers often relying financially on domestic labour, for example, are those likely to lack any household support in the first place. This can exacerbate inequality for them as they may be pushed towards precarity by increased reliance on debt to access that support. We operationalize inequality by class, conceptualizing it as an 'opportunity construction' which shapes 'sorting mechanism into class locations' (Wright 1997: 118–19). In a discussion of gender differences in occupational distributions that resonates with a contemporary focus on intersectionality, Wright brilliantly notes that 'forms of inequality and domination' can have direct effects on the different opportunities people encounter 'by affecting their acquisition of relevant resources' (1997: 122).

In the next sections of this chapter, based on these arguments, we delve into an approach explaining how and to what extent unpaid labour can help address inequality in precarious work. This approach is informed by the political dimension of unpaid labour which we portray as the 'politics of unpaid labour'. To develop a theory of such politics, we proceed in two analytical steps. The first explores the motivations and meanings individuals associate with unpaid labour by fleshing out the 'ideal worker' norm and ideological process motivating the occurrence of unpaid labour by introducing punishment and reward practices which we see as underpinning stigma. In the second step, we examine the concept of resilience, looking at how resilience is dependent on the existence of resources to sustain unpaid labour, whereby these resources are themselves class based. Importantly, we look at both the macro-level regulatory arrangements (welfare and employment through state policy and other institutions) and the micro-level individual support from family income and reproductive labour as well as cultural capital as important resources to sustain unpaid labour.

A Theory of the Politics of Unpaid Labour

The 'Ideal Worker' and Stigma

The concepts of the 'ideal worker' and 'stigma' guide the theorization of the meanings workers attribute to unpaid labour, deepening our understanding of the form and conditions of exploitation which sparks unpaid labour. As indicated in Chapter 1, unpaid labour is understood as *the time and effort people invest to undertake tasks which relate to the work implicitly or explicitly assigned to them, but for which they are not paid.* Importantly, we use stigma to refer to the ideological function explaining why a worker undertakes unpaid labour in the first place. The 'ideal' (i.e., the 'virtual') norm (Williams et al. 2013) attributing an 'actual identity' to a worker (Goffman 1963) can generate stigma when s/he does not adhere to it. As such, this norm implies the existence of a 'work devotion schema' (Blair-Loy 2003) reflecting deep cultural and ideological assumptions that work demands and deserves undivided and intensive loyalty, obedience, and trustworthiness. This schema thus specifies the cognitive belief, moral commitment, and emotional salience of making work the central focus of one's life.

Mary Blair-Loy (2010) has explored how the workplace can be a potent site of moral prescriptions, experienced as externally binding mandates and subjectively compelling schemata. Accordingly, the author explains how the work devotion schema can fulfil both a 'coercive' role—as workers feel forced to comply—and a 'seductive' role—as workers may also believe that a strong work ethos helps shape their sense of 'self' and 'self-worth'. Consequently, non-compliance with specific work arrangements can be interpreted by superiors, co-workers, and even the employee in question as a violation of the 'work devotion schema' and therefore 'morally' lacking. In *The Problem with Work*, Kathi Weeks (2011) develops a theoretically sophisticated argument around the 'work ethic' stemming from Weberian and Marxist theories of ethical and moral responsibility as well as exploitation and subordination. In accordance, what is considered to be 'morally correct' becomes a 'contradictory instrument of subordination ... *which* serves the more disciplinary function *to* construct docile subjects' (Weeks 2011: 51–6—italics added). Thus, work as a 'field of individual agency' becomes 'the problem' exactly because it entails meanings which are grounded in 'ideological hegemony' (2011: 51 6). Fleming (2014) uses Foucault's concept of *biopower* to develop a powerful critique of this hegemonic 'work ethic' by emphasizing how our life abilities and extra-work qualities (bios or 'life itself') become key objects of exploitation—particularly under neoliberalism. As he argues, 'in order to gain the most from the concept of biopower ... we must position it within the context of capitalism proper—that is to say ... exploitation', with *biopower* considered as potentially entailing unpaid labour as the former 'makes use of efforts and innovations among groups and individuals beyond this remit' (2014: 883–5).

We locate, and further theorize, the meanings workers attribute to the unpaid labour they perform within this ideological assumption as framed within existing debates and theories of governmentality and work. In reference to Williams et al. (2013), we argue that the 'ideal worker' norm has the ideological function of normalizing unpaid labour by making the worker prioritize work in the public employment sphere over work in the private home sphere. Drawing on Fleming's (2014) analysis of *biopower* and its evolving resemblance to a concept of 'living', we adopt the author's recommendation to examine its manifestation within socially constructed patterns of inequality. This approach suggests expanding the Foucauldian framework of power to encompass elements of class—an aspect historically overlooked by Foucauldian theory. We do this by examining how the hegemonic ideology works within three specific work areas or occupational fields, each reflecting different occupational class-based structures with distinct resources (or types—or a combination—of capital; see Hilgers and Mangez 2015): creative dance, residential care with a focus on the human concern for the vulnerable, and online platform work performed by self-employed entrepreneurs. As such, we argue that unpaid labour is rationalized, meaning it is produced, maintained, and normalized by the 'ideal worker' norm which makes 'work' the responsibility of a *self*-responsible, *self*-reliant, and *accountable* individual. In so doing, the 'ideal worker' assumes certain features characterizing the self-employed. In the context of freelancers engaged in online platform work, Foucauldian theories of governmentality have been instrumental in addressing the coercive entrepreneurial ideology of the 'enterprising' and 'accountable-*self*', as elucidated by McNay (2009). We add and explain how this understanding extends to other occupations, such as those within the realms of art and care.

Accountability calls for people to 'account for' their actions (e.g., O'Neil 2002, 2014; Banks 2004; Lunt 2008), i.e. to assume responsibility for them. Du Gay (1996) explains how accountability has emerged through changes in work arrangements within firms since the introduction of total quality management (TQM), just-in-time (JIT) systems, and lean systems in the 1990s. These changes have led to increased accountability and have, to a certain extent, pushed employees into a situation similar to that permanently experienced by the self-employed. In so doing, employees have become responsible for translating internal organizational life into the language of customers and suppliers. Consequently, organizations have undergone various structural changes, such as the introduction of project teams and peer review systems for skill assessment and evaluation, thereby significantly increasing worker accountability. As Clegg and Baumeler (2010) argue, they have raised expectations of workers dedicating themselves to meeting customer demands. In so doing, employers have increasingly cultivated workers to become 'enterprising subjects', 'driven by the desire to optimise the [*self*] worth of his or her own existence' (Du Gay 1996: 181—italics added). In the author's view, the entrepreneurial turn represents a qualitative shift in the nature of both organizations and the subjectivities they promote: 'the character of the entrepreneur can no longer be seen as just one among a plurality of ethical personalities *but must rather be seen as assuming an ontological priority*' (Du Gay 1996: 181, in Vallas and Cummins 2015). Here, Vallas and Cummins (2015: 3) use the concepts of the 'enterprising self' and 'self-entrepreneurial rhetoric' to explain how existing norms produce, maintain, and reproduce the employment relationship by placing significance on worker subjectivity.

This relates to literature showing how 'normalization' under the 'expectation of a high reward' (Neff et al. 2005: 310–29) is the way in which workers bear the risk within distinct jobs and occupations. Whereas distinct work situations shape workers' identity, identity norms also account for specific work situations and different arrangements. Indeed, as Vallas and Cummins (2015) powerfully argue, the rise of extreme uncertainty and precarity potentially makes workers more vulnerable to the discourse of accountability. They base their analysis in part on Collinson's influential analysis (2003) which connects the development of employee subjectivity to a modern era characterized by precarious conditions.

Our argument is that unpaid labour normalized by the 'ideal worker' norm is influenced by a 'self-entrepreneurial rhetoric' (Vallas and Cummins 2015) encouraging workers to take personal responsibility and be accountable for their work, including unpaid labour, by giving it meaning. Especially, we suggest that this rhetoric has the symbolic power to legitimize unpaid labour through a system of rewards and punishments. In other words, individuals engaging in unpaid labour are less likely to be subject to the stigmatization associated with not meeting a specific 'ideal' norm which comes in the form of societal expectations. Moreover, unpaid labour becomes part of an individual's identity, seen as a rewarding aspect of someone's work and even as a moral duty (e.g., in caregiving or artistic pursuits). Therefore, individuals readily undertake unpaid labour to avoid penalties in the present, such as being shamed, discredited, or isolated, in the hope of a future where their efforts will be recognized and valued without shame.

Hence, the dimension of 'hope', which is centred on the *self*, is key to understanding why someone embarks on a career possibly involving unpaid labour. In her 'From "Having" to "Being"', Lamont (2019) memorably illustrates how the centrality of the 'narratives of hope'—as centred on the 'self-worth'—is important for building resilience against the accelerated diffusion of inequality under neoliberalism (we discuss the relevance of resilience for unpaid labour and how it relates to inequality in precarity in greater depth in the following section). At this juncture, however, we contend that the *self* is both a product of and shaped by the 'dominant symbolic' (Skeggs 2004). This is in line with Foucault's (1979, 1988) early understanding of the *self* as not just a discourse, but as a whole system of inscription, exchange, value attribution, perspective, and practices that make it possible. Thus, to become a *self* is premised upon the availability of and access to cultural resources (e.g., existing ideologies, constructions of belongings, and stigmatized conditions) which are equally important to secure access to the economic and material resources needed to acquire the knowledge for *self*-responsibility, *self*-reliance, and accountability (Vitellone 2002).

Nonetheless, the production of the *self* requires the creation of conditions servile to the logic of capitalist accumulation. As Rose (1989, 1992) remarkably argued, a whole range of technologies, and in particular knowledge, are designed to produce a *self* that fits the capitalist system, providing new profit-generating resources and services. The 'self-entrepreneurial rhetoric' (Vallas and Cummins 2015) is the symbolic power that explains how unpaid labour becomes surplus value through the exploitation of labour within capitalist accumulation. This draws on Foucault's early contention that we live in an era in which power has been 'governmentalised' (Foucault 2010), i.e. invisibly shaped by structural apparatuses and discursive practices at the level of the state, firms, and society at large, and in line with neoliberal principles. In particular, literature focused on the career building increasingly required in some jobs and occupations has showcased the role of neoliberalism in shaping work orientations, generating a 'passion paradigm' which makes workers all the more susceptible to exploitation. Gina Neff's (2012) concept of 'venture labor' powerfully highlights the exploitation stemming from the risk assumed by workers in various occupations and industries under 'discursive entrepreneurialism'. The evidence presented in this book on creative dance, residential care, and online platform work provides empirical support for this argument, illustrating how unpaid labour encompasses a shared system of individual meanings linking the experience of workers to something worthwhile and useful to them in the present and the future. Thus, whereas workers derive meanings from contingent and future situations of 'hope', they also frame these meanings within a structured situation of a continuous 'present' (Laaser and Karlsson 2022). The process of 'meaning making' is a deeply 'human feature' that enables workers to build a strong connection between work activities and their wider life purpose and hope in life (Yeoman 2014). Accordingly, individuals pursue the narrative of the 'ideal' as something in line with the efforts and abilities of human beings to enjoy success in the future (Lamont and Hall 2009; Warikoo 2016; Mijs 2018).

However, workers' pursuit of and access to material resources plays an equally significant role in mediating and reshaping these meanings. This occurs through both formal and informal social practices and relationships within the complex and contested realm of social dynamics (Thompson and Vincent 2010). It is within this context that capital exerts social control by disciplining workers' effort through punishments and rewards (Edwards 1979). In a recent study on gender inequality, for example, Cohen et al. (2023) draw upon Ackers' (1990) application and representation of the 'ideal worker' to define and legitimize 'the ways in which power is defined and deployed ... *by* valuing some qualities and ways of being and penalizing others' (Cohen et al. 2023: 538—italics added). Therefore, the meanings assigned to unpaid labour are influenced by economic, social, and institutional factors, as individuals require access to resources in order to sustain their unpaid labour and minimize the risk of social stigma in the present. However, not everyone has the same access to these resources. Thus, the cultural and social structures—which in his *Theory of Communicative Action* (1981) Jürgen Habermas defined as the 'levels of the systems'—within which individuals strive to achieve their desired and meaningful goals play a significant role in shaping these dynamics. Consequently, the extent to which unpaid labour can contribute to inequality in precarious work depends on an individual's ability to access the necessary resources to sustain unpaid labour.

To conclude, whereas reframing or retuning a *self*-image by subjective experiences of identity (i.e., the 'ideal worker' norm) may allow workers to define their jobs as meaningful, valued, and fulfilling, such epithets are dependent on the material, exploitative, and class-based structural conditions of the work. Social relations of exploitation reflect inequality, as power is intertwined with class-based and gendered differences in social status. The following section therefore uses the concept of resilience and theories of class reproduction to theorize how and to what extent unpaid labour, stemming from the nature of the work in the three described work areas or occupational fields, accounts for inequality in precarious work, examining resilience in the form of the resources able to sustain people's capabilities to undertake unpaid labour in the run-up to or while performing paid employment.

Resources for Resilience and Class

Resilience is defined as the capacity to cope with different kinds of challenges (Hall and Lamont 2013). It is built upon resources allowing people to live a secure and meaningful life. These resources refer to financial and social capital used in pursuit of favour and advancement (Bourdieu 1986). Either individual (i.e., social, cultural, or economic) or collective (i.e., institutional) resources function as the financial and social underpinnings of unpaid labour. As constituents of individual resilience, financial and social resources relate to income and social reproductive labour support within families. Cultural resources are further constituents.

Offering a society collective resilience, institutional resources take the form of redistributive and generous welfare benefits, employment protection in labour markets, and state policies (albeit for the most part limited to those within an employment relationship). Beginning in the 1980s–90s, state-based neoliberal policy reforms in Europe led to important transformations enhancing precarious conditions in labour markets due to cuts in institutional resources. Welfare, social benefits, and employment protections of various kinds were all pruned, while in many cases the state withdrew from funding various sectors. Yet all these institutional resources were key to the collective resilience inherent to a welfare state. In other words, the partial dismantling of the welfare state under neoliberalism can also be seen as a reduction in collective resilience and a concomitant rise in self-responsibility. Furthermore, these neoliberal cuts fostered precarious work. For example, care services became 'marketable goods' (Ungerson 1997), with new competition- and cost-based market forces exerting downward pressure on working conditions (Hermann and Flecker 2012). Likewise, the increasing influence of market-driven principles and reduced public funding in the creative and cultural industries (CCIs) led to a rise in project-based employment (Whiting and Symon 2020). While CCI project work itself is not inherently precarious, studies have shown that the combination of flexible schedules and unpaid overtime has created unstable conditions for workers involved in projects (Greer et al. 2018). This situation has resulted in workers having to juggle multiple jobs to make ends meet (Taylor 2004). These challenges are particularly evident in cases where state funding has been replaced by private funding (Pulignano, Dean, et al. 2023), leading to heightened competition among project workers seeking opportunities in the market (Greer and Umney 2022). While a worker may compete for work under precarious conditions in the public sphere, what happens in the private domestic sphere relates to how a family adapts to the insecurities and uncertainties manifested in the labour market by offering the resources to sustain this work (Pugh 2015). As indicated in Chapter 1, Beckman and Mazmanian (2020) talk about 'scaffolding', defining it as the patterns which emerge in how families distribute and manage precarious work by offering different support structures. Middle-class families and individuals with resources and fungible assets are able to provide support to sustain family members in precarious work, while working-class individuals and families without such resources and structures become increasingly impoverished and pressurized as they seek to deal with the insecurities they face. Moreover, when faced with an unstable income, variable work schedules, and requirements to qualify themselves for work, for example by acquiring their own tools of the trade, the latter are rarely able to mitigate the financial and material consequences of unpaid labour alone. Mitigation is thus managed within families and households (where such exist) where efforts to erect 'scaffolding' to cope with the uncertainties of the precarious work often reflect the different socio-economic class-based positions of the individual, household, and family. In a nutshell, resilience is thus dependent on available resources and is thus class based.

Building on Bourdieu's notion of the fluid and evolving nature of class formation (1986: 12), Wacquant (1991) demonstrates that the middle class has no fixed boundaries but rather undergoes continuous production and transformation. Research into understanding the composition and function of cultural capital in the reproduction of class inequality (Lamont and Molnár 2002; Lamont et al. 2014) has focused on how symbolic boundaries produce, reproduce, and/or follow from in-group social differences, or exclusion from positions requiring material resources. Symbolic boundaries are conceptual distinctions devised to categorize objects, people, practices, and even time and space (Lamont and Molnár 2002: 168; see also Pachucki et al. 2007). Importantly, they are considered the 'cultural processes [that] are a crucial missing link between cognitive processes and macro-level inequality' (Lamont et al. 2014: 8). Symbolic boundaries differ from—but are also typically seen as congruent with—social boundaries (Sherman 2018), which are defined as 'objectified forms of social differences manifested in unequal access to and unequal distribution of resources (material and non-material) and social opportunities' (Lamont and Molnár 2002: 168). Whereas symbolic distinctions may or may not correspond to material ones, they always recognize and legitimize unequal allocations of resources (material and non-material). Nonetheless, structures of power and domination are maintained and reproduced by the legitimacy which attributes recognition to some groups and misrecognition to others. Bourdieu and Wacquant (1992) argue, for example, that power works through (mis)recognition whereby cultural privilege, social status, and power are seen as ascribed rather than achieved, and therefore thought of as natural and legitimate. Importantly, Bourdieu associates this (i.e., the 'essentialising of value') with the powerful, whose power can be hidden and hence misrecognized.

In her book *Class, Self and Culture*, Beverly Skeggs (2004) extends this argument by illustrating how the process of class formation operates in reverse as well. She reveals that individuals on the bottom rungs of the social hierarchy are also subject to misrecognition, ascribed with essential characteristics imposed and fixed by societal values. This form of (mis)recognition goes beyond concealing the workings of the powerful; it also conceals the systems of inscription and classification serving the interests of the powerful. The latter not only justify their claims to power by legitimizing their own interests but also by denying access to or recognition within systems of symbolic domination. These systems enforce a sense of fixity upon those from whom the powerful derive their authority and claim moral distance. As Chapter 5 (in Part II) illustrates, and this is more accentuated in the United Kingdom (UK) than in Germany, the relatively limited resources available to working-class women in residential care in terms of access to alternative good-quality jobs, and the relatively limited support for domestic work and childcare (care work is considered a vocation for women), explain why these workers experience a binary relationship between unpaid labour and precarious work. Yet care workers associate meanings of genuine attachment and altruistic motivations to the unpaid labour they perform despite the poor working conditions and pay for this type of work (see also Hebson et al. 2015). We conclude that discerning how social positioning, movement, and exclusion are generated through systems of inscription, exchange, and value is key to understanding how inequalities are produced, lived, and read by workers. This book addresses these aspects in relation to precarious work and unpaid labour, identifying the structures of power and exploitation which account for how unpaid labour, stemming from the nature of the work in the three described work areas or occupational fields, helps address inequality in precarious work, in different forms and among different domains where resources to sustain unpaid labour are differently available. In so doing, we theorize how unpaid labour is both shaped by class and serves to reproduce class structures, examining how and to what extent individuals and workers sustain unpaid labour. This involves focusing on the class divisions of unpaid labour, the role played by unpaid labour in the distribution and exchange of both economic and symbolic resources and various forms of capital (Bourdieu 1986).

As indicated above, our focus is not solely on symbolic (cultural) and social resources for individuals to sustain unpaid labour. This book also examines the institutional frameworks within labour markets at both country and sector levels able to provide individuals with ways of sustaining unpaid labour. We observe that, under the influence of neoliberalism, these regulatory arrangements have undergone significant changes, for example, transitioning from collective to individualized approaches to risk. In the following sections, we provide an overview of these changes in the investigated sectors (i.e., creative dance, residential care, and online platform work) and countries where empirical fieldwork was conducted between 2020 and 2022. These investigations are presented in detail in Part II of the book. In this chapter we confine ourselves to showing how these changes have involved diverse arrangements at the level of welfare and employment regulation, as well as state policies in relation to investment and state funding and the emergence of digital technologies.

Creative Dance

'Project Work' between Market and State Policy

Cultural and creative industries (CCIs) cover a wide range of occupational activities (Campbell et al. 2019). However, the term is used here in sole reference to dance (ballet). The work is predominantly 'project work' performed by freelancers. As indicated above, although not all project work is precarious, it is well established in the literature that project work can raise uncertainties by shifting risk away from an employer to the freelancer.

CCIs utilize project work to achieve flexibility within a volatile and unpredictable market for creative products (Hesmondhalgh and Baker 2011) to minimize costs, while encouraging and enabling reliance on trust and commitment in relation to whom is hired (Antcliff et al. 2007). CCI project work is usually linked to an individualistic mode of existence, often including working for free as this is associated with the 'vocation' of being an artist. This vocation is normalized by what Millar (2014: 48) has called 'an art of living in a precarious present'. Yet, and importantly, precarious work in CCIs emerges from market-based organizing principles. These principles shape the 'social framework' (Sydow and Staber 2002) in which project work takes place, subordinating creative workers to national arts (funding) policies and employer demands. The latter are intermittent, temporary, and unpredictable, making work arrangements casual (McKinlay and Smith 2009; Kunst 2015). A growing strand of research points to the activities of policy formation by the state as an important factor accounting for precarity by shifting risks through the organization of transactions between self-employed service providers and clients (Greer et al. 2009). Broadly speaking, national governments in Europe have provided little support to self-employed CCI project workers (Khlystova et al. 2022), generating precarity for these workers—especially during the Covid-19 pandemic (Pulignano et al. 2021).

The case of creative dancers in the Netherlands and Sweden presented here (see Chapter 4) takes a perspective encompassing the cultural processes of an artist's vocation or 'virtual identity' and a state's arts policy to account for the precarious nature of project work in dance. Studies have shown that the rise in precarious project work in CCIs has often coincided with cuts in public funding (Umney and Symon 2020). They have also shown that these cuts have spurred dance companies to increasingly resort to project-based work performed by freelance dancers (Pulignano, Dean, et al. 2023). Whether such work translates into precarious employment conditions will likely depend on how and to what extent the funding organizations and institutions are able to shelter project workers.

Moreover, the extent to which project workers are able to cope with the precarious conditions of their work (their 'resilience') is likely to be dependent on the resources available to them. As dance is an occupation requiring substantial and permanent personal investment in training (as a 'tool of the trade') which is not always reflected in the rates attained by the dancers, and as the majority of dancers are self-employed project workers with little access to the institutional resources generally reserved for employees, dance—and importantly ballet—tends to be a field of work populated by non-working-class artists, i.e. those with access to the requisite socio-economic resources provided by the household.

One further aspect of the 'resilience' needed when working as a performing artist is the ability to come to terms with the hierarchy of dance where only a select few dancers reach the pinnacle of their profession and thus enjoy immunity from its financial and social downsides. For the rest, perseverance and hope constitute the personal 'resources' needed to cope with unsocial working conditions in a field where family life takes a backseat.

Residential Care

Labour Shortages, Working Conditions, and Covid-19

Residential elderly care faces important challenges. In particular, privatization and corporatization (Farris and Marchetti 2017), whereby large multinationals are investing in long-term care by acquiring assets in national (health)care systems, have arguably disrupted the quality and stability of care service provision. Importantly, work in residential care has become increasingly pre-defined, standardized, and fragmented (what we term '*stopwatch care*'), with care providers often lacking a supportive human resource management infrastructure. This is leading to heavier workloads for carers, in turn contributing to endemic staff recruitment and retention problems. For example, Skills for Care (2021) estimated that the turnover rate of directly employed staff working in adult social care in the UK was 28.5% in 2020/1, equivalent to approximately 410,000 leavers over the year. Looking at this figure in greater detail, average staff turnover was 31.5% in care homes with nursing (i.e., nursing homes) and 29.6% in care homes without nursing (often referred to as long-term residential homes) (Devi et al. 2021). On average, 6.8% of roles in adult social care were vacant in 2020/1, equivalent to approximately 105,000 vacancies (House of Commons 2022).

The main reasons for staff leaving care include pay, hours of work, poor working conditions, and feelings of burnout and stress. Brexit has aggravated the widespread staff shortages in the UK, with European Union workers withdrawing from the UK labour market (Johnson and Pulignano 2021). Germany likewise faces a shortage of care staff, a phenomenon set to grow since the number of people needing home care is estimated to increase from 2.3 to 3.4 million by 2030, according to the German Statistics Institute (Knaebel 2022). As of 2019, over 4.1 million people nationwide were in need of care in Germany, while over 36,000 care positions were vacant in 2022 (Bundesagentur für Arbeit 2022). Low wages, a high level of responsibility, and long working hours under intense time pressure discourage people from entering the sector. What further complicates the matter in Germany is that residential care homes compete for staff with hospitals which are generally able to pay higher wages (Wichterich 2019).

Although the poor pay and working conditions in residential care may prompt dissatisfaction among care workers, research has shown that care workers consider their work to be meaningful. Analyses of the choices of working-class women entering care point to their otherwise limited employment opportunities, with care work possibly offering them some rewards in comparison to previous and alternative employment (Hebson et al. 2015). These analyses also indicate that care work does not preclude the possibility of genuine attachment and altruistic motivations, and is often considered to be a vocation reflecting women's natural predisposition and justifying not only their attraction or suitability for such work (Folbre 2012; Palmer and Eveline 2012), but also their 'acceptance of poor working conditions and pay for this type of work' (Hebson et al. 2015: 32).

The challenges already weighing down on the quality of care services and working conditions for care workers became even more pressing during the Covid-19 pandemic when residential care homes found themselves inadequately prepared and underresourced to deal with the crisis, placing inordinate and intense job demands on workers (Barnett and Grabowski 2020). In 2020, for example, 25,000 untested patients were rapidly discharged into residential care in England and Wales between mid-March and mid-April (BBC 2020), laying the foundations for a residential sector crisis that saw 27,000 'excess deaths' in 2021 (compared with the five-year average) (in accordance to the Office of National Statistics). In Scotland, too, residential care was at the centre of the first-wave crisis. In the first week of April 2020, 'care home deaths were more than 160% higher than the historic average of weekly deaths in care homes' (Bell et al. 2020). To our knowledge, there are no official statistics on Covid-19-related mortality rates in Germany (Fischer 2022), although they can be expected to be similarly high.

Broadly speaking, the high death toll in residential care presented care workers with an extreme form of 'emotional labour' (Hochschild 1983), with them finding it difficult to cope with the increased workload and daily deaths in underfunded and understaffed care homes. Moreover, local authorities' revenues and local government spending power (i.e., government funding, council tax, and business rates) dropped by 29% in real terms between 2010/11 and 2021/2 in the UK (House of Commons 2023). While the government in the UK provided short-term emergency funding to local authorities to deal with the social and financial consequences of the pandemic, this funding proved to be insufficient (Health Foundation 2021).

The German government provided a fast response to the crisis in care which, together with the guidelines from the European Centre for Disease Control and Prevention and the strong support for care homes to implement them (Ellison et al. 2022), helped monitor the spread of the infection, particularly in residential care settings (Fischer 2022). The German trade union Ver.di, which represents health and care workers, has secured an agreement with the employers' organization BVAP to provide a €1,500 bonus to nursing staff and caregivers for their contributions during the COVID-19 crisis. Additionally, the agreement includes extra payments for part-time workers and trainees.

Online Platform Work

Competition and Self-Employment

Catering for freelancers operating from home, online platforms have to a large extent replaced traditional agencies as intermediaries between clients and service providers (Lomax 2017). They are attractive for freelancers because they in effect take care of the marketing (the search for clients) which freelancers would otherwise have to perform themselves. Platform business models are designed to generate profit through charging commissions for their intermediation services, whereby the commissions may be paid either by the freelancer or the client. Typical fields of work include information technology (IT) (e.g., programming or website design), graphic design, and language processing (e.g., translating or proofreading).

As freelancers, online platform workers are not subject to any working time restrictions and are thus free to 'make hay while the sun shines', such as working long hours when demand for their services is high, and short hours when demand is slack. Despite such fluctuations, they aim to generate—averaged over time—a living income. However, this 'perfect world' is being undermined by technological developments, whether in the intermediation phase in the form of automated algorithm-driven work assignment or in the actual conduct of the work in the form of artificial intelligence (AI)-driven service automation, as seen increasingly in the field of language processing (e.g., DeepL and Google Translate).

Our focus is on how the operations of online platforms are impacting freelancers' ability to attain a living income. Several factors need to be considered here. First, the fact that the platforms are online basically means that they are open to service providers throughout the world, including those in countries in different time zones and with lower costs of living, thereby allowing other deadlines (deadline competition) and lower rates (price competition) to be offered. Second, rating systems have become transparent, meaning that freelancers are under even more pressure to deliver excellent work to attain and maintain their reputation, and thus their access to paid work. Any dent in their ratings can have a major repercussion on their income. Furthermore, this transparency enables clients to make opportunistic demands, for example requesting freelancers to perform work unpaid in return for a good rating. Third, platforms are squeezing their rates, whether by the above-mentioned price competition, by the commissions charged to freelancers, or by certain platforms' requirement for freelancers to purchase platform currency to bid for jobs.

As we will see in Chapter 6, these developments are eating into freelancers' incomes, making their living situations increasingly precarious. Though the causes differ, the repercussions are the same as those experienced by dancers. With no institutional resources available due to the online platform workers not having an employment relationship, external (household) resources are needed to sustain the work. This in turn makes online platform work a class-based domain, as only non-working-class households have the necessary resources available.

Summary

In this chapter, we defined a theory of the politics of unpaid labour, developing a framework exploring how unpaid labour can contribute to inequality in precarious work. We started by examining the concept of the 'ideal worker' norm which establishes a standard and carries a stigma. We conceptualized this norm as a form of symbolic power serving the logic of capital accumulation and making workers strive to avoid being disrespected or stigmatized by prioritizing work, including unpaid labour. We then went on to look at the concept of resources for resilience and class, explaining how unpaid labour contributes to the social reproduction of class-based stratification in precarious conditions. Unpaid labour is socially and economically costly, as it often requires support behind the scenes, such as that provided by a stay-at-home spouse, or other financial and institutional resources. These resources sustain individuals during periods of inactivity or other challenges. Overall, our framework highlights the interplay between the 'ideal worker' norm and the costs and support associated with unpaid labour, shedding light on the dynamics and processes driving inequality within precarious work. We argue that how unpaid labour is handled plays a crucial role in understanding how inequality unfolds within a context of precarious work. It is important to recognize that not everyone possesses the same resources to sustain unpaid labour. This unequal distribution of resources reflects class-based power structures that are historically exploitative and perpetuated over time. By illustrating how unpaid labour contributes to the reproduction of class-based structures and the resources it necessitates, we contribute to ongoing discussions on precarious work and inequality. Importantly, we shed light on how precarious work generates unequal effects through the lens of unpaid labour. Furthermore, our work adds to the debates surrounding precarious work and unpaid labour by theorizing the extent to which unpaid labour contributes to precarity.

We back the theorization developed in Part I by empirical case studies in Part II of this book. As explained in the section of the methodology used (see Appendix), our case studies were based on 129 interview and thirty-eight audio diaries with employees and freelancers working in the areas of dance, residential care, and online platform work in various European countries. These case studies look at the working conditions of these often-precarious workers, with a focus on unpaid labour, the social, financial, and institutional resources at their disposal to cope with it, and their social backgrounds. In doing so, we draw a connection between resource availability and class (and gender).

PART II

THE EMPIRICS BEHIND THE THEORY OF THE 'POLITICS OF UNPAID LABOUR'

4

Dance 'for the Sake of Art'

A Non-Binary Relationship between Unpaid Labour and Precarious Work in Swedish and Dutch Dance Organizations

Dance in the Netherlands and Sweden

Dance as an 'art form' has an uneasy relationship with the market in terms of financial support through public or private patronage (Wulff 2014), a finding significant for assessing employment outcomes. Ballet, as one form of dance, is a poignant example.

Unlike in Sweden, public funding in the Netherlands is not allocated to individual dancers, but mainly to organizations at national, regional, and municipal level. Only two leading ballet companies, the National Ballet and the Scapino Ballet Rotterdam, can apply for long-term public funding from the Ministry of Education, Culture and Science (Rijksoverheid 2020). All others must apply for short-term project funding. There are a small number of arms-length public-funded bodies, such as the Performing Arts Fund, as well as a host of private funders such as the Prins Bernhard Cultuurfonds. As the Dutch government emphasizes notions of the 'cultural entrepreneur' in awarding public funding (Ministry of Welfare, Public Health and Culture 1999), cultural organizations have to privately fund 15% of their total budget before being able to receive public funding (Pots 2000). Such thresholds are absent in Sweden where organizations such as the Royal Swedish Ballet are largely state subsidized. Public grants are also available for individual dancers, providing them with a regular income (SOU 2009). However, a mixed public-private funding model was introduced in Sweden as an austerity measure in 2009 (Myndigheten för Kulturanalys 2017), emphasizing the role of the 'artist as entrepreneur' (SOU 2009: 16). Fund distribution at national, regional, and municipal levels has shifted to project-oriented funding, increasingly resulting in short- and fixed-term work and self-employment (in the form of freelancing) via grants and scholarships.

The Politics of Unpaid Labour. Valeria Pulignano and Markieta Domecka, Oxford University Press.
 DOI: 10.1093/oso/9780198888130.003.0005

Project work in Sweden increased by 59% between 2010 and 2017, while permanent employment in contemporary dance and ballet organizations decreased from 81 to 57% between 1999 and 2018 (Tillväxtverket 2018). Nevertheless, private funding in ballet remains limited, with public funding predominating (Flisbäck and Lund 2015).

Over the past two decades in both the Netherlands and Sweden the role of funding bodies has become more significant in determining dancers' working lives. However, the two countries had different starting points. Taking the form of (arts) budget cuts, Dutch government responses to financial crises fuelled the already fierce competition for funding among ballet companies, leading to an increased proportion of dancers working as freelancers: between 2010 and 2015, for example, freelance project work in dance increased in the Netherlands by 20%, while the number of dancers in permanent employment decreased by 30% (Lahaut 2019). Conversely, in Sweden, regular and stable employment retains its importance in traditional ballet companies (Wulff 2014).

Studies also report that the way in which funding bodies have helped shape the organization of service transactions has generated inequality. Importantly, new forms of funding have impacted hiring practices in dance—to a large extent network-based—generating disadvantages related to ethnicity/race, gender, and class status (Pulignano, Dean, et al. 2023). In the Dutch and Swedish dance scenes, where approximately three-quarters of dancers are women (CBS 2020; Statistiska Centralbyrån 2021), female dancers have a higher share of self-employment. In Sweden, however, male dancers tend to earn more, with the top income bracket consisting of 59 percent men and 41 percent women (Konstnärsnamnden 2016).

Furthermore, the projectification of work in dance and the limited role of public funding, especially in the Netherlands, have encouraged trade unions to conclude collective agreements in order to create a level playing field for decent working conditions for performing artists. They are based on a July 2019 recommendation developed by the Dutch Authority for Consumers and Markets (Autoriteit Consument en Markt) and re-interpreting competition law under certain conditions, for instance when freelancers work side by side with employees (Van Andel and Loots 2022). The collective agreement for theatre and dance negotiated between the Nederlandse Associatie voor Podiumkunsten (NAPK) as the employer organization and the Kunstenbond as the worker organization has introduced minimum pay rates and regulated working hours, travel time, rest periods, and leave. Rates for freelance dancers should be 150% of the remuneration of salaried workers to compensate for the higher personal costs a self-employed individual has compared to a salaried worker, for instance in terms of spending on (disability) insurance and savings for pensions. However, this only applies to freelancers replacing employees within a sector where a high proportion of workers (63%) in the Netherlands earned less than two-thirds of the national mean in November 2018 (Been and Keune 2022). In Sweden, in addition to the collective agreements concluded between the Danscentrum, the Swedish Performing Arts Association, and the Swedish Union for Performing Arts and Film, the Swedish Arts Council developed an action programme in 2003 for professional dancers. Its aim is to guarantee universal access to social protection for dancers, irrespective of whether employees or freelancers, in public-funded dance organizations. As a result, in 2006, a dance alliance (the Dansalliansen) owned by the above three organizations and Trygghetsrådet TRS (The Job Transition Foundation – TRS) was introduced to extend social protection to freelance dancers in state-based dance organizations (also called dance institutions) in Sweden.

The distinction between the more encompassing protection offered to dancers in Sweden and that in the Netherlands was reflected in the measures introduced by the respective governments to support both freelance and employee dancers during the Covid-19 pandemic. In the Dutch performing arts, including theatre and dance, there were no ad hoc measures introduced. The only measures available were those generally foreseen for the self-employed. Given how difficult it was to exercise in such an environment, with lockdowns negatively impacting skills and shortening an already short career, government funds were obviously insufficient to allow dancers to reskill. Even dancers able to benefit from general government funds, being self-employed they found themselves having to practice to keep in shape in often small apartments, often together with children learning remotely from home. In Sweden, the government introduced extra funding for the dance alliance, while arts councils and private dance organizations provided compensation for income lost due to cancelled performances. While not alleviating all problems, this covered dancers' training and other needs. However, the processing of applications for unemployment funds in Sweden often proved to be lengthy for dancers with multiple contracts and mixed contractual statuses (either fixed-/short-term employees or freelancers). These long administrative procedures meant that both fixed-/short-term and freelance dancers had to save for the eventuality of unemployment, even if they officially had access to unemployment insurance funds (Pulignano et al. 2021).

To gain an insight into working conditions in dance, with a focus on what motivates dancers to perform unpaid labour, what resources they have available to sustain it, and how they deal with any ensuing precarity, we conducted twenty-five biographical narrative interviews with dancers (thirteen in Sweden and twelve in the Netherlands) and collected eight audio work diaries (five in Sweden and three in the Netherlands). The results are presented below.

Results of Our Study in the Netherlands and Sweden

Precarity for Whom? The Biographical Case of Lisa Who Can Sustain Unpaid Labour in Dance

Thirty-six years old and white, Lisa (NL03) is a freelance dancer of Canadian origin. Her family moved to the Netherlands when she was 5. She started her 'serious' dance training at the age of 10 at the Royal Conservatorium in a large city in the Netherlands. Her parents are professional dancers who later in their careers started a private dance school in the Netherlands. During her dance training in Holland, Lisa realized she was much more interested in contemporary dance than classical ballet, leading to her decision to continue her training in New York. She did not stay for the full four years until graduation, as she received a job offer from a dance company in France. She accepted it, following her teacher's advice that she would learn more in the real dance world than at a dance school. The job in France was without a contract: 'we were housed there, we were given food and we got just a little spending money, but nothing you could live on'. It was also a short-term job and soon Lisa needed to look for new work opportunities, doing auditions and unpaid internships: 'Both of my parents come from the dance world, so I had a huge advantage of having some connections and private auditions. I feel very lucky about that'. Lisa's 'luck' also stems from the fact that continuing support from her family makes it possible for her to sustain the unpaid and unpredictable work arrangements. Lisa subsequently worked in Spain, in an organization bridging apprentice dancers and professional dancers. She did not receive a salary there but 'a scholarship like financial aid', which meant it was very low, keeping her dependent on her family's support: 'I was getting help from my parents to pay the rent'. Lisa tried to find something positive in these frequent changes and short-term poorly paid contracts by saying: 'When you start in one company, it just narrows you down as a dancer. And I can try many different things.' After a year in Spain, she went to Israel, following the choreographer she collaborated with. She worked there in a dance company where 'conditions were very different from what we're used to in Europe. There were no contracts at all, there was no payment at all'. For Lisa, who was not paid much before, working now completely for free came as a shock, especially as it was 'a widely respected choreographer and a famous dance company'. Her work schedule was very hard: 'We had the shows three or four times a week, two children's performances in the morning, which often meant getting onto a bus at 4am, driving somewhere, having the first show at 9:30 and the second at 11:00. And then driving back and still having rehearsals.' Nevertheless, Lisa was 'happy' to be there as she could 'learn so much'. To generate a modicum of income, she took on a side job as a dance teacher, while continuing to receive financial help from her parents in the Netherlands. When Lisa's Israeli company went on a tour of Northern Europe, work conditions became even more difficult:

> This time I got paid but also you are not at home, you're on the road the whole time and it's the North, so cold and dark. It makes a difference, especially if you work with your body. I would sit on the bus for many hours, then do a performance and sit on the bus again for many hours. Physically traveling is the hardest thing for your body.

During the tour, Lisa sustained a knee injury: 'very frustrating, but it's part of the job'. Lisa needed knee surgery but as she was working without an employment contract, she had no health insurance abroad. She travelled to the Netherlands for the surgery, afterwards receiving some physiotherapy at her parents' private dance school: 'At the age of 23, I went back to live with my parents—with no income, no company's support, no insurance, just nothing'. On recovering, she started working as a freelance dancer on a number of projects, first in the Netherlands, then internationally. Lisa keeps comparing the working conditions of freelancer dancers in the Netherlands and elsewhere: 'In France, dancers are more protected than in Holland. When they don't earn, they have fantastic support there. The same is true in Sweden. But here in Holland, there's nothing'. In her periods without income, Lisa received financial support from her family: 'In my unemployed moments, when I went around auditioning, any other dancer would have had huge costs in taking classes. I didn't, because I could always get classes in my parents' company. They also helped me pay for the auditions and travelling'. Now working as a freelance dancer, Lisa is participating in several international projects which are crucial for applying for funding abroad: 'We kicked off a series of projects, as culture funding in Holland got cut like crazy. In 2013 things were closing right and left. Opportunities were taken away, so we had to start building something with others, to be able to dance at all'. Lisa's partner works in dance too, as a choreographer. Likewise, many of her friends do so as well, forming a 'community of mutual support'. Lisa sees dancing as difficult to be combined with motherhood: 'My choices so far mean that I am now 36 and without a kid. And I don't know if I will ever have one. It's difficult to imagine it'.

Why Unpaid Labour? The 'Ideal Dancer' Norm and Sacrifice for the 'Sake of Art'

The pinnacle of success in the creative industries in general, and in dance in particular, is to be recognized as a 'real' artist. To earn confirmation as such (i.e., complying with the 'ideal' worker norm for a dancer), dancers are ready to put in untold hours, responding as 'real' artists to what 'real' art asks for, i.e. sacrificing themselves *for the sake of art* (Bourdieu 1986). As Jane indicates 'They say jump, we only ask how high. We're trained all our lives to say yes' (NL02_Jane).

Students and graduates from dance schools report that 'dance is the art you need to make sacrifices for' (SE22_Anna), as it requires a serious investment from childhood onwards and involves constant body work. One way of showing that one is able to make sacrifices is to work for free. At the same time, doing free or unpaid work can result in someone making another feel inadequate or unworthy as Nadja states: 'They make you believe you're never really good enough, so you kill yourself with work (SE21_Nadja). Likewise, the expectation to have to invest in oneself, eventually spending time doing unpaid work, is framed within ongoing changes in the institutional and structural conditions—including policy and funding interventions—underpinning the creative and cultural industries (CCIs). These changes are leading to employment in the industry becoming increasingly precarious, very often taking on a 'project' form.

Cuts in public funding are leading to dance companies reducing employment contract lengths or switching to service contracts for self-employed dancers (see Chapter 3). In the latter case, dancers are considered to be autonomous service providers theoretically choosing between working time and free time and setting their rates. However, in practice they often end up working permanently with little influence on their rates as the market they depend on for earnings is increasingly competitive: 'If you want money, you need to make the money happen. You need to contact the right people, you need to collaborate with people, you need to think constantly how you can reinvent yourself. And you can't ask for too much [money], otherwise people won't work with you' (NL04_Sara). All of this self-marketing work is unpaid, falling under the category of the 'personal investment work' required of any freelancer, irrespective of the profession.

Freelance dancers have different types of contracts. In some, they are paid for nearly every step needed to achieve the final product (a performance close as possible to perfection). The money they receive at the end of their work is sufficient to cover rehearsals, conceptual work, the performance itself, and possibly even the rest time they need after each show. In other types of contracts, freelance dancers are paid mainly for the performance. This remuneration does not cover rehearsal time or the conceptual work they do with choreographers, helping them to develop the piece. They are not paid for rest time and for extra tasks they do, such as cleaning the stage and preparing their own costumes. In this case, if the hourly remuneration (total remuneration divided by the hours worked) is below the country's respective minimum wage, we contend that they are performing unpaid labour (cf. our definition of unpaid labour in freelancing in Chapter 1). Nevertheless, despite being aware of the unpaid consequences, they often have no other option than to sign such contracts, as they have no access to the first type. They are basically faced with the choice of dancing and performing some unpaid work or not dancing at all.

Through their personal investment work in keeping their bodies in shape, rehearsing to attain perfection, travelling (where only the most basic costs are covered), and participating in auditions (which they have to pay for) and the many promotional events, they 'hope' to demonstrate the 'right' attitude and be rewarded (recognized as 'real' artists). Similarly, they do everything to avoid being penalized, for example by being labelled as a 'troublemaker' and/or having their artistic identity questioned. By sacrificing themselves *for the sake of art*, they eventually build meaning into their work and life through having their identity reconfirmed. Yet, this constant reconfirmation comes at the cost of being expected to work untold hours and accept their work situations, 'gaining experience, connections and good advice but earning no money' (SE08_Nikola).

Dance has become synonymous with untold hours with meagre compensation, leading in many cases to precarity. For a handful of classical ballet and contemporary dancers lucky enough to find employment in state-funded dance companies, the situation is relatively manageable, but for those working—generally as freelance dancers—for underfunded small companies without the financial muscle to adequately remunerate their workers, the situation is characterized by ongoing uncertainty: 'It's very scary when you don't have a contract and you don't know if you will earn enough to cover your expenses' (NL06_Alessandro). Subject to a constant struggle to get a gig, they are under constant pressure to agree to training and rehearsals, rest time, travel time, and extra tasks ranging from stage lighting to stage cleaning, all within the scope of their employment or service provision contract, such as without any supplementary payment. In many cases, this is due to the dance company operating on a shoestring budget, and thus being unable to pay for all work put in by the dancers.

> Every four years the government decides which company gets the big money, and the big grant allows them to continue existing for four years. They make plans for four years. If you have a small company, you can try to ask for a one- or two-year grant. The big companies continue to have money, allowing them to employ their own manager, PR people, directing and technical staff, all this kind of things that a small company may not have. Maybe the choreographer is also the director and the costume designer. They do everything to try to survive, meaning that dancers do lots of things. Lighting, makeup, costumes and so on. And we're not paid extra for doing that. (NL06_Alessandro)
>
> I feel devalued at my workplace. It's something common because when the cultural sector goes under, it is difficult for our employers to try to be human and generous. But they're also trying to save their own asses, so everything goes downhill. (SE28_Jaime, diary)
>
> Working in a small theatre I started doing this ... extra work. They didn't have money to employ everybody. So I had to clean the stage before the performance. I had to do the lights with the technician. Especially during the tour this was very tough because I had to unload the car, help set up everything ... I was exhausted even before the performance started. (SE11_Fabiano)

Unpaid extra tasks are well documented in dancers' diaries as they form part and parcel of dancers' everyday life:

> Today I started the day by cleaning the dance halls. I did that between about 7:30 and 9am. And that was just regular housekeeping. Mopping, vacuuming, dusting, cleaning toilets, cleaning the kitchenette. The usual things. (SE10_Isabelle, diary)
>
> I was answering lots of emails on the [dance] company's website. I compiled and sent out various offers and took pictures for the website. I did that between about 12:30 and 17:30. I didn't get paid for that. (SE10_Isabelle, diary)

> I was sending some emails this morning to keep in touch and I sent some flyers about the new show. I booked the tickets and a room in [name of the city] where we perform. (NL07_Francesco, diary)

For dancers—whether freelancers or employed on short-term contracts—with no other means of support, either institutional (i.e., unemployment and other social benefits) or family based (e.g., reliance on an earning partner), such unpaid supplementary work translates into financial instability and existential insecurity. As we will illustrate in this chapter, the degree of access to resources determines whether dancers fall into precarious work and life trajectories. In this case study, we consider dancers of different ages, gender, ethnicity, class background, and whether able to rely on family support, in two distinct institutional contexts, Sweden and the Netherlands, showing the opportunities available to some categories of dancers and unavailable to others. In particular, different degrees of commodification in power structures, reflected in different levels of public funding and access to social benefits in the two countries, affect the extent of, motivation for, and the possibility of putting in untold hours in adherence to the 'ideal dancer' norm. The latter is the parameter used by those in key positions in dance and by dancers themselves to assess their 'real' artist identity earned through sacrificing themselves *for the sake of art.*

In both countries, many young people try to enter dance, following their passion for dancing and their dream of a fulfilling artistic career. They hope that their sacrifice in the form of working untold hours for little or no compensation at the start of their careers will pay off in the future:

> I did many unpaid jobs. In some cases, I had to pay for the possibility to work, to meet people, to learn. I paid for auditions. I paid for my training to be able to participate in a show in New York for different audiences. It was an important experience, but I had to pay for it. I thought it was some kind of opportunity. I knew I couldn't afford it, but I thought I could learn something, which I did. I got to rehearse for a show, together with a choreographer. I saw what it's like to be on stage, but … I had to pay for it. (SE02_Sandra)

Later on, dancers discover that these untold and unpaid hours are not an initial stepping-stone to a dance career, but are expected and required at all stages of their careers, with constant pressure to carry on working without remuneration in adherence to the norm of the 'ideal dancer'—a norm in the sense that it indicates the sacrifice to be made *for the sake of art* on three levels: excellent skills, hard work, and the 'right' attitude. In so doing, the norm resembles a Weberian 'ideal type'. There is no place in dance for workers who are less than 'ideal'. An 'ideal dancer' is supposed to have the skills necessary to deliver beauty and perfection, to work very hard at all times, as well as to have the 'right' attitude. This last aspect involves subordination and compliance (i.e., a readiness to follow the vision of others), all with a view to delivering on time and according to plan. Deviating from the 'ideal' incurs the risk of being taken away from the stage, losing employment and the status associated with on-stage presence, and thereby foregoing the prospects of future dance jobs. One is no longer considered as 'one of us', as a 'real' artist. The dancer's very identity is questioned. The excellent skills, hard work, and 'right' attitude shaping the 'ideal dancer' create the cultural and practical pressure forcing dancers to consent to personally invest untold hours in training and extra ballet classes to keep in perfect shape, to rehearse and travel without any supplementary pay, to prepare and wash their own costumes, to do their makeup, to help with stage lighting and cleaning, as well as tasks related to self-marketing and digital visibility:

> Travelling time is unpaid, even though it's part of the job. All the admin work I do is unpaid. Going to performances, doing classes, training. These are hours of work every day that you don't get paid for. When you have time off between one project and another you can't stop training. It's not an option to go to the gym or do dance classes, it's a necessity. Then you have to pay for things like treatments, depending on your insurance which most freelance dancers don't have. Sometimes there's no work contract. You work ten hours, yet get paid for six. Generally, dancers are financially undervalued, especially freelance dancers as they do so much work that is not accounted for. (NL03_Lisa)

> This morning I did the self-training and extra ballet class to prepare for the day, and of course, it's not paid. These are the things I need to cover myself but there's no choice. Self-training is something I have to do to be at the top of my profession. (NL06_Alessandro, diary)

> We do professional photo and video shoots to have something good to put online. I'm not getting paid for my own promotion or company promotion, or for putting videos on Instagram. All the PR is of course unpaid, and we have to do it by ourselves. (SE02_Sandra)

As stated in Chapter 1, from a legalistic point of view there is no such thing as unpaid work when working as a freelancer under a service provision contract. The rate of pay agreed between the freelancer and the client should be sufficiently high to allow the freelancer to attain a 'living income', as for instance reflected in the Dutch collective agreement for dancers which states that freelance dancers are to be paid a rate 50% higher than that for salaried dancers as compensation for their supplementary expenditure. However, competition between dancers combined with funding cuts mean that dancers are often unable to achieve an income covering all their costs, in turn meaning that much of their time investment goes unpaid:

> The pay was not that good. It was around // I mean if you consider per hour, it was quite a bit. But we were supposed to perform, and it was €175 for the day. But this also includes the training I had to do, the cost of the room I use for training, the cost of the train that it would be around €25 between everything. So, it's a bit under my, say, amount that I should get for a performance. (NL06_Alessandro, diary)

> The payment today is really a good payment because I'm getting paid around €300 for this performance, that is likely over my /ehm/ percentage that I normally get paid. So, it's kind of good money. And it definitively covers also for- example the training that I had to do in the morning. (NL06_Alessandro, diary)

> The daily income today was around €100 for the rehearsal. It was 9am to 4pm, so something like 7 hours, so not so much but still okay. It's much lower than what I should get, but in some projects I don't get paid for rehearsals at all, so ... (NL06_Alessandro, diary)

> Daily income. Difficult to put a value to it. And with rehab, I've just lost money. I went minus on that one because it costs kr740 [€65] each time. So, it was kr740 minus today. I did a workshop today so I earned kr2500 [€215] there. kr2500 before tax. I don't know how planning meetings can be of any value. I do not get paid for the meetings, but it will be a future project that I needed to do that. (SE28_Jaime, diary)

> I was working with [name] dance and theatre today between 9am and 2pm. We were supposed to finish at lunch, but we were pretty slow, so we didn't have lunch, but we kept going until about 2 o'clock. So, yes, it was overtime. We were rehearsing for performances and workshops that we'll be doing this week. I worked 5 hours, but I got paid for half a day. And the compensation for half a day is kr574 [€49]. (SE10_Isabelle, diary)

Moreover, the 'ideal dancer' works to the norm of prioritizing work over private and family life, reflecting the need to be constantly available, in shape, and ready to dance, and to execute tasks 'professionally' to the best of one's abilities, including investing in one's personal development and making sacrifices. Any deviation from the ideal is penalized by the non-recognition of one's identity as a 'real' artist. Reflecting gendered expectations of women being the ones who care for the family and rear children, married dancers are the ones usually penalized by the norm. By contrast, single women with no family responsibilities, as well as men in general, are the ones able to comply with the 'ideal' and therefore rewarded. Hence, gendered punishment and reward structures are the tools used to discipline and control dancers in dance production circles. Reflecting compliance or non-compliance with the norm, dancers are assessed as 'fitting in' or 'not fitting in', with the latter stigmatized through punitive measures of exclusion.

Stigmatization through Punishments and Rewards

We reconstruct punishments and rewards from the perspective of dancers, i.e. how they describe them and how they interpret and attribute meanings to them. For a dancer, not being considered a 'real' artist—a person willing to spend time performing tasks necessary for work but not directly associated with dancing—means having one's status suspended or lost (i.e., moving down a rung on the status ladder), having one's skills and attitude questioned (i.e., being labelled as not having the 'right' attitude, not sacrificing enough, not putting the 'love of art' in first place), and therefore being side-lined and excluded and eventually made unemployable through being sentenced to 'professional death'—in short, stigmatized—in the dance field.

Dancers' narratives draw a picture of highly hierarchical power relations where choreographers and artistic directors exercise control in almost limitless ways. They manipulate dancers by making them feel 'ashamed' and 'guilty' in order to force them to work longer and harder. In so doing, choreographers and directors discipline dancers by discouraging them from making any demands and forcing them to sacrifice their private lives and free time for prolonged rehearsals, travel, and networking activities. The threat of failure is used by those in key positions in the dance hierarchy: dancers are repeatedly told they will disappear from the stage with the stigma of a 'failed artist'. This threat becomes internalized by dancers themselves: 'not working fulltime as a dancer would be a failure' (SE06_Arianna).

Punishments

Punishment for non-compliance with the sacrifice expectation takes the form of judgement and exclusion, experienced by dancers through stigmatizing looks and comments. They see their professional skills being questioned, they are labelled as not being 'good enough' or 'difficult', they hear gossip about them 'not being capable', 'not working hard enough', or 'being a princess'. They experience being treated very differently when not complying with expectations: 'they started being mean when I questioned something, they changed their behaviour towards me' (NL09_Alba). Stigmatized dancers are taken off the stage and experience a loss of status: 'I was cast aside, looked down on, treated like shit' (NL04_Sara); 'they never casted me again' (NL09_Alba).

> Well, they came to me /eh/ to ask me to do it [stand in for another dancer], But that I was supposed to perform that very day, supposed to learn the piece in one day. And I was really, you know, I said I've done it many times before but with that piece specifically I didn't want to look bad. I didn't want it to be bad. So, I said no. But then after that they were—then they were mean, they changed their behaviour towards me, you know? Like okay, we'll ask someone else, and they make you feel like—you know? Bad. They would not cancel the piece, they wouldn't, because it was just like a 15-minute piece, they could just arrange it. They will not /eh/ change that part and you know cut this and do it and just, they will just make you feel like—because you didn't want to do it, now you're out. (NL09_Alba)

> I just looked at the clock, looked at them and very respectfully said like: 'Can we continue with the rehearsal, please? And if not, can I leave this room?'. And that was it. I never entered the room again when they were there. They never casted me again. Never. I never did that piece for them again, which in our company ... we don't have that. But also, there is no hierarchy. But with them there was a clear-cut hierarchy. (NL09_Alba)

> After three years of work, you're either asked to join the main company or to leave. I knew very early on that I wouldn't be staying. I knew I wasn't what they needed. I didn't feel appreciated. For three years I was being side-lined, looked down on, treated like shit, sorry for my vocabulary. So, I had no other choice but to go free-lancing ... That was a phase in my life I refer to with a lot of darkness and bitterness. (NL04_Sara)

To avoid being stigmatized as a 'troublemaker', dancers refrain from voicing their claims and complaints. To avoid being labelled as 'difficult' and potentially blacklisted (SE11_Fabiano), dancers often do not even protest in the face of injustice experienced by themselves and/or their fellow dancers. As the risk of punishment for voicing their concerns is real and high—'I've heard of freelance colleagues who did speak up, and then the next time they didn't have a job' (SE22_Anna)—dancers tend to keep their mouths shut, as in the case of Fabiano, trying to protect his partner at the cost of his own employability in dance:

> Then I moved, with my /eh/ fiancé [also a dancer], to the South of Sweden where I met some great choreographers. I was [in a dance theatre] there for two years. Then I got injured. That confronted me with the reality of how fragile the dance world is. Because as soon as I got injured /eh/—at the same time the artistic director changed—they didn't renew my contract. Even though I was there for two years. In Sweden if you're under contract for three years, then you get long-term employment ... My wife was in the same company. She was pregnant and they didn't give her a permanent contract. She found out that, after she'd left, they gave two permanent contracts to other dancers. So it was ... not the best feeling. Of course, we couldn't do anything ... I mean I wanted to ... but my wife said to drop it. And I did that ... So, we were both freelance ... struggling. Now I think I should change professions. (SE11_Fabiano)

There is also a stigma attached to a dancer 'not sacrificing enough'. For example, starting a family may be a reason to become side-lined. There is no flexibility in dance: 'nothing will adapt for you in your job so that you can have a family. Nothing' (NL09_Alba). If a dancer cannot cope, s/he gets replaced. Female dancers find it more difficult to comply with the norm of the 'ideal dancer', and especially with the expectation of being permanently available, as care responsibilities make it difficult for them to be always available for extra hours of rehearsal. Under these circumstances side-lining can be seen as discrimination. While there is obviously an inherent contradiction between parenting obligations and the imperatives of dance, Sweden tends to do more to alleviate the problems through its higher degree of regulation featuring proper maternity leave, long enough breaks during the day, and practically no overtime. Dancers in the Netherlands, however, are left to themselves to come to terms with their consciences:

> I was working a lot, doing many, many ballets, many, many performances. I had just returned to work with my first child, so I was taking her on tour with me and it was fine. Then I became pregnant again. I danced up until five months or a bit longer but then after that. you know, you don't fit anywhere. And my second child was more difficult, like Jesus Christ, bloody hell! She would cry every night, oh my God. And I was going back to work and straight into a tour. While they were still young that was relatively okay. We had this rule at NDT that your kids could come with you until they were two years old. After that, I had to leave both of them at home. And that was my last year, and it was so hard, so very, very hard. Like—feeling so guilty

for—not only being away so much but even when I was in the country, I was working such long hours? I would drop them off at nursery in the morning and then wouldn't be back 'till late, Quite often, even on a normal working day when we didn't have a show it was after seven. And then it was basically half an hour and then it was bedtime. I had … huge amount of guilt about that. Huge … It was just pushing it, pushing it, pushing it. Always pushing it. For some silly notion and I don't really know why I kept pushing it. (NL02_Jane)

If I hadn't had kids, I'd have been offered ballet master jobs in other countries … but I don't wanna move right now. So, you have very limited options now. (NL02_Jane)

When we tour, we're away for a month or five weeks, here and there. I got my first child when I was 27. I have three kids now. And of course, it's out of question to be a mother and a dancer. It's just—impossible. I did and some people did it too but it's rare and extremely difficult. If you want to have a family that's practically impossible in this career. Because if I'm on tour for five weeks, I don't see my kids. And we don't get any benefit, like maternity leave. It's different than other professions. They say we have to stop 6 weeks before birth and come back 6 weeks after. But that's practically impossible because it takes 6 weeks to get up on my feet again. Instead of paying for maternity leave, they say a person is sick. She gave birth but she's not feeling well, she's sick and she can't come back to work. So It's the insurance that actually pays my salary, not the company … If you need to breastfeed, you have to do it in your lunch break. We have 45 minutes lunch break and I had to pump my milk then. But [after dancing] you're exhausted, so there's no milk coming out and you have to come back for rehearsal. You know that if you are late there's pressure because you need to learn a choreography or create a choreography. And if you are late for a rehearsal then it's much more work mentally than if you're there from the start. So that's a lot of pressure … From the company there's no help with childcare. You have to figure out what to do. After my second child I got divorced and for me it was impossible to pay half of my children's nursery. With my salary. I mean just impossible. The nursery is extremely expensive because the hours that you work are extremely long. (NL09_Alba)

Those unable to adapt, which is frequently the case for women when they become mothers, get shifted to other roles, replaced, and/or excluded. Some women postpone the decision to become a mother as long as possible or don't have any children at all:

A lot of dancers try to become parents after their career. But then it's too late. I know many dancers who wanted to become mothers but couldn't because the career just

> took too much of their time and afterwards they were not able to conceive children. (NL09_Alba)

Dancers working in different contexts, as freelancers in both private and state-funded dance organizations, spoke of their experiences of injury and abuse. Such cases were more common in the Dutch sample where dancers found it more difficult to have their rights protected:

> There was this audition, lasting two days. I think at least 200 dancers were invited. We were divided into small groups of about 10. And they had then max. 5 minutes to show something . . . We were invited back into the hall and then it was announced that they were actually looking for women who could dance on pointe shoes, were super slim and preferably naked. But this had not been said beforehand. So I spent my whole day there, actually just losing my energy on something that didn't make any sense at all. But that's how dancers are treated. And it was such a big dance institution . . . (NL05_Leen)

> I had this really bad toe . . . I went to the physio, we're very lucky having a physio on campus, so he sent me for a scan and /ehm/ it turns out I have like massive degeneration of the joints. That came as a shock. But I felt there is no way this is going to stop me, you know. They offered me this cortisone injection and that was brilliant actually, it was very, very painful but it gave me almost instant relief. At that stage I was working a lot, doing lots of ballets, lots of performances. Also, I had just got back to work with my youngest, so I was still taking her on tour with me. I just carried on. Nine months after the first injection, it slowly started to wear off and then for the next two years I got an injection every year. But the amount of time that it gave me relief was getting shorter and shorter. And they said to me like: 'Listen you can get these forever if you want because there's no joint to be saved, so you should be thinking about stopping'. That was an orthopaedic specialist saying that. I remember being very emotional . . . I remember at one point, oh God . . . I was working with one of the choreographers . . . It was a rehearsal for this really difficult duet, and it was of course all on that foot and she just came up to me, put her foot under mine and just cracked it over and I remember like . . . I almost cried out, it was just the most painful . . . she found the most sensitive spot. (NL02_Jane)

We encountered experiences of dancers feeling unsupported, unprotected, and 'powerless' more frequently in the Dutch context, where dancers were forced to withdraw from a particular dance context in order to keep on dancing:

> At some point I had to leave the [dance] company ... I had a conflict with a choreographer ... and I chose to leave the company, despite having a stable position. I didn't have any other job to go to. I knew I was powerless. There were many things I wish I could've been able to express but I couldn't do it. It was better I kept all that to myself, it was better to leave. (NL07_Francesco)

> Here in the Netherlands, there is no union for dancers, so everybody is like on their own ... I really felt the need to be appreciated in that company. After three years of being side-lined, looked down on, treated like shit, I decided to leave and do freelancing, which seemed very hard and very insecure. (NL04_Sara)

Neither Francesco nor Sara quit dance completely. They left the dance companies where they felt 'powerless', 'left on their own', and unappreciated, and became freelancers.

Rewarding

Dancers are rewarded when they show the 'right' attitude. With positioning in the creative field based on the reproduction of dominant practices, compliance with formal and informal rules means that those in key positions can continue employing people similar to themselves: those in their own image, with a similar background and easily able to 'fit in'. The greatest reward in the dance field is to be recognized as an 'excellent' dancer and a 'real' artist. This recognition is crucial as it confirms dancers' own identities and their social identities linked to prestige. Beside the rewards in the immediate work context—in the form of recognition by choreographers, artistic directors, and colleagues—there is also the social status and prestige granted by society at large, especially in the case of dancers performing in top locations. The prestige is confirmed by having a regular on-stage presence in leading roles. Dancers consequently try to secure their stage time, often at the cost of great sacrifices.

This struggle to gain recognition as a 'real' artist means that dancers must adapt to the requirements of the dance field. This is facilitated by early socialization with 'body work'—as Anis (NL01) describes: dance is 'a long and ongoing investment in physical capital', the result of 'discipline, ongoing exercise and continuous diet you learn since you are a child' (NL01_Anis). This discipline over one's body and attitude becomes translated into subordination, following orders without questioning them, and never saying 'no'. It includes agreement to do unpaid labour being treated as part and parcel with dance. The dancers we interviewed were intrinsically highly motivated, driven by their passion for dance and by a sense of a Weberian calling (implying a fulfilment of duty). They adapt, out of love for their profession, to be able to do the type of work they are so passionate about:

> While dancing, I feel the most like myself. I love entertaining people, I love sharing emotion or energy, being able to give a part of me, that I see that people grasp and understand and take on and then evolve within themselves, that is something I really enjoy, and the stage is the best way to do it. I love communication in general and communicating through art and dance is really thrilling. (NL04_Sara)

> We're from all over the world and super dynamic and enthusiastic and so committed to dance, so passionate. (NL04_Sara)

Dancers adapt because they hope to find fulfilment in their professional field and recognition by 'adding something new to the dance scene, reinvigorating it, changing things' (SE06_Arianna). Unpaid labour is performed in the 'hope' of finding (paid) work—that is why Swedish self-employed dancers start developing a piece before handing in applications for funding. Yet sometimes this does not pay off and becomes a risk for the worker because funders often want to see proof that a dancer has already started working on a project. Therefore, there is a transfer of risk from the funder to the dancer: private and state funders do not want to take the risk of subsidizing a project where they cannot judge the actual artistic quality. Instead, they would like some indication that the dancer is serious and will be able to complete the project. This means, however, that dancers are faced with the risk of investing time and money by themselves (doing residencies, paying for travel/studio/equipment) without knowing if they will be funded at all (SE06_Arianna). Applying for grants is 'hope work' as 'everything is put into work, all the passion and enthusiasm, all the time, the weeks of only work, sleep and eat' (SE06_Arianna).

Beside adaptation out of their passion for dance, there is also adaptation out of fear. Dancers adhere to expectations, no matter the cost, as they are scared of being stigmatized: other important figures in the field may think that they are 'not good enough', their attitude is 'not right', or they are not 'real artists'. Adaptation brings not only reward in the form of recognition, but also incurs physical and emotional costs as dancers sacrifice their health to meet expectations. The long training needed to achieve excellence can lead to strains and injuries. It may also entail emotional ups and downs in relation to the artistic production cycles, consisting of lighter days of rehearsals and very intense days before a première. The long hours and overtraining take their toll, with many dancers needing physiotherapy or psychotherapy (SE22_Anna), the costs of which must often be covered by the dancers themselves. There are also relational costs involved, as relationships and childbearing decisions are very much affected by where and when dance work can be performed. As such, dancers' capacity to show that they are willing to sacrifice themselves, their health and well-being, as well as their families is not equally distributed. As indicated, women who had decided to become mothers, despite the expectation of sacrifice to adhere to the 'ideal dancer' norm, spoke of the suffering caused by their adaptation efforts:

> There's this pressure ... that your body needs to be perfect but after becoming a mother, your body has changed, and you don't know if you'll be able to recover ... I also had postpartum depression after my first child because the birth went really bad, I almost lost him ... And my mind was going over and over again throughout the birth and through the fact that I almost lost him ... but I had to go back to work. After just three, no, two months, after my caesarean I was actually on stage doing my first performance ... In the dance world you find very few women who actually have families. You find some but—there are very few. This means it's really difficult to find any understanding. (NL09_Alba)

By adhering to the norm of sacrifice *for the sake of art*, dancers are pressured into things that are not of their choice, including performing unpaid labour. The pressure they feel to say 'yes' and thus kowtow to the expectations of those in key positions in dance leads to a perception of unpaid labour as undesired but 'unavoidable'. Long-term kowtowing leads to disillusionment, burnout, and withdrawal, or in rare cases, contestation. There is an illusion that unpaid labour is part of the 'rite of passage' in the creative sectors, only a temporary phase in one's career usually associated with a junior status. However unpaid labour has a systemic character, with even experienced dancers finding themselves pressured to perform it. In retrospect, many perceive themselves as having been 'naive' for not voicing their concerns earlier:

> I hadn't been very vocal about my injury. I had kind of kept it to myself because I didn't want it to influence people's perception of me, because people are very judgemental and so flippant with how they talk about you ... Like oh you see she's always injured or oh she's always faking it, or you know and it's so painful. So, I was very concerned with keeping that to myself ... That's just part of being a dancer. Sometimes you feel like there's no other choice for you but ... to do it. You work

> around, you know? But maybe there's a choice? Maybe it's just our stupidity to agree to all that? (NL02_Jane)

Respondents refer to *subordination*, *striving for perfection*, *permanent availability*, and *permanent competition* as characterizing the *sacrifice for the sake of art* and explaining why they perform unpaid labour. These characteristics offer crucial insights into what the norm of the 'ideal dancer' is about, i.e. what is expected from them and what they believe is needed in order to be considered a 'real' artist. It is these meanings that we turn to now.

The Qualifying Meanings of Sacrifice 'for the Sake of Art'

Permanent Availability: Having the Body Always 'Ready' to Perform

The production cycle in dance ranges from shorter days when dancers mainly train to keep their bodies in shape to extremely long days on tour and before premières. There is an expectation that dancers will be permanently available and ready to work at any time in accordance with frenetic project work. Professional dancers are often treated as free atoms, unconnected to anybody else and unburdened by any obligations. It is assumed they will be ready to jump into a new project at any time, that their skills will be kept up to date, that their bodies will be well trained, and that they will keep on investing their own resources in daily training—no matter how challenging it is to keep the body in shape:

> It's a profession where you have to be in shape ... I've often seen dancers coming back after some leave and injuring themselves as soon as they're back, because they've been at home with their kid. Then you're supposed to come back ready and do a lot of physically demanding stuff. (SE04_Jon)

> I'm really lucky because I still live in the city where the company I used to be with is, so they're allowing me to take a ballet class every month. I've been keeping my training up by taking classes with them. I also create my own exercise, it's something that I have to do by myself. I have to figure out how to prepare properly for the work that I'm doing at the moment. And now, during Covid, everybody is panicking that everything needs to be done at home and online and it's a big thing, but freelancers have always done that. Their situation has always been like that: training at home, on their own and for free. It's not a new concept. (NL04_Sara)

The need to keep one's body in shape requires not only daily training but also regular physiotherapy in order to deal with recurring injuries:

> The day started at 8:20 with rehab work that I have to go to because my work depends on my good physical condition. So, I worked with a physiotherapist for my injured knee. It was a couple of hours consultation plus workout, rehab workout in the gym. (SE28_Jaime, diary)

While training and preparation as well as rehabilitation work for dancers employed in state-funded dance organizations in Sweden is included in their employment contracts, for self-employed dancers working in private-funded dance organizations in the Netherlands keeping their bodies in shape is unpaid labour, their 'personal investment work'. The expectation of permanent availability is understood as a commitment, with unavailability tending to be interpreted as being 'not keen, not having the right attitude' (NL11_Bart). Permanent availability requires self-discipline in keeping oneself physically and mentally fit. This self-discipline is a product of dance school discipline: very intense days with up to ten hours of training, and the experience of an exhausted body and mind at the end of the day. Some dancers reported feeling like 'a superhero' (SE06_Arianna), 'achieving the impossible' (NL08_Mia) after a première. It is common for dancers to be very well prepared, physically and emotionally, for their work as professional dancers, 'feeling strong, fit and confident' (NL10_Dominika) after graduating from dance school. However, dance schools do not prepare dancers either to work or to combine dance with poor-quality side jobs. Instead, they prepare dancers for paid employment within dance organizations. Self-discipline is needed to keep 'strong and fit' when dancers leave academy and enter the labour market. Self-employed dancers say: 'it's much more difficult to stay fit when you start working: you can never train as much as you do at school and you need a lot of self-discipline once the structure is no longer there' (SE06_Arianna).

The expectation of permanent availability means that 'dance is a job where you can't be sick' (SE22_Anna), with dancers made to believe that no cancellations are possible:

> The day of the show I had a very high temperature. But I didn't want to say // I don't want to let everybody down and say, you know, I can't come . . . but I was so sick that I was almost unconscious when I got home. (SE22_Anna)
>
> It's common to work even though you feel you actually need some rest, or to work while you're sick. I've even danced with stitches on my foot. (SE04_Jon)

In both the Netherlands and Sweden, dancers reported feeling pressure to be permanently available, sometimes resulting in them working while sick. The difference between the two contexts lies in the frequency of overworking: while in the Netherlands—at least outside the two national ballet companies—it is almost a norm to overwork (with little time for rest and family life), in Sweden the boundaries between work time and rest and family time are easier to maintain due to collective agreements guaranteeing paid rest time and the state (welfare) supporting periods of inactivity for both freelancers and employees in state-funded organizations:

> I got up at 7am, prepared my food, took a train at 9am and before noon I arrived at [name of a city]. We had a class from 12 till 1pm, a class plus a warm-up. Then from 1pm till 6pm, we had time to work and then from 6pm till 7:30pm we had a dinner break. After that we had some time to prepare for a première, preparing for the show, costumes and stuff like that. Another warm-up and then the show from 8:30 till 10pm. Then the train back home. (NL07_Francesco, diary)

> I don't overwork because my body needs time to rest. Otherwise, I'll get another injury. Today I did my training till 4pm and then came back home, I cooked and took care of my flowers and plants. But on the days we have a show I don't get home until after 10pm. (SE28_Jaime, diary)

> I take my breaks. Today I had a lunch break and I had dinner break. I need to eat responsibly. Today I also took a one-hour nap before the evening show. (SE08_Nikola, diary)

Striving for Perfection: Achieving Excellence in Order to Deliver the 'Perfect' Product

The emphasis on excellence and perfection means that dancers need to practice as long as it takes to achieve this:

> You just have to work very very very hard. Even if something is extremely difficult, you just work harder, even harder and until it actually looks very good, perfect. (NL09_Alba)

> The dance world is mentally and emotionally draining but physically … It's just too much. People in the dance company work six days a week, up to four shows a week. It's like ongoing, ongoing, ongoing. And there's so much pressure on excellence. (NL04_Sara)

In Sweden, collective agreements regulating employment relations in the dance sector cover the extra hours of rehearsals performed by dancers employed in the state-funded dance companies. Conversely, in private dance organizations in the Netherlands, self-employed freelance dancers are not paid for the extra hours of work they perform, as is the case in Sweden with self-employed dancers working on projects: 'you are paid for the whole project, no matter how many hours you've worked' (SE06_Arianna). Moreover, in all dance contexts, dancers are expected to work very hard, otherwise their attitude will be questioned:

> Many times, I've been overworked in this company [NDT]. They just ask you to do more and more. There's this pressure to always be working and if you're not, if the director looks at you and you're not moving in the studio then you're like at fault and you're wrong and you're being looked down on. (NL04_Sara)
>
> We work as much as 150%, but we're only paid for a fraction of the work we're doing. (SE02_Sandra)

Striving for perfection is part of an artistic (work) ethos in dance, and thus resourced and tolerated by dancers. But it is also a way of securing free labour. Made to believe that they are 'never really good enough' (SE21_Nadja), dancers agree to striving for perfection by investing their personal time. This often means 'killing themselves with work' (SE21_Nadja) in order to prove they are able to reach the level of perfection required from them and thus be recognized as 'real' artists. Striving for perfection means that each day is filled with long training hours and rehearsals, as illustrated in the working diaries:

> Today, the day was quite intense, like most days. I ((sighing)) left home quite early around 7am. I had a lesson from 8 to 9 in the studio and then I went to my rehearsal from 9am till 5pm. (NL06_Alessandro, diary)

The perfection ideal is especially difficult to attain when dancers need to take on side jobs to supplement their income. While in Sweden freelance dancers can combine various sources of income (including state support, dance jobs, and side jobs in the wider market), in the Netherlands dancers excluded from formal employment and without access to individual state grants struggle to earn sufficient income from dance jobs and depend on their side jobs or other personal financial resources (e.g., a partner's income) to the point of overexploitation:

> Then I had to run to the studio to start teaching at 6pm. I had 3 classes, one after another, till 9pm. I arrived home after 10pm. And I still had to prepare my food, proper food, for today's dinner and tomorrow's lunch. After all that, I was shattered. (NL06_Alessandro, diary)

It is a balancing act between the need to secure sufficient income (by doing side jobs) and having enough time for training and rest: 'I often risk overworking myself—and that's when injuries happen' (NL06_Alessandro, diary).

Subordination: Never Saying 'No'

The dance hierarchy makes dancers dependent on choreographers' and artistic directors' decisions. Any act of insubordination may bring punishment in the form of being taken off the stage, excluded from dance networks, and thus losing future job opportunities. Dancers are supposed to be silent: 'I was told that I should be careful what I say if I want to work here again' (SE21_Nadja), and to follow orders: 'There's not much autonomy here. We're just supposed to follow the people we work for' (NL06_Alessandro), 'everything you do needs to fit the choreographic choices and vision' (NL07_Francesco). This translates into it being impossible to question dominant ways of working, including the pressure to do unpaid labour:

> As a dancer you're always afraid that if you say what you think, if you don't agree with something, you'll be taken out by the network. Meaning someone else will do that piece, someone else will be performing instead of you. Just because you didn't think something was right. Or you didn't accept certain way of working. (NL09_Alba)

> It's all psychological … manipulation. They're playing on your emotions. You feel this constant pressure to give in. You go to an employer as an employee but you're also a very passionate artist who will do anything they say. You know that is essentially our job as a dancer. They say jump, you say how high and you say which way and they say: smile or be sad. You know, we're trained all our lives to say yes. (NL02_Jane)

Dancers' passion and love of dance are used against them, to discipline them and create the constant threat that 'someone else will be performing instead of you' (NL09_Alba). Having been trained to be submissive and say 'yes', dancers agree to unpaid labour. Their attitude is constantly controlled: they are rewarded for subordination and punished for voicing their concerns. Many of the dancers we interviewed reported being treated 'instrumentally':

> For many choreographers you are an instrument. Your body is just a tool to express their vision. (NL09_Alba)

> I got some time off /sighs/ but suddenly I had to cover, I had to be second cast for a new role. It was kind of a backup plan, but Jesus I was unlucky because the girl got injured two days before the première! /sighs/ I didn't know the steps. I just didn't know them. So I spent ... They pushed me for maybe 24 hours to try and figure it all out. And I just couldn't do it. Like they'd have to cut sections, I could do some sections but not others. The most stressful 24 hours of my life! But that was a consequence of not being able to say 'no'. I should've said 'no'. I should've said: 'You let me go or I quit and that's it'. (NL02_Jane)

Dancers do whatever needs to be done to allow for a show to be successfully delivered. Doing 'everything that needs to be done' and the difficulty to say 'no' to those higher up in the hierarchy translate directly into performing many unpaid tasks, especially for self-employed dancers in work contexts characterized by budget constraints:

> Once I worked with the theatre, where we had to perform [children's shows] at 9 am. At this theatre, they didn't understand the need for a dancer to warm up properly. Every morning you have to train one hour at least before being ready to perform. It was hard for me to tell them I also needed to train to keep in shape. They didn't understand that. So, I had to train myself. Which was not the best condition. And I had to do it for a performance early in the morning, tough. In addition, I had to help the technician with the scenography. I got injured and they were really mad. And then I cracked, One day I had to go out, do the big performance and set up everything. Put up the performance, then take everything down. That was hard. I complained but they said that it's normal. Well, it's normal to you but ... It was just too much. They want you to do too many things. (SE11_Fabiano)

The subordinated position of dancers *vis-à-vis* those higher in the dance hierarchy, their training to follow instructions, and the punishments for not conforming with the norm of the 'ideal dancer' result in dancers keeping silent even when their rights are violated. Dancers are forced to perform while they are sick or injured:

> There was one performance when I got sick. Before the première. I said: 'I have fever, I don't feel good'. I said all this one week before, I asked: 'Let me rest', 'No, you must go on because we have a première'. So, I had to continue. But one evening it was too much. I just dropped everything and said: 'I have to go home. I can't go on like this'. But they made me come back because it was two days before the première. I said: Let me rest one day, let's see'. Then the fever went down a bit and I knew how important it was for them. Moreover, I love premières. I love performing.

> So, I said: 'Okay let's do it'. Then we did the premiere. And I had so much pain, I couldn't even enjoy the party after the premiere. Everybody was happy, drinking champagne. I said: 'I can't stay. I need to see a doctor right now because I don't feel that good'. I was coughing. Then I went off to hospital. But the next day I had to perform again. (SE11_Fabiano)

Moreover, unpaid labour puts a question mark over a dancer's professional value:

> When you sign the contract, you're basically saying that you agree to do anything that is good for the company. Like the last time I had a performance I wasn't even paid for that because you're doing it for the company. Even if you don't know why you're doing it. Even though it's extra time, you are not getting paid for that. The photographers wanted to take pictures of you, but you don't think about the image rights or anything. You accept these photographs and later on you realise that I just gave my time, my image. Everything for no money. And this happens a lot. (NL09_Alba)

Subordination is clearly visible in the work diaries kept by dancers. They tell of dancers' inability to express their 'strong emotions' (NL06_Alessandro) in order 'not to create trouble' (NL06_Alessandro):

> The director of the company … is not really fantastic. So, there's a lot of stress and … frustration. And anger. But it's not something you can express. You need to keep it bottled up. I have a lot inside me but I just can't show it. (NL06_Alessandro, diary)

In both contexts dancers report 'a constant struggle' (SE11_Fabiano) not to be side-lined or even excluded from the most prestigious dance genres and venues. However, this struggle has several nuances. Opportunities to enter dance in the Netherlands are relatively limited due to the lack of individual state grants. Conversely, dancers in Sweden have better chances as they can apply for grants for dance projects (i.e., providing regular income) and for funding for attending auditions and networking events: 'My Dansalliansen ... Månadslön [monthly salary] that I'm receiving—on the 22nd of December ... the total amount I'm receiving is kr25,235 [€2,157] So, a total after taxes that I will receive is kr12,943 [€1,106]' (SE08_Nikola, diary). This form of state-based support is crucial in the case of dancers coming from lower classes and ethnic minority groups, for whom state grants may be the only way of entering professional dance. In the Netherlands, dancers unable to rely on family resources (as is often the case among working-class and non-white dancers) and thus unable to sustain unpaid work over longer periods of time become excluded. They are deemed to 'not fit in' due to their 'wrong' attitude or non-compliance with 'classical ballet body', though the core of the problem may be their inability to sustain unpaid labour due to the very limited family and institutional resources they have access to.

Permanent Competition: Everybody Is 'Replaceable'

Dancers constantly compete against each other, as they are made to believe that everybody is replaceable:

> I see a lot of colleagues who are burnt out. There's this pressure to keep going because, if you can't manage, there is always someone else who can. You live constantly with this idea that you are replaceable. (NL06_Alessandro)

> As a dancer you can be replaced at any moment. Don't ask for anything, don't expect anything because you can be replaced. (NL03_Lisa)

What counts in dance is to be on stage—as much as possible, preferably in leading roles and at prestigious venues. As the stage space is very limited, dancers 'live in permanent rivalry' (NL09_Alba) as 'everyone wants to be on stage' (SE12_Hiroko). Dancers are prepared to compete from the very beginning of their dance education. They are pitted against each other and continually told that very few of them will eventually become professional dancers:

> In the first week [of dance school] the headmaster gave a speech. He said that some of us wouldn't even graduate and only a few would make it and become professional dancers. I also remember a teacher saying that what matters most is perseverance. Those persevering are the ones who will get the jobs. It's not about having the biggest potential or being the most talented, it's about perseverance. (SE02_Sandra)

Perseverance is important within a context of permanent competition for stage space, but there is also a clear advantage in having the right gender, class, and ethnicity:

> There are many more women coming out of dance schools. And they're all applying for the same jobs, whereas the boys, the men, are harder to find and they have a much higher chance of getting a job. (NL02_Jane)

> If you are a good and a well-resourced male dancer, you are definitely luckier than if you are a well-resourced female dancer. Being a man in the dance world is always advantageous, like you're more important. (NL07_Francesco)

> I'm coloured, so there's no place for me in ballet. There are so many stereotypes in the industry ... I dance and I'm like curvy, I'm like not this typical example of what a dancer is. I only find jobs in musicals as everybody expects I'll be good at singing. (SE21_Nadja)

Dancers not meeting up to expectations regarding their physical appearance (not white, not petit) or their available income support (i.e., not middle- or upper-middle-class, and also including income from a partner and/or other family members) find themselves at a disadvantage. Their precarious conditions prevent them from making headway in the dance scene, as they cannot afford to perform unpaid labour—this being the doorway to entering and competing in dance. This is a problem particularly for those not enjoying state support in times of inactivity, as for example among freelance dancers in the Netherlands, in contrast to dancers in Sweden who enjoy generous unemployment and other social benefits, irrespective of whether they are self-employed or an employee. In the Netherlands, ballet dancers experience 'permanent rivalry' (NL09_Alba) to get a role and have their contracts renewed: 'even after 20 years, when a new choreographer comes in, I still have to audition' (NL09_Alba). Hence, although someone could work for free by subsidizing their passion for dance with 'poor-quality side jobs' away from the dancefloor, in the long run unpaid labour will likely push such dancers into precarity. As we will explain in the next sections, resources are crucial for dancers in order to build resilience. Those with limited access to family-based and country-based resources are those who find it most difficult to build up this resilience, and who are more likely to slip into precarity when performing unpaid labour while trying to adhere to the 'ideal'.

Unpaid Labour, Resilience, and Precarious Work

When dancers get older and more experienced, they reflect more on their efforts to comply with the 'ideal' and the costs of their compliance, including their sacrifice *for the sake of art* and the unpaid labour it involves. This reflectivity helps them develop resilience, which in turn is a condition for coping with the hierarchical pressure and the conditions of unpaid labour:

> When you start getting older, you start to question things and make demands. You don't want to be treated just like ... teenagers in pyjamas. (SE04_Jon)

> Dancers are a bit … naïve. We love our profession so much, we're so passionate about our profession that sometimes things … Then, later on in life, you realise how stupid that was. Basically, they were just taking advantage of you. Perhaps not in this aspect because maybe this gave me some professional experience, but in many other ways like doing little jobs or doing photography. Like you want to feel like you're doing some kind of self-marketing. So you do everything for free. Of course. You're just happy to dance, basically. You know? And they take advantage of that. A lot of people take advantage of that. (NL09_Alba)

From the perspective of time, dancers perceive themselves as 'naïve' or even 'stupid', sacrificing their lives in the name of art and then coming to the bitter conclusion that: 'you have to sacrifice many things and then there is nothing' (NL09_Alba). Nevertheless, many of them stay in the dance field as choreographers or teachers, as they find it difficult to give up the identity they have developed and their passion for dance: 'The feeling dance gives you is incredible. I don't think you can experience anything like this elsewhere' (NL09_Alba). Via their dance work, dancers build their identities, possibly making them resilient to the punishments and rewards described above and in turn underpinning their compliance with the 'ideal' of sacrifice and the associated unpaid work. Those showing resilience are often the ones not falling into precarity as they are better able to cope with working for free because they have institutional and family resources that make unpaid labour affordable in the long run. Those without such resources are the ones more likely to experience precarity resulting from their difficulties to make enough out of their dance work to immunize them against the penalties entailed by performing unpaid labour.

Institutional Country-Based Resources: Funding and the Role of the State

Dance is an extremely competitive field and aspiring dancers are already warned in dance schools that only a few of them will become professional dancers. Even before graduating, young dancers therefore apply for a handful of vacancies in state-funded dance institutions. Those who manage to get taken on find themselves in 'protected dance shells' (NL02_Jane)—the only chance for longer term employment in dance. Respondents report differences between how dance institutions work in Sweden and in the Netherlands:

> It's so nice to come back, you realise there are many things that are better in the Swedish institutions when compared to the rest of Europe. Maybe working conditions are just better because in Sweden there are many laws, maybe the trade unions are stronger here. People here don't work overtime without being paid extra. If that happened, someone would complain to the trade union. And that's the

> reason why some choreographers from other countries feel it's weird in Sweden: 'How can you do that, I want to work more now, why is it so restricted?' (SE04_Jon)

> Here in the Netherlands, there is no union for dancers. So, everybody is like on their own. I know that in Sweden most companies have incredible unions, that's the difference. I have a good friend who's in a company in Gothenburg and—they seem to have a healthy system there. (NL04_Sara)

> I did a workshop in the Netherlands and through that workshop I got a private audition for [name] dance company, one of the biggest in the Netherlands. I was very happy that I managed to get in, I was really lucky, but I wasn't paid a full salary. I got a contract for 700 or 800 euros, something between an intern and a professional and I don't know how it was possible. I don't know whether it was even legal—I was working full-time as a professional dancer. But I said nothing, I needed that job. (NL06_Alessandro)

State-funded dance institutions have gone through significant changes in both Sweden and the Netherlands. In the Netherlands, stable employment has been gradually replaced by temporary and on-call project work where pay is lower:

> At a certain point the law changed here. Before, even if they were taking you on for a project, the big companies would always offer an employment relationship. You were employed as employee, even if it was only for two months. But now they don't do it anymore. Now you just get paid, you do your part and goodbye. I've had quite a few contracts like this and I knew I was paid less. (NL07_Francesco)

In Sweden, dance companies offer employment within a standard employment relationship. Nevertheless, dancers also realize how working conditions have changed over time:

> When I was working at Opera [the Royal Swedish Opera] I realised they were trying to cut costs or find some way to cut our rights . . . They started counting every penny. If they want to buy some famous choreographer, then they pay a lot, but when it's someone who's in the house then they don't want to pay that much. (SE04_Jon)

Dancers unable to find employment in state-funded dance organizations become freelancers, working from gig to gig. Self-employed dancers describe facing 'an ongoing struggle' (SE11_Fabiano), though our respondents also reported that self-employment was bolstered by the funding opportunities available to dancers in Sweden:

> There's more funding available in Sweden, so it's been easier to do my own work here. But of course, writing applications is a never-ending task. I'm always working on something. One application can take two weeks of full-time work. (SE06_Arianna)

Moreover, the Swedish organization Dancealliansen[1] employs freelance dancers during periods of inactivity. Our interviewee sample included several dancers and dancing families (SE11_Fabiano; SE12_Hiroko) whose livelihoods depended on the income from Dansalliansen. Dancers are hired on two-year contracts, during which they have to work a certain number of days for their contracts to be renewed. Fabiano's contract has been renewed five times, for a total of ten years. Dansalliansen becomes dancers' 'main source of income' (SE11_Fabiano) or 'the second biggest contributor' (SE08_Nikola) to their income. In this way, dancers do not automatically fall into precarity between dance jobs. Their income and that of their households are protected by the contract with Dansalliansen.

Self-employed dancers in Sweden can also apply for unemployment benefits from the insurance fund (Unionens A-kassa), insofar as they are members of the basic fund. Some of our interviewees reported having 'applied for the unemployment fund soon after they lost their "side jobs" or after having been unsuccessful with their grant application' (SE06_Arianna). This insurance fund provides additional protection against precarity for dancers in Sweden, in contrast to dancers in the Netherlands who have no such protection.

In both countries, dancers need to attend auditions for dance jobs. Auditions can 'take weeks of work to prepare' (SE02_Sandra). In Sweden, dancers can apply for grants to cover the audition costs (travel and accommodation), while, in the Netherlands, dancers need to cover all these costs themselves, using their personal resources. Having worked initially in France and the Netherlands, Fabiano (SE11) told us about using up all his savings to cover the costs of auditions all over Europe:

> I had 30.000 SEK in my account that I'd saved while I'd been in school and worked extra. Because of the auditions, all my money went on travelling to Stockholm, Norway, Denmark, Germany ... We didn't have any left ... Now with Arbetsförmedlingen [the Swedish Public Employment Service], you can get some help, at least they pay for your travel. (SE21_Nadja)

[1] '*Dansalliansen* provides freelance dancers with basic employment and offers competence development, matching and collaborations with other actors in the field. Dansalliansen is a state-funded organization owned by Danscentrum, Swedish Performing Arts Association, The Swedish Union for Performing Arts and Film and TRS' (https://dansalliansen.se/english).

Moreover, in Sweden freelance dancers can apply for public grants for their projects, thereby increasing their chances of staying professionally active while developing some new organizational and artistic forms—a type of adaptation that does not challenge the 'status quo' but allows them to do what they have been trained to do.

> It's a very difficult industry with a lot of competition. I was quite young, and I wasn't prepared for what was ahead of me. But it was becoming easier and easier every year. I learnt how to negotiate how much I got paid. I made sure to sign contracts in accordance with the union's rules. I'm getting more jobs now, most of them on project contracts. I've been freelancing for nine years now. I've also been able to quit most of the side jobs I've had over those nine years. The older you get the more you think about possible injuries, about what happens if you're unable to work. I realised that I should become a member of an organisation such as Dansalliansen, which is available for all freelancers. I'm also a member of an unemployment fund. It gives me a feeling of safety. (SE02_Sandra)

The more comprehensive social security system in Sweden means that dancers can relatively easily go through different 'turning points' in life (such as parenthood, sickness, or unemployment) without the risk of falling into precarity.

> I'm very lucky to be in Sweden, because paid parental leave here is another thing that I'd never have been able to benefit from in Italy or in the Netherlands, where I used to live. Free nurseries for children. Even child-related housing benefits, that's something that is quite rare. (SE22_Anna)

Anna told us of her twenty-year-long career as a dancer in a state institution in Sweden where she could afford to have two children without destabilizing her professional or household situation. Generous maternity leave, coupled with free childcare and a housing allowance for families with children, provided an efficient safety net for her family. When she experienced work-related health issues, she was able to access physiotherapy and psychotherapy free of charge.

Hence, the difference in the institutional resources available to employees and freelancers in Sweden and the Netherlands explains the different meanings attributed by dancers to precarity and how they cope with it. In Sweden, respondents emphasize that economic independence is achieved by combining income from dancing jobs, state grants, and benefits as well as 'side jobs' or 'breadwinning jobs' (SE21_Nadja). These include jobs in cafes, restaurants, shops, schools and museums, or babysitting. Such jobs contribute to providing a sense of security ('earning enough') and enable planning:

> I started working extra at a clothes shop and continued taking on different projects. I also took unpaid projects which I was managing and would apply for grants. Many jobs were unpaid. Sometimes I worked extra in a shop to make sure I earned enough to cover my needs. Sometimes I would take a job to be able to go to free dancing classes in summer to keep up my training. Some months I would have dancing jobs that I was able to invoice, in accordance with the collective agreement. In other months I'd just stick to breadwinning jobs which are always easy to find. (SE02_Sandra)

It is reported that finding a side job is quite predictable in Sweden due to their widespread availability (they are 'always easy to find') and their regulated conditions concerning pay and hours. The situation in the Netherlands is different. There we see dancers either relying more heavily on family economic and social resources (i.e., unpaid social reproductive labour)—a situation indicating that they belong to the middle or upper-middle class—or facing the unpredictability and precarity of 'side jobs'. In Sweden, dancers also need to make sure that they do a certain number of hours of paid work per month (in dance or elsewhere) to qualify for the state insurance, which does not apply to dancers in the Netherlands. In both contexts there are nevertheless also dancers with a strong commitment not to do 'side jobs' at all, as they want to preserve their image and the associated prestige of being 'real artists' (SE10_Isabelle). According to them, 'breadwinning jobs' could hinder the construction of a convincing professional identity. This is more likely affordable in Sweden than in the Netherlands.

Household Wealth and Social Reproductive Labour

A dance career requires a major financial investment in the form of participating in numerous workshops, often led by well-known coaches (dominant network gatekeepers), as well as numerous auditions involving fees and travel costs. Whereas middle-class dancers may be given several opportunities to sell their 'body work', working-class dancers may have only one chance or may be pushed out of the dance field altogether. Class at the intersection of gender and ethnicity (race) defines for whom it is going to be most difficult (or impossible) to be immunized against punitive non-adherence to the 'ideal'. This results in classical ballet being populated predominantly by middle- and upper-middle-class white dancers. Moreover, these dancers find it easier to build individual resilience and therefore to carry on performing unpaid labour as they can rely on their family's wealth and support for social reproductive labour.

Family resources make all the difference to survival and progress. These resources are not only of a financial nature, but are also represented by the social capital of the family of origin, especially in terms of having an 'insider status', making it easier to enter dance as well as to perform social reproductive labour:

> My parents come from the dance world. So, I had a huge advantage and opportunity to have some private auditions ... My parents worked here in the theatre, so I had access to the physiotherapist and to the workout studio. And so many choreographers had already known me since I was a kid. (NL03_Lisa)

Middle- and upper-middle-class dancers find it much easier to cope with unpaid work than dancers with a lower class background. The latter, especially when lacking generous country-based social benefits and/or a partner's income to subsidize their unpaid labour, are more likely to fall into precarity and may even be forced to quit. Working for free in dance is unsustainable for them. This situation helps maintain the status of classical ballet and contemporary dance as a fairly elitist field, with restricted possibilities for access and progression. Compared to the Netherlands, the greater Swedish institutional support available to individual dancers in the form of grants for dance projects (providing regular income) and funding for attending auditions and networking events better allows those from a lower class or an ethnic minority to enter the dance field. The resultant intergenerational effects are relatively stronger in the Netherlands than in Sweden. In the Netherlands, working-class kids understand that dance in general, and classical ballet in particular, are 'not for them'. They are not sent to ballet schools by their parents, and they do not see dance as a feasible career option. There are however cases of working-class kids who, despite ballet not featuring in their upbringing or one of the scenarios structurally and culturally ascribed to them, develop a great passion for it and start dreaming about becoming dancers like Billy Elliot. They encounter all sorts of obstacles on their way, with a lack of money for ballet school fees being the very first of them:

> I remember my parents [in Spain] counting every penny to pay for the school. Sometimes when I was in bed I would hear them with a calculator trying to figure

> out how to do it. Because when I started, there was this very cheap place and then I was so good that they wanted the best for me. People said, 'she's very gifted', so I guess my parents felt pressure to go on … My parents didn't have enough money for me to go for auditions. Indeed, they took out a small loan for me to come to Holland and audition here but I basically did only one audition because that's all I could afford. There were 366 girls. Only girls. And they needed just two. But thank God I was lucky enough and I entered the company. (NL09_Alba)

The situation is very different for dancers coming from middle- or upper-middle-class families. Here, family resources in the form of savings for education (NL03_Lisa) and a budget for the necessary travel play a crucial role:

> All that stuff costs money. First of all, ballet school and then travelling. We stayed in London, which was great, but it cost a ton of money. My mum was very supportive, she convinced my dad to pay for everything, and my grandfather would fly with me to auditions. (NL02_Jane)

> I always had in mind that in case I ever got into trouble or needed money, I could always reach out to my parents. (NL10_Dominika)

The parental home, especially when parents are well-off, is a safe haven for self-employed dancers. In later life, this supportive role may be taken over by a partner whose income compensates for any unpaid labour performed by the dancer:

> My partner is richer than me, he has a better income, which helps. (NL03_Lisa)

> I was lucky I met my husband, financially it was a huge relief. (NL02_Jane)

Resilience is built upon the support provided by well-off and double-income households, providing shelter from precarity. Especially, family financial resources ('being lucky to have supportive parents' and a 'partner with a better income') are essential for subsidizing the unpaid labour required to enter dance (e.g., dance training, auditions, travelling, work to gain experience and network). At the end of the day, a dancer's capacity to afford to perform unpaid work determines his/her chances to gain a foothold in dance, especially in the absence of other institutional forms of resources.

A different case is where both partners are self-employed dancers and where the income of one is not sufficient to subsidize the unpaid labour of the other. Devoid of family resources, dancers report being forced to take on 'poor-quality side jobs' (e.g., working as a waitress in a restaurant or doing babysitting) to gain some regular income:

> We both started work and then had breaks. Now, we'll see how things go ... My partner decided to also work in a restaurant. She has a passion of cooking ... And it's also good to do something different in case there are no dance jobs. I started a course in yoga, and I give Pilates classes as well. In case something happens, I think both of us are prepared for it. (NL07_Francesco)

Two-dancer households are particularly precarious in the Netherlands, especially those with children, as they cannot count on generous state support in the form of child benefits, housing allowances, and free childcare as found in Sweden. Some of the self-employed dancers we interviewed in the Netherlands were not covered by social security as they could not afford the contributions. In case one partner got injured, the household would have to survive on a single income:

> If something happens like it happened to my partner now ... He injured himself. He's pretty much screwed because he can't dance anymore ... He only gets like €40 help a month, so with my income I have to maintain the entire family of five. (NL09_Alba)

If in a two-dancer household one of the partners is employed in a state-funded dance organization, while the other one does project work, the situation may be still manageable, as regular employment provides predictable income. Things are very different when both are freelancers with fluctuating incomes. If such a household also contains children, dancers may feel the pressure to change career: 'it is very stressful, I'm thinking about changing my profession' (NL07_Francesco) in order to have a more stable income and avoid household precarity.

Due to having to offer constant physical and mental availability (impossible during pregnancy and birth) and due to cultural expectations regarding motherhood, female dancers struggle the most in the Netherlands, reflecting the high costs associated with childbearing and the inflexibility of dance organization:

> I was going back to work [after maternity leave] and straight into a tour. So, I'd take my babies with me on a tour until they reached the age of two. Then I couldn't take them anymore. There's no chance to negotiate anything. There was this tour

> in China. Three weeks! I had to leave both my kids with my husband at home and it almost killed me. That was so so so hard. I felt so guilty for—not only being away so much, but even when I was in the country, I was working such long hours. On normal days, when we didn't have a show, I'd pick them up from the nursery after 7pm. When we had a show, I wouldn't see them at all. (NL02_Jane)

Combining dance jobs with family life is difficult in both contexts, but in Sweden it is a bit less so due to the more regulated working hours and moderate childcare costs. In the Netherlands, the long hours together with high childcare costs make it almost impossible to cope:

> The nursery is extremely expensive because the hours that you work are extremely long, meaning that basically the baby has to be in the nursery as many hours as you work. (NL09_Alba)

Creative Dance: Conclusions

Young people enter creative dance 'for the sake of art' and not for the sake of financial reward. Indeed, only the top echelons of the dance hierarchy experience any great financial benefits, while the majority of dancers work on the breadline, eking out a precarious existence in the hope of gaining future recognition as a 'real' artist.

Funding changes in the creative industry in recent decades mean that increasing numbers of dancers are now working on freelance contracts, without the security of a standard employment relationship. Due on the one hand to competition among dancers and on the other hand to funding constraints, remuneration in dance is generally low. Those lacking personal (for example, in the form of other household income) or institutional resources to subsidize their dance careers are often forced to quit dancing. This leads to a classed structure in dance, where only (upper-)middle-class dancers endowed with the necessary resources are able to survive. We found this to be the case in ballet, a dance 'niche' where (upper-)middle-class dancers—the majority—enjoy access to resources which can help them cope with the precarious employment conditions of their jobs. Here, unpaid labour itself is a privileging resource allowing workers to build resilience against such precarious conditions, even if this privilege does not eliminate the inherent job insecurity that comes with employment conditions in dance. Thus, we conclude that a non-binary relationship exists between unpaid labour and precarious work in dance.

Furthermore, resilience is needed in a world characterized by 100% subordination to producers and choreographers, while the burning desire for perfection and recognition requires a great amount of personal investment work, a lot of which goes unpaid on account of the low rates attainable by freelance dancers. Dance is thus a 'calling' requiring great personal sacrifices 'for the sake of art' which dancers in their narratives associate with meanings of stigmatization through punishments and rewards. For a dancer, being discounted as not a 'true' artist—i.e., someone willing to invest time in tasks crucial for his/her craft but not directly linked to dancing—results in a loss of status (i.e., going down a level in the status hierarchy). A question mark is placed on his/her skills and commitment (i.e., s/he is seen as lacking the 'appropriate' dedication, not sacrificing enough, or not prioritizing the 'passion for art'), leading to him/her being marginalized and excluded by the dance company and co-workers. S/he ultimately suffer a stigmatizing 'professional death', becoming unemployable in the dance sphere.

5

Care 'for the Sake of Others'

A Binary Relationship between Unpaid Labour and Precarious Work in Residential Care in the United Kingdom and Germany

with Me-Linh Riemann

Residential Care in the United Kingdom and Germany

In the United Kingdom (UK), publicly funded residential care is mainly financed through local government revenues. In search of cost savings and efficiency gains, local authorities have outsourced most of elderly care to the private sector, thereby exacerbating the extent of low pay (Rubery and Urwin 2011; Butterick and Charlwood 2020). At the end of the 2000s, 81% of places in residential care homes were in the private for-profit sector, compared with 13% in not-for-profit sector and 6% in care homes funded by local authorities (Land and Himmelweit 2010; Shutes and Walsh 2012). There is evidence of low pay, the use of zero-hour contracts, skills shortages, high staff turnover, and low self-esteem in residential care settings in the UK (Skills for Care 2021). Importantly, zero-hour contracts come with subjective experiences of unpredictable shift patterns and incomes and eventually in-work poverty due to workers not being given sufficient hours to work. Involuntary part-time (hours) and irregular shift work are the 'normality' for several workers in residential settings in the UK (Low Pay Commission 2021). Moreover, there is no national accreditation for residential care staff and care settings are often underfunded. The UK Health and Social Care Committee estimates that an additional £7 billion per year is required by 2023/4 to meet care needs—a figure it describes as a 'starting point'. The Health Foundation has suggested that an additional £14.4 billion a year would be required by 2030/1 to meet future demand, improve access to care, and increase care wages (House of Commons 2023).

Valeria Pulignano and Markieta Domecka with Me-Linh Riemann, *Care 'for the Sake of Others'*. In: *The Politics of Unpaid Labour*, Oxford University Press. © Valeria Pulignano and Markieta Domecka (2025).
DOI: 10.1093/oso/9780198888130.003.0006

In Germany, local authorities and municipalities have neither responsibility for nor authority over the health services provided in their jurisdiction. The system is supervised by the self-governing bodies of the statutory long-term care insurance (Pflegeversicherung) introduced in 1994 and the statutory health insurance at state level (Bundesländer). Providers are reimbursed from long-term care and health insurance funds on a fee-for-service basis and have no role in the delivery of public-health-oriented services, like community health assessments or community interventions for health promotion and prevention (Fischer 2022). Privatization is taking hold of German care homes too. In 2017, 63% of care settings were private for-profit, 36% private non-profit, and 1% public (Spasova et al. 2018). As regards training, there are several qualification levels for carers in Germany. These range from care assistants who have completed a one-year formal training programme or gained the same status through work experience, to qualified care workers who have completed a three-year training programme in elderly care or healthcare or have a university degree. The latter (qualified care workers) account for 35.3% of the total residential care workforce. People with another care or social qualification account for a further 26.3%. However, the biggest share (38.4%) are those without a recognized qualification or still in training. These are the ones with the lowest wages and often working part time (Gruber et al. 2021).

In response to the Covid-19 pandemic, minimum wages in care settings in Germany have gradually increased to €12.55 for unqualified social care assistants, €13.20 for care assistants with one year's training, and €15.40 for professional caregivers (Bundesagentur für Arbeit 2022). Nevertheless, average hourly wages in the feminized care service sector remains lower than those in industry-based male-dominated sectors in Germany. Moreover, the training of social care assistants is not regulated at national level and pay and working conditions vary between regions.

To gain an insight into working conditions in residential care, with a focus on what motivates caregivers to perform unpaid labour, what resources they have available to sustain it, and how they deal with any ensuing precarity, we conducted thirty-nine autobiographical narrative interviews with caregivers (nineteen in the UK and twenty in Germany) and collected seven audio work diaries (four in Germany and three in the UK). The results are presented below.

Results of Our Study in the UK and Germany

Precarity for Whom? The Biographical Case of Tina Who Cannot Sustain Unpaid Labour in Residential Care

Tina (UK15) was born in London in 1958 and adopted by a couple, both of whom were artists struggling financially. She developed an interest in working in the healthcare sector at an early age. After finishing her A-levels, she enrolled in a Christian college to study nursing. At the age of 19, she became unexpectedly pregnant and was forced to leave school. Tragically, her baby died shortly after being born. As a coping strategy, she focused on 'having a family', getting married, and having five children in rapid succession in her 20. Her first husband was not a very 'conscientious' person and constantly in and out of work. Tina had to find a way to provide for her family financially, while at the same time shouldering most of the childcare and housework responsibilities. In this context, she discovered the possibility of working nightshifts at a local elderly care home. This option allowed her to be economically active while taking care of her children during the day. Due to the severe labour shortage in this sector, Tina knew that 'care work was something that is *always* available', even without formal qualifications. It was also related to her original intention of becoming a nurse and her identity as being 'always good at looking after people'. Her first workplace was a small, privately run nursing home with about thirty residents. A typical nightshift lasted from 8pm to 8am, during which Tina was required to give out medication, wash residents, and put them to bed, and take care of those who wandered around at night or who were incontinent. In addition, she also had to do some domestic tasks such as cleaning and preparing breakfast. While Tina enjoyed the care-related aspects of her work, she was irritated by being asked to do additional tasks (e.g., baking cakes) not covered by her employment contract and the associated job description, but nevertheless expected of a good carer.

Due to her first husband frequently changing jobs, the family moved around a lot. In the 1980s, Tina consequently also frequently changed employers, gaining work experience in both private and public care and nursing homes across the UK, and combining part-time employment with more informal agency work ('it all overlapped quite a bit'). The agencies sent workers to care homes and hospitals hit by high workloads and understaffing. In theory, these agency workers were supposed to offer only 'very basic' care services given their lack of training, but in reality, they are frequently assigned medical tasks for which they were not qualified. Tina continued working nightshifts to be able to take care of her children during the day. She also tried to fit in some extra care work during the day to make ends meet. As a consequence, she suffered from severe sleep deprivation for several years. Her workload was so high that Tina had the feeling she 'works for two': 'there should be four people on, and it's only two of us doing everything'. The only way to get everything done was to work faster and longer: 'I try and start earlier than I should in the morning, so I've got a little bit of leeway. And I carry on working afterhours, otherwise I won't be able to finish all that needs to be done. I also work through lunch breaks'. Tina often found herself in situations of emotional blackmail when asked by her manager to work overtime. She tended to accept, knowing that her refusal would hurt the elderly residents as 'there's nobody else to take up the slack'. She also saw that tight scheduling had an impact on the quality of care, as she was unable to spend as much time with individual residents as she deemed necessary: 'It's all too rushed. You can't spend the time that you want to. And then you go home and you're not happy, you don't feel rewarded'.

In 2006, Tina moved to another city in the UK together with her new partner (who worked as a self-employed builder and decorator) and her two youngest children. She found an administrative position in sheltered housing, while also working weekends at a nursing home which she described as '*really* badly managed'. As a way to make some additional money, she also worked informally with a few private clients she found through newspaper ads. In 2010 she had an accident at the sheltered housing facility. As she lived in a flat on the sheltered housing estate, she felt pressure to be available at all times. The accident occurred while she was officially 'off-duty', visiting an isolated resident on a weekend and taking him out for a walk on the facility's premises:

> I had an accident; I fell over and shattered my leg. So, I couldn't do the private work, and they were quite cross about that. And the local authority, because it was quite well regulated, they had to pay me for being sick. I had a lot of operations during a year, and they paid me for being off ill for about six [months] and then sort of half pay. And then basically they decided that they had an awful record of sickness with people there and basically sacked me. They said: 'You had so many days off sick in the last year!' (UK15_Tina)

With the help of the trade union, Tina took legal action but lost as the accident did not happen 'during working hours'. Tina's willingness to perform work outside the scope of her employment contract out of empathy was thus held against her in a situation of conflict. At the time of the interview—eleven years after the accident—Tina's leg needs to a further operation as she suffers from chronic pain. For Tina, the accident marked a turning point as she felt deeply demoralized by her employer's lack of support. No longer able to perform intense physical labour, she moved to live-in home care. Due to her frail health, she would prefer to take early retirement, but she cannot afford it. At the moment, her pension would be around £800 per month, while her partner, who has worked as a self-employed builder his whole life, would receive an even smaller pension.

Why Unpaid Labour? The 'Ideal Carer' Norm and Sacrifice for the Sake of Others

The highest stakes in the care sector are defined around the questions: who cares and who can be recognized as truly caring, whether at the level of the state, the municipality, care organizations, or care workers themselves. Society as a whole—with the direct participation of care recipients and their families—is constantly creating and recreating definitions of who cares and who is truly caring—or just caring enough. When we try to understand why people (mainly women) enter care work in the first place, and why they work so many hours without receiving pay that reflects the many hours of work they do, we see—after listening to their work and life stories—that they do it because they care and want to be recognized as truly caring. Women are channelled towards care work as it is assumed that this is something they do 'naturally' and well—as if they have some 'natural' capacities to look after others. These capacities are framed by the identity women develop early in their lives as a result of their socially constructed gender roles involving taking care of their young and elderly family members (i.e., 'care for care'). Thus, women enter care because of their 'caring identity': 'I've always been a caring person' (UK01_Sophia); 'I've always had that caring nature' (UK02_Mary); 'Caring is in my genes. Whenever anyone needs help, I do what I can' (DE12_Marianne).

Ever ubiquitous in residential care, the Covid-19 pandemic put a spotlight on underpaid or unpaid care work. It takes on many different forms including underpayment (as pay is just above the minimum wage and care jobs are paid less well than male-dominated industrial jobs), working through normal breaks (e.g., baking cakes or shopping for residents), working outside (i.e., before and after) regular working hours, constant physical and emotional availability which often includes paying informal extra visits to elderly people outside regular shifts, the use of private financial resources, e.g. buying items residents need or are especially fond of like a particular type of cake or materials for arts and craft: 'I buy the craft material that we use with the residents. They love arts and craft, and I pay for it out of my own pocket. Each time it is £4, £5, £6 worth'. (UK17_Tara, diary). The work intensification during Covid-19 also meant unpaid labour, with care workers investing more time in complying with government hygiene rules, such as even more frequent handwashing and cleaning, preparing meals for residents (as external catering companies were not allowed to enter the homes), and doing the laundry (washing their own uniforms as well as residents' clothes, towels, and bedsheets). A well-known form of labour not financially remunerated in residential care is emotional labour in the form of the feelings, emotions, and expressions used in fulfilling one's work. These can be described as productive work coming under the header of the 'commercialization of intimate life' and which are used to 'get the job done' (see Hochschild, 1983). Yet, there are no definitive dividing lines between the public and private worlds of emotions, as workers enter care organizations with life histories and certain innate forms of behaviour. For example, the management of feelings and emotions is work: it can refer to the regulation of a worker's own emotions and/or the regulation of emotions in others, whether they be customers, co-workers, or managers (see Bolton 2005). We found evidence of the importance of this emotion management work; yet this work often went unrecognized, and therefore unpaid.

We also found that the pandemic represented an extreme form of emotion management where it was difficult to manage the emotions of care recipients due to the restrictions on personal care disrupting the routine and meaningful rituals of these intense daily interactions. Even before the pandemic, there had not been enough staff to handle everything. The pandemic meant that those available were often forced to work faster and longer, prioritizing the needs of residents over their own needs and those of their families. Workers were often confronted with the dilemma of whom to protect more: residents or themselves and their families. Sacrifice *for the sake of others* is part of the 'ideal worker' norm in care. Workers trying to adhere to the norm, through meeting the expectations of their managers, their residents, and their colleagues, want to demonstrate that they are 'caring carers' capable of sacrificing themselves *for the sake of others*. In performing this balancing act, workers work unpaid overtime, coming to work before their shifts start and leaving late. Experiencing frustration, they are purposive agents forced to hide their emotions from residents in the face of multiple deaths, as witnessed during Covid-19. They stay on at work in order to have a chance to do what they have been unable to do during their hectic shifts, sitting with residents or having a chat with them to keep up their spirits and courage during such a dramatic period. They also do admin work after normal working hours, including taking paperwork home. Paid the minimum wage, care workers told us about being 'flooded with tasks' (DE08_Susanne) and about their managers refusing to recognize how difficult it was for them to complete all the tasks in time. This ended with them clocking up unpaid overtime, trying to tie up loose ends afterhours to feel respected and recognized by meeting their own expectations and those of 'others'.

Unpaid labour in residential care thus arises at the intersection of biographical, cultural, and structural dimensions. Biographically, from an early age and throughout their lives, care workers develop their 'caring identities', prompting them to go beyond their job description to gain a feeling of work 'well done' and to provide care at a level personally satisfying and meaningful to them and consistent with their 'caring identities'. This includes performing unpaid labour. Culturally, care workers are presented with norms of conduct, including the 'ideal worker' norm, in the knowledge that adhering to the norm will be rewarded in the form of recognition and respect as a 'caring carer' by care home residents and their families and by their employers. However, in order to meet these normative expectations, they feel forced to provide unpaid labour. Structurally, care workers work in a context of underfunded and understaffed organizations, where the workload is much greater than the capacity of the workforce, consequently creating pressure to perform unpaid labour in order to meet residents' care needs.

The choice of taking up care work is related to a combination of practical and biographical (identity-related) motivations providing carers with a meaning to their lives. Several interviewees stated that they were 'not great academically' (UK01_Sophia), preferring 'to do practical things rather than writing things down' (UK01_Sophia), or having to combine work with childcare responsibilities, or not being able to find other jobs locally. Moreover, there is no accreditation for care workers in the UK, resulting in residential care work being perceived as something practical, with only minimal entry requirements and—due to permanent labour shortages—always available: 'I didn't want to do cleaning anymore. And I thought: I'd work in care, it's easy to enter, they're always looking for people to work in care' (DE06_Zarima).

In Germany, we have examples of women (and people with a migrant background) being directed towards the care sector by unemployment agencies. After experiencing difficulties on the labour market, they were offered 'free training to become care assistants' (DE08_Susanne). Alongside such practical aspects, there may be a 'caring identity' developed early on in people's lives, especially when they take care of young and elderly members of their families:

> I've obviously always looked after my nieces and nephews; I've always looked after my stepchildren. I've always had that caring nature. My granddad used to call me an angel on Earth. Because I always wanted to look after my family. (UK02_Mary)

> My grandma needed a bit more help as she got older, and I just really enjoyed spending time with her and sort of helping her out. So in the school holidays, when I was younger, I used to go up every Sunday and help her go shopping, cook lunch ... I just liked helping her and I enjoyed her company. She had like endless stories ... But that's how I got into care: it was my grandma. But also, when I was probably 10 or 11, our next-door neighbour, the lady was married but her husband was working, and she had lots of little children and I really liked helping her look after them. I was like, looking out for them, I would help with bottle feeds and baths and so I think I've always been a caring person. (UK01_Sophia)

There are the stories of intergenerational transmission, with different generations of women in the same family working as professional carers, offering each other understanding and emotional support:

> My grandmother, on my father's side, she's worked in care all her life, also in an elderly care facility, and I often talk to her about the job and all. And I basically always get applause from my family, and my mother always says she really respects me for being able to do that. She always says she thinks it's really tough for me to do this. But, to me it's just perfect, I love it. (DE20_Lilly)

There is common awareness that care wages are low, but at the same time, as the care sector constantly suffers from labour shortages, care work for female careers is considered always available: 'they are crying out for people' (UK02_Mary).

> I just went on a few job sites and started applying for jobs. It was very difficult because of the money [in care], you know, to take sort of pay cuts and stuff. But I just applied. I was applying to supermarkets. I was applying to estate agents, I was applying to factories, I was applying to cleaning companies, anything. And obviously that's when I found out like there was a lot of jobs for the care sector. They were like crying out for people, and I know a lot of people, like a lot of my circle of friends, they're in the care sector and you know, one of my best friends said: You'd be amazing at this job, Mary, come and come on work for us, you'd be brilliant! (UK02_Mary)

Women enter care in the hope of arranging working hours around their child-care responsibilities: 'After having my children, I got involved in the care side of things. I went for the weekend and evening shifts' (UK01_Sophia). We also have a few cases of women who, as graduates, had other career options and had previously worked in office or management jobs and who had consciously opted to work in care, following their vocation (understood as Weberian calling). With their biographies including taking care of family members (DE18_Eva), they developed empathy towards vulnerable and suffering people. As a consequence, they turned their proficiency in private matters into their occupation. One such example is Beate (DE02), a care worker in Germany in her early 60s, whose previous career in human resources (HR) and the good income of her household allowed for a comfortable life without any need for her to work. Nevertheless, Beate decided to enter the care sector after being a full-time carer for her mother-in-law and after realizing how much meaning 'helping others' had for her:

> My husband was working, and I decided to take care of my mother-in-law. I left my job. And I was helping her to wash, I was feeding her, and while I was giving her food ... or when I was holding her hand ... giving encouragement, exchanging memories, I realised ... that it was important. And that I enjoyed doing it. You know, not always I had a great relationship with my mother-in-law. Just like in other families, there were ups and downs. But people have their needs ... And I was thinking: 'How would you like to be treated in such a situation? Would you like to cry ... And say: "I have to go to the toilet, but I can't leave the bed on my own. I am scared that I'd fall"'. And if no one is coming, what should you do? Pee in your bed? Do you want that? And it was clear that I don't want that. And other people don't want that. I wouldn't wish anyone to feel so helpless. So, I did it and it was natural for me. I took care of my mother-in-law ... I was 50 at that time and I faced a question: 'Do I want this office job I had before, or do I want to work with elderly people?' And it was clear to me that I wanted to work with elderly people. (DE02_Beate)

Despite easy access to care work, without formal requirements, credentials, and qualifications and with minimum training (or no training at all), care workers soon become deluded, experiencing difficulties in having 'care work' acknowledged as a formal 'profession' by others, and often finding themselves unprepared for the challenges they encounter at work:

> I've done training, but that's like very standard, basic training. For the 'others' I am not in a 'profession' ... I really felt ... sort of helpless dealing with dementia patients because ... sometimes you have people who would revert back to their childhood, or they wouldn't recognise their family who were visiting. You've got lots of people who forgot they had their meal ... Sometimes people are aggressive. I had a woman

> running at me with the pointy end of an umbrella. But you get used to people hitting or throwing things at you. There are people who suffer from hallucinations, like at the moment, we have this lady who screams that she's left the oven on, and the house is gonna burn down and you need to deal with all of it. I've had all sorts of things thrown at me, I've been pushed, I've been kicked, I've even had people trying to bite me. (UK01_Sophia)

Nonetheless, female care workers consider themselves 'professionals' who nurture their love for the job to cope with the complexities of not having enough training and support, lacking recognition, and being underpaid. In their narratives they kept reminding us and themselves why they had chosen this kind of work in the first place and what care was really about:

> I learned from my godfather that it is important to help if someone has an accident, not to look away and I have always been enthusiastic about that. I have always said: Our 'profession' is defined by just a smile from the older folks, whether it is someone who can speak or not. That is already worth a lot . . . you realise that, when they smile, you are doing it the right way and that they feel comfortable. And that is what defines this profession. (DE04_Sonja)

Whereas our interviewees' specific work arrangements vary, there is a common thread connecting their experiences of care work, such as the need to 'do as much work as possible for as little pay as possible' (UK05_Lynn). Alongside the time pressure ('it was so busy and so stressful today that I only took three cigarette breaks. Each time smoking the cigarette very quickly' (DE07_Julia, diary)), workers find themselves subjected to emotional blackmail and moral pressure against the backdrop of organizational deficits. They know that a refusal to do unpaid overtime would most likely harm the elderly more than their employers, which is why many refrain from challenging the status quo. Unpaid overtime is therefore frequently undertaken to mitigate the worst repercussions of unfavourable structural conditions, such as severe labour shortages. In many cases, our interviewees felt that they had no choice, knowing that a refusal to do unpaid overtime would be considered immoral and incurred the risk of being sanctioned. At the same time our interviewees also emphasized that they could not bear the thought of leaving residents in an unkempt state, e.g. at the end of their normal shifts, a scenario which often drove them to invest their own time and resources. The ubiquity of unpaid overtime in care raises important questions about the power structures triggering the exploitation of such a feminized workforce. The criteria defining what makes an 'ideal care worker' are deeply intertwined with gendered notions of what makes a 'caring woman' and/or a 'decent human being'.

Despite sometimes only having received minimal formal training, none of the care workers we interviewed described their jobs as easy, trivial, or unskilled. On the contrary, they viewed it as complex, very challenging, and therefore requiring high practical and emotional skills. One theme dominating our sample was that, due to the low pay, tough working conditions, and having to do 'dirty' tasks (e.g., changing adult diapers), care work was sometimes perceived as an inherently unattractive job, chosen only as a 'last resort'. Our interviewees however dealt with the misconceptions of their occupation by means of identity work. Through the combination of their personal identity ('being a caring person'), their calling ('it is not a job, it's a calling'), and their professional identity ('it's not about money, it's about helping those in needs'), care workers construct and defend the meaning of their work. The other side of the coin is the unpaid overtime—as the caring, dedicated workers are expected (and expect of themselves) to do things for which they will not be remunerated. At the same time, they are aware that their underpayment goes hand in hand with a lack of recognition:

> Somebody said to me before: 'What job do you do?' And sometimes I felt shame to say … that I am a care assistant, because it's always been so much negativity about carers, and our value in a job. I've had people say to me: 'Oh, you're just a bum wiper. That's all you are as a job!', you know … But in fact I'm dealing with … I'm someone's probably last port of call, I'm there with somebody, while they're taking their last breaths. I've been there, why they've been in pain. I've been there when they've been frightened. I've been there when they've been happy and joyful. I've seen them, you know, I've seen their new great grandchildren being born. I've been someone's support worker, someone's friend, someone's everything. (UK03_Diana)

> The work is so hard … so overwhelming. And the type of money you get … It just doesn't balance out at all, like it should not be minimum wage. A lot of people think like a care job's so easy. They see people just having a cup of tea with an old person. And then they think: 'Oh, that's all they do, they sit around just eating cakes and coffee and stuff'. But it's actually nothing like that. (DE18_Eva)

There are contradictions between how care workers see themselves and their work, and how they think they are perceived by others. The unpaid labour care workers are supposed to perform to comply with the 'ideal worker' norm contributes to the perception of their work being of little value, despite being ‘someone’s support worker, someone’s friend, someone’s everything’ (UK03_Diana).

The image of a care worker sacrificing herself *for the sake of others* is not only constructed by care workers and care recipients, but also propagated by employers. It is used instrumentally to promote an attractive image of a care establishment. For example, care homes often advertise their services by promising prospective residents a safe and comfortable environment, where they will be taken care of as if they were family. Such advertisements often feature photos of mostly young, smiling, and emotionally devoted women, to whom the elderly look up to full of gratitude. Although such advertisements fail to grasp the complexity and lived reality of care work, they nevertheless deserve attention as they embody important ideals which care workers are expected to strive for in their everyday duties. Not only are they supposed to provide the elderly with practical and emotional support, they are also expected to do so in an efficient, subordinate, and attentive manner—and all of it, as Mary (UK02) commented: ‘for the money that’s so low that it’s shocking’.

Despite the high level of responsibility and the long and intense hours, care workers are notoriously underpaid. Our interviewees were no exception in this regard, with their wages either at or slightly above the minimum wage level in both national contexts. In Germany, the workforce is made up of care assistants (*Pflegehilfskräfte*) and fully qualified care workers (*Pflegefachkräfte* who have completed an apprenticeship). Due to the severe labour shortage, some of our interviewees who worked as care assistants were assigned tasks and workloads very similar to those of their fully qualified colleagues, despite earning significantly less:

> This head of the ward saw everything I do. And she said: ‘This is not possible. Zarima, I haven’t seen everyday companions like you. You do everything! And there are everyday companions who just wait until the nurse comes’. But what do I do? I go there straight away and I ask: ‘Do you need help?’ And I help, and I do this, this and that. But a nurse earns €17 and I earn €10 … And I do the same job. (DE06_Zarima)

Since completing our data collection in 2021, the pay structure in Germany has changed. The national minimum wage was increased from €9.60 in 2021 to €12 in 2023. Not least in response to Covid-19, the wages of care workers were increased above the minimum wage. Several interviewees commented that this increase in pay above the minimum wage was symbolically important for them, as it entailed a modest recognition of their work:

> Well, if all people who work in Germany get at least €12 an hour from next year on, then what does it matter if I work at a Lidl cash till for €12 an hour or if I take care of the elderly for €12. Or if I go clean somewhere for €12. That the elderly carer needs €2 more, or that he has to do a lot more, work longer hours, that's also quite clear. (DE18_Eva)

While these changes were welcomed, care wages remain low, particularly in comparison to those in male-dominated occupations. A further factor impacting some of our interviewees' financial situations was that they only worked part time due to caring responsibilities at home. Unless they had other financial support (e.g., through a partner's income), these interviewees struggled to make ends meet. The situation for care workers in the UK looks relatively worse, as care assistants are rarely paid more than the minimum wage of £9.50, and are often employed on zero-hour contracts. These interviewees had to cope with a lot of income insecurity, as they needed to stay 'on call' without a guarantee of getting paid. The well-documented drawbacks of zero-hour contracts in the UK were confirmed by our interviewees. The unpredictable working hours, and thus income, made individuals particularly vulnerable to precarity. However, in Germany, despite minimum wages in the care sector (the 'Pflegemindestlohn') having increased in the face of increased demand during Covid-19, they were often still considered by our respondents to be insufficient to guarantee a decent life as they did not reflect the amount of work spent caring: 'We got paid a bit more but there was suddenly much more work. One had to do everything much faster to stay within the timeframe' (DE07_Julia, diary). Moreover, care assistants ('Betreuungsassistenten/innen' or 'Alltagsbegleiter/innen') are often hired. These are expected to help with physical care tasks (e.g., accompanying people to the toilet or giving them food), something which belongs to the job description of a professional (not assistant) caregiver, meaning that the 'value of their small pay rise' (DE11_Sinem) is not commensurate with the work they perform.

Stigmatization through Punishments and Rewards

Care workers are supposed to cater for the physical and emotional needs of the elderly, yet they report that this is very difficult (or impossible) 'within very tightly allocated time slots' (UK05_Lynn), described as 'Minutenpflege' (DE19_Alina) or 'stopwatch care' (UK05_Lynn). Furthermore, they are expected by their employers to always be available, to prioritize work over private life, and to subordinate themselves to their superiors. As they work in understaffed organizations, they are expected to 'work for two', filling all the gaps in care. If falling short of any of these ideals, care workers risk being stigmatized as 'not truly caring' or letting residents down: a guilt-inducing technique meant to discourage care workers from challenging the status quo. Despite this threat, several interviewees shared incidences when they resisted the pressure to conform, only to be subsequently penalized.

Punishments

None of our interviewees took care work lightly. Keenly aware of residents' dependence on their services, they were intent on doing their best to meet everyone's demands. This was, however, not always possible. Our interviewees frequently recalled situations where they contested—often unrealistic—expectations. These 'acts of contestation' covered a wide spectrum, ranging from distancing themselves from criticism, downright refusal to do certain tasks, whether individually or collectively (e.g., when work became dangerous both for care workers and care recipients), or even reporting an employer to the local authorities. Resisting the 'ideal worker' norm by not conforming to expectations induced processes of stigmatization intended to punish such behaviour and bring carers 'back in line'. The perhaps most difficult challenge was to reconcile the requirement to work fast ('working for two') and the wish to provide 'high quality care'. Care workers were often forced to prioritize, meaning that they were inevitably falling short of somebody's expectations. This in turn left them with a feeling that they are 'not caring enough'. Moreover, they were shamed individually by management and in front of others:

> My manager at the time ... she was horrible. I witnessed her ringing up caregivers and having a go at them for not taking care shifts. And it wasn't a private conversation between her and the caregiver. She would put it on loudspeaker so that everybody in the office could hear. (UK01_Sophia)

The difficulties of maintaining high ethical standards under intense time pressure was evident throughout the German and UK samples. Several interviewees recalled situations where their own definitions of good quality care deviated from those of their superiors, whose main priority appeared to be the speed of work needed to deal with the high workload ('working for two'). Many interviewees valued the emotions expressed during social interactions with the elderly which they believed to be essential to maintain care recipients' well-being—and thus implicit in their job descriptions. Several recalled situations where they were criticized by superiors and co-workers for spending too much time engaging in social interactions at the expense of speed of work. Interestingly, this criticism was not limited to working hours *stricto sensu* but also to the labour performed by carers in their own time (e.g., during normal official breaks):

> There is criticism which is hard to stomach. For example, last time I was criticised in front of everyone in a meeting. That I made waffles for all the residents ... that I made fresh waffles for all the 45 residents, during my lunch break. That I could have cared for the people suffering from severe dementia during that time ... And then I said: 'It was just more important to me that the residents get a fresh waffle and are happy about it and ... Well, during my lunch break and she [the manager] also ate some'. ((annoyed)) You know, stupid cow. Things like that. Such ridiculous criticism, which every now and then hits you very, very hard. (DE12_Marianne)

Many interviewees portrayed their workplaces as very hierarchical and at times intimidating environments where they could expect little sympathy in case they needed time off:

> And we got this new manager, and she absolutely micromanaged us, she was on our back all the time, do this, do that, paperwork hand written this and the other, And she started going through people who're going out sick, and the sickness red card ... so if you weren't one of them that didn't have any time out sick, she was a nice as anything to you', and if you were one of them that did, she was awful to you. So, anybody who was off sick *she was just awful to* and the staff were getting upset. (UK09_Joan)

Care workers are regularly shamed and made to feel guilty for getting sick and asking for sick leave: 'they try to make you feel real bad for being off' (UK09_Joan). Moral pressure is used to make absences as short as possible: 'who's going to take care of these vulnerable people while you're away' (UK13_Lina). Even in cases of work-related health problems, such as back injuries caused by heavy lifting, the pressure remains. Workers are also made to feel guilty when they admit they cannot cope with the type of work or the type of residents they have been assigned. Instead of receiving support, they are often shamed and ridiculed:

> I told the company: 'I'm sorry but I can't cope with it', 'Oh, you need to do it anyway'. I said: 'No, I can't do that', 'Oh, you need to give it a try'. I said: 'I did give it a try. I can't cope. I am not well'. And of course, I came again and again. I asked for a meeting

> with the main manager. They said: 'Who will do that if you don't? You're a carer; you really need to be caring'. (UK19_Marija)

The moral pressure described by Marija (UK19) is a common phenomenon in both the UK and Germany, though its intensity differs. All UK interviewees described situations where their superiors engaged in moralizing forms of argumentation to silence workers, to force them to do more work, and to maintain the status quo. This moralizing criticism is viewed by workers as very hurtful, due to their deep identification with their chosen profession. In Germany too, staff shortages lead to unpaid overtime ('It's normal to work overtime because something has to be finished' (DE03_Doreen)), as well as to the recruitment of less qualified staff and an increase in part-time jobs. Contrary to the UK, however, we found examples of workers feeling satisfied with their work environment, especially in the case of small-scale shared-living units where workers reported enjoying good relations with management.

Despite the sanctions experienced at work for not complying with the 'ideal', many care workers stay in their jobs. Care work is described as being 'sticky to leave', with workers 'prisoners of love', unable to leave due to personal attachments (Folbre 2012). The emotional bonds with care recipients make it difficult to quit, as described by Lynn (UK05) who reflected on being torn between love for residents and hate for the organization:

> I was unhappy at that company. Because they were just obsessed with money, you know, just wanted you to do as much work as you could for as little pay as possible. And then they got my wages wrong, they owe me hundreds of pounds. But I had to wait until the following week to get it. I had so many issues. And like at the time I didn't have, you know, I was living with my parents and things so I didn't have bills to pay. I wanted to leave for a long time, but I was so attached to the residents, you know, I've gone through years with them. They were like my second family. And I just didn't want to leave them, so I stayed with the company. (UK05_Lynn)

Lynn was keenly aware of the exploitative structures of the organization which apparently took advantage of their workers in the form of unpaid labour: 'I don't think anyone does care work for the money, but we're not superhumans' (UK05_Lynn). Leaving this company was, however, a complicated process as it entailed 'abandoning' vulnerable residents with whom she shared a long history ('I've gone through years with them'). She did eventually quit, having reached breaking point ('getting too much') due to money and mental health concerns:

> I don't think anyone does care work for the money, because the money isn't that great for the amount of things you do, but … It got to the point where I couldn't make ends meet. Money wasn't enough. It was a bad company to work for. There were no benefits, no rewards or anything. I also knew that I had to think about my own mental health, I had to leave because … it got too much. (UK05_Lynn)

Quitting, however, was not so easy. Lynn got caught up in a situation where whatever she decided to do felt wrong: she was unable to stay because her working conditions were unsustainable, yet she could not leave as that made her feel guilty:

> For a long time, I wanted to leave but I didn't tell anybody. And then I told the people I worked with and one of the supervisors … she understood my reasons for wanting to leave but I felt like she kind of made me feel guilty because I was a full-time worker. And she was sort of saying: 'Well, who's going to cover your shift?' … I was sort of talked into not leaving for a bit more, I was *made to feel guilty for leaving*. And then when I told some of the staff I worked with, they were quite sad to see me leave … I remember the day I did my last shift, it was really, really emotional. Because the residents … they were like my family. And I was crying, they were crying. And I remember thinking, like: I'm doing the wrong thing, I shouldn't be leaving. (UK05_Lynn)

There were several interviewees in our sample who felt morally obliged to stay in work arrangements they were unhappy with. The reasons were numerous, ranging from frustration over apparent mismanagement to witnessing cases of abuse and negligence of residents. For our participants, these situations were very difficult to cope with. They felt torn between not wanting to be part of an organization they perceived as exploitative and feeling that they ought to stay on to mitigate the effects of, e.g., mismanagement on the elderly. As the boundaries between one's personal and work sphere became increasingly blurred—especially after working with specific residents for prolonged periods of time ('they were like my family'), our interviewees worried about what would happen after they left. Their superiors commonly employed guilt-inducing strategies to make their workers stay on despite being unhappy with working conditions. Withdrawal was thereby construed as an act of abandonment—not only of the residents but also of co-workers left with double the amount of work. This disturbing prospect deterred many care workers from leaving.

Rewards

When speaking about what makes care work rewarding, many interviewees referred to the deep satisfaction they derived from making the elderly happy: 'I realise again and again how grateful the elderly are for what you do for them' (DE02_Beate). They consider this appreciation as confirmation that they are 'caring carers' complying with the 'ideal worker' norm. Being popular among residents often serves as a source of recognition and self-esteem. Since the atmosphere among colleagues was often described as competitive, it could furthermore serve as a mark of distinction: indeed several interviewees took pride in being especially caring and competent care workers:

> My relationship with every resident is something special, I'd say. Thank God, I have the ability to accept every person the way they are. Without judging them in any way. I'm very empathetic. I can empathise with everyone. For my residents every day without me is a terrible day /laughing/ So, I basically can't go on holiday. Many people also tell me that they love me. And those are exactly the moments where I think: Yes, I did everything right. They value my commitment. They say ... there's one resident, she is blind, she always says: 'When you are here, there is life in the home'. She said: 'It starts when you walk through the door and say "good morning"' ... It's not my job, it is my calling. (DE12_Marianne)

To cater for the emotional needs of residents, our interviewees deemed it necessary to spend sufficient time with them. This was not however always possible as severe labour shortages translated into rigid schedules, leaving only limited time for each individual. Being rushed off their feet, care workers felt frustrated and unable to 'do their work properly'. Going against the ideal of a 'caring carer', this lacked any reward:

> I remember feeling frustrated a lot of the time, because I felt like I didn't have enough time to do what I wanted to do. And I think a lot of people if they had a choice to not have a wash so that you could spend more time just sitting with them and having a cup of tea, I think they'd choose that, you know, because they just wanted a bit of companionship. And I'm an overthinker, I'm a worrier. And I am very emotional and caring, so there was a lot of times when I would come home,

> and I'd be drained because I didn't feel like I had done my job properly. Because I just didn't have enough time to do my job properly. (UK05_Lynn)

In response to the time pressure and unfavourable structural conditions, including the severe labour shortages, many care workers invest different forms of unpaid labour to compensate for organizational shortcomings—including arriving earlier and staying longer (working before and after their official working hours, making unofficial extra visits to the residents, and working through their official breaks). These were not isolated incidences, but had often become part of workers' everyday routines to make workloads more manageable and to have a chance to 'do their work properly':

> When you come in at quarter to 8 then you might find that everyone is already there and they're waiting for breakfast. That's why I always come in at 7:15. So, for five years I've been gifting my employer half an hour each and every day. So that I don't have this stress. You know? I come and everyone is waiting for breakfast and quick, quick, quick, I don't like it. I like to do it calmly, that's why I come earlier and distribute breakfast in a proper way or prepare it carefully. I also have to make breakfast bite-sized for many people. Because of this half an hour that I always come earlier I have some room to do something with people, to ask them how they are. (DE12_Marianne)

> The early shift starts at 6:30am, but I'm always there earlier because I can't be there at half past 6 and start immediately, I always need to prepare things beforehand so that I don't need to run. So, I'm there at 6, do my things and then start on the wards. (DE11_Sinem)

Unpaid labour is an example of how care workers strive to meet the ideal of being 'caring carers' by doing their work properly. The 'caring' identity developed by workers through performing their work 'properly' regardless of the money and in line with their intrinsic motivation reinforces individual resilience, immunizing them against being considered 'not a good carer'. This intrinsic motivation pushes workers to put in unpaid hours as they genuinely care about residents' well-being and believe it is their moral duty—responding to an 'ethic of care' (Tronto 1993)—to help those in need. Sacrifice *for the sake of others* is not only a matter of personal choice dictated by their identity of good and caring workers, but also a response to working conditions that leave very little room for social interactions and providing adequate emotional support to care recipients. The reward for going above and beyond one's official duties takes the form of seeing the elderly happy and well taken care of. Complying with expectations is also a way of avoiding stigmatization and maintaining a positive reputation *vis-à-vis* superiors, colleagues, residents, and their families. Carers are intrinsically rewarded when they see that their patients are well taken care of ('professional satisfaction') and that the latter and their families appreciate the work done for them ('personal satisfaction'). For a care worker, being rewarded means going the extra mile to see residents happy:

> I love to do some activities where I bring ingredients and cook for residents. Because I've been to Morocco, I do the Moroccan meals. And one resident said to me: 'It's like going out for the night'. And I was happy to see how much she enjoyed it. (UK07_Marc)

Carers are rewarded when they see how important they are for residents, to the extent of being 'their whole world': 'We are their children and their friends and their parents and their ... everything. Because many of them, they don't have any family, they don't have anyone who'd come to visit them. You're everything that they see' (UK19_Marija). The situation of being 'their whole world' is rewarding as it adds to the meaning built by carers around their work. But at the same time, it creates a lot of moral and ethical pressure, as carers feel morally and ethically obliged to provide care even outside their working hours, as 'there's nobody else who could do it' (DE07_Julia). Unfortunately, this sense of obligation is often instrumentalized by organizations to compel workers to perform unpaid labour.

The Qualifying Meanings of Sacrifice 'for the Sake of Others'

The meaning of sacrifice *for the sake of others* is constructed around care work 'having priority' and needing to be 'done properly' with dedication and love and realized through permanent availability, 'working for two' accountability, and subordination.

Permanent Availability: Physical and Emotional Presence on and off Work

Sacrifice *for the sake of others* is realized through permanent availability, meaning that care workers wanting to be recognized as 'caring carers' need to prioritize work by being constantly available, both physically and emotionally, no matter whether they are on or off duty. Physical availability means workers work extended and often unpaid hours. It intersects with emotional availability in the sense that workers regularly visit residents outside official working hours to keep them company and provide them with emotional support in different ways, even as simply as having a cup of tea or watching TV together. Nonetheless, physical and emotional availability implies that careers are 'always on call', as described by Sophia:

> Now I work in a nursing home, so the nurses deal with medications and there are also doctors. So, I can just go to work and then leave and not to worry too much. But in my old job, in the dementia care home, I was a senior, so I was always on call. I had to deal with things when the manager wasn't there so I could never switch off from work and it started to invade my home life. I had to step away. (UK01_Sophia)

Both residents and colleagues ask care workers to remain available at all times. In their eyes, an 'ideal' care worker should be constantly available, both physically and emotionally, selflessly giving up family life and leisure activities. Even if workers are legally entitled to take time off, non-compliant actions, such as going away for a weekend, can be morally penalized by peers: 'We didn't like that' (UK15_Tina).

Permanent availability is required by management too. It takes the form of constant calls and last-minute requests, as there seems to be a permanent state of emergency. For care workers, it is very difficult to resist such requests, especially as they understand how much their physical and emotional presence is needed. They also want to demonstrate to themselves and to others that they are 'caring carers'. They thus agree to last-minute extra shifts, depriving them of a chance to get some rest. In some cases, they even offer extra visits during their non-working hours. Prioritizing work over family life by being constantly available, physically and emotionally, sometimes means not being able to 'see one's children' enough:

> When you have a new care worker, or a new member of staff and they're really keen, they won't respond that like, you say 'yes' to everything. You want to be seen and help people and so you'll be like, yeah ok, I do this or, yeah ok, I'll do that shift. And I was very quick to get to the point where I wouldn't see my children, /uh/ I always just seemed to be working. (UK01_Sophia)

Being 'really keen', Sophia refers to sacrificing herself *for the sake of others*—in the form of the devotion (including being unable to say 'no') shown to one's residents (and their families), colleagues, and management, as a way of demonstrating and having reconfirmed one's professional identity as a 'good carer'. Identification with the professional role is very high, to the extent of calling residents 'my second family' (DE06_Zarima):

> I enjoy working with my … people. They are like my … second family. From family you go to work. And your family is also there. Every day I look forward to seeing my people and when they see me—they are also happy and laugh. I always know when they are feeling bad or when they need something … I just see that these people need help. And I like helping. (DE06_Zarima)

> My son is now 9 years old, Covid really separated us from the elderly care facility, but my son was going with me to work since he was little. He plays the flute, so he played there at Christmas, he sang Christmas songs. He was there when we had tea and danced with the people. He was always there, or he played board games or sang children's songs, he was really very present, and they always ask about him: 'How's school?', 'When is he coming?', while he keeps on asking: 'Is this person still there?', or 'What is he doing', and it's a really nice connection. (DE11_Sinem)

Genuine care is expressed by doing things 100%, without cutting corners and by making oneself available, even outside working hours. Such dedication and affection towards one's elderly patients ultimately result in unpaid labour:

> I just can't walk in and clean and go out again, it's not possible. You can't do things half-assed. You go on, and still, you don't say: 'oh I did 15 minutes of overtime now'. No! You just do it because you think it's important, and because you *like* the residents. And sometimes you develop some more affection, and you want to visit them outside of your working hours, in your free time, right. I mean, that's lovely, I think that's great! Yes, it is. But sometimes it's just too much, too long and too often as nobody pays you for it. (DE15_Michaela)

'Working for Two': Doing Everything That Needs to Be Done

'Working for two' is the requirement for care workers to do everything necessary to provide a certain standard of 'quality care'. Nonetheless, the severe labour shortages in the care sector in both Germany and the UK translate into pressure on workers to take on a physical and emotional workload for which two or more care workers would normally be needed. This results in such extreme time pressure that doing one's work 'properly'—providing 'caring care'—becomes impossible. At the same time, the hourly wage remains the same, meaning that the extra workload and extra time pressure become a form of unpaid labour.

> And *everywhere* was so short-staffed. Let's say there should be four people on, and we got two and that was fairly normal, you know? People wouldn't want to pay out or the management wouldn't pay out any extra to get extra agency staff in and quite often no one was available anyway. So, you would rush around. (UK15_Tina)

> Each resident has their own different needs. So it's very, very difficult to spread your time that you have with everybody. And I do find that very challenging. And when I come home, I just feel like I'm very, very tired, I'm physically exhausted. I love this job but I don't think I'm going to be able to do it for a long time. It's so tough. Sometimes I come home and have a shower, and just cry and cry, and have a big cry. (UK02_Mary)

> I followed a nurse for two days. And then they said: Well, /eh/ now it is the morning, there was a team meeting at around 6am and then they said: 'Beate, you go there and there. You have to finish up this person in the morning. Then you have to make the bed. To see that the room is okay. And then the people have to be taken downstairs into the breakfast room. You need to wash them, take off their sleepwear, help them brush their teeth, and shave them'. We were supposed to have the residents downstairs in the breakfast room at 7:30. But I didn't manage to do that! I was downstairs with everyone at 7:50, drenched in sweat. And they immediately said: 'It is not okay! You have to work harder. You have to do it faster! (DE02_Beate)

The pressure to 'work for two' reveals the perverse effects of structural changes over the last decades in the care sector in both the UK and Germany (see Chapter 3). Labour shortages, on the one hand, and the logic of increased efficiency and profitability in care organization, on the other, resulted in a care environment where everybody is rushed:

> I've been working in care since 2004 and I see that a lot has changed. Back then, it was all better organised. And we had less time pressure, because we had a time plan and we had to stick to it. It was possible to work in a relaxed way, to talk to people during your shift, and no one was rushed. But now you rush yourself, you rush your residents and your colleagues. And when I look at it now, we're all at our limits. We're running all the time. The interpersonal aspects suffer. It's difficult to take your time to chat with people, but you can't just go in and do your thing, automatically like a robot ... Times were different then. If you wanted to stay in one room

for 10 extra minutes, to chat a bit, it was possible. But now, we feel we just can't afford that anymore, to say: 'Come let me just stay for a moment'. (DE11_Sinem)

In each of our field sites, our interviewees reported on the effects of this increased time pressure. For the organization, efficiency seems to be the decisive criterion in terms of determining workers' capacity to perform all the prescribed tasks in a timely manner, especially if a single worker is capable of 'working for two'. Carers are expected to wash, dress, and feed residents to a tight schedule, without compromising on the 'quality of care'. Since this type of labour involves dealing with complex human (emotional) needs, workers found it extremely difficult if not impossible to meet such demands:

We are running everything according to a schedule. At the end of the day, we need to make sure that the residents are happy and have everything that they need. We try to go with the flow, to follow the needs of our residents, but of course there are some tasks that you have to do at certain times, like preparing meals or giving medications. Sometimes some of the residents might need some more time for personal care, or they feel upset and they call you. And if you can, you go to them, but sometimes there's just no time. Not enough time at all to do it all. (UK17_Tara, diary)

Today I couldn't fulfil all residents' wishes. They weren't doing so well today, and they were asking me for things but I just couldn't be there all the time, because there's so much to do. Sometimes they need more help, and I don't know what to do. But today it was still okay, because the residents were actually sympathetic about it that you just can't jump like that regardless of the normal schedule. (DE07_Julia, diary)

The care home providers in our sample differed in terms of how they responded to residents' emotional needs. Several facilities hired extra staff (especially in Germany) specifically responsible for social activities such as arts and craft sessions. While our interviewees generally welcomed such initiatives, they lamented the increasing fragmentation of their work into social and care tasks; a division that felt somewhat artificial and made it more difficult to build trust relationships with residents. In the narratives, they commonly drew comparisons with earlier stages of their careers when high efficiency and profitability had apparently not played such a central role:

Well, I have quite a big period to span, from 2004 to 2021, and I feel like you used to have less time pressure. And in my mind, the interpersonal aspect was more

> important before. Now we've got social carers for that, which I approve of, because anyways you never have enough people, but it would be nicer if you had *more* colleagues able to pick up the slack. To help me if I don't have enough time to finish. (DE11_Sinem)

The pressure to 'work for two' was exacerbated during Covid-19 as care workers were expected not only to provide extra tasks related to social distancing, PPE (personal protective equipment), and additional cleaning, but were also required to provide more emotional labour in order to sooth their distressed patients. They were expected to manage their own emotions (staying calm despite increasing risks) and the emotions of others. The experience of working under immense time pressure, however, is not limited to the pandemic. In fact, it has become so common that care workers have developed their own vocabulary for it. The understaffing and increased workload are termed 'classical situations', while care timed down to every minute is called 'Minutenpflege' (DE19_Alina), 'stopwatch care'. Some organizations have installed software to calculate timeslots in minutes for the most efficient care provision. This approach, however, puts care workers under additional pressure. We had expected to observe such phenomena predominantly in large care homes designed for high numbers of residents, but we discovered that 'stopwatch care' was also occurring in small homes:

> My shift started at 7am, but I arrived there at 6:35 and the nightshift would leave at 6:45. The next staff member came around 9am, which meant I was alone for two hours as a student. I prepared the normal tasks for the day, made breakfast and stuff. And when my colleague came, and if we were lucky, we were three people working. Every patient had to get out of bed quickly, because the nursing management could show up, and they don't appreciate it if patients are still in bed. All residents are supposed to be sitting at the table by no later than half past nine, and they have to have eaten whether they want to or not. Plus the housekeeping, laundry, cooking, etc. Then people were supposed to take a nap in the afternoon, right. No matter if they wanted to or not. We had to put people to bed for an hour and a half, so that the living area could be cleaned. It was very important for it to look clean, and to do your documentation at a set time, the games at a set time and treatment at a set time. (DE19_Alina)

The pressure to work faster has a direct impact on the quality of care and residents' quality of life. Through calculated and meticulously measured series of tasks ('stopwatch care'), space for abuse may be created. To meet targets and get their work done, care workers depersonalize care recipients to make their work more time efficient. Residents may be put to bed during the day 'for a nap' irrespective of whether they want it or not, just because it is faster to do other tasks when they are not around. They may also be fed in inhuman ways, just because there is not enough time for proper feeding:

> In the home it was really, really horrible ... And the carers ... there was no team spirit. We worked there together, but somehow also against each other. And the way people talked there ... how they treated the residents ... No, it didn't work for me. I just went to the HR department. Then they said to me: 'We don't want to work with you any more'. I said: 'Yeah, I don't want to work with you either. That's actually why I'm here'. I said: 'The way people are treated here; you should be sued'. Yes. I was kicked out of the place. /laughing/ I thought that was pretty bad, yeah. There are cups with mouth caps for when residents are in bed, you know? So that when they drink, nothing is slobbered in bed. Then they just put the cup in their mouth. The residents couldn't do anything, they couldn't move or anything. And then they left the cup in their mouth until it was empty. They didn't remove it, nothing and /desperate/ oh, I thought: Help! I think if I had been lying there, I would have spat at them. You just can't do that. Because it also spills. There's a big hole. It's not like the drinking bottles for babies, where they have to suck, you know? It is running out of the mouth and as much as it was running, they also had to swallow constantly. Yes, and that's how it was done also with the food. They didn't check that they first swallow ... or whether they even like it and want to eat. So, the residents were completely ignored. In terms of their will, their existence and their humanity. (DE08_Susanne)

Eva (DE18) who used to work in the same shared-living home for dementia patients as Alina (DE19), describes herself and her colleagues as 'Mädchen für Alles' ('an all-rounder'):

> In the flat share we were all-rounders: we provided basic care and companionship, did the cooking and housekeeping. I stopped because we were permanently understaffed. The promised second worker was on duty less and less. The cleaned staircase and the ironed laundry were the most important things for our bosses. We're supposed to do everything while taking care of 9 patients. But you can't be everywhere at once. How can you keep an eye on all 9 people with dementia while cleaning the windows? (DE18_Eva)

The preoccupation with cleanliness referred to by Eva is not about residents' comfort but about the building's external appearance which needs to remain attractive to families and potential clients. In the interview Eva reported that the private home was sold to a financial investor in 2017. At this point, interest in residents' well-being decreased rapidly as the new owner had no education in or understanding of care, being predominantly focused on making a profit: 'They are managers and financial advisors who've never heard of care, except that you can make a lot of money there' (DE18_Eva). The profit-oriented perspective also resulted in care workers' wages being reduced to a minimum care-sector level. This view is shared by other care workers, both in Germany and in the UK: 'Owners just reap in the money; the rest doesn't matter' (DE08_Susanne).

The expectation of 'working for two' leaves carers feeling exhausted, both physically and emotionally. Those who have experienced working in both large care homes and small shared-living places describe distinct working systems resulting in different types of pressure; while in the former, care workers suffer physical exhaustion (as they need to deal with so many patients, lifting and holding them), in the latter, they experience more emotional pressure as they need to deal with a whole variety of tasks and demands all at the same time:

> In this shared flat, it is more … the psychological things that are stressful. Not the physical things. Let's say this lifting, carrying, putting down or whatever. What happens on the ward. Where you are also sometimes really physically reaching your limits. (DE07_Julia)

In both contexts the physical and emotional pressure increases when the staff-resident ratio is raised (DE07_Julia).

Not only are workers expected to work for two, but they are also held accountable for everything they do. Working with frail elderly people entails high risks, as mistakes can have devastating—at times fatal—consequences. The narratives contained detailed descriptions of dangerous situations where residents suffered serious injuries and sometimes even died (e.g., choking on food or falling down). For the care workers, this is an additional stress factor, as they can be held accountable for such incidences in cases where these happened 'under their watch':

> And *then* she choked on something. And then /in panicked voice/ 'Mrs ?, Mrs ?', you know, 'Mrs?, Mrs?!' And then I scream: 'This woman is choking on something!' And then I check: 'Oh, she's already turned blue'. I call 112. The emergency doctor arrives. I say: 'I don't have time to explain, come here real quick' … And they came … Unfortunately [it was too late] … And then the doctor said: 'You have to call the police'. When the police came, I told them what really happened there. And

> the police said: 'Yes okay. It is believable what she's saying'. Everything was fine afterwards, but still /sighing/ I had like … for a week I had so many thoughts about it, you know? It's a tough experience. You know, it's such backbreaking work. And so emotional. (DE10_Ruby)

The risk of potentially harming residents in association with understaffing and overworking significantly increased after the onset of the Covid-19 pandemic. The fear of infection—and potentially provoking a chain reaction—very much overshadowed our interviewees' everyday life, especially during the early stages of the pandemic, prior to the introduction of vaccines. To prevent outbreaks, workers had to adhere to very strict social distancing rules, wear PPE, and step up hygiene—measures that added stress to their routines. Despite taking precautionary measures, several interviewees experienced Covid-19 outbreaks at their workplaces, many with tragic consequences.

Subordination: Having Nothing to Say

Our interviewees described the division of labour in care homes as very hierarchical. The hierarchy is topped by managers and (paying) clients. In cases of conflict, the 'client is the king' (UK19_Marija), indicating a power imbalance between care workers and residents. Workers feel unheard and unprotected when subject to accusations (e.g., of stealing or negligence) or in cases of sexual harassment or being attacked verbally and physically by patients suffering mental disorders. Care workers shared their sense of powerlessness with us. The experience of being placed at the bottom of the hierarchy goes hand in hand with the perception of being excluded from decision-making ('one has nothing to say' (DE06_Zarima)) and of being subordinated and exploited:

> I am subordinated and exploited here … It doesn't matter what I do. When they ask: 'Will you do this? Will you do that?', 'I will. I will. I will.' And … /sighing/ for years already … I also have a child, but for years, I've always been the last one to take days off because I have nothing to say. They are always right, and I am always wrong. (DE06_Zarima)

Care workers have a good understanding of what is expected from them in order to comply with the 'ideal care worker' norm and with their own professional standards on the quality of care they want to provide. They are also bitterly aware that meeting all expectations does not always bring recognition, whether at work or in society at large. Many carers told us about their distant and strained relations with their superiors who were apparently quick to criticize but never to praise. Throughout our cross-national sample, interviewees pointed to a lack of reciprocity in their work relationships. They were expected to 'do a lot' while not being granted the same privilege of making demands themselves. It was notable how even modest requests like taking a day off were met with indifference or even hostility by superiors. Many care workers in our sample claimed that their superiors lacked empathy and a deeper understanding of what this type of labour involved. In several cases, those in charge had no care background, instead approaching their work from a purely managerial perspective of minimizing costs and maximizing profit. This approach often translated into a very authoritarian leadership style discouraging workers from making demands or suggestions. This pattern was very demoralizing for our interviewees, who spoke openly about situations where they felt they had 'no voice' due to their low standing. A picture was painted of management who 'don't care' (UK19_Marija) about either workers or residents:

> When you're a good worker, a good carer, if you come on time, if they don't have any problems with you, if you put in a lot of effort, so people like you ... if you really know how to do the job and you love the job like I love my job ... I love to help people ... I thought that the office people would come together and say: 'Oh she's such a good carer', you know, 'She's good'. But no! They never did. And when I was there with them [working in the office], I was shocked. I was literally shocked because they don't care. If someone is a good carer or a bad carer. They just don't care. (UK19_Marija)

There is an ongoing narrative, appearing in all interviews, about management being out of touch with the reality of care work, especially higher management ('people in London') giving orders and issuing new regulations without understanding the nature of care work. This results in care workers not feeling appreciated:

> What I myself and my colleagues dislike at the moment is the lack of support from the people higher up ... sort of the people in London ... we just don't feel appreciated by them. I mean we feel completely appreciated by our manager and ... the residents and the residents' families, but sometimes it feels like they're not supporting us. They just keep giving us more stuff to do or having restrictions on what we can and cannot do. We have to follow strict procedures for instance about rings we're not allowed to wear. There's quite a few people who ... the way they say things, they shouldn't be in care ... because they *don't care*. (UK01_Sophia)

It was fairly typical for our interviewees to use terms like 'fear' and 'intimidation' when describing the atmosphere at their workplaces. There appears to be a double standard in how carers are expected to be selfless and kind, yet cannot count on receiving the same treatment themselves. If the mere sight of a superior already induces anxiety, workers are unlikely to resist. They accept working unpaid overtime as they fear experiencing negative consequences for saying 'no' to their superiors. We also have examples of carers being treated without respect, being shamed for occupying a low position in the organization, and being ridiculed for not earning much by a superior:

> I never say 'no', I do everything, and this means working longer hours, longer than what should be foreseen (8h a day??) ... but even so, I'm treated like crap. Sometimes, the head of the ward makes fun of my salary. It is now the fourth time that he's said 'Yes, you get here €2000.' And I say: 'Which €2000? What are you talking about? Why are you making fun of my salary?' /agitated/ Because he gets €2400 a month and I ... /sighing/ [€900] And it hurt me so much that I cried on my way home. They don't appreciate people ... They say: 'It's good that this woman is fighting for a piece of bread and does so much and doesn't receive anything from the state.' And on top of that, the director makes fun of your salary. (DE06_Zarima)

The 'ideal worker' norm presents a list of expectations that are impossible to meet, no matter how hard workers try. It sets such high standards for physical and emotional labour that, in the current work context of high time pressure and understaffing, are impossible to achieve—as care workers are not superhuman: 'they expect us to be superhumans, but we're only humans' (UK19_Marija).

Unpaid Labour, Resilience, and Precarious Work

When care workers get older and more experienced, they become more reflective about their efforts to comply with the 'ideal' and the costs of such compliance, including their sacrifice *for the sake of others* and the unpaid labour it involves. This reflexivity helps them to develop resilience which in turn is a condition for coping with the hierarchical pressure and the conditions underpinning unpaid hours. Interviewees stated that, on entering care work, they tended to take up a lot of shifts and work very hard, wanting to show that they were truly dedicated, that they were 'caring carers'. But over time they learned to be more assertive:

> As I got older, as I know the care system, I do sort of now tell myself to take a step back and that I can actually say 'no'. But when I first started the care thing, I just thought it was wrong to say 'no'. But yeah, I've had people phone me up and say: 'Can you work a shift tomorrow?', and I'm just like: 'No I can't'. And I don't feel bad saying 'no'. (UK01_Sophia)

Nevertheless, unpaid hours in care are a way for care workers to gain job satisfaction:

> Often, I'd just stay longer. Not as a worker but as a visitor. And it was so lovely to sit together like this. With no rush because you weren't on the clock at that moment. You were a part of it, you got integrated. If you're in a household for eight hours every day, it feels a lot like your home. (DE18_Eva)

However, the low pay (possibly in combination with unpaid overtime) may lead to precarity. The workers' narratives and work diaries suggest that they can hardly get by while doing this type of work, and they are aware that if something unexpected happens, they will be left extremely vulnerable:

> For today's shift, which was a seven-hour shift I earned just over £64. We are paid at a rate of £9.25 an hour. Is this sufficient to cover my basic needs? No, it isn't. So, if I have ... If something happens ... It is already a struggle paying my bills despite the fact that I don't have a mortgage. My energy bills have gone up by £100 per month. Also, if I get sick ... or if I have any problems with my car, I don't have savings and I don't earn enough to be able to pay for something expensive to be done to my car. (UK17_Tara, diary)

We found this precarity to be nested in gendered identities which in turn are often combined with limited class-defined access to resources and limited work opportunities available locally. As a consequence, we see working-class women entering care as they feel this is what they can access and what they can do very well, as they have been socialized to take care of others from their early childhood. They know that the care sector is 'always hungry for people' (UK15_Tina) and that care work is associated with the expectation of selflessness and sacrifice 'for the sake of others' (DE12_Marianne). Women, and especially working-class women, relate this sacrifice to both the private and the public sphere of work, independently of the country context.

> I grew up on a farm in Poland and constant work was just part of it. You know, for a child of a farmers' family. You get up in the morning with the chickens and go to

> bed in the evening after a day of hard work. The motto of my mother was: 'Always go to bed with a good feeling'. You know, no matter what you did, whether you tidied up your house, you worked in the field, do it best you can. Work hard, be self-reliant, independent, take care of others. So, I was always very diligent, hard-working, I always did a lot ... Before I ask for help, I try to do it on my own. And ... I graduated from school ... I was very eager to learn, I enjoyed going to school. I was dreaming about entering university but as soon I turned18, my mother said: 'You need to start earning money. We need help'. And I didn't go to school anymore ... because we were four children and we all had to eat. (DE01_Renata)

> I'm from a large family and I'm very family orientated. I'd do everything for my siblings and for my children. Before, also for my parents and my husband. My husband was a drug addict. I took care of him for years. His family sort of turned against me, which was fairly strange. My mum-in-law was just demanding things, cuz she was quite involved in his life, obviously. I mean she paid for him to go to rehab God knows how many times. So she was a very involved person, but /um/ there was lots of disagreements over things. She demanded so much from me ... My husband died and I had to take care of my kids. yeah ... it was a really difficult time and it was really difficult not having support from his family. But I was not lying in bed and wallow for myself, I'd rather be out, doing something, taking care of my kids. I went for a job in care because I knew about care, right? (UK01_Sophia)

At the same time, the gendered expectation of doing care work is framed within ongoing changes of the institutional conditions, including policy and funding interventions characterizing the care sector in both the UK and Germany. These transformations—together with demographic changes—have led to care being underfunded (see Chapter 3) in both the countries. As a result, care work has become increasingly un- and underpaid and precarious, with the UK suffering more due to the precarious contractual conditions in care employment and the absence of a national government budget for adult social care (House of Commons 2023). In particular, care work in the UK is poorly paid and often performed by workers on zero-hour contracts. Carers on zero- or low-hour contracts are likely to experience unpredictable shift patterns and low incomes. The late payment of the hours worked means that there are often times when carers are 'left without enough money to get through the month' (UK18_Edith), forcing them to use the days of their annual leave to cover unavoidable situations such as sickness, or leaving them reliant on other sources of income within the family and state benefits. However, welfare provisions in terms of disability allowance, child benefit, and childcare assistance in the UK are insufficient, with UK participants reporting that working unpaid in care was quite tough considering that private childcare was 'extremely expensive' (UK01_Sophia).

Institutional Country-Based Resources: Funding and the Role of the State

In the UK, care workers are more likely to experience precarity due to zero- or low-hour contracts and low pay. In the last two years, the median hourly rate for UK-based care workers has decreased by 1.5% in real terms, driven by a high (7%) rise in the cost of living (Skills for Care 2022). Care workers can have their income topped up by universal credit (a state benefit), but this is considered insufficient in the context of rapidly increasing costs of living. In both countries, care workers living in single-income households and with a migrant background experience relatively higher precarity than non-migrants living in a double-income household. For example, Zarima is a 41-year-old woman from South-Eastern Europe who earns €900 for a five-day week with six-hour shifts. This puts her in a precarious situation, requiring her to take on a second job to be able to make ends meet:

> I work 6 hours a day, from Monday to Friday, what do I earn? Hmm ... €900. So, I also need a part-time job so that I can get by, pay my rent. So that I don't have to live off the state. And for seven years, I haven't taken one cent from the state. But it also hurts me when I see that my colleague has 4 hours and gets €1000. And she doesn't do more than me. I do the same job as her, just because these papers ... my training papers are not recognised here in Germany. And many foreigners from Russia, Bulgaria, Rumania, Croatia, they have honest experience with care abroad, but it's not recognised here. (DE06_Zarima)

Despite years of experience in her home country and a one-year training programme in Germany to become a care assistant, Zarima earns no more than she did before as a cleaner, namely €11.40 per hour (she started at €9), even though she does the same work as other care workers whose training has been recognized. Zarima's bitterness is well grounded as she is aware that the minimum wage in Germany's care sector is much higher: €12.55 for unqualified social care assistants, €13.20 for care assistants with a one-year training programme, and €15 for fully qualified care workers. Non-European Union migrant workers in Germany report having their qualifications hardly recognized at all and struggling to obtain a legal status and work permit. Rashid (DE09), a 29-year-old man of Pakistani origin, experienced years of legal battles, bringing him to the conclusion that in Germany 'everything is broken':

> I worked as a care worker in Pakistan. And I worked as a care worker in Germany. In March 2019 I was at the foreigners' registration office to get my ID card extended. And the foreigners' registration office ... it withdrew my work permit. Because of the passport. They said: 'You have to clarify identity and then you can continue working here'. And after that ... I went to the embassy ... the Pakistan embassy in Berlin. I requested the passport there. I requested a Pakistani passport and then it took 6 months. They first /eh/ have to send the—request to Pakistan, they have to check something like a criminal record or things like that. And then I received the passport. I think in September 2019 I submitted my passport. And in October I received a letter that I'm allowed to work again, and I can get my work permit. Then I went there, to the registration office to pick up my work permit and a lady said: 'Sorry, something was printed wrong'. And I didn't get it! And until now I've been fighting to get my permit. I also applied to be a hardship case. It was also denied. I also submitted a request with a lawyer, applying for the permit because then Covid started in March and I knew in Germany more staff were needed in the care sector, but the court rejected my request. I sent lots of e-mails to the foreigners' registration office because of the permit. I said: 'Can you give me the permit in Covid times because I'm trained, experienced and I just stay at home. I see people dying every day, thousands of people died, I want to help, I want to work'. I wanted to work but I couldn't, I wasn't allowed to. (DE09_Rashid)

The situation described by Rashid is paradoxical: during a time of dire need for care staff, he (an experienced and eager care worker) was not allowed to work. The withdrawal of the work permit had immediate consequences for his financial situation: 'Previously when I was working in the care home, I was earning €1,500. That was enough for me. When I lost my work permit, I lived on social benefits of €170' (DE09_Rashid).

Care workers with a migrant background earn less as they tend to work on the lowest rungs of the care ladder due to the fact that their experience and qualifications gained abroad are not recognized. In the UK, as indicated, many such care workers earn less due to their zero-hour contracts, as in the case of Marija, who moved to Britain from South-Eastern Europe:

> I came here in this country two years ago. I don't have rights or benefits here. I can't get a flat, I live in a shared house, it is £800. And I was earning £1,000, and I have a

> car and I need to pay, you know. Month after month after month, I said: 'I can't do it like this, I can't live like this you need to give me more hours to work'. (UK19_Marija)

Care workers wonder 'where all this money goes to' (UK15_Tina). It does not go to them, as their wages are very low; and it does not necessarily go to the residents either as 'they eat very little, so the portions are minimal, and the food in these homes is not great' (UK14_Marta). Nor does it go to the care facilities themselves as there are constant cost savings being made there:

> Savings are being made everywhere. Those who own the facility, they collect the money, and the rest doesn't matter. So, something needs to be changed here. It shouldn't be allowed to work for profit in care. It's not right ... Everything we use at work needs to be saved. And some things are poor quality, not really usable. You have to save money and you have to use it longer, even though it might be a disposable product. The money certainly doesn't go into what we need and what residents need. (DE08_Susanne)

> I understand some money is needed for the infrastructure, for central heating, for some repair works from time to time, but ... I think the bosses are taking it all. The manager, the owner of this home. Because for a week in a nursing home people pay £800–1,000. *For a week!* (UK14_Marta)

Several women we interviewed had spent several decades working in care in the UK and Germany, and continued to do so well into their 60s, developing various work-related health issues. Some were worried about their pensions, especially if they had taken career breaks or worked part time due to child-care responsibilities. Some were in a better position to cope with the financial insecurities than others, depending both on their contractual arrangements and access to state support. For example, while in Germany workers could largely rely on state provision in case of health emergencies, in the UK they experienced difficulties even in obtaining paid sick leave, forcing them to use their annual leave to cover any sickness.

Several interviewees in our sample were at the lower end of the economic spectrum, making enough to cover their bills but not much more. This was especially problematic when having to provide for family dependents. The narratives provided insights into the long-term developments of how the care sector and access to governmental support in Germany and the UK has changed over the last decades. Several interviewees compared how they struggled to feed their families, for example in the 1980s in the UK under Thatcher when less regulations (e.g., in terms of minimum wages and access to benefits) were in place, and how they now struggled:

> I think when I first started work, I don't think there was even a minimum wage, I think they could choose whatever they wanted to pay. I'm sure I was on less than £3 an hour, I was on something really, really ridiculous ... Now, it's just a bit above the minimum wage. I've cried myself, so many times, when I look at what's in my bank account. And I need gas, I need electricity, I've got to put food on the table for the kids and I didn't have the money. You know, I've been working every hour I could physically work. And it doesn't matter how many hours I worked, the pay's so low that I couldn't afford to live. I've been having to borrow money from my family, just to be able to sometimes put food on the table. But I have to pay that money back. So it's a vicious cycle. You know, it's extremely hard. Obviously, I have a husband, he's a transplant patient. At the time, he couldn't work, he was paid their Disability Living Allowance. But because he was stable, it was a very, very low, low income that he got. And he probably paid one bill. And that was it. You know, and that was it. You know, and for me, we couldn't afford for me to pay for childcare because it was extremely expensive. So the truth was, he stayed at home with the children. And I went out, and I was the one who went to work. So, you know, financially, that strain was all on me. So when I couldn't bring in any more money, I couldn't do any more hours. I was feeling like I was failing ... Looking in your freezer and your cupboards and thinking: what we're going to do the kids for tea tonight, you know. It's really, really heart-breaking. Let alone anything else that they wanted or needed. You know, that didn't even come into thought: what's for tea? It's really, really hard. Really, really tearful quite a lot. Like say now looking back on it, it was like, how did we ever manage? How did we ever do that? But you do, you find a way. Whether it means you give the kids something to eat and you don't eat that night. You know? That before now, you know, piece of toast maybe for yourself and you put the hot meal in front of the kids. That's very, very hard times. (UK03_Diana)

This example illustrates the insufficient state provision, and the phenomenon of families slipping into poverty despite one parent working full time. The wages paid in the care sector are often insufficient to make ends meet, forcing workers to take on debt which then needs to be repaid. They thereby enter a 'vicious circle' of need, debt, and need again. As Diana received no state support to help cover her bills and her husband's disability living allowance was so low that it 'paid one bill', the family was pushed into poverty, with parents having to choose between feeding their children and eating themselves.

Another example of insufficient state provision is maternity leave: how it is calculated and how much it actually covers:

> I got paid maternity leave, but it was worked out on an average of the previous 12 weeks that I'd worked. And you know, I'd done a lot of extra shifts, but they worked out my maternity pay on the lower part of my hours. So I could have got more money if they'd done it over the whole year. Towards the end of my pregnancy, you know, I was more tired physically, I didn't feel like I could do as much, so I didn't put myself down for as many hours and then when they worked out // when they worked out my maternity pay they did it off the reduced hours that I was doing. So I got maternity pay for it // yeah, it was the it was like basic // It was basic maternity pay. I ended up getting this statutory maternity pay. So then, over time my maternity pay got lower and lower. In the final week they paid me 30 pounds. /laughs/ 30 pounds maternity pay. That wasn't great. (UK05_Lynn)

In Germany, we see greater reliance on a male breadwinner model, with women leaving the labour market for three years or longer after giving birth to children. They are also more likely to work part time than women in the UK who struggle to work sufficient hours to make ends meet. According to Germany's national statistics, about 80% of employees in residential care work part time (Statistisches Bundesamt 2018). In the UK this percentage is much lower: 51% for care workers and 28% for senior care workers (Skills for Care 2021).

Household Resources and Socially Reproductive Labour

Some of our interviewees were still in their early 20s and living with their parents who covered most of their bills, especially in Germany. Furthermore, there was a clear divide between double-income and single-income households. In the first case, the care worker's wage was commonly regarded as a supplementary income for the family. These interviewees were in a more privileged position, as they were able to reduce their workload and have more time to rest. Respondents considered this an advantage, albeit giving rise to jealousy and resentment among colleagues. Beate (DE02) was one of our interviewees in Germany who came from a middle-class background. Her husband held a managerial position at a well-known automotive company, and the couple had recently returned from a year in India (where her husband had been sent for work). Prior to moving abroad, she had had a well-paid office job unrelated to the care sector. On her return to Germany and backed by the experience of taking care of a family member, Beate decided to quit her office job and become a full-time care worker. Although her motives for entering the residential care sector were well intentioned, she remembers how her arrival at her first workplace was met with suspicion, as from a financial point of view she did not have to work:

> They were asking me: 'Where are you from?', 'I'm just back from India.', 'What do you mean, India?'. My colleagues were so surprised. It's not common that someone comes from India. 'And what did you do before?', 'I worked in an office', 'Oh, so why are you coming to us now?'. They couldn't believe it. And kept asking: 'And your husband? Do you still have a husband?', 'Thank God, I have a husband', 'What does he do? He works at Mercedes', 'Oh!' And then I had this feeling ... there were these prejudices: She doesn't have to work. Why did she come here? (DE02_Beate)

Beate's position is privileged and quite uncommon. Indeed, we had very few cases like Beate in our sample. Many respondents relied on a male partner's income, though this was more the case in Germany where a higher percentage of carers work part time. We also see double-income households (in both countries) where a partner's income is low due to his precarious work situation, health issues, or addictions (alcohol or drugs). Importantly, in the UK we also have examples of double-income households where both partners are in precarious employment or self-employment, facing the possibility of losing income any time:

> My husband and I came back from Poland, it was October. We came back from a short holiday, and it turned out that I lost my job, so suddenly! My husband broke his leg. As he was self-employed, he didn't get any money ... from insurance or sick leave. We were both unemployed. The end of that year was ... very very tough. No benefits. I knew I had to find a new job very quickly. (UK14_Marta)

The 'no benefits' referred to by Marta encompassed three aspects: (1) a lack of generosity in terms of institutional support ('you can't survive on a benefit'); (2) difficulty in accessing support—as Marta had previously worked for less than two years on a zero-hour contract and her husband, as a self-employed truck driver, had not been able to pay his contributions; and (3) the shame associated with 'living on benefits':

> I haven't used any benefits yet, because fortunately we can work with my husband and it's probably a last resort, I think. At least for me, taking advantage of these benefits is a last resort. When you can't find a job or when it is really hard to make ends meet. (UK14_Marta)

Still, single-income households are in a very different position. After the loss of the second income due to separation, sickness, mental issues, addiction, or a partner's death, women care workers take on extra shifts to 'earn enough money to keep the family afloat' (UK01_Sophia). They do 'everything possible to put food on the table' (UK08_Monica) and use all available help: 'My husband died. I had a lot to deal with. It was really difficult. Without the help of my mum, I wouldn't have made it' (UK01_Sophia). Nonetheless, we also see less dramatic cases where women are the breadwinners (DE19_Alina) while the partner takes care of the household and childcare. With her full-time work and hourly pay of €15, and her husband's unemployment benefit, Alina says they have enough to get by on. However, as soon as her husband starts working again, she plans to reduce her working hours as she feels exhausted.

None of the care workers in the UK used full-time daycare for their children as private nurseries were way too expensive. We therefore saw women juggling being a parent and being a care worker, taking evening or weekend shifts and organizing their work around childcare. They also resorted to help from family members. Though childcare costs are lower in Germany than in the UK, many interviewees based in Germany reported that they could not afford full-day childcare, especially when they had two or more children (DE18_Eva). Their way of dealing with this was to extend their maternity leave for up to three years and then to opt for part-time work.

Residential Care: Conclusions

Residential care involves providing a home environment for elderly people no longer capable of living alone. Creating this home environment is mainly the (emotional) responsibility of caregivers, the majority of whom are female and poorly paid. Working not for financial reward in a sector characterized by low wages but *for the sake of others*, caregivers perform labour considered to be emotional, intrinsically guided by a vocation or calling, and hence often unpaid. The narratives we collected underline this, pointing to the complexities and contradictions of unpaid labour in care work. They indicate that unpaid labour in care settings is often the result of interpersonal relationships, while also revealing that caregivers are having to work harder and longer under new market-oriented (i.e., cost-cutting) business models resulting from shrinking public investment and mounting private investment in care. This has led to a polarization between professional care workers ('Pflegefachkräfte') and care assistants or helpers

('Betreuungsassistent/innen' or 'Alltagsbegleiter') in Germany, and to a virtual collapse of the hierarchical structure in UK. In Germany, while care professionals are relatively well paid on account of the minimum care wage (*Pflegemindestlohn*), their numbers are decreasing in favour of much more poorly paid helpers. In the UK, there are no great financial incentives for professional carers, leading to them being paid wages at the same low level as those without any credentials.

We found a binary relationship between unpaid labour and precarious work, meaning that doing unpaid labour is more likely to entail gendered precarity. This outcome is in line with early debates on the motivations and meanings of care work. These debates point to gendered values and norms as well as the limited opportunities available to working-class women—constituting the majority of the care workforce—to access cultural and social capital, explaining why people take up care work despite the poor pay. Narratives reveal how caregivers struggle to meet highly gendered double standards of work, whether in the care home or at home, often leading to them working part time and/or unsocial hours in order to provide the elderly with 'human' care. Such caring for *the sake of others* sees caregivers working to the 'ideal' of being a 'good carer' in the eyes of their peers, the elderly, and their families, management, and society overall, in the face of demanding work conditions featuring hardship, overwork, and little defence of their rights and dignity. Despite care workers generally having employee status, the majority have variable and uncertain working hours due to their contractual status (e.g., zero-hour contracts in the UK) which translates into unsecure income.

Many reported feeling deeply frustrated about what they referred to as 'systemic problems' in the sector, such as the low pay and the lack of respect from superiors. Aware that any acts of rebellion would likely cause more harm to the residents than their employers, they 'suffered in silence', investing their own unpaid resources. Respondents spoke of their own ethical standards on how they wanted to take care of the elderly and of a deep emotional attachment to them, commonly using very affectionate terms when speaking about them. Caregiving is thus one of those social occupations crucial to the functioning of an (ageing) society, but little rewarded by capitalist society.

6

Freelancing 'for the Sake of Reputation'

A Binary/Non-Binary Relationship between Unpaid and Precarious Work in Online Platform Work

Online Platform Work in Belgium, France, Italy, the Netherlands, and Poland

Online platform work covers a variety of tasks accessed by self-employed workers ('online freelancers') through an online labour platform. In many cases, the work is short term and highly uncertain (so-called 'gigs'), while in others the tasks may be more complex and longer term, even to the extent of those performing them becoming 'semi-employees' of the client commissioning them. This wide range of task duration and complexity has led to the emergence of different types of platforms used by different categories of workers. On the one hand, there are easy-to-access platforms with a business model focused on earning commissions from freelancers for short-term tasks. These platforms pay little attention to checking freelancer credentials, meaning that they are often accessed by people without formal qualifications and/or beginners. Intent on exploiting freelancers, they have little interest in establishing long-term relationships with either clients or freelancers or in offering good working conditions. As freelancers are required to bid for gigs, we refer to these platforms as 'digital tournament' platforms. On the other hand, there are more professional platforms focused on longer term assignments with repeat clients. As their business model is focused on having clients pay for their services, they are interested in both establishing long-term client relationships and developing the portfolios of the freelancers whom they are able to offer to their clients. The latter aspect translates into relatively good working conditions for freelancers and greater rate-setting autonomy. As these platforms are oriented towards having clients select possible freelancers from tailored lists compiled on the basis of their portfolios, we refer to them as 'non-tournament' platforms.

Labour platforms have existed in the form of agencies for specific services (e.g., translation agencies) for many decades (Lomax 2017). Their main

The Politics of Unpaid Labour. Valeria Pulignano and Markieta Domecka, Oxford University Press.
 DOI: 10.1093/oso/9780198888130.003.0007

benefit for any freelancer is that they assume responsibility for finding a freelancer's clients. Without them, a freelancer is forced to go 'knocking on doors' in search of work—a time-consuming, often frustrating, frequently unsuccessful, and unpaid task. In return for this marketing service, agencies charge a commission, generally reflected in the difference between the amount paid to the freelancer and that charged to the end customer. However, in the online platform world, this 'knocking on doors' has—as we illustrate—been replaced by freelancers having to submit bids, which can be just as frustrating, frequently unsuccessful, and unpaid.

The one main feature distinguishing these traditional platforms from the online platforms investigated in our study is the exacerbation of the general working conditions characterizing all agency work, especially among those platforms focused on casual work. For example, while freelancers working for traditional agencies have always been rated by an agency's clients, the rating systems used by online platforms are much more transparent and open to client scrutiny, meaning that freelancers become forced to invest significantly more effort in building and maintaining a reputation. Similarly, rates can often be negotiated with a traditional agency, whereas this is frequently not the case with anonymous online platforms.

While freelancers have always been subject to competition, it has been exacerbated by the ease of access to platforms (especially those offering 'casual' services) by freelancers throughout the world, and importantly those from low-wage countries like India or Pakistan, or within Europe from countries with less strict taxation and social contribution regimes. This increased competition is leading to freelancers experiencing market uncertainty due to volatile demand. Uncertainty is further enhanced by arbitrary job assignment and performance measuring rules to which online freelancers have to adhere 'for the sake of their reputation'. As such, platform rules, for example in the form of metrics and ratings calculated by algorithms, point to a system of punishments and rewards used to control and discipline workers. Put in a nutshell, freelancers find themselves held 'hostage' by rules over which they no longer have any say.

We selected four labour platforms on the basis of their business models: Upwork, AddLance, Malt, and Jellow. Upwork and AddLance operate as 'digital tournament' platforms, while Jellow and Malt operate as 'non-tournament' ones.

Upwork was created through the merger of Elance and o-Desk, one of the first online staffing agencies. As of early 2022, the platform hosted over 800,000 freelancers and over 150,000 active clients. Offering one-off short-term gigs, Upwork operates globally as a marketplace for online freelancers, matching them with clients by bidding and algorithmic management. Freelancers access work on a casual basis depending on a performance rating system which combines data on speed, response rate, task completion, communication, complexity, and availability of jobs. Upwork ranks the profiles of outstanding freelancers using ratings and 'job success scores' (based on jobs completed/cancelled within a rolling twenty-four-month timeframe). Rankings are visible to clients. To achieve and maintain high ratings and avoid deactivation, online freelancers need to keep themselves constantly active by logging in frequently, applying for tasks, and performing work. Contacting clients outside the platform is punished through warnings, fines, and eventually deactivation. To achieve a high rating, online freelancers commonly perform unpaid labour by offering to complete tasks below their normal rates. They also use their own financial resources to pay for 'connects' (i.e., Upwork currency) to apply for paid tasks. Workers are charged a commission of 20% of their fee when the transaction is completed.

Working with over 50,000 freelancers in 2022, *AddLance* operates as a meeting place for online freelancers, matching them with clients through bidding but without the use of algorithmic management. Online freelancers access work on a casual basis and there is no commission on awarded tasks. However, similar to Upwork, they buy platform credits (i.e., As You Go credits) to increase their chances of accessing tasks.

Hosting over 300,000 freelancers and 40,000 registered companies in 2022, *Malt* operates as a labour intermediary, matching online freelancers with clients via algorithmic management but not using bidding. Freelancers do not send in job applications or bid for tasks but are contacted directly by clients. Malt supports portfolio building by incentivizing long-term relationships between freelancers and their clients. Workers are charged a commission of 12% of their fee. This decreases to 7% when repeat work is done for the same client. Freelancers construct a detailed profile listing their competences, work history, and education. This helps Malt to improve matching. Freelancers are offered training in portfolio building and rate setting, as well as support in dealing with administrative issues.

Hosting 50,000 freelancers in 2022, *Jellow* operates as a headhunting agency matching online freelancers with highly specific offers from clients. In doing so, it uses neither bidding nor algorithm-based performance measurement. It is an example of a largely automated, yet personalized, system of matching clients (including businesses) with freelancers on the basis of portfolios, for example in the form of work experience. Workers do not need to purchase platform currency (there is no bidding) and they do not pay fees, as only clients are charged. Online freelancers enjoy access to the full database of clients and tasks as members of the 'Jellow club' (registration is free of charge and voluntary). They can also keep their profiles open without the need to be permanently active.

To gain empirical evidence of how these platforms operate and what consequences this has for those concerned, we conducted sixty-four biographical interviews with online freelancers (fourteen in Belgium, fifteen in France, fourteen in the Netherlands, fourteen in Italy, and seven in Poland) working on the four above-described platforms. We focused on translators, copywriters, graphic designers, and information technology (IT) specialists as these are the most common professions performed online; thirty-nine of our interviewees were translators and copywriters (eight in Belgium, ten in France, nine in Italy, seven in the Netherlands, and five in Poland) and twenty-four graphic designers and IT workers (five in Belgium, five in France, five in Italy, seven in the Netherlands, and two in Poland). The gender split was thirty-seven women and twenty-seven men, while ages ranged from 20 to 66. We also collected thirty audio work diaries.

Results of Our Study on Online Platform Work

Precarity for Whom: The Biographical Case of Paulo, an IT Freelancer Stuck on Upwork

Paulo (FR02) is a 38-year-old Portuguese man living in France who has worked as an IT freelancer on Upwork for the last fourteen years. He specializes in web development, server maintenance, and programming. From his early childhood, Paulo was fascinated by technology. At a time when no one in Portugal knew how to use a computer, he was already building his own from old parts. He always knew that technology was 'his thing' and it was 'what he was meant to do'. After high school, he enrolled at university to study computer science. Coming from a working-class background and without financial support from his family, he had to work during his studies to make ends meet. On weekdays he worked in a factory producing plastic moulders, while at weekends he worked in a supermarket. Studying was a night activity and this turned out to be unsustainable. Paulo dropped out of university and started working full-time, first at the factory for two years and then at the supermarket. This was frustrating as he really wanted to work in IT. In 2006, at a time when, as he says, computers and the internet were still not widespread in Portugal, Paulo started doing small IT jobs, first in computer repair and maintenance and then in website development. Those side jobs were not well paid, but after experiencing 'really low pay', unfair treatment, and 'terrible unscrupulous bosses yelling and yelling at you for no reason' in the factory and supermarket, he wanted to go freelance. Paulo had just got married and his wife, even though against the idea of freelancing, was to become a 'financial anchor' thanks to her stable employment. Paulo appreciated her help but at the same time he suffered from social and family pressure to provide for his family. He felt stigmatized as 'a loser' as his 'wife paid the bills'. As Paulo was not able to find enough clients where he lived, he decided to join ODesk and Elance (now Upwork) to try his luck online. On joining the platforms, he immediately experienced extremely high competition from Indian and Pakistani IT workers who charged low rates and reacted very fast to all the job offers on the platforms. He soon realized that he would never be as competitive as them and that he needed to somehow start building a reputation (through clients' positive feedback and ratings). After weeks of brainstorming about what he could do that others could not, he concluded that he could leverage his knowledge of languages (he had managed to teach himself English and French) and coding to perform translation tasks—especially translations in coded patterns, as in websites. He worked the next two years mostly on translation tasks, expanding his competences to proofreading, copywriting, and video subtitling. Having gained a good online reputation (a top-rated score), he was able to charge slightly higher rates and to start working mainly on IT tasks. This, however, proved to be very difficult: the minute an IT task was posted on the platform, fifty or more applications were immediately lodged. This, Paulo said, happened because freelancers based in India and Pakistan seemed to apply for every job available with pre-defined application formats, thus scuttling any attempts to make a more tailored application. According to him, the approach used by platform workers in South Asia 'polluted the system'. He thus understood that the introduction of the Upwork currency ('connects') needed to send in applications might have changed the situation. Though Paulo was not happy to use his own money to bid for tasks, at the same time, he hoped that the 'connects' would squeeze out low-price workers. Throughout the interview (which lasted over three hours), Paulo kept coming back to the importance of client reviews and ratings on Upwork, as well as the difficulty of setting one's own prices on the platform. He found he was able to gradually raise his rates as his reputation improved but was repeatedly forced to lower them when he was unable to gain any new tasks. Paulo argued that Upwork 'never managed to educate its clients' who frequently asked freelancers to perform tasks for free in exchange for a five-star review. The power of reviews was so great on the platform that Paulo felt his situation was 'precarious', being 'totally dependent on clients' good or bad will'. He gave examples showing that 'one single negative review can destroy your reputation, and restoring it requires lots of time and effort'. Using his IT skills, Paulo tried to find out how the Upwork's rating system worked but ended up with more questions than answers:

> it's impossible, really, to understand why your total rating doesn't correspond to the sum of all your ratings. Recently I also discovered that my communication rating was only 3.5, not 5, even though I'm always very fast in replying to all my clients' requests and I'm very kind with them.

Paulo also spotted 'a few bugs in the system' that wrongly lowered freelancers' ratings. He reported the issue to Upwork's support system, but never received any answer or saw any changes. Despite all these difficulties, Paulo continues to work on Upwork: 'How can I leave? I've made my reputation here'.

While working as an online freelancer, Paulo went back to university but then dropped out again. After the birth of their child, his relationship with his wife progressively deteriorated and eventually the couple got divorced. Due to financial constraints, they remained living in the same flat after the divorce:

> I was still on Upwork, but things were not going well. I moved in with my sister, and then with my grandmother. I was just paying for my food, stuff like that. And the internet, I needed that. I was always scared because I couldn't go back to my parents or my sisters and just ask them for money. They don't have any money. They're poor like me.

Via a dating app, Paulo later met a young Brazilian woman whom he decided to marry and with whom he moved to France. As his second wife's Brazilian teaching qualifications were not immediately recognized in France, she started working as a translator on Upwork. Living with two unstable incomes, Paulo and his wife tend to overwork to make ends meet. Paulo accepts every task he finds on the platform and agrees to 'impossible deadlines' as he needs to cover the costs of 'one home in France and one in Portugal' where his child lives. At the end of the interview Paulo said: 'I'm stuck on Upwork. I can't become more than this, but I can't leave it either. I'm stuck doing multiple small things without being able to specialise in anything. And the money ... well, it is as it is'.

Why Unpaid Labour? The 'Ideal Platform Worker' Norm and Sacrifice for the 'Sake of Reputation'

Digital labour platforms hold platform workers hostage to a set of rules measuring their performance. While compliance brings rewards in the form of good ratings and access to paid tasks, it also requires personal investment work not always recoupable through the rates charged and is thus unpaid. Focusing on two types of platforms, 'digital tournament' platforms (i.e., Upwork and AddLance) and 'non-tournament' platforms (i.e., Yellow and Malt), we show how different platform rules force workers to invest varying levels of unpaid labour to build their reputations and gain access to paid work. 'Digital tournament' platforms generate very high competition by organizing casual transactions using technology to match supply and demand through bidding and not investing in developing either workers' portfolios or long-term relationships with clients. On 'non-tournament' platforms, on the other hand, the platform actively supports portfolio building and does not match supply and demand through bidding (see Table 6.1).

Table 6.1 Distinction between 'digital tournament' and 'non-tournament' platforms

	'Digital tournament' platforms: Upwork and AddLance	'Non-tournament' platforms: Jellow and Malt
Target client base	Freelancers providing services	Clients (mainly companies) seeking services
Investment in workers' portfolio	No active support for portfolio building	Active support for portfolio building
Bidding system	Bidding system generating high competition among workers	No bidding system
Algorithmic control	Algorithmic control resulting in workers' dependence on Upwork No algorithmic control on AddLance	Algorithmic control on Malt No algorithmic control on Jellow
Tasks	Short-term, casual gigs	Long-term, regular tasks and jobs
Relationships with clients	Short term, casual	Long term, regular
Return on investment	Hardly possible; resources difficult to be converted into capital	Possible and attainable; resources can be converted into capital
Unpaid labour	Relatively high	Relatively low
Relationship between unpaid labour and precarity	Binary	Non-binary

Source: Author's elaboration.

A portfolio refers to a platform worker's whole work experience, their achievements and their skills developed both online and offline in the wider labour market. In many ways, it resembles a CV. Portfolio-building support goes hand in hand with greater autonomy for workers and their capacity to establish long-term relationships with clients. We found that platform workers providing services through Jellow and Malt were able to showcase their 'education, work experience, expertise' (NL10_Martine) on their platform profile which could then be used as a 'bargaining chip' (PL28_Nina) and 'business card' (BE10_Jamal) in relations with clients. There are 'examples of the work you have done, companies you have worked for' (FR19_Nunzio) as well as links to personal websites and LinkedIn profiles. Portfolio-building support is also about encouraging regular and relatively long-term jobs (as opposed to casual short-term gigs) and long-term relationships with clients which may be maintained even after a worker leaves the platform. We also found that, despite the potential portfolio-building advantages a non-tournament platform offers to freelancers in comparison to a digital tournament one, the platforms within each cluster differ with regard to the presence (or not) of an algorithm-based performance system.

A 'digital tournament' platform using algorithmic control (as is the case with Upwork) may potentially enhance autonomy for a small number of high-performing workers. Yet for the majority of freelancers active there, it generates high unpredictability as there is no transparency on how exactly a reputation is generated through client reviews submitted after services have been provided via the platform. The performance measurement system features rewards and punishments. Using ratings as their basis, algorithms make decisions on freelancers' positions and future task assignments. Through their use of algorithms to determine a worker's performance, platforms incentivize workers to act in accordance with company objectives, and in particular to maximize economic transactions. Greatly influencing their prospects for employability and income, the algorithms are designed to coerce workers to defend and improve their performance ratings, in turn forcing them to 'toe the line' and deliver high-quality services speedily and at competitive rates which may easily translate into undercharging. This is indeed the case with Upwork where algorithmic control results in workers' dependency and a high level of personal investment work to comply with platform rules and with the norm of the 'ideal platform worker'. Through their compliance, workers demonstrate that they are professionals able to sacrifice themselves and their family lives *for the sake of their reputation*. To build a reputation on Upwork, workers agree to unfavourable conditions, including underbidding, undercharging, and unpaid labour: 'While you're building a reputation, you work for next to nothing! You charge the bare minimum, you work your ass off because you need those five stars' (FR02_Paulo). Importantly, reputation is platform specific and is immediately lost (together with all the ratings) on quitting the platform.

On 'non-tournament' platforms, when no algorithmic control is used (as is the case with Jellow), reputation takes on a different meaning. More attuned to that of traditional freelancers, a reputation depends not on ratings but on high skill levels, reliability, and a professional work ethos. Not forced to strive for 'five-star' ratings, freelancers can focus on presenting their skills and work experience in the best way possible, and on developing good (preferably long-term) relationships with clients. Workers are incentivized to regularly update and improve their profiles to increase their chances of finding clients, knowing that 'you're in a huge pool of freelancers and you have to stand out' (BE14_Jasper). Freelancers working on Jellow can be contacted by their clients on and off the platform (while on Upwork only on-platform contacts are allowed). They 'receive emails directly from businesses' (BE10_Jamal) when they are selected, and they arrange the terms and conditions of their work 'independently from the platform' (BE12_Ben) and get paid directly by clients. In some cases, Jellow freelancers may work for longer periods on client premises as self-employed workers or even as fixed-term employees (BE14_Jasper). Their reputations are developed as a result of frequent direct interactions with clients, and are thus not platform specific (see Table 6.2).

The online workers we interviewed told us about their experiences of and motivations for undertaking unpaid labour. Their narratives are sanguine insofar as they point to unpaid labour being to some extent the 'natural' consequence of platform work due to the rules laid down by platforms and negatively impacting workers' autonomy and freedom. While these rules vary between platforms in the scale and form of unpaid labour experienced by workers, we observe that workers try to comply with platform rules in order to build and defend their reputation—even if this is done at the price of working for free. For example, platform workers report that positive reviews from clients generate high rating scores which translate into a good reputation, while negative reviews can create a real stigma preventing them from gaining more work (or getting stuck in under- and unpaid work) in the future. To reduce stigmatization, workers comply with the 'ideal platform worker' norm, sacrificing themselves for the *sake of their reputation*. In their experience, undertaking unpaid work is necessary to secure future paid gigs. However, respondents also highlighted differences in relation to the forms of unpaid labour and the platform rules either impeding or enhancing

Table 6.2 Distinction between platforms using (or not) bidding and algorithmic control

		Matching freelancers with clients through bidding	
		+	–
Algorithmic control: using algorithm-based performance measurement	+	**Upwork** Freelancers buy platform currency to increase their chances of winning tasks. Matching is facilitated by the platform's use of algorithm-based performance measurement (a score based on various factors including client reviews)	**Malt** Freelancers do not buy platform currency as they don't bid for tasks. Instead, they are contacted directly by clients who use the platform's search engine. Clients can use algorithm-based performance measures (scores based on various factors including clients' reviews) to decide whom to contact
	–	**AddLance** Freelancers buy platform currency to increase their chances of winning tasks. Matching involves clients selecting freelancers based on their offers and is not backed by any algorithm-based performance measurement	**Jellow** Freelancers do not buy platform currency as they don't bid for tasks. Instead, they are contacted directly by clients who use the platform's search engine, with additional platform support. Clients select freelancers based on direct interactions

Source: Author's elaboration.

freelancers' autonomy. These differences reflect a platform's organizational context.

On 'digital tournament' platforms such as Upwork and AddLance, unpaid labour takes the form of constant online presence and availability, with freelancers subordinating themselves to both platform rules and client requirements. They work hard to deliver good results, striving for perfection in order to secure clients' full satisfaction and gain the 'five-star' reviews necessary for future access to tasks. In so doing, they 'sacrifice' their time and resources to be constantly ready to reply to client requests irrespective of the time of day/night. Such constant availability is important to compete with thousands of other platform workers scattered around the world on price, quality, and delivery deadlines.

Conversely, on non-tournaments platforms where workers do not bid for tasks (Jellow and Malt), freelancers report experiencing relatively less risk of unpaid labour related to searching for gigs and applying for tasks. In concrete terms, this means that freelancers can recoup their investment through their capacity to set prices *vis-à-vis* clients, as for example stated by this freelancer:

'Jellow is actually the only platform where I gained some good assignments ... I found a really good client there—they pay on time and good and I regularly receive assignments' (BE13_Kaat).

Freelancers have always performed 'free' labour which they have then been able to recoup through their rates. The upsurge of platform work and the accompanying competition has however constrained such recouping, with our findings showing that this is dependent on the organizational rules applied by the platform. Freelancers working on Upwork and AddLance spend a lot of time responding to generic enquiries that may never result in paid work. This is not just limited to newcomers, as Anita, an experienced Upworker, explained in her work diary:

> Today as well I did things that I'll never be paid for, in the sense that I'll never recoup all this from what I'll be able to price into my rates and therefore eventually earn. In the morning I was doing research for my new assignment. I was looking for the key words, I was checking the websites of the competitors, and so on. It took me about an hour and it's for the assignment I hope to be offered. (PL04_Anita, diary)

On Jellow, much less time is spent on applying for tasks or responding to general enquiries as freelancers receive tailored assignments delivered directly to their mailbox, as in case of Carine, a 26-year-old copywriter working on Jellow in Belgium: 'I check my email and I see what clients want me to do. There's no fuss. I do it quickly and get paid without any delay' (BE13_Kaat). As a reputation on 'non-tournament' platforms is understood in terms of professional work ethos, freelancers on Jellow invest additional effort to show how reliable, highly skilled, and 'nice to work with' they are. While building a reputation also requires unpaid labour, it is experienced not as a 'loss' but as an investment in developing lasting relationships with clients, possibly opening access to well-paid regular tasks and jobs:

> Today I started writing my New Year cards for my clients, which I think is important to do just out of politeness. I want to show that bit of extra gratitude. So, I write a separate card for everybody, matching the text to the person. I also put my business card in there. So, it's partly ... out of humanity and gratitude, but of course it's also a smart thing to do because they are reminded of me and we can keep in touch. (BE13_Kaat, diary)

Contrary to 'digital tournament' platforms (Upwork, AddLance) where the investment in reputation building is lost on quitting the platform, this is not the case on Jellow and Malt where the investment may result in lasting networks equally valuable on-platform as off-platform. Workers on Upwork and AddLance experience difficulties capitalizing on their on-platform investment due to platform rules keeping workers in a position of dependence on the platform for income, in the sense that a worker's gains are strictly related to following platform rules (e.g., permanent availability for tasks posted on the platform). By contrast, freelancers working on Jellow and Malt reported that their investment can easily be converted into capital, consistent with the platform logic of investing in portfolio building and long-term relationships with clients. Consequently, Jellow and Malt freelancers reported that waiting times (between tasks) and the time needed for communication with clients were a 'normal feature of freelancing' and that they would generally recoup their investment through well-paid work in the present and future. Support for portfolio building means that freelancers can develop their professional position and non-platform-specific relationships with clients for use in the wider market. Jellow is an example of how a platform can facilitate cross-referencing (combining the data from various freelancers' profiles), helping new platform workers to gain access to clients and encouraging both on-platform and off-platform communication, but without burdening them with fees and the requirements of speedy performance and permanent activity, as in case of 40-year-old Jeff, who works as a graphic designer:

> Immediately after my studies I moved to West Flanders because my wife and her parents had a printing company there. But I specifically didn't want to work in that print shop, so this is how I started to be interested in design, marketing, video editing to become a freelancer, and Jellow was the digital place where I started to look for clients. After a little while clients also started looking for me as I became well-known for my quality of graphical design ... Jellow allowed me to import data from LinkedIn, for example, contributing to my development ... I do not have a family who can help me, my wife works in that print shop, she does not earn much, I had to build my position on my own. (BE05_Jeff)

In contrast to Upwork and AddLance which make money through charging a commission on jobs performed by freelancers, clients on Jellow pay a monthly fee to access freelancers' profiles: 'they chose not to earn money through us, freelancers, but through businesses' (NL06_James). Jellow workers thus have lower costs *per se*. Moreover, they receive personal support in searching for tasks and clients, and advice on what to charge and how to improve their profiles. They gain knowledge of client requirements at the early stage of initiating the transaction by communicating directly with Jellow supervisors. This results in a significantly lower level of unpaid personal investment work, especially with respect to communication with clients, searching for jobs, and applying for them. The transparency of the economic transaction is key here: 'Following the advice of Jellow management I have developed my Jellow profile and now I see it really pays off' (BE46_Romi). Freelancers compete by developing their portfolios which give access to work: 'Jellow is part of my freelance network. Everything I publish on other sites, I also publish here. All I achieve elsewhere, I put on Jellow as well. It's all connected, which increases my visibility to my potential clients' (BE10_Jamal).

The investments made by freelancers in relation to skills and reputation are recognized by the 'non-tournament' platforms and converted into capital they can actively use for self-promotion, social media presence, networking, communication, and cultivating lasting relationships with clients: 'I really invest a lot of time in personal contact with my clients and it pays off' (NL04_Dirk). Working on Jellow enhances a freelancer's overall competitiveness—whether on this particular platform, on other platforms, or on the wider labour market: 'I got some really good translating jobs and that was because I stood out' (NL07_Jamie); 'I was contacted directly by clients who appreciated my experience and liked my profile' (BE46_Romi). Their educational credentials, skills, previous work experience, and professional identities are cultural resources which freelancers can convert into platform capital, as Jellow actively supports this conversion: 'Jellow is actually the only platform where I gained some good assignments because my profile was good ... I found really good clients there—they respect you, pay on time and I regularly receive assignments from them' (BE13_Kaat). Freelancers enjoy more autonomy here, which translates into their ability to negotiate the terms and conditions of their work, including setting prices and contacting clients freely (on- and off-platform), as platforms are interested in fostering regular and long-term transactions between workers and clients.

On 'digital tournament' platforms not supporting portfolio building, workers reported being constantly under pressure to perform and compete. They experienced difficulties setting their prices, as platforms cultivated conflict by fostering one-off transactions via price-based competition, with workers matched by bidding. Reputation and pay are platform specific: 'Without good ratings, I can't increase my rates' (NL02_Marie). Upwork freelancers, for example, are not encouraged to show their non-platform experience and they believe that showing their external portfolios in their Upwork profiles 'doesn't look very professional' (BE02_Laura). Workers find themselves subordinate to platform rules due to the algorithmic management driven by clients' reviews. It is not the portfolios but client reviews that make and break careers on Upwork:

> A client ended the contract prematurely and gave me three stars, that's not even a negative score: it's three out of five, it's decent. But for months to come, I got people asking me what it was about. They were very suspicious about me ... One bad review can make you jobless. (FR02_Paulo)

On AddLance, freelancers 'can upload a digital portfolio for clients to look at ... which has logos and projects you did' (IT07_Ugo) as well as the links to their 'LinkedIn, Instagram, and personal websites' (IT26_Angelo). This can open the door to well-paid tasks but it is unsure for how long and how much work is being requested because of the bidding: 'AddLance gives you the possibility to get some potential clients but on a non-regular basis. You never know how much you'll work; how much you'll earn' (IT08_Marta).

The 'ideal platform worker' norm, based on sacrifice *for the sake of reputation*, takes on slightly different forms depending on the platform model. While reputation on 'non-tournament' platforms is understood in terms of reliability and a professional work ethos, on 'digital tournament' platforms it is understood purely in terms of ratings, with the 'ideal platform worker' norm expressed on various levels: attitude (compliance with platform rules), availability, competitiveness, and hard work at all times. There is hardly any place for platform workers who are less than 'ideal', as competition is fierce, and the supply of online workers outstrips client demand. Workers on 'digital tournament' platforms thus find themselves between 'a rock and a hard place', as any deviation from the 'ideal' brings the risk of stigmatization; at the same time, complying with expectations requires personal investment work without any guarantee of this being recoupable in the form of income. Such investment takes the form of (1) *time*: applying for jobs, waiting time, preparation time, communication time, administration/paperwork, travel time (travelling to clients when necessary), networking, and maintaining relationships with clients over time; (2) *tasks*: overworking in order to meet very tight deadlines (unrealistic timeframes accepted due to high competition), emotional labour invested in 'making clients happy', self-marketing (constantly updating one's online profile: adding jobs and tasks recently completed), extra work to deliver a perfect product/service, and extra tasks performed at a client's request (not included in the previously agreed job description and budget); (3) *equipment/tools/fees*: arranging a home office, buying hardware and software, paying for specialist courses and workshops to upgrade one's skills; paying platform fees, banking fees (for currency conversion and international bank transfers); buying platform currency in order to increase bidding power (with higher chances to win jobs). These are all out-of-pocket expenses on top of the unpaid labour. In the 'good old days' of non-platform freelancing, such costs would be recouped through the rates set by freelancers. Due to the heightened international competition on such platforms, however, it has become increasingly difficult for freelancers to set a 'living rate' high enough to recoup these costs.

The *ideal platform worker* on a digital tournament platform is thus someone who needs to (1) be permanently available, responding very fast, and working day and night (including weekends and holidays) to meet tight deadlines; (2) be attentive to all client wishes at all times, responding positively to all client requests (including for extra tasks not previously agreed and not budgeted for); (3) keep silent, as any conflict or complaint may lead to severe consequences, such as lowering a worker's rating score or even suspension; and (4) participate in permanent competition which requires (self-)investing and self-improving in order to gain an advantage over other freelancers. Complying with all these expectations leads to a situation where work is given permanent priority over all spheres of private and family life. This is a sacrifice platform workers make in order to stay afloat: to keep their position on the platform and secure enough income to support themselves and their families. Awareness of the existence of these expectations is part of their tacit knowledge. On the other hand, non-compliance entails stigma from the platform (for instance by deactivating the profile of the worker who consequently loses the reputation they have built on the platform) and the client (e.g., low ratings translating into fewer gigs and a lower income).

Stigmatization through Punishments and Rewards: When Unpaid Labour becomes 'Income Theft'

We reconstruct the platform stigmatization process of penalties and rewards from the perspective of workers, i.e. how they describe the penalties and rewards they experience, and how they interpret and attribute meanings to them. Platform workers expect a return on their personal investment in the form of income. However, when the rates chargeable preclude such a return, the result is unpaid labour which can be described as 'income theft' for the freelancer. This 'income theft' is often seen as either a penalty or an outcome of platform actions. The latter is particularly the case with platforms using algorithm-based performance systems where freelancers report having to invest unpaid labour to avoid being penalized in the form of lower ratings and 'reputation loss'.

Importantly, complying with platform rules brings rewards in the form of higher ratings, in turn giving better access to paid work on a particular platform (but not in the wider labour market). Non-compliance, on the other hand, is penalized. Freelancers unable to follow platform rules are likely to find an algorithm downgrading their status (i.e., having their ratings lowered or entirely wiped out), questioning their skills and attitude (i.e., being labelled as not having the 'right' attitude, not sacrificing enough, not being permanently available, and thus not putting work obligations first), and therefore sidelining and excluding them (i.e., not being one of us, the 'reputable' professionals)—in short, stigmatizing them. The consequence of stigma is 'professional death' on the platform: unemployability due to low ratings or account deactivation (as in the case of Upwork where freelancers may have their profiles deleted as punishment for contacting clients off-platform). Any deviance from the 'ideal platform worker' norm is stigmatized (in the form of a damaged platform reputation) and puts pressure on workers to do more work—even if it is unpaid. Compliance with platform rules and the 'ideal platform worker' norm, on the other hand, are rewarded in the form of recognition and a higher reputation (as expressed by Malt's 'Rising Talent' and 'Top-Rated' badges), thereby increasing workers' chances for more regular and better paid tasks.

However, on digital tournament platforms using algorithm-based system, such as Upwork, a reputation is platform specific, meaning that, on quitting the platform (by one's own volition or after being punished), workers cannot make use of it: the platform reputation is deactivated together with the platform profile. 'You invest so much in all the ratings and badges on Upwork that it means you have to stay on the platform. If you're out, all of this is lost' (NL02_Marie). The pressure to comply with platform rules to avoid penalization is especially strong here. The narratives of freelancers working on 'digital tournament' platforms using an algorithm-performance system draw a picture of highly hierarchical power relations where clients and platforms exercise control in almost limitless ways, holding freelancers hostage. The rules and expectations of platform work are so clear to workers that they know and fear what is going to happen to them when they do not comply. There is a constant fear on Upwork that non-compliance with platform rules will translate into joblessness.

Findings illustrate that there is a fear of joblessness also in non-tournament platforms, as in the case of Malt where one freelancer had this to say: 'I'm scared when I come back from vacations that I'll have no more work'

(FR15_Fanny). This is because of the use of the algorithm-based performance system which penalizes the lack of permanent availability and non-compliance by lower rating statistics, in turn impacting access to paid jobs. The pressure to be permanently active and always ready to work results in stress and a feeling of a lack of agency in the face of platform rules: 'All I want is to put myself offline sometimes, but if I do that, I'll lose my competitiveness and it'll take me three weeks to regain it' (FR15_Fanny). The platform algorithm calculates a 'job success score' based on each freelancer's activity within the last twenty-four months. This is an individual worker metric that monitors the share of jobs successfully completed. It goes down when freelancers cancel tasks assigned to them, with no opportunity for human mediation. The statistics gathered by a platform contribute to a 'point-based' system of badge assignment, enabling the platform to rate worker performance. The ratings are based on speed (response and task completion), communication, complexity of the job, and availability. These criteria are pre-defined by the algorithm, generating a rating score of up to five stars. Failure to achieve 'those five stars' (FR15_Fanny) 'puts my future income at stake' (BE02_Mathieu). Thus, stigmatization in the form of a 'less-than-five-star' review and 'less-than-highest' statistics translate into a 'reputation loss', ultimately meaning the loss of income ('income theft').

Freelancers reported that attaining the 'top-rated status is the only thing that matters' (NL01_Jan). The goal of accessing more clients and tasks is achieved by beating competitors on price, speed, and quality. Badges are difficult to win but easy to lose, as ratings can be lowered if workers are not regularly available: 'It's the replying speed that gets your profile highlighted. As soon as I have a request, I feel stressed because I know it needs to be answered as quickly as possible' (FR05_Max). The constant requirement to be available and active makes it difficult to take time off: 'I can't remember the last time I took a holiday' (FR02_Paulo). In the case of inactivity or a low job success score, platform workers are asked to improve: 'If you are non-active, they contact you. If you don't react, you get expelled' (NL01_Jan). The threat of being downgraded keeps freelancers in 'the whirl of competition and unpaid' (FR05_Max).

The situation is different on Jellow, the 'non-tournament' platform which does not use an algorithm-based performance system. Here freelancers report enjoying autonomy in how they can organize their work (e.g., the freedom to use samples of their previous work which are already included in their profiles and which makes them independent of the platform). This is different to Malt where the platform's support in portfolio building is conditional on them being constantly available online as their rating depends on their speed of response and availability to clients.

We now describe the punishment and reward processes in both 'digital tournament' and 'non-tournament' platforms before delving into the qualifying meanings of the sacrifice *for the sake of reputation.*

Punishments

Freelancers on 'digital tournament' platforms are constantly afraid that less-than-total compliance with platform rules and expectations will result in punishment. Knowing that they need to be regularly available online, the fear of a bad review drives them to be available all the time, as in the narrative of Ludovica, a translator working on Upwork:

> I'm supposed to be available all the time, replying immediately, and even if I'm not, I still have it at the back of my mind because I received a message from the client, so I need to reply, there is really no boundary there. I'm also afraid they'll give me a bad review. (IT25_Ludovica)

This resembles the narrative of Marie (NL02), a 20-year-old university student from Italy who joined Upwork in the hope of finding work as a translator. This attempt turned out to be very difficult, as she got continuously rejected due to her lack of reviews. She adjusted her strategy by accepting extremely poorly paid assignments from developing countries. She tried to comply with expectations, making herself available and doing unpaid labour, but still she experienced constant fear of receiving a bad review:

> Some clients don't even live where I live so there is a jetlag, so maybe I get a message at 2am ... there's really no boundary maybe for them it's like a 1 pm [and] for me it's 8pm. So I'm supposed to be off work and study, but then I get a message so there is really no ... no balance between work and private life ... I also fear that they would leave me a bad review ... So I try to do my best to be always available, and not so expensive, and to do everything as they like, I like to be precise and to deliver the work if I can ahead of time and at a good price, so that maybe they notice and they give me better review. But it's not always the case. (NL02_Marie)

'Non-tournament' platforms encourage portfolio building and direct interactions with clients, rather than penalizing freelancers. However, when the platform uses an algorithm-based performance system, freelancers fear that non-compliance with platform rules will result in bad reviews, potentially leading to exclusion, as stated by this Malt freelancer:

> My profile worked super well during the Christmas holidays because I think that I was the only one who replied and who was available. Starting from the first of January, or from the second of January, my profile went back down actually. I used to be third in the WordPress ranking for the whole of France, but on the second of January I moved to the twelfth (position) ... Plus, on Malt I think that the algorithm really has a vicious circle side to it. There are certain moments when I have started some missions, so Malt put me in front. But in the month of December, I got just two missions, as people started going on holiday, so I was pushed down. Then I started accepting more missions and now I have too many requests which I am no longer able to manage. Actually, I have now already four projects, I am full until the end of January. I can't take on any other projects because I couldn't do them—and now I start to refuse—and I clearly see that I am no longer put in front. It's complicated because to be able to always be in front and to always have jobs with Malt—you have to constantly accept missions, sign them but if we sign them, we can't—humanly (speaking), we cannot do the work that is demanded from us in terms of time, in terms of number of hours we can work. I want is to put myself offline but if I do that I lose my profile strength and so it will take me three weeks to regain it ... that's what I find really complicated. (FR15_Fanny)

Despite working with similar algorithm-based performance systems, platforms vary in the degree of freedom they give freelancers to address any negative reviews. For instance, on Upwork, a 'digital tournament' platform, freelancers have only limited opportunities to contest client reviews. By contrast, on 'non-tournament' platforms like Malt, workers retain a higher degree of autonomy, underscoring the platform's commitment to portfolio building:

> A client once posted a negative review, and I asked Malt to evaluate the situation, to look at my profile and to delete that review ... they saw my profile, my way of working, and that all the other reviews were 100% satisfied ... They deleted the bad review very quickly. (FR04_Milena)

Rewards

There is no difference between 'digital tournament' and 'digital non-tournament' platforms when it comes to rewards. Freelancers are generally rewarded by the platform (e.g., by providing more work) and the clients (e.g., requesting services) when they show the 'right' attitude, meaning that they are ready to sacrifice themselves *for the sake of their reputation.* Their platform positioning is based on their capability to fit in, resulting in the reproduction of dominant practices. Compliance with platform rules on a 'digital tournament' platform means that freelancers follow the path ascribed to them: they bid for tasks, pay platform fees, buy platform currency, do their work to the best of their abilities, collect the reviews—which praise the quality of their work, their speed and dedication—and build their platform-specific reputation: 'Everything is centred around ratings: if your ratings are good, clients will come, and pay you; if your ratings are bad, they go away' (NL03_Hendrik). The greatest reward is to be recognized as a 'reputable platform worker': fast, skilful, reliable, always available and ready to work, as reflected in ratings confirming their personal and social identities as 'good professionals'. The best-performing freelancers on Upwork enter a select group of top Upworkers who get directly recommended to clients, thereby facilitating their access to work. 'Digital tournament' platforms are recognized as 'a sort of a game where you have levels, you have scores, you have reviews' (FR06_Bel). Freelancers believe that, by playing the 'platform game' (FR18_Timothy) and focusing on improving their ratings, they can achieve a 'price that really corresponds to the added value and the quality that I propose' (FR17_Oliver). In many cases, however, this never happens.

The Qualifying Meanings of Sacrifice 'for the Sake of Reputation'

Respondents refer to *permanent availability*, *subordination*, *striving for perfection*, and *permanent competition* as the qualifying meanings of their sacrifice *for the sake of reputation*, explaining why they perform personal investment work which, if they are unable to recoup the costs through their rates charged to clients, eventually becomes unpaid labour. These meanings offer a crucial insight into the 'ideal platform worker' norm, i.e. what is expected from a freelancer and what s/he believe is needed in order to be considered reputable—a synonym for reliability and professionalism, especially on the 'digital tournament' platforms (like Upwork and AddLance) and those using algorithm-based performance measurement (like Upwork and Malt). It is these meanings that we now turn to.

Permanent Availability: The Impossibility of Switching Off

Many of our interviewees were lured by the promise of autonomy and flexibility into taking up platform work. They believed that the technology used by digital labour platforms would allow them to work anytime from anywhere, in turn enabling a good work-life balance. One significant motivation to join the platform economy is based on the narrative of the entrepreneurial self: constant demands for individuals to become more than they are, to become self-entrepreneurs, to maximize and optimize their capacities, to invest relentlessly in themselves, their skills, and their online visibility through self-marketing. The imperative to act like an entrepreneur equates to a drive to orient one's thinking and behaviour towards the objective of market success, in line with the vision of the flexible and autonomous life seemingly offered by labour platforms. Some of our interviewees saw online freelancing as a stepping stone to entrepreneurship:

> At the moment I'm happy to be doing what I'm doing, which is platform freelancing. But eventually I want to start a company and do that, i.e., not being a programmer but actually being part of a company which I own and have founded. (NL05_Stefanos)

> I was still doing my own webstore but also taking up freelance work in combination with three other entrepreneurs. We would offer a full service to companies that wanted to do something online but did not have the knowledge or the skillset in-house. And I was doing that for two years . . . after which—I separated from the three other entrepreneurs and carried on individually. I set up my own company also to do freelance work and I have been doing that ever since. (NL03_Hendrik)

While there are narratives of struggle to enter a regular employment relationship due to such stigmatizing obstacles as age, inexperience, or a lack of academic credentials (e.g., for university drop-outs), most interviewees were drawn to platform freelancing for its alleged freedom. Some were lured by the vision of liberating themselves from the increased competition of the liberalized services market (e.g., translators), rigid work structures, or dysfunctional or even 'toxic' (FR15_Fanny) working environments where they faced discrimination (due to their ethnicity, nationality, and gender), and/or where their work efforts went unrecognized. This group was particularly attracted by platform promises of being able to 'control when, where, and how you work' (cf. Upwork website, 2023). These promises also appealed to those wanting greater autonomy and flexibility at work in order to better combine it with family responsibilities, as in the case of Jan (NL01), a 43-year-old translator working on Upwork in the Netherlands:

> I needed flexibility and I didn't mind having to work on weekends or evenings. With my girlfriend we have a little baby and I needed to plan out a little bit, figure things out . . . I guess I wanted to be my own boss, so I wouldn't really have a boss that orders me to do things. Because, for example, if I know I'll have to take care of my

> little one, I can't take on an assignment. And I'm not being pushed by my employer to do that anyway. (NL01_Jan)

For those with very limited job opportunities, online freelancing seemed to be the only viable option, as in the case of Viola (IT27), a 25-year-old translator living in a small town in Italy:

> I live in a small, isolated town, in the middle of nowhere ... And then the pandemic started, and I was thinking: 'What can I do? Let's see if I can find an online job, to work flexibly from my computer'. The thing that seemed most feasible was translation as I could use my language skills I'd got when I'd stayed for a year in England. I knew at the beginning I might be paid close to nothing, but I had no choice. (IT27_Viola)

The promise of flexibility, however, was rarely matched with sufficient worker autonomy over when and how to work. Enabled by technology, 'digital tournament' platforms impose permanent availability on workers, irrespective of the time of day or night:

> You always have to be available, so obviously that makes us stay in front on the phone, in front of the computer all the time, just in case. And clients really love us being immediately available. (FR15_Fanny)

> We're in three different time zones. All across the world. So it means that there's always gonna be new work every few hours because someone's working in their time zone. And there are requests, and you need to react quick. (NL09_Sasha)

As a result, platform freelancers work long and unsocial hours to comply with erratic and last-minute demands from clients around the world, and to compete with thousands of other workers by offering a lower price and shorter delivery deadlines. Client reviews and platform ratings rewarding their availability, adaptability, and speed are increasingly central to work allocation. On both 'digital tournament' and 'non-tournament' platforms using algorithm-based management system (i.e., Upwork, Malt), freelancers' response time is precisely measured and displayed on their profiles. Not responding fast enough downgrades workers in search lists, while going on holiday for a week means having to spend several months rebuilding the score defining their platform position. Platform freelancers are often forced to work nights and over holidays to keep their clients happy and maintain their ratings. Otherwise, they risk being penalized by the platform. Upwork and Malt nudge their workers to respond swiftly and complete tasks as quickly as possible.

The pervasive nudging system consists of tracking the speed of response: this metric not only contributes to the worker's overall score on the platform but is also displayed on their profile so that clients know how quickly workers reply.

Jan (NL01), the previously quoted Upwork translator who joined the platform hoping for a more flexible work arrangement, soon found himself in a situation of permanent work while trying to build his platform rating:

> There's been a few times that I took on an assignment that was really tough and then ... yeah ... I got a reaction from the home front because—then I'm // because yes, you kind of know it beforehand, but it's always more work than it seems. But then I'm, for example, working one or two weeks from 9 in the morning until 9 in the evening. I was supposed to help with the baby, but it's difficult. (NL01_Jan)

On Jellow, a platform with no algorithmic control and supporting freelancers' portfolio building, there is no expectation of permanent availability, meaning that freelancers can decide themselves how much work they want to take on. On Malt, however, where workers' performance is measured through an algorithm, high pressure is felt to be permanently available, possibly resulting in a loss of social life: 'friends just call you less, then they don't call at all' (FR15_Fanny). Fanny, a 29-year-old IT specialist from France working on Malt, told us about her inability to switch off even during holidays, and her feeling of alienation from her own family. She particularly criticized the dominance of response times in algorithmic rating calculations and the consequences of not keeping up with the system:

> [Your] average response time becomes a criterion and so then obviously I get class requests on Sunday at 11pm, on Saturday at 6am there you go! On Friday at 10pm it's terrible because if we worsen response time, then the algorithm likes you less and puts you less in the front. (FR15_Fanny)

If Fanny (FR15) had worked as an employee in a regular company with a line manager, she could have at least tried to ask not to be contacted on weekends. The platform, however, measured her work performance (including her response time) automatically. Acts of non-compliance were immediately punished, creating a work atmosphere that she experienced as 'authoritarian and non-responsive' (FR15_Fanny). After a few years on Malt, Fanny decided to leave online freelancing, a decision she openly reflected on:

> I have to be available to respond to a request and that puts me in a sort of wait in my head like a sort of on-call duty as if I was a fireman. And I know that now they

> could call me at any moment and that feeling never leaves me and that is one of the reasons that pushed me to revert to being a salaried employee. (FR15_Fanny)

To improve their platform-specific reputations, freelancers feel pressure to always be 'on call' to respond to prospective clients, even during unsocial hours. As a platform reputation is extremely volatile (being 'top-rated' one week does not mean that this status is maintained in the following weeks), it is not safe to take breaks from work. Freelancers in general, except those working for Jellow, had the feeling that platforms colonized their free (life) time, due to (a) the fear of bad reviews, (b) a lack of regard for any form of regular or social working hours, (c) working for clients in different time zones, and (d) a fear of missing out on new opportunities. The technology enabling permanent connectivity combined with the expectation to be always 'on call' makes it impossible for online freelancers to clearly distinguish between work and non-work (life) time. They work 'whenever possible' ('make hay while the sun shines') and 'at whatever rate' to meet clients' expectations and to improve their rating scores. The work diaries draw a clear picture of the financial costs in the form of time pressure, under- and unpaid tasks experienced by freelancers who are often required to work at high speed in order to meet very tight deadlines, as reported by Anita:

> I had just four hours to finish a translation today. I felt frustrated because I had so little time. I think I was hitting the keyboard with more intensity. (PL04_Anita, diary)

Both narratives and work diaries show how the financial costs which platform work entails are interwoven with social costs. For example, participants reported working early mornings, evenings, nights, and weekends, admitting that, while they might 'take it easier' (IT03_Jessica, a translator on Upwork) on a Saturday or Sunday, they still had little time for their families or for social and leisure activities. Freelancers declared being 'fully autonomous' in their work, while reporting numerous unpaid assignments and that the boundaries between working and non-working times are increasingly blurred, as in the case of Diana, a 33-year-old Belgian translator and copywriter who works for a translation agency as well as on Upwork:

> I promised my client to deliver the work by tomorrow, not realising that it was already Friday night. But of course, I also deliver on weekends if necessary ... Sometimes I have no time to see my boyfriend or my friends, but I need to keep my top-rated status, which implies I often have to give up on what I can price into my rates to clients, I need 5 stars, always. (BE01_Diana)

The narratives reflected whether online freelancing was worth the significant social and financial costs it implies. Making oneself permanently available to clients incurred significant costs, including a deterioration of social relationships, the neglect of caring responsibilities, and/or having to give up important personal interests and meaningful activities, as reported by Nina (PL28) who was candid about the encroachment of platform work into her private life:

> My boyfriend thinks I'm a workaholic, because even on a trip, I take my laptop with me and I need to have a hotspot to stay online. We go out with friends to get a pizza or see a movie, and I can't take my eyes off my phone, I'm waiting for an email, I want to reply right away ... As my friend once called it, I'm always on stand-by. For me, there's no line between work and free time, or to be more accurate, between looking for work and free time. (PL28_Nina)

Freelancers who are uncertain about their platform position (as a 'top-rated' status is not guaranteed) and uncertain about when a next assignment will come along, tend to accept all jobs, irrespective of whether they have realistic timeframes or not. They thus often struggle to meet the deadlines, working twelve hours a day or longer, sacrificing their family life and all other aspects of their private life, as in the case of Jan, a 43-year-old translator working on Upwork in the Netherlands:

> Sometimes I say I'm going to deliver 10,000 words of a certain technical text within 2 days. I know up front it is not possible. So then indeed you exert a lot of pressure on yourself. Sometimes there are also assignments that are not realistic, but I still accept them. Even though I know I'll get in trouble with them. But once you have an assignment, you work 9 to 9. And I accept it, knowing I had to communicate it somehow at home. (NL01_Jan)

Due to the algorithmic control and the uncertainty as to when the next assignment will land on their desks, freelancers working on Upwork remain trapped in a whirl of irregular jobs, making the boundaries between their working time and private time impossible to maintain. The penalties for not meeting a deadline or lowering one's response rate are severe, as negative client reviews result in a lower rating and a damaged platform reputation. The fear of even greater 'sunk costs' keeps them attached to the platform, trapped in the constant race for jobs, reviews, and scores which do not necessarily yield any prizes. Despite the algorithm control, freelancers on Malt experience relatively less uncertainty due to the relatively higher regularity of the jobs due to the platform's investment in portfolio.

Subordination: Doing without Questioning

If we see subordination and autonomy as the opposite poles of a continuum, freelancers closest to the subordination pole are those working on 'digital tournament' platforms which do not invest in portfolio development or long-term relationships with clients. The use of algorithm-based performance measurement (as in the case of Upwork) enhances price-based competition while exerting downward pressure on freelancers' rates. Online workers are entirely dependent on platform rules for gaining jobs, creating income, and developing their rating-based reputation. There is no room for negotiation here, as questioning the rules immediately brings about the risk of being punished by bad reviews and lower ratings. Subordination, on the other hand, is rewarded, so freelancers learn that 'doing extra work for no extra pay' is a rule to comply with, as it 'may be rewarded in the future, perhaps' (BE01_Claire).

> I promised my client to deliver the work by tomorrow, and it doesn't matter it's the weekend ... Sometimes I have no time to see my boyfriend or my friends, but I need to keep my top-rated status, I need those 5 stars, always. I may not get back now what I am investing in, I always lose, I do hope once with 5 star I will, who knows. (BE01_Claire)

Hourly rates charged by online freelancers are relatively transparent on platforms, but the actual money they get paid (based on billable hours and subject to deductions) is often not shared, meaning that competing workers do not know the true extent of the 'prizes' on offer. This means that they accept jobs with very few details about what exactly will be required. On completion, they are frequently asked by clients to do some 'extras' which were neither mentioned nor budgeted for beforehand. This is one of the most common forms of unpaid labour on 'digital tournament' platforms as freelancers are unable to recoup their investment through fair prices due to the fear of getting fewer gigs in the future.

The impossibility to negotiate platform rules means that freelancers on 'digital tournament' platform never say 'no'. They are silenced and discouraged from making any claims by the prospect of punishment. Instead, they are encouraged to keep their heads down as they 'may be rewarded in the future, perhaps' (BE01_Claire). Upwork and AddLance freelancers reported in unison that 'reviews are everything ... And there's always a fear of bad reviews' (FR02_Paulo); 'It all comes down to my Job Success Score, that's what really matters' (IT21_Nadia); 'It's mostly short-term projects on Upwork and all your rating is there, so that means you have to stay on the platform' (NL02_Camila). Upwork 'offers no real support for workers' (NL03_Dano), putting them in an asymmetrical relationship with clients where 'the platform is not freelancer-friendly' (PL06_Barbara); 'if there is a problem, the client is always right according to Upwork' (NL02_Marie). The platform 'turns us [workers] more and more into some sort of milking cow' (NL02_Marie).

Freelancers on 'digital tournament' platforms spend their own money and set their prices through subordinating themselves to the in-house software and its bidding system: 'I spend money to buy credits' (IT08_Marta), 'I buy credits to offer myself to the clients' (IT19_Sabrina), treating this as 'covering costs of investment' (IT16_Carla), while the price-based competition induced by the platform limits their ability to set higher prices. Freelancers on Upwork and AddLance face a 'lot of competition, especially when there is someone who'll do the job for a lower price, which often happens' (NL02_Marie). The same freelancers also depend on gaining high ratings on the platform to access more and better paying clients, as dictated by the algorithm-based performance measurement system where it exists—as on Upwork: 'your rate reflects the quality of your profile' (IT03_Jessica); 'clients rarely choose someone without a rating' (NL02_Marie). 'Companies try to choose from the 50 top-rated profiles, they go to the top of the list, so you'll always have the ones with higher rating there' (BE02_Laura).

On 'digital tournament' platforms, there are limited channels for recourse if freelancers disagree with a client's rating or want to better understand how the algorithmic management works. When they contact platforms for support, they receive little reassurance. Constantly changing reviews, performance metrics, and opaque algorithmic operations contribute to reputational insecurity: an ever-present fear of bad reviews and their effect on future earnings. The rating system generates workers' subordination in several ways. First, it limits freelancers' control over pricing. The platform tells them how they should price their work: '[Upwork] recommended getting started by setting a very low rate' (PL04_Anita). Second, their actual ability to influence pricing is strictly tied to ratings, since 'without any reviews from clients it's hard to get ahead' (PL02_Matylda). Without a good platform-specific reputation built through the ratings, freelancers 'can't increase their rates' (NL02_Marie). Third, the way the algorithm functions is not fully comprehensible: 'the logic they use for calculating the rating isn't very clear' (IT27_Viola). The algorithmic control is based on asymmetrical relationships with clients where the latter can 'force you to do jobs for 5 dollars by threatening to give you a bad review' (IT27_Viola). The rating system forces workers to lower their rates to get positive reviews. This is particularly the case at the beginning of a platform career, as when 'you're starting, you quote the lowest rate just to get a job' (FR06_Bel), while only freelancers who 'got very good feedback ... could charge a bit more' (FR02_Paulo). Work is governed by the hope that better reviews will lead to better paid jobs. Nevertheless, the capacity to raise prices remains limited as 'clients are price-sensitive' (FR05_Max) and 'I can ask for a fair rate, but I cannot go higher than that. There are many who tell me: you're too expensive!' (FR27_Jule); 'you cannot really ask for a higher price' (NL03_Dano), 'you cannot renegotiate prices' (FR28_Deepa) and there is a 'race to the bottom on Upwork' (FR02_Paulo).

Subordination is also experienced on Malt where freelancers, while getting support for portfolio building, depend on client reviews for their reputation building. Nevertheless, as there is no bidding on Malt, freelancers do not have to purchase platform currency to gain access to paid tasks. The situation is different on Jellow where there is neither a bidding system nor algorithmic control. Freelancers supported by the platform have more opportunities to access regular tasks and jobs on the basis of their non-platform-specific reputation and with a lower investment in unpaid labour.

Striving for Perfection to Make Clients Happy: Extra Tasks for No Extra Pay

The fear of a bad review predisposes freelancers on 'digital tournament' platforms to do everything possible to make their clients happy. On 'non-tournament' platforms, the wish to deliver the best service possible explains why freelancers strive for perfection, in line with their professional identity (their work ethos and professional standards). For example, on Jellow, freelancers strive for perfection not out of fear of a bad review leading to a bad rating, but in their general attempt to demonstrate their professionalism. Some of the freelancers we interviewed had experienced being headhunted by the platform: 'Jellow contacted me as I had the skills they needed' (BE10_Jamal). Likewise, another freelancer reported that she was invited to join a platform, receiving 'an e-mail asking if [she] wanted to work for them as a freelancer' (BE01_Claire).

Conversely, freelancers working on 'digital tournament' platforms reported that delivering perfection was part of the platform game, with clients needing to be pampered all the time. Freelancers determined to maintain high ratings are ready to invest in preparing, proposing, correcting, and polishing their work (even if this work is not covered by the rate charged) in order to make sure their clients give them a five-star review:

'I always feel the pressure to please my clients and do everything possible to make them come back' (FR28_Deepa). Anything less than five stars and Upwork freelancers risk seeing their ranking drop. Just one bad review can send them spiralling—and then it takes months to get back up. The client-friendly design of the rating system results in clients often demanding more than they actually pay for. Upwork freelancers reported carrying out free supplementary work and giving clients the option to pay less than the agreed amount in exchange for a five-star review.

> There's always this fear of a bad review, so I try to do my best, to do everything as they like, to be precise, not too expensive and to deliver the work ahead of time wherever possible. All of it to keep my clients happy, to avoid getting stuck, with no work in the future. (IT01_Mirko)

Permanent Competition: Investing and Self-Improving to Gain an Advantage over Other Online Freelancers

For online freelancers, competition is a challenge: they all face the presence of others with similar skills and reputations. For those working on 'digital tournament' platforms, however, competition means extremely high pressure and a continual struggle. They describe 'absurd competition against people who are lowering prices a lot ... I managed to get some assignments but in return for some really unreasonable prices' (IT07_Ugo). This was due to the 'unfair competition', 'the competition [which] is fierce and dishonest' (IT19_Sabrina), and competition from 'many young unexperienced professionals', resulting in a 'race to the bottom' (IT08_Marta). Many of the interviewed Upwork and AddLance freelancers had a feeling of being forced to settle for 'rock-bottom prices' (IT16_Carla) in order to win any tasks at all:

> On AddLance, you are cannon fodder, you have to work for peanuts, struggle, do the interview with a client, use all your time, do all the work ... it's us workers who are supporting the platform, not the other way round. (IT08_Marta)

Similarly, freelancers on Upwork struggle to set prices and experience conflicts of interest as the platform incentivizes one-off, casual transactions with clients through price-based competition. Freelancers on both Upwork and AddLance reported 'needing to lower the price' (IT07_Ugo), having to set only 'affordable prices' (IT19_Sabrina) as these platforms do not incentivize workers to gain recurrent transactions from regular clients by investing in portfolio building. Freelancers end up finding mostly short-term assignments with 'non-regular' (IT08_Marta), 'one-off clients' (IT19_Sabrina), and clients 'who are in a hurry. And once the job is completed, no one cares, no one is interested in further collaboration. They just say goodbye' (IT16_Carla). Within the platform game, workers feel they are played against each other for client satisfaction and platform profit:

> I see a race to the bottom. People are being played off against each other to see who can offer the lowest price. You can lose your ratings anytime and therefore people compete to get the best reviews. It's awful. (NL04_Dirk)

To gain a competitive advantage on 'digital tournament' platforms, freelancers invest extra time for 'client satisfaction' and 'good reviews'. Their work gets intensified and extensified; they spend hours and hours communicating with clients, searching and applying for tasks, sending free samples of work, and doing extra tasks. All this is treated as a personal investment in ratings, possibly helping them to increase their rates. But even this is uncertain. While young workers may treat it as 'part of the game' or simply 'the reality of freelancing', established freelancers are more prone to contest it: 'we don't accept that unpaid anymore' (BE12_Ben).

On 'non-tournament' platforms, competition takes a different form. Clients contact freelancers directly on the basis of a list provided by the platform when a client enters a job request. Freelancers neither send in job applications nor bid for tasks but are contacted directly by clients who 'send the request directly to different workers' (FR19_Nunzio). The parties then enter into one-to-one negotiations where 'freelancers can't undercut each other' (FR03_Marisol) since they 'cannot compare prices' (FR05_Max). On Jellow 'it is not possible for the applicant to see how many workers react to a certain task' (NL10_Martine). Moreover, the platform curbs excessive competition between freelancers by providing clients with 'more specific' (BE46_Romi) search templates. For workers, this means that clients are more likely to be interested in their services, as the platform's search engine 'very specifically looks at what I do, what are my availabilities, specialisation and reputation, where I live, what kind of clients I want to work with' (BE46_Romi). The 'advantage for workers is that they know that they don't have to respond to requests on the entire internet' (BE44_Gloria). Instead, they belong to a pool of experts suitable for a particular job. Moreover, they do not need to invest time and financial resources to find clients as 'this is clients who search on Jellow and dig up our profiles' (BE44_Gloria). As the platform supports portfolio building and thwarts price undercutting, freelancers on Jellow experience some degree of price-setting freedom: 'I can choose my own price' (BE14_Jasper) and 'set a high rate' (NL05_Stefanos).

They can also develop long-term relationships with clients as 'big companies search here for semi-employees' (BE13_Kaat) and 'we can work for them long-term' (BE13_Kaat).

The situation is slightly different on Malt where the platform helps 'to update portfolios and gain projects' (FR13_Pierre), but where there is also algorithm-based performance measurement: as 'there are lots of people on Malt, we are all competing in accordance with the gamification system where rating depends on reviews' (FR15_Fanny). Freelancers' way of dealing with high competition is to go off-platform once stable relationships with clients have been developed: 'it is normal to get to know a client on Malt and then to work with them directly outside the platform' (FR13_Pierre), thereby 'avoiding Malt's 12% commission fee' (FR09_August), while the platform is 'not aware that I have redirected clients away from it and that I am earning good money' (FR15_Fanny).

The sacrifice *for the sake of reputation* made by online freelancers to attain high ratings is not necessarily recouped in the form of increased autonomy, guaranteed work, or more lucrative jobs. They invest in building a reputation, hoping that this in turn will give them access to better paid tasks enabling them to recoup their investment and gain a living income. In our sample, we found examples of successful freelancers on both types of platforms, though it was easier to find them on those platforms that support portfolio building, such as Jellow and Malt. On 'digital tournament' platforms such as Upwork and AddLance, freelancers attaining positions of autonomy and gaining easily accessible and better paid work are few and far between. The years of permanent availably, subordination, perfection seeking, and fierce competition leave many empty-handed or stuck with getting by on casual tasks, and struggling to make ends meet.

Unpaid Labour, Resilience, and Precarious Work

The chances of complying with the 'ideal platform worker' norm are not the same for all. Those most dependent on platform work for income find themselves in the most difficult situation: forced to comply with platform rules and last-minute client requests, they are most likely to experience 'income theft' in their attempts to protect their platform-specific reputations and access to future tasks. On the other hand, those with additional sources of income (savings, household income, earnings coming from other types of jobs, or institutional support) and able to treat platform freelancing as an supplementary activity have more room for manoeuvre—they can be more selective in accepting tasks and clients (avoiding underpayment) and can invest more in equipment, skills, and platform currency to gain access to better paid tasks and better (possibly repeat) clients. After an initial period lasting from a few weeks to a year or longer, freelancers become more realistic about the opportunities and constraints provided by digital platforms. They see how unbearable the sacrifice *for the sake of reputation* can be, especially on 'digital tournament' platforms. This reflexivity helps them decide whether to continue with online freelancing (and if so, in which form) or to quit.

Freelancers with access to resources allowing them to sustain 'income theft' may decide to stay in online freelance work, working on different platforms, developing their skills, and investing in lasting relationships with clients. The resources they have at their disposal, whether financial (household income and property), social (networks), or cultural (skills and professional identity), can help them build resilience. However, such personal resources are not enough as freelancers cannot be 'liberated' on their own. The organizational structures of the platforms, their rules and functioning are equally important. Freelancers on 'non-tournament' platforms are comparatively less precarious than those on digital tournament ones as they incur relatively less risk of 'income theft' when complying with platform rules. This is because these rules enable them to build a career and to compete in a transparent and fair way in the freelancing market by supporting portfolio building. Using Jellow and Malt as the facilitator for building their portfolios and client bases, freelancers are more likely to gain a return on their investment, both online and offline. When the platform rules turn out to be too restrictive, as in the case of Malt with its algorithmic control, freelancers can just leave, taking their clients with them.

In the case of freelancers active on 'digital tournament' platforms, freelancers are less likely to be in a position to build resilience. Even for those with personal resources to sustain 'income theft' over time, we found many cases of these resources being time limited, for example when savings ran out or when a partner refused to continue subsidizing the platform work. This lack in ability to build resilience may also be due to platform rules. Freelancers here are more likely to get crushed by the reviews machine, gaining no return on their initial investment of time and other resources. Chasing gigs, spending their own money to apply for them, trying to comply with platform rules of permanent availability, striving for perfection to make clients happy, and competing on time and price with thousands of other online freelancers, Upworkers and AddLancers are likely to experience sunk costs. Stuck in the whirl of casual, underpaid tasks, unable to contact their clients off-platform, and unable to develop the type of portfolios that would count in the wider market, freelancers find it difficult to escape precarity while incurring 'income theft'.

Binary Relations

We observed a binary relationship when precarious work unfolds from income theft, as in the case of 'digital tournament' platforms whose rules constrain the capacity of freelancers to recoup their personal investment in freelance work by exerting much greater pressure on their capacity to control the conduct of their work (especially setting their own rates), while at the same time not providing enough support for portfolio building or developing long-term relationships with clients. Freelancers on Upwork and AddLance commonly invest personal resources when applying for paid tasks: 'every time you apply you have to buy these things called "connects" (the Upwork currency), which you pay for out of your own pocket' (BE0_Diana); 'I started by applying for many jobs, wasting many "connects" on clients who never got back to me' (IT27_Viola); 'the first money I earned I just used to buy more connects' (IT27_Viola). Here, 'freelancers are the only ones paying' (IT04_Danilo) to get access to clients as 'workers are not allowed to contact clients directly' (IT29_Zuzka), and the platform 'does not allow clients to see a freelancer list' (IT04_Danilo). Some freelancers reported spending substantial amounts (over €100) without gaining any clients at all (IT27_Viola)—a clear example of sunk costs. Those who declared having made a profit also reported having to spend as much as €500 on credits (IT27_Viola). On 'digital tournament' platforms, freelancers are under constant pressure to perform (to receive the highest ratings possible), but all the ratings and reputation they invest in are platform specific and lost as soon as workers leave the platform. Unpaid labour is treated as a 'necessary' investment here: 'At first ... I was working for far too little, but this was sort of the price that I had to pay for being new and having to get these reviews' (PL07_Anna).

With unpaid labour not being a resource for building a client base, precarity unfolds, as in the case of Anita (PL04), for whom unpaid labour directly translated into precarity:

> Actually the majority of my work today ... I mostly replied to some calls from clients, I already had three meetings, and three more big meetings planned ... so this was the time when you had to explain it all ... the time, which is not compensated ... So my daily income? Well, zero! Yeah, zero ... (PL04_Anita, work diary)

Rates were further eroded by the fees paid to platforms, for currency conversion, bank and PayPal services, as well as micro pay for micro tasking, as reported in the diary of an Italian translator, Jessica: '74.72 dollars for today. But if we deduct fees and exchange rate, I've earned around 60 euros' (IT03_Jessica, work diary).

Paulo (FR02), a 38-year-old Upworker living in France, explained how his work was divided between various paid and unpaid activities. Despite his fourteen years' experience, he still only earned €70 for a full workday and spent a significant portion of his day working 'for himself' (FR02_Paulo, work diary), as he put it, while foregoing payment. These sunk costs cannot be covered by freelancers' rates due to high competition, as reported by Dano (NL03), a 30-year-old IT specialist working on Upwork in the Netherlands:

> You pay for a lot of stuff on Upwork, so I put up my prices to cover for it. And there was one person interested in my work but he said: 'Yeah you're good, but you're too expensive.' He didn't give me the job. (NL03_Dano, work diary)

Beside the investment in time, effort, and one's own money (in fees and connects), there is also another type of investment needed: in skills development, office equipment, hardware, and software (the 'tools of the trade'), all of which are deemed 'necessary' to work properly and stay competitive. These investments are not covered by their rates, as reported by Paulo (FR02) in his work diary:

> I spend all of my working time sitting, so I had to invest in a good chair and good office materials. Also, for this new assignment, I was not entirely skilled for some things, so they suggested I do a course on Udemy. This is an online course which I can take in my own time. I thought the course was worth the investment. So, I paid for the course, I didn't discuss this with the client and so this is something I'm doing for myself and I could use for other clients, potentially. (FR02_Paulo, work diary)

Even after investing in office equipment and skills development, Paulo charges his clients the same rates as before as he 'always feels the pressure to please his clients and make them come back' (FR02_Paulo). Freelancers on 'digital tournament' platform can easily become stuck between the need to invest in new skills and the need to be permanently available for work. We have a story of James (NL06), a 28-year-old Ghanaian working as a self-taught IT specialist on Upwork in the Netherlands. Given the importance of ratings, James interlaced periods of training (up to ten hours per day at his own expense) and platform freelancing. While further training would have improved his marketable skills, he found that taking time off to study meant his response rate went down and his profile became less visible to clients, thus reducing his access to paid work. To become active again, he had to rebuild his platform profile from scratch, taking on small tasks that did not cover his costs. He gained no return on his skills investment as he got punished for his insufficient availability and got stuck in unpaid and underpaid labour.

We observe that the binary relationship between unpaid labour and precarity on 'digital tournament' platforms is especially strong in the case of those relying on platform income for their survival. This was the case with Max (FR05) who had no access to institutional resources in the form of benefits or tax exemptions and did not live in a double-earner household. If Upwork or AddLance freelancers cannot rely on savings or a partner with a stable income to cover unpaid periods, they fall into precarity. Average net income per working day on Upwork was €71.54, compared to €143.36 on Jellow. When we relate the lower pay to the higher incidence of unpaid work, it is easy to appreciate that many Upwork freelancers struggle to make ends meet: 'I work a lot just to pay my bills and buy my food ... Working eleven hours today I must have made €50, if I count how much I get for completing my tasks minus the platform fees' (FR04_Milena).

One way to escape the binary relationship between unpaid labour and precarity is to work off-platform: 'you need to move work outside AddLance ... the work relationship doesn't have to stay there' (IT07_Ugo); 'You meet your clients on AddLance and relationships continue outside the platform ... You just create a connection for future projects' (IT26_Angelo). On Upwork, however, freelancers are prevented from moving client transactions off-platform, as 'the chat is closely monitored, you risk getting blocked' (IT02_Marco). Some, however, try 'moving away from Upwork and just work normally on B2B terms' (PL03_Krysztof), but this means the loss of a hard-earned platform-specific reputation.

Non-Binary Relations

On 'non-tournament' platforms supporting portfolio building (i.e., Jellow and Malt), we observe a non-binary relationship where precarious work does not automatically unfold from unpaid labour. Here, the importance attached to freelancers' portfolio and client base development often translates into regular, long-term assignments, meaning that any unpaid labour may be covered by future paid work. Jellow matches freelancers' experience and skills with tailored offers from clients searching for specific and often very high skills. Freelancers enjoy access to the full database of clients and tasks as members of the 'Jellow club' whose registration is free of charge and voluntary.

They can also keep their profiles open without the need to be permanently active. The platform charges no fees or commissions from freelancers: 'it's the clients that pay' (BE01_Claire). While clients rate workers through reviews submitted to the platform, performance ratings do not determine whether or not freelancers gain access to work. Freelancers are free to establish rates and prices in a way allowing them to recoup their personal investment and therefore reduce the risk of 'income theft'.

On Malt as well, freelancers do not send in job applications or bid for tasks but are contacted by clients who 'send the requests directly to different workers' (FR19_Nunzio). Importantly, and similarly to Jellow, Malt supports portfolio building and the development of long-term relationships between freelancers and their clients. The platform 'normally charges 12%, but if you work more than 3 times for the same client, this decreases to 7%' (FR09_August). Freelancers construct a detailed profile listing their competences, work history, and education. This helps Malt improve matching between workers and clients as 'it is easy, you have your photos, examples of your work, and companies you've worked for, all displayed there' (FR19_Nunzio). Freelancers are offered training in portfolio building and how to set rates: 'There's the Malt Academy, there's webinars where you learn how to work on a platform' (FR03_Marisol); 'Malt's support is via phone and email, they reply within a second, it's nice, and works very well' (FR27_Jule). Malt workers are able to overcome administrative difficulties and handle troublesome clients as 'Malt advisors help us solve problems' (FR03_Marisol). On both Jellow and Malt, freelancers have much greater scope to recoup their investments in freelance work through their freedom to set their rates and thus reduce the risk of income theft. As a result, the relationship between unpaid labour and precarity is non-binary. Platform workers are able to set their own prices from the very start, for instance by replying to client proposals and saying: '"Look, this is very specific and you'll need an expert for this", which is something clients understand and agree to increase prices' (BE05_Jeff). Freelancers can thus 'set prices independently' (NL06_James), 'in negotiation with a client' (BE05_Jeff), utilizing rates convenient for them and clients, such as 'per hour or per project' (NL10_Martine). In this way unpaid labour takes the form of an investment, recoupable by higher rates in the future.

Household Resources and Socially Reproductive Labour

On first joining a platform, many online freelancers lack any knowledge of what it really takes to succeed there. Our 'digital tournament' respondents soon found out that skills are primarily recognized through positive client reviews and a platform's rating system rather than formal qualifications, job descriptions, or career ladders. This is particularly the case for those workers with no parallel stable employment in the wider market, and whose income is largely dependent on the platform. Nevertheless, even freelancers able to rely on another source of income soon become aware of the platform rules they have to obey in order to be able to gain access to tasks there. Clients are generally less interested in applicants' academic credentials than in their online reputation, largely derived from quick response rates, efficiency, and low rates. However, without any ratings, our respondents, irrespective of any stable employment in the wider market and across different countries, found it extremely difficult to attract prospective clients, stressing how getting the first five-star review was a crucial milestone to get their workflows going. At the same time, freelancers reported accepting low rates or underpaid assignments for the sole purpose of gaining the first positive reviews and being able to boost their metrics. Despite experiencing this initial phase as very frustrating, our respondents viewed it as something 'necessary', 'a rite of passage' to develop and establish their online reputation. However, while some participants traversed this initial phase comparatively quickly, others spent months on the platform without receiving more regular or more lucrative assignments. This prolonged period of learning platform rules and trying to win tasks was easier to sustain for those with supplementary sources of income, while those reliant solely on platform income tended to adopt a strategy of undercharging and overworking. If it worked and they received their first positive reviews, they could continue applying for further jobs. However, if this period of very low income lasted too long and was thus unsustainable, they would quit a particular platform or the platform economy in general, disappointed and angry, as their investment in time and effort had not borne fruit.

> My income is impossible to determine. I'm below the living wage on an annual basis, that's usually the case. The entire 22,50 euros from today is net. (BE41_Sigrid, work diary)

Financial resources are needed to sustain freelancing without any (or just a low) return on investment over time, and few have such resources at their disposal. Jan (NL01), a middle-class translator working on Upwork, told us about having 'a financial buffer' (NL01_Jan) in the form of savings and living in a double-income household which made work on Upwork possible for a while: 'Both me and my wife have an income where we can help each other out. And it makes things a little more feasible for us. But I don't know how long I'll be able to do it' (NL01_Jan). Jan contrasts his 'well-resourced' position with that of his colleague who was forced to leave online freelancing altogether due to a lack of financial resources:

> I had a colleague, who was copywriter, and he had exactly the same situation [on Upwork, doing unpaid labour]. And I can imagine that in his case, he was the only one who brought in some money. And he had a mortgage, a wife, a kid, so he couldn't take it for long. He started looking for a salaried job. (NL01_Jan)

Some of our interviewees were still in their early 20s and living with their parents who covered most of their bills. Many of them were full-time students, so they were not required to pay social security contributions and taxes as long as their income was below a certain threshold. For students, online platform work is initially a side job, helping them to make ends meet, but frequently it becomes their main source of income after graduation when they have difficulties finding work in the field they were studying. Since there are periods of low income on the platform, or no income at all, it is crucial to have a support system in place: 'You need to be in a comfortable situation where you can survive even if you don't earn any money at all. You just can't work on Upwork if you have to pay rent, food and bills all by yourself. You just can't do it', says Viola (IT27), a freelancer with a working-class background. It also takes time to get repeat clients: 'It took me a year to get the right clients on AddLance. Before, my gigs were very small, one-shot work really, badly paid tasks that led nowhere' (IT08_Marta). For older freelancers, the family support system moves from parents to a partner:

> I understood I always had to have some financial reserve to cover for a month or two of not having any income. I saved as much as I could. And I'm also in a relationship and my girlfriend also has a job, and we have some savings and support from parents. Otherwise, it would be too scary, not being able to pay the rent. (NL08_Alma)

As some platform workers need to pay fees to submit project proposals and buy platform currency to increase their chances of winning a bid, it means that, alongside skills, they also need to have financial resources at their disposal in order to be able to do platform work. This potentially creates entry barriers for workers from low-income households, who cannot rely on family resources to subsidize the initial investment in launching a platform career (resources needed to pay platform fees and to purchase platform currency), and the further investment in reputation building (e.g., doing unpaid labour in exchange for five-star reviews). Consequently, it can lead to the exclusion of some categories of workers. Such entry barriers are less pronounced on the platforms that do not require immediate cash transfers, as in case of Jellow. Here, freelancers do not pay any platform fees, do not buy platform currency (as there is none in place), and do not participate in bidding as they are selected on the basis of their portfolio. Still, it is easier to launch a freelancing career having some household resources at hand, but the lack of this does not translated into exclusion: 'My partner is a bartender and he'll be a bartender forever, so I won't be able to fall back on his income. Still, on Jellow I manage to get some good assignments. They are well paid. I just wish there were more of them' (NL10_Martine).

Platform freelancing, even when it allows for a basic level of income, is often experienced as a dead-end path by working-class and lower-middle-class freelancers, such as Max (FR05) who argues: 'I couldn't work towards building anything, I could only survive' (FR05_Max). This, however, does not necessarily lead to exit. The family dynamics (the birth of children, the loss of a partner's income) and difficulties with finding alternative job opportunities can make freelancers stay on platforms despite the clear disadvantages:

> We already pay rather high contributions, here in France. We also pay platform commission fees ... On top of that, competition with other translators makes us lower our rates regularly. These are translators based in other countries, where they perhaps pay no contributions at all. And we see that clients are sensitive to prices. For me, my way to counteract this, is to propose to the client: Listen, I suggest you do a test because you clearly asked several translators for a quote, so anyway, I suggest you do a little test of a 100-word sample and that will allow you to evaluate the quality beyond the price aspect. But well ... there are a lot of contracts that I don't win since I don't want to go down, I don't want to lower my rates endlessly. If I go under 10 cents per word, I do it against my will. But it's difficult to make a living here. And I have a family with three kids, so I am not a single student, I have my responsibilities. But it's really difficult. (FR05_Max)

Not only is it difficult to support a family on the basis of platform freelancing where the income is rather low and uncertain, but also the platform requirement to offer constant availability makes it difficult to combine online freelancing with family life. From the narratives of platform freelancers, we get a picture that, even when they are not doing 'productive labour' on the platform, they do not dare to go completely offline: 'it's 7pm, you are making dinner for your kids and then I have a request from Malt. Of course, I have to respond immediately' (FR05_Max). The clashing expectations of availability on the platform and at home is the source of work-life conflict involving the entire family:

> That's how it works. I need to generate some income, so I find myself with a lot of work, then I work late on the evening, then I also work on the weekend, then my wife is not very happy, nor my kids. (FR05_Max)

Institutional Resources in Different National Contexts

The four selected platforms operate in varying institutional contexts. As we show below, differences in institutional regulations in relation to welfare and self-employment may lead to differing resources to counteract—albeit to different extents and forms as indicated—the threat of income theft which freelancers may incur when providing online platform services. This in turn explains the inequality in precarity. Moreover, different taxation and social contribution regimes can provide competitive advantages or disadvantages to freelancers in different European countries.

Looking first at institutional resources, unemployment benefit received following the end of a standard employment relationship can act as a temporary resource boosting income and thus resilience *vis-à-vis* any income theft, as can child benefit or a state and/or company pension (for older freelancers). Where such options do not exist or are financially inadequate, workers have to search for alternatives. For example, our findings suggest that freelancers may underreport their income in order to remain registered as unemployed while working on a platform, thereby maintaining free access to health insurance, as was the case with one of our respondents, 30-year-old Upwork translator Anita (PL04). If she decided to do platform work legally, paying her taxes and social security contributions, the work would no longer have been sustainable for her. As Upwork does not require its workers to officially register themselves as self-employed, such options are open to Upworkers.

Turning to taxation and social security contributions, Belgium, the Netherlands, France, Italy, and Poland present differences in their regulation of self-employment. In Belgium, the self-employed are exempt from taxation up to €25,000 per year but have to pay (on a quarterly basis) social security contributions to the tune of 20.5% of previous-year earnings. In Italy, regular self-employment, which is subject to 15% income tax up to €25,000 and biannual social contribution payments (around 25%) that are calculated on the basis of earnings from the previous year, is complemented by the contractual arrangement of 'independent casual work' (*contratto di prestazione occasionale di lavoro autonomo*). This allows citizens to perform own-account work at a minimum tax rate (20%), with no social contributions payable on earnings of up to €5,000 per year. This amount rises to €6,666 for specific categories, such as retirees, students below the age of 26, and recipients of income support benefits. In France, the self-employed (i.e., *auto-entrepreneurs*) are exempt from tax when their income is below a specific threshold, but they pay social contributions directly to the national welfare institute. Different to Belgium and Italy, social security contributions in France are calculated on the basis of effective current earnings, making it easier for self-employed workers in times of low income. Moreover, under the so-called 'ACRE system', starters benefit from a reduced rate (11%) for the first three quarters. Finally, in Poland, self-employed workers pay tax at a 19% flat rate and are exempt from paying social security contributions for the first year. Importantly, Poles can work as freelancers through two categories of civil law contracts: contracts 'for mandate' that do not require the specification of a particular outcome, and contracts to perform 'specific tasks' where the outcome is set from the start (Lewandowski and Magda 2018). The latter are particularly appealing because they benefit from a low rate of tax and are also exempt from social security contributions.

Dependent on the institutional context, there are different levels of control over the self-employed and their compliance with taxation rules. We observed that tax avoidance is easier and more frequent in some countries (e.g., Poland, Italy) than in others (e.g., France, Belgium, the Netherlands), giving Polish and Italian freelancers a clear competitive advantage—they can charge less as only part of their income may be taxed due to underreporting. In this way, freelancers enhance their attractiveness to potential clients at the expense of freelancers in other national contexts. In addition, freelancers can leverage the different strategies utilized by online platforms in different countries. For example, in France and in Belgium, Malt checks if all freelancers are registered as self-employed and provides online tools to facilitate tax payments. Exploiting transnational differences, these checks are not performed by Upwork. Our interviewees reported that Upwork maintains a certain level of opacity regarding invoicing. Freelancers wanting to comply with taxation and contribution rules in their countries, such as Paulo who works in France, find it difficult to invoice clients whom they do not even know. Upwork solely provides a total payment: 'It's not that evident to have a clear idea of who you are working with, and this of course increases the perception of a lack of transparency in your work and it may get you into trouble' (FR02_Paulo).

Online Platform Work: Conclusions

As an entrepreneur, a freelancer working in one of the occupations referred to in Chapter 6 is for all intents and purposes a one-person company. Like any company, a freelancer performs administrative and productive tasks. Whereas the former (tasks like invoicing, tracking payments, or VAT declarations) are by nature unpaid and thus to be covered by the fees charged (as discussed in Chapter 1), the latter should, as far as possible, be paid. While obviously covering any work commissioned by a client, productive tasks also include marketing endeavours to acquire work, for example in the form of issuing quotes, not all of which will be successful. The time and effort invested here must also be covered by the fees charged. As with any company, factors influencing the chances of a quote being successful include the price quoted, the level of competition, and availability. How then does working for a platform impinge on the entrepreneurial freedom of a freelancer as a one-person company?

Ultimately, the success of any freelancer working on an online labour platform—in contrast to an offline freelancer—is dictated by their online reputation established by the scoring mechanisms increasingly prevalent in the online world, whether for example for hotels (e.g., booking.com) or for online marketplaces (e.g., eBay). Without a reputation, adequately paid work is difficult to find. Freelancers thus invest a lot of unpaid or underpaid labour *for the sake of their reputation.* When working for 'digital tournament' platforms fostering casual, one-off transactions and not interested in career development, a reputation is built solely through positive client ratings. With these ratings dependent on availability, response times, competitive rates, work outcomes, and subordination to platform rules, reputations are hard to earn but easily lost. Even a short holiday can send one's reputation spiralling downwards and, with it, future earning opportunities without which a freelancer working solely on a platform may be doomed to precarity. Similarly, 'digital tournament' platforms do not require freelancers to formally register their activities, meaning they have no incentive to report their earnings. This is deleterious for 'real' (i.e., officially registered) freelancers who find themselves at a disadvantage when it comes to having to pay tax and social security contributions and pricing these into their rates.

On the other hand, when working on a 'non-tournament' platform without bidding, freelancers do not participate in bidding as they are selected on the basis of their portfolio. Moreover, they are supported by the platform in building up their portfolios and establishing long-term relationships with clients. Their reputations thus reflect their qualifications and professional work ethos, thereby enabling them to charge higher rates, and in turn to avoid precarity. Such platforms thus tend to be the home of 'real' freelancers, showcasing their entrepreneurship spirit while respecting their 'self-employment status'—i.e., considering it as 'real' employment without wanting to treat freelancers as something they are not, such as dependent employees. Studies on stigma and self-employment have emphasized how any stigmatization of self-employment draws upon a general misrecognition of 'real' self-employment work *vis-à-vis* regular employees, meaning that having previously been self-employed may even be perceived by the job market as sending a negative signal (Koellinger et al. 2012).

As the work performed on digital 'tournament' platforms is more casual, freelancers' incomes tend to fluctuate more than on 'non-tournament' platforms. As a result, the level of external resources needed to sustain the work is higher. We found many respondents mentioning receiving support from a partner, although this often led to personal relationship problems. However, as the work is casual, it is fairly easy to avoid reporting it to tax and social security authorities. Indeed, non-reporting may be viewed as a resource, even to the extent of giving non-reporting freelancers a competitive advantage. As opposed to the other two work areas studied (i.e., dance and residential care), we found no sharp evidence of any class-based distinctions when examining the conditions—especially in the long-run—of freelancers working on platforms belonging to the same cluster, i.e. 'digital tournament' platforms or 'non-tournament' platforms. However, it can be assumed that, as discussed by Martindale and Lehdonvirta (2023), platform work—especially on 'digital tournament' platforms—retains class-based difference upon entrance (see the introductory Paulo (FR02) story) but disguises it through the (semi-)anonymous manner of working after someone enters the platform world. Nevertheless, we did find that business models tended to polarize class-based differences between digital platforms. For example, when comparing class structures, we observed a notable difference between freelancers belonging to the same class operating on 'non-tournament' platforms versus those on 'digital tournament' platforms. This suggests that, when freelancers on non-tournament platforms have better access to resources, such as household income and support, often reflecting their class background, they are better able to sustain unpaid labour and distance themselves from precarity. Conversely, freelancers on 'digital tournament' platforms, who share the same class background, often face persistent financial pressure. This is attributed to the highly competitive nature of these platforms, eventually depleting the resources they possess.

This leads to a different relationship between 'digital tournament' and 'non-tournament' platforms with regard to how and to what extent unpaid labour relates to precarious work. In essence, we found a binary relationship between unpaid labour and precarious work on 'digital tournament' platforms where even the wealthier freelancers experience their resources depleted by platforms which do not sufficiently support them in portfolio building. Freelancers are likely to experience their work as precarious when undertaking unpaid labour because of the significant non-recoupable 'sunk costs' invested in skills and reputation building. Unable to charge 'living' rates, they are prone to precarity when regularly using their personal resources to sustain themselves and the unpaid labour they perform on the platform.

PART III

THE IMPLICATIONS OF THE 'POLITICS OF UNPAID LABOUR' AT THE CROSSROADS OF SOCIOLOGY AND ECONOMICS

7
Unpaid Labour, Labour Markets, and Capabilities

with Bernard Gazier

The Theme

This book started by asking why workers in different sectors and countries perform unpaid labour within and/or in the run-up to paid employment, and how this unpaid labour is interlinked with precarious work. Based on our inductive qualitative study involving a large number of work diaries and biographical narrative interviews with workers in creative dance (in our specific case, ballet) in Sweden and the Netherlands, residential care in Germany and the United Kingdom (UK), and online platform work in Belgium, France, Italy, the Netherlands, and Poland, our answer is that workers undertake unpaid labour in adherence to an 'ideal worker' norm to avoid being stigmatized through punishments and in the hope of being recognized and rewarded for the work they do for the *sake of art*, the *sake of caring* for others, or the *sake of reputation*. The unpaid labour is thus meaningful—i.e., it has social value—for them.

We also found that not everyone performing unpaid labour, stemming from the nature of the work in the three described work areas or occupational fields, and in adherence to the 'ideal worker' norm, subjectively experiences precarity in the same way and to the same extent, despite the objectively precarious conditions of their jobs. The analysis captures this by describing as 'binary' or 'non-binary' the relationship between unpaid labour and precarious work. Essentially, we found that whether this relationship is binary or non-binary is dependent on how precarity is subjectively experienced, a factor which in turn relies on the individual and collective resources available to those concerned to sustain unpaid labour. In other words, having access to such resources, a factor often associated with class background, can help them cope with the precarious employment conditions of their jobs. Indeed, unpaid labour itself can also be a privileging resource allowing

Valeria Pulignano with Bernard Gazier, *Unpaid Labour, Labour Markets, and Capabilities.* In: *The Politics of Unpaid Labour*, Oxford University Press. DOI: 10.1093/oso/9780198888130.003.0008 workers to build resilience against such precarious conditions. While this privilege exists, it does not eliminate the inherent job insecurity that comes with the employment conditions. Workers persist in undertaking precarious jobs in the 'hope' of a better future. Our analysis shows that this is possible insofar as individuals possess the resources enabling them not only to sustain the unpaid labour, but also to capitalize on it. We found three forms of resources relevant to sustaining unpaid labour: individual income (including self-owned property), social support from family/household members (including childcare and housework usually referred to as socially reproductive labour), and social benefits provided by the state directly or through other collective bargaining arrangements, whereby the latter are subject to institutional national labour market contexts (see Table 7.1 for a summary of the findings).

As findings have shown, in creative dance there is an overarching occupational ideology prioritizing the pursuit of a career *for the sake of art*. This ideology reflected through the meanings people attribute to unpaid labour (i.e., permanent availability, striving for perfection subordination, and permanent competition) intersects with the significant influence of resources and privileges which in creative dance resemble class privilege. These resources are crucial because they directly affect an individual's ability to handle the unpaid obligations involved in creative dance. Conversely, the paucity of resources in residential care reduces the capacity of caregivers—the majority of whom are lower-middle- and working-class workers—to sustain the unpaid labour stemming from the extremely demanding conditions of their work, with much hardship. Despite the adverse conditions of care work hindering their ability to manage unpaid labour, caregivers continue to engage in caregiving out of a commitment related to the idea to caring for others (i.e., working *for the sake of others*). This underscores an occupational ideology in care based on a professional 'work ethos', which reinforces altruistic motivations and meaningfulness attributed to unpaid labour, making it purposeful for those who view it as part of their skilled professional 'ethos'. However, whether that professional 'ethos' is considered worthy of respect and thus rewarded by 'others' is uncertain. It recalls Sayer's (2005b) analysis of the moral dimension of class where the author states that 'one of the most important features of class inequalities is that they present people with unequal bases for respect' as often these people are confronted with 'unequal access to the practices and goods that allow them warranted respect or conditional recognition' (Sayer 2005a: 959). Finally, in online platform work, it is the ideal of employability, demonstrated by the importance of maintaining

Table 7.1 Summary of the findings in creative dance, residential care, and online platform work

	Creative dance	Residential care	Online platform work
'Ideal worker' norm	Sacrifice for the *sake of art* Permanent availability: Having the body always 'ready' to perform Striving for perfection: Achieving the excellence in order to deliver the 'perfect' product Subordination: Never saying 'no' Permanent competition: Everybody is 'replaceable'	Sacrifice for the *sake of others* Permanent availability: Physical and emotional presence on and off duty 'Working for two': Doing everything that needs to be done Subordination: Having nothing to say	Sacrifice for the *sake of reputation* Permanent availability: Impossibility to switch off for fear of losing work Striving for perfection to make clients happy: extra tasks for no extra pay as 'sunk costs' or self-rewarding and learning experience Subordination: Doing without questioning Permanent competition: Investing and self-improving or not
Stigma	Not being 'good enough', being 'difficult', being a 'troublemaker', 'not being a real artist', 'not being capable', 'not working hard enough' or 'being a princess'; exclusion: 'never being casted again'	'Not truly caring', 'not doing their work properly', inducing guilt and shame; moral pressure: 'the elderly will suffer'	Bad reviews ruining reputation, 'not being reliable', loss of employability
Unpaid labour	To show one is able to sacrifice for *the sake of art* To avoid the stigma of not being a 'real artist'	To show one is able to sacrifice for *the sake of others* To avoid the stigma of not being a 'truly caring carer'	To show one is able to sacrifice for *the sake of reputation* To avoid the stigma of not being a 'reliable and reputable professional'
Relationship between unpaid labour and precarious work	Non-binary	Binary	Binary or non-binary, depending on platform rules and resources

Source: Author's elaboration.

one's reputation (i.e., working *for the sake of reputation*), which reveals the motivation behind the performance of unpaid labour.

This book has introduced and discussed a theory of the 'politics of unpaid labour', advancing our understanding of how inequality in precarious work occurs. The central thesis is that exploitative unpaid labour is triggered by class-based power structures reflecting an intrinsic inequality in the distribution and possession of resources. Accordingly, the book defines the politics of unpaid labour as the power dynamics and policies surrounding the use and exploitation of labour power that is not monetarily compensated and which therefore remains unpaid. In other words, we argue that the study of unpaid labour is important to address and advance our understanding of inequality in precarious work by uncovering both the resources needed to support and the dynamics underpinning the 'doing unpaid'. In particular, our study uncovers the ideological (i.e., the 'ideal worker' norm reflected through the working for *the sake of art*, *the sake of others*, and *the sake of reputation*) which shares an idea of the meaning of work—under neoliberalism, digitalization, and to a growing extent demographic—which is considered a site of 'ideological hegemony' (see the debates and theories of governmentality and hegemonic 'work ethic' in Chapter 3), and structural power dynamics, including the role of labour market institutions and state policy at the crossroads of micro-individual and macro-regulatory structures, that perpetuate unequal and class-based outcomes for workers, whether they are employees in a waged-labour relationship or self-employed in a service provision relationship with clients mediated (or not) by a digital platform.

Hence, the book suggests a theory of the politics of unpaid labour to explain how unpaid labour and precarious work are connected. It does this by examining the governance structures and policies steering the labour market and the ideological forces or ideas that make unpaid work seem acceptable in the occupational fields or work areas of creative dance, residential care, and online platform work. These ideas influence why people in these areas perform unpaid work. At the same time, the book adds knowledge to theories and debates on unpaid work in the three investigated occupational fields by illustrating how this unpaid work, stemming from the nature of the work in these fields, in turn entails inequality in precarity by reproducing social class.

A Snapshot of Unpaid Labour from Work Diaries

In creative dance, we found that unpaid labour is undertaken by both employees and freelancers (for the most part 'project workers'), and that it takes the form of time spent on preparing, planning, training, and rehearsing, on self-promotion work (e.g., marketing and branding), on travel, on performing additional tasks (i.e., work intensification), and on working longer (i.e., work extensification), as revealed by our ballet dancer work diaries. Much of the unpaid work is 'personal investment work' not adequately compensated by the fees chargeable by freelance project workers: specifically, on 64% of person days, dancers who kept work diaries for ten working days mentioned preparing and planning work, while on 62% of the person days, they reported investing in keeping in shape (see Table 7.2).

Turning to residential care, we found that unpaid labour is mainly associated with working longer hours (i.e., unpaid overtime), with work intensification ('stopwatch care') meaning that care workers are unable to complete the assigned work in a manner in line with their work ethos, thus obliging them to work longer without being paid. Work intensification includes working faster and performing tasks not belonging to their profile or job classification. One respondent described this as 'working for two'. It is important to state that, while managing emotions ('emotional work') often implies performing unpaid labour in accordance with the work ethos mentioned above, such unpaid work increased significantly during the Covid-19 pandemic when our study was undertaken. Care workers mentioned in their work diaries the unpaid labour performed to manage their and residents' emotions on 74% of the person days (see Table 7.3). Significantly, the narratives shared by care workers on the work before and during the Covid-19 pandemic highlight a crucial distinction. In contrast to the pre-Covid-19 era, care workers found themselves making decisions during the pandemic, often together with their co-workers, concerning the appropriateness of their interactions with residents in terms of emotion management (see Pulignano, Riemann, et al. 2024). All indicated significant amounts of emotional work being performed in accordance with the nature of the presentational and philanthropic 'social feeling rules' (Bolton 2005) underlying their motivations. They described various forms of such rules, for example 'modifying their voice', 'holding together', and 'leaving their home to go and sit with residents'.

Freelancers have always 'made hay while the sun shines', working long hours when work is available. They have also always invested time and effort to network with clients and thus gain access to paid work. In principle, unpaid labour is part and parcel of freelancing life. In pre-platform times, many freelancers worked via agencies, 'outsourcing' their self-marketing to an agency in return for the agency charging a commission (the difference between the amount paid to the freelancer and that charged by the agency to the end customer) on the work performed. Rates were high enough for

Table 7.2 Prevalence of unpaid labour in creative dance (percentage of person days, by form of unpaid labour)

Work sector	Forms of unpaid labour	Example quote	Percentage of days this form of unpaid labour was mentioned by workers
Creative: dance	1. Personal investment work: preparation, planning, rehearsals, promotion, and networking	'There are years of gaining experience, connections and good advice but earning no money' (SE08_Nikola) 'We do professional photo and video shoots to have something good to put online. I'm not getting paid for my own promotion or company promotion, or for putting videos on Instagram' (SE02_Sandra) 'You need to contact the right people, you need to collaborate with people, you need to think constantly how you can reinvent yourself. And you can't ask for too much [money], otherwise people won't work with you' (NL04_Sara)	64%
	2. Keeping in shape: training (physical and mental), rehab, warm-ups, diet, and rest	'You need to do classes and keep training. These are hours of work every day that you don't get paid for. When you have time off between one project and another you can't stop training. It's not an option to go to the gym or do dance classes, it's a necessity' (NL03_Lisa) 'There's discipline, ongoing exercise and continuous diet you learn since you are a child' (NL01_Anis) 'The day started at 8.20 with a rehab work that I have to go to because my work depends on me feeling good physically. So, I worked with a physiotherapist for my injured knee. So, it was a couple of hours consultation plus workout, rehab workout in the gym ... I also need time to rest. Otherwise, I'll get another injury' (SE28_Jaime) 'Self-training and extra ballet classes are not paid. These are the things I need to cover myself but there's no choice. Self-training is something I have to do to be at the top of my profession' (NL06_Alessandro)	62%

3. Travel time: touring and commuting	'When we tour, we're away for a month or five weeks, here and there. You don't see your kids, you travel during the day and preform every night. It's exhausting and you don't get any extra money for that' (NL09_Alba) An employed dancer referring to the fact that there is no extra pay for extra effort which sometimes results in injuries, due to the strain: 'travelling is the hardest thing for your body' (NL03_Lisa) 'Travel time is unpaid, even though it's part of the job. All the admin work I do is unpaid. These are hours of work every day that you don't get paid for' (NL03_Lisa) 'I got up at 7am, prepared my food, took a train at 9am and before noon I arrived at [name of a city]. We had a class from 12 till 1pm, a class plus a warm-up. Then from 1pm till 6pm, we had time to work and then from 6pm till 7:30pm we had a dinner break. After that we had some time to prepare for a première, preparing for the show, costumes and stuff like that. Another warm-up ad then the show from 8:30 till 10pm. Then the train back. I arrived home after midnight. The travel time was not paid. I also had to buy my tickets' (NL07_Francesco)	34%
4. Doing extra tasks: building the scene, doing the lightening and cleaning, replacing colleagues, additional admin work, etc.	'[The theatre] didn't have money to employ everybody. So I had to clean the stage before the performance. I had to do the lights with the technician. Especially during the tour this was very tough because I had to unload the car, help set up everything. I was exhausted even before the performance started' (SE11_Fabiano)	30%
5. Creating job opportunities: networking, self-promotion	'I had to pay for the possibility to work, to meet people, to learn. I paid for auditions. I paid for my training to be able to participate in a show in New York for different audiences. It was an important experience, but I had to pay for it' (SE02_Sandra)	36%

Continued

Table 7.2 *Continued*

Work sector	Forms of unpaid labour	Example quote	Percentage of days this form of unpaid labour was mentioned by workers
	6. Overworking to reach perfection	'You just have to work very very very hard. Even if something is extremely difficult, you just work harder, even harder and until it actually looks very good, perfect' (NL09_Alba) 'The dance world is mentally and emotionally draining but physically ... It's just too much. People in the dance company work six days a week, up to four shows a week. It's like ongoing, ongoing, ongoing. And there's so much pressure on excellence' (NL04_Sara) 'We work as much as 150%, but we're only paid for a fraction of the work we're doing' (SE02_Sandra)	8%

Note: On the basis of an analysis of eight audio diaries recorded for ten consecutive working days by freelance ballet dancers.
Source: Author's elaboration.

Table 7.3 Prevalence of unpaid labour in residential care (percentage of person days, by form of unpaid labour)

Work sector	Forms of unpaid labour	Example quote	Percentage of days this form of unpaid labour was mentioned by workers
Residential Care	1. Unpaid overtime: staying at work after a paid shift is finished	'It's normal to work overtime because something has to be finished. We're not paid extra for that' (DE03_Doreen)	32%
	2. Coming to work early and working during breaks	'For five years I've been gifting my employer half an hour each and every day. I come to work half an hour earlier, so I have some room to do something with people, to ask them how they are' (DE12_Marianne)	40%
	3. Buying what residents ask for (pastries, socks, craft materials) out of one's own pocket	'I buy the craft material that we use with the residents. They love arts and craft, and I pay for it out of my own pocket. Each time it is £4, £5, £6 worth' (UK17_Tara)	4%
	4. 'Working for two' due to understaffing	'We're so short-staffed. Let's say there should be four people on, and we got two and that was fairly normal, you know? The management wouldn't pay out any extra to get extra agency staff in and quite often no one was available anyway. So, you would work for two' (UK15_Tina)	14%
	5. 'Stopwatch care' ('Minutenpflege'): the pressure to work fast in order to meet the targets	'You're drenched in sweat, and they say: "You have to work harder. You have to do it faster!"' (DE02_Beate)	28%
	6. Working as an all-rounder ('Mädchen für Alles'): doing everything that needs to be done, irrespective of the official job description	'We were all-rounders: providing basic care and companionship, doing the cooking and housekeeping … We're supposed to do everything while taking care of 9 patients. But you can't be everywhere at once. How can you keep an eye on all 9 people with dementia while cleaning the windows?' (DE19_Eva)	48%
	7. Emotional labour: taking care of residents' emotional needs and managing one's own emotions	'Often, I'd just stay longer or come on my day off. Not as a worker but as a visitor, just to sit together. With no rush' (DE18_Eva)	74%

Note: On the basis of an analysis of seven audio diaries recorded for ten consecutive working days by employed care workers.
Source: Author's elaboration.

freelancers to recoup any unpaid investment in labour or the 'tools of the trade'. The market entrance of digital platforms has changed all this—and not for the better. Unlike freelancers employed by conventional agencies who are typically discretely rated solely by the agency's clients, online platforms employ more transparent rating systems open to client review. As a result, freelancers working on such platforms are compelled to dedicate considerably more effort in establishing and maintaining their professional reputation and they may face difficulties to build portfolio and career perspectives. Furthermore, while freelancers can to a certain extent negotiate rates when dealing with conventional agencies, this practice is frequently unavailable when working with anonymous online platforms.

Our study focused on two types of labour platforms: 'digital tournament' platforms where freelancers bid for (mainly short-term) 'gigs' and 'non-tournament' platforms without bidding. Much more focused on long-term client relationships, the latter are willing to invest in helping freelancers develop their portfolios, thereby increasing their attractiveness *vis-à-vis* clients. The different rules used by platforms, as well as the possible existence of an algorithm-based performance system, bear witness to the heterogeneity of platform business models. These range from Uber-like models focused on casual transactions performed by non- or semi-professional freelancers to what are basically traditional but automated agencies targeting professional freelancers and long-term transactions, preferably with repeat clients. Whereas 'digital tournament' platforms foster (worldwide) competition and thus exert downward pressure on rates, thereby nullifying any attempts to recoup the cost of any unpaid labour invested in accessing the work, 'non-tournament' platforms do their best to offer freelancers a proper deal. Indeed, freelancers working on such platforms report that they do not experience any (or less) unpaid labour as deleterious due to the platform's investment in portfolio development. Moreover, they report a significantly lower incidence of unpaid work, especially with respect to client communication and searching and applying for jobs. Conversely, freelancers on 'digital tournament' platforms register a relatively higher incidence of unpaid labour: client communications (83% of person days), searching and applying for 'gigs' (40% of person days), buying platform currency to bid for tasks (3% of person days), and working longer and faster (work intensification and work extensification) (97% of person days). Nevertheless, they consider this a natural consequence of freelancing (see Table 7.4).

Table 7.4 Prevalence of unpaid labour in online platform work (percentage of person days, by form of unpaid labour)

Work sector	Forms of unpaid labour	Example quote	Percentage of days this form of unpaid labour was mentioned by workers	
			'Non-tournament' platforms: Jellow & Malt	'Digital tournament' platforms: Upwork & AddLance
Online platform work	1. Communication with clients	'I received a message from my English client, he wanted me to do a transcription of a video. We talked for an hour and then he changed his mind. He didn't give me this job' (FR16_Namita)	32%	83%
	2. Buying platform currency to bid for tasks	'What bothers me is buying the currency, paying the commission fees and covering the transaction costs, like the exchange rate' (IT16_Carla)	0%	3%
	3. Job searching and applications	'All the work I've carried out today was not paid for. It was just searching for jobs and applying for transcription and translation jobs. Nothing came out of it. And I earned nothing. Zero' (NL08_Lorenza)	2%	40%
	4. Sending free samples of work	'They ask you to send things and then they actually use parts of the texts that I have written without paying me anything' (NL01_Jan)	6%	5%
	5. Work intensification & extensification	'Today I had to work for four hours without a break because the client was in a great hurry' (IT16_Carla)	60%	97%
	6. Doing extra jobs to keep clients satisfied	'I am scared to say "no" to the client as that may close some doors for the future' (FR13_Pierre)	19%	40%
	7. Investment in reputation building	'Your reputation is totally dependent on clients' good or bad will … one single negative review can destroy your reputation, and restoring it requires lots of time and effort' (FR02_Paulo) 'I keep adding things to my website, my Instagram, doing a bit of marketing, a bit of connecting with people. I wrote a bit for my blog, which I hope will be paid for one day. I also wrote Christmas cards for my clients' (BE13_Kaat)	4%	15%

Note: On the basis of an analysis of twenty-one audio diaries recorded for ten consecutive working days by online platform workers.
Source: Author's elaboration.

The Theory of the 'Politics of Unpaid Labour': Unveiling Inequality in Precarious Work

Our analysis of creative dance, residential care, and online platform work introduced the theory of the politics of unpaid labour to explain how the study of unpaid labour, stemming from the nature of the work in the three described work areas or occupational fields, helps address inequality in precarious work. The book does this in two ways.

First, the book shows that socially reproductive labour outside the market is increasingly an important resource supporting unpaid, under-, or poorly paid labour inside the market in light of the transformations facing work and employment. Performing unpaid labour within or in the run-up to paid employment requires a precarious worker's household to be able to adequately manage its finances to cope with irregular or low income. Households and individuals without adequate (financial) resources may be pushed into dependence on state welfare systems with their associated disciplinary regimes. This creates new interdependencies between paid and unpaid labour, due to unpaid labour constituting both socially reproductive labour outside the market and unpaid labour time inside the market, with the former often needed to sustain work which, in relation to the paid and unpaid time and effort invested, is poorly remunerated (Pulignano and Morgan 2023). Consequently, it is not only work within the public sphere of paid employment, but also domestic work associated with household arrangements that is becoming more precarious. Managing household finances under these conditions leads to multiple potential disruptions to domestic arrangements. These come at a cost to individuals and households, as witnessed by household breakups, mental health and addiction issues, minor criminal offences, and ultimately 'deaths of despair' (Case and Deaton 2020). While well-endowed middle-class families may be able to supply the necessary support, we suggest that unpaid labour is deepening inequalities in precarity between households. One further aspect relates to individuals without any household support. As Molyneux (1979) argued:

> Single workers, and migrants, whose labour power is usually reproduced on a daily basis without the benefit of female domestic labour, are invariably paid below-average wages. Even supposing that they were able and willing to afford the necessary appliances, such categories of workers live in conditions (slums, hostels, shanties) which make it difficult for them to perform their own domestic labour; as a consequence, they tend to rely on services and food obtained on the market. (1979: 11)

Second, the book argues that, to comprehend the extent to which unpaid labour contributes to inequality in precarious work, it is crucial to consider how social norms legitimize certain individual behaviours. It is well documented that people working in creative domains willingly embrace uncertain job conditions in return for meaningful and fulfilling work, as highlighted in studies by Banks (2006) and Coulson (2012). Similarly, there is an analogous observation in social care research, as indicated by Baines (2004). One recent study refers to the 'legitimate frames' (Trappmann et al. 2023) in which precarity unfolds. Our analysis provides a finer grained analysis, revealing how these legitimate frames are operated by stigma. It also explains how institutions in labour markets and state policies can bolster existing hierarchies and class-based structures by restricting resources for individuals in different ways. For example, the transformations caused by national governments' legislative and policy changes, themselves dictated by European Union deregulatory policies in the early 2000s, have helped justify and institutionalize austerity measures, including the marketization and privatization of many public services, in many countries. The imperative at the core of these transformations is a neoliberal 'regime of competition' (Pulignano 2018) triggering a downward spiral of wages and working conditions by fostering a trend of workforce flexibilization, against which collective bargaining systems across Europe had little to offer (Voss et al. 2015). The challenges posed by the Covid-19 pandemic and its aftermath, combined with surging technological advances, demographic trends, armed conflicts, energy concerns, the resurgence of inflation, and climate change, have retained the spotlight on social issues, especially wages, as witnessed by recent waves of strikes and policy developments, for example on minimum wages.

Drawing on the notion of the politics of unpaid labour, the following sections examine the implications of our theorization for the theory of capability in labour economics.

Enriching the Capability Approach by Shifting the Focus to the Labour Market

Labour markets in capitalist economies are socio-economic structures where changes are often associated with inequality. The inequality debate revolves around the 'equality of what?' question once posed by Amartya Sen (1980), with the alternative philosophical answers being 'resources' (or 'opportunities'), 'welfare', and 'capabilities'. The answers that policymakers have been concerned with relate to income, wealth, housing, access to the labour market and jobs, life expectancy, social protection, and access to public services such as education, healthcare, police protection, or public transport. Sen's question leads us to a distinct conceptualization of inequality where equality is defined as the equal opportunity for individuals to pursue 'freely chosen life plans' (Sen 1980, 1985, 1992).

Chapters 4, 5, and 6 in Part II present empirical evidence illustrating how unpaid labour can both result from and serve as a prerequisite for these life plans. This duality arises because unpaid labour presents a landscape filled with both opportunities and threats, demanding the strategic allocation of financial, social, and institutional resources. These resources encompass various aspects of life, including socially reproductive labour within the domestic sphere, and employment and welfare structures concerning pay, income, benefits, and protection through state policies and other institutions, such as collective bargaining, within the public sphere. The distribution of these opportunities throughout society determines the extent to which unpaid labour can serve as a resource for individuals seeking to realize their freely chosen life plans.

In a broader context, as we have demonstrated, both ideological processes and material conditions form the foundation for the role of unpaid labour in perpetuating inequality and precarity. Through a holistic analysis, Parts I and II of the book have explored the 'politics of unpaid labour' at the intersection of individual and collective resources and social institutions, revealing the interconnectedness of various work forms across diverse spaces and domains, and shedding light on the complex dynamics contributing to inequality and precarity. The ability to sustain unpaid labour is contingent upon socially reproductive labour in the domestic sphere as well as household income and the labour market institutions. The book has shown that unpaid labour is embedded in different ways in social practices within labour markets, highlighting that, at the end of the day, someone needs to sustain it (and 'to pay for it'). In so doing, we have shed light on the operation of structural inequalities and the different ways in which occupational opportunities and resources, as circumscribed by class, risk limiting the freedoms that the capability perspective in economics—described in the following section—relies upon.

In other words, while capabilities depend on opportunities within labour markets, we claim that the former are structured by income- and identity-based social classes, as seen in the field of dance where we identified a structured hierarchy or system of social class based on the perpetuation of prestige and advantage through family connections and resources. In this structure, only dancers belonging to the (upper) middle class and possessing the necessary resources are able to thrive in the dance context. In other words, individuals from higher socio-economic classes enjoy an advantage or privileged position in the world of dance due to the resources they are able to access. Likewise, we identified gendered values and norms as well as the limited opportunities available to working-class women—constituting the majority of the care workforce—to access cultural and social capital. Caregivers, poorly paid and primarily from working-class backgrounds, grapple with the burdens of the highly gendered double standards of work, both within the care home and their own households. This struggle may lead to them readily taking on part-time work and/or night shifts. Despite the fact that care workers technically have employee status, they may also face variable and uncertain working hours—in the UK this is often tied to precarious contractual arrangements such as zero-hour contracts—in turn resulting in an insecure income for these workers. Finally, we found that business models seem to polarize class-based differences on digital platforms. For example, when comparing class structures, we noticed a notable difference between freelancers belonging to the same class (mainly of middle class or lower middle class with very few of working class) operating on non-tournament platforms as compared to those on digital tournament platforms. This suggests that, given the same middle- or lower-middle-class background, the former have better capacity to capitalize on their access to resources, such as household income and support, enabling them to sustain unpaid labour and create some distance from economic necessity, while the latter, with similar class background, might experience continuous economic pressure due to the highly competitive nature of digital tournament platforms depleting the access workers have to resources. This adds to arguments that how and to what extent digital transformations of labour markets reduce some class-based differences in the selection of workers (Martindale and Lehdonvirta 2023) depends on the platform business model.

Instead of veering away from labour markets, therefore, this chapter strongly advocates understanding labour market institutions and policies through the lens of 'emancipatory capabilities' (Gazier 2022a), enhancing conventional economic perspectives on 'capability' by comprehending how opportunities within labour markets shape class-based inequality in precarious work—a concept at the core of the theory of the politics of unpaid labour presented in this book. We use this lens to further develop our analysis in the following sections at the crossroads of sociology and economics.

Labour economists and economic sociologists have traditionally captured the class divisions correlating with income and security by taking a labour market 'segmentation' perspective (e.g., Doeringer and Piore 1971).

Accordingly, workers may find themselves in secure, well-compensated roles or trapped in more precarious, low-paying jobs, largely contingent on the specific labour market 'segment' in which they operate. Thus, there seems to be agreement among theorists from an economic and sociological perspective that 'class' positions, with their accompanying resources and limitations, correlate with individuals' occupational positions in the labour market. In other word, 'occupation is a central indicator of class position' (Oesch 2006: 14). A brilliant illustration in sociology is Pierre Bourdieu's early ambition to bridge the relation between the economic and the symbolic by treating 'occupation as an indicator of both the (economic) degree of the market power and (symbolic) secondary properties such as level of education or geographical distribution' (Bourdieu 1984 in Oesch 2006: 14).

Our analysis is guided by two interlinked reflections. The first focuses on the labour market institutions and policies responsible for how and to what extent unpaid labour shapes inequality in precarious work, as the resources needed to sustain unpaid labour are made available and distributed in accordance with these institutions and policies. The former include labour law, education, training, collective bargaining, wage determination, and social security. The latter refer to those shaping and implementing these policies, i.e. a government's legislative and executive arms, as well as management strategies and business models positioning jobs and their holders in firms and other organizations, and labour unions' capacity to affect those strategies. The second reflection is that capabilities and opportunities—as individual freedoms for people to achieve what they wish to do and to be ('functionings') in accordance with their preferred 'life plans' (Sen 1980, 1992)—are dependent on a set of collective material and ideological arrangements made up of policies, institutions, and norms providing (or not) people with generous and appropriate opportunities.

Hence, we argue that the freedoms people enjoy—and which theories of 'capability egaalitarianism' consider important for explaining equality in society (Sen 1992)—cannot be built 'in silos' as they are contingent upon a set of capability-providing collective arrangements of which labour market institutions and policies are a key factor. The argument is put forward that labour market institutions and policies are just as important as civil, social, and political rights to guarantee equality in opportunities as they account for how far these rights are equally exercised. The evidence presented in this book supports this argument by illustrating that freedoms, including the performance of unpaid labour, are a necessary but insufficient condition for guaranteeing equality in society. This is because exercising these freedoms also depends on the availability of individual and collective resources, including labour market institutions.

Developing these reflections, the following sections construct an argument on the significance of integrating and promoting a labour market focus within the broader framework of the theory of capability in labour economics.

Capabilities and *Functionings*: The Challenge

Amartya Sen (1980, 1992) and Martha Nussbaum (2003, 2011) introduced the concepts of 'functionings' within the theory of capability in labour economics in order to assess the freedom and well-being of individuals. In the capability theory, 'functionings' represent any state of an individual's existence, reflecting the set of functions an individual performs, while capabilities encompass the entire range of potential 'functionings' for the same individual. This approach places a strong emphasis on freedom, whether in the negative sense ('freedom from want') or the positive sense ('freedom to do'), rather than solely focusing on the possession of goods or subjective feelings of happiness. Empowerment goes beyond observed preferences or behaviours, focusing on the 'real freedom of everybody'. One example is the much higher income and special help needed by a disabled person to achieve 'functionings' similar to those of a non-disabled person. The theory also emphasizes adaptive preferences in the sense that individuals' negative expectations may end up in a lack of empowerment (Gazier 2022a).

The capability theory considers 'decent employment' as an important factor shaping individuals' capabilities under the broad theme of 'having control over one's environment', alongside political participation and property rights (Nussbaum 2003). Nevertheless, considering access to 'decent employment' as a core dimension of the capability approach remains problematic. While there would seem to be agreement that the context of employment, such as the labour market where individuals make their choices, influences the nature of capabilities, the capability theory has limited application to the labour market as an institution. Conversely, as the theory of the politics of unpaid labour illustrates, the labour market is the primary avenue through which individuals either secure or miss out on their livelihoods and autonomy. This is because 'the institution of the labour market is the primary mechanism for producing and distributing welfare' (Bartelheimer et al. 2012: 93–4). Therefore, we argue that not considering the labour market risks missing out on how social redistribution occurs.

Leveraging the theoretical foundation of this book on the politics of unpaid labour, this chapter crafts a counter-narrative underscoring the analytical importance of the concept of capabilities and 'functionings' within the labour market. This exploration unfolds in four steps. First, we embark on a critical examination of the labour market in its role of shaping both individual and collective capabilities. This analysis engages with the capability theory in labour economics, with particular attention accorded to Amartya Sen's insights on employment and work, on the one hand. As a second step, we investigate how labour markets shape individual and collective capabilities by introducing the segmentation approach and exploring its integration into the analysis of class dynamics. In a third step, we use the 'employability' theory within socio-economic perspectives to illustrate how labour markets shape both individual and collective capabilities. Finally, we discuss how individual and collective capabilities influence the living and working conditions of individuals by attempting an alignment between the capability approach and the perspective on 'Transitional Labour Markets' (TLM) (see Schmid and Gazier 2002) through the use of the concepts of 'exit', 'voice', and 'loyalty' (Hirschman 1970). We conclude by highlighting a policy pathway under which the book's main theoretical argument of the politics of unpaid labour can help enhance the collective capabilities approach.

Step 1: Employment and Work in the Capability Theory

Capability theory focuses on discrimination, exclusion, and mutual recognition between co-workers and between employers and workers which it considers as key features in the definition of employment and work. As Nussbaum argues: 'individuals have the right to seek employment on an equal basis with others ... they have the freedom from unwarranted search and seizure. In work, workers are able to work as humans exercising practical reason and entering into meaningful relationships of mutual recognition with other workers' (Nussbaum 2011: 34). Here, the labour market is considered an 'external' or 'conversion' factor and therefore its effects on capabilities and 'functionings' is not assessed (Stephens 2023: 324).

Within the framework of justice and capabilities, the exploration of employment and work by Amartya Sen (2009) takes on a nuanced perspective. While the central problem of how workers are treated is acknowledged, insights into the labour market, including the roles of collective players, such as labour unions, are notably sparse. The emphasis consistently leans towards a broader viewpoint, advocating the inclusion of all worker categories—from peasants and sharecroppers to housewives engaged in unpaid domestic work, precarious workers, and those formally employed. In essence, within Sen's (2009) classification, these groups are characterized as the 'traditional underdogs' sharing a category with 'oppressed minorities in intolerant communities' and 'sweated workers in exploitative business arrangements' (Sen 2009: 282–3).

Although the overarching perspective stresses the importance of avoiding favouritism towards any particular group, the challenges experienced by these groups, including issues of skills, impartiality, and discrimination, are underscored. For example, Sen (2009) occasionally broadens the scope of 'functionings' to encompass achievements ranging from being well nourished and avoiding premature mortality to community participation for pursuing work-related plans and ambitions. However, he refrains from further exploring their implications for skills development within the labour market. At the same time, the author draws on traditional arguments of potential pitfalls within labour unions prioritizing the interests of their members (insiders) over others (outsiders) to explain inequality. In addition, the assertion that capabilities involve achieving various combinations of 'functionings', subject to comparison based on valued outcomes, legitimizes a focus on complex and pluralistic sets of 'functionings'. However, there is limited exploration in Sen's work into how these 'complex *functionings*' contribute to or hinder autonomy and decent work. This is particularly the case when referring to developing countries.

These gaps might be attributed to Sen's (2009) consideration that 'individual freedoms' are means aimed at challenging the conventional neoclassical approach to decision-making in economics. Consequently, the conceptualization of 'functionings' overlooks the role of a labour market's collective players and institutions, for example labour unions and collective bargaining. Nevertheless, labour unions fulfil various essential roles within labour markets. In the seminal work of Richard Freeman and James Medoff, *What Do Unions Do?* (1984), labour unions are seen as non-competitive bodies seeking advantages for stabilized and unionized worker groups. On the other hand, they play a pivotal role in articulating collective preferences among workers, potentially encompassing all workers, and steering them towards operational aims through inclusive collective bargaining structures (see also Doellgast et al 2018). Sen (2009) emphasizes the non-competitive and potentially discriminatory aspects of labour unions while disregarding their other constructive facets. This unilateral stance is unjustified against the statement that labour unions play a central role in combating adaptive preferences—an issue which Sen (2009) highlights when examining 'real freedom'.

In line with Sen's concern over 'real freedom', we therefore advocate integrating the study of the labour market, with its segmented (class-based) structures and collective players, into the capability debate in labour economics, thereby contributing to a more comprehensive and contextualized understanding of the challenges and potentials surrounding individuals' capabilities and freedoms.

Step 2: Labour Markets, Segmentation, and Capability

Some three decades ago, Robert Solow (1991) challenged the notion of the labour market as a natural state of affairs, instead proposing to view it as a 'social institution'. Accordingly, a labour market represents a dynamic mix of multi-level individual and collective players, structures, and rules that evolve over time. Among the players, companies and their strategies stand out. While they strive to achieve their individual goals, such as maximizing profit and fostering innovation, the far-reaching effects of their accomplishments significantly influence the welfare of both their employees and society at large. Taken together in a given economic and social context, companies can thus account for inequality by pursuing more or less stabilizing and enabling strategies and policies contributing to labour market segmentation (see Box 7.1: 'The Labour Market Segmentation Perspective').

Box 7.1 The labour market segmentation perspective

Definition and Labour Market Inequality

The labour market segmentation perspective (see Doeringer and Piore 1971) highlights the stark differences evident among various job types within companies. It not only emphasizes the barriers existing between different job groups—such as disparities in educational qualifications beyond skill requirements or instances of discrimination—but also places significant focus on the distinct adjustment mechanisms operating within these submarkets. Central to this perspective is the differentiation between what is termed the 'primary' segment and the 'secondary' segment within the labour market. The 'primary' segment encompasses jobs characterized by stable career trajectories within companies, displaying minimal wage fluctuations and typical of larger companies with an established workforce, whether skilled or unskilled. The 'secondary' segment exhibits contrasting features, including job instability, limited career progression prospects, and substantial wage variation. The labour market segmentation perspective ultimately converges on the concept of a 'dualistic' or unequal labour market, delineated around two poles, one stable and the other unstable. Over time, subsequent studies exploring labour market segmentation have transcended this binary delineation, introducing subsegments within the 'primary' sector, such as the 'upper primary' segment which caters to highly skilled and/or executive-level workers. This subsegment is characterized by strong job stability, ample mobility opportunities, and wage variability. By contrast, the 'inferior secondary' segment represents informal and extremely unstable jobs devoid of any semblance of security or adherence to labour laws.

Core Argument
The socio-economic discussion surrounding the segmentation perspective is rooted in two fundamental arguments. First, the 'techno-social' argument stresses that numerous large companies, equipped with substantial fixed capital, seek to stabilize their workforce by structuring internal career paths and engaging in collective bargaining with labour unions to meet their objectives. Conversely, other companies operate within a competitive context, relying on wages to attract workers but lacking structured career advancement opportunities and often maintaining an adversarial stance towards labour unions. The second argument delves into power dynamics, emphasizing the 'divide and conquer' concept. This viewpoint contends that the dichotomy between a stable workforce and an unstable one serves as a dual mechanism for employer control over employees. Stabilized workers may fear potential dismissal, relegating them to unemployment or the secondary job market. Meanwhile, workers in the secondary segment find themselves ensnared in restrictive 'mobility chains', transitioning from one unstable job to another or facing repeated spells of unemployment.

Developments
While the reality of segmentation persists, its nature has undergone a significant evolution (e.g., Rubery and Wilkinson 1981; Gazier and Petit 2007). Several phases have marked the evolution of the segmentation. The initial phase involved the flexibilization process, expanding the 'secondary' labour market while shrinking the 'primary' one. The subsequent 'outsourcing phase' saw major shifts as large companies strived to just retain 'core' activities, handing over non-core activities to subcontractors offering less favourable employment terms and remuneration. This period also witnessed the emergence of new forms of control, evaluating individual worker performance and fostering the individualization of work relationships. Recent changes include the expansion of self-employment and platform work, alongside the emergence of complex employment networks involving 'third-party' intermediaries between workers and end users. While temporary employment agencies represent an older example of such arrangements, they now coexist with various for-profit or non-profit 'third-party' players. Segmentation continues to exist

continued

Box 7.1 *continued*

in diverse forms, often resulting in additional divisions within segments. Some previously stabilized workers in the 'primary' sector face constant threats of displacement, being forced into direct competition with lower cost producers abroad, particularly if they have remained in low-skilled roles. These workers find themselves in a superficially stable 'segment', yet are subject to precarious and potentially unstable work relationships (akin to the 'secondary' segment), often experiencing wage cuts and intensified workloads. At the same time, each segment is becoming more heterogeneous, offering opportunities for some workers to establish a livelihood and advance in their careers, while others struggle to navigate the pressures and constraints they encounter, unable to progress to more favourable positions.

As indicated, there is agreement among theorists in sociology and economics that class positions in society and segment positions within the labour market are somehow aligned. In essence, the upper middle class is typically aligned, metaphorically speaking, with the upper 'primary' segment, while the traditional working class is predominantly aligned with the central 'primary' segment. Less stabilized groups, such as migrants and the lower middle class in service-oriented roles, tend to belong to various versions of the 'secondary' or informal segment. When someone safeguarded within the 'primary' labour market loses his/her job, the protection afforded by the previous job ensures temporary replacement income. However, if there are no alternative jobs within the 'primary' segment, that person will be relegated to the 'secondary' segment where s/he contends with less stable and lower paying jobs, and the risk to experiencing periods of unemployment.

Equating social class with labour market segments is not a straightforward or purely mechanical exercise. Numerous influencing factors come into play to define the nature of the relationship between social class and labour market segments. Discussed in analyses of social (im)mobility, these factors include an individual's educational trajectory, family culture, the place of individuals within a family structure, group demographics and culture, and geographical location (for a summary, see Oesch 2006). At the same time, several countervailing factors impact the relationship between social class and labour market segments. They include opportunities for intensive retraining, assistance from nearby or distant associates, and decisions to relocate to different regions or areas (e.g., Martin 1994; Bauder 2001). This points to contextual circumstances shaping individuals' willingness and capabilities in the labour market.

The concept of 'mobility chains' (i.e., constraining mobility paths for the majority of workers in any group) within the labour market segmentation perspective has provided a useful framework for analysing the capabilities enjoyed by different groups of workers within the labour market from a labour economics perspective. For example, Korver and Schmid (2012) have elaborated the concept of 'transition capacity' to explain the contextual socio-economic conditions underpinning different workers' capabilities. Certain groups of skilled workers possess a robust 'transition capacity' due to them belonging to the upper primary segment or the upper middle class, enabling them to benefit from re-employment opportunities within the labour market. Other groups of workers with relatively low skills are rarely able or willing to engage in intense retraining as they are trapped in a shrinking labour market where their jobs become obsolete. Their transition capacity is therefore low. Within labour market segmentation debates, competition to access the primary segment is considered a key factor shaping the 'transition capacity' of any worker. In accordance with Doeringer and Piore (1971), low-skilled workers recruited in 'primary' jobs are allowed to gain higher skills through on-the-job and formal training. Accordingly, workers can access the primary segment after a transition period in the secondary one. Under contemporary changes occurring in labour markets, this is becoming more unlikely as companies increasingly demand high skills right from the beginning of any individual career. In addition, the empirical evidence presented in this book illustrates that, although unpaid labour may occur in any segment of the labour market, for some groups of workers who have access to individual and collective resources (potentially enabling capabilities) due to their socio-economic position within a distinct (class-based) segment of the labour market, unpaid labour is likely to be experienced as not deleterious but as an instrument of personal autonomy. Here, we also show that company strategies may intersect with country-based state policies, potentially shaping different workers' experiences of autonomy, as seen in dance (greater public funding in Sweden than in the Netherlands) or in state-supported care marketization and privatization processes (more accentuated in the UK than in Germany).

Personal autonomy, which the capability theory considers an individual and final *functioning*, is thus intricately linked to the resources shaping the opportunities and constraints within a distinct (class-based) segment of the labour market and/or work environment. To conclude, we argue that the capacity of workers to acquire and develop capabilities—in turn entailing the achievement of certain 'functionings'—pertains to the extent to which labour markets and company strategies empower or constrain workers' choices about their work, efforts, and career orientation. As such, in line with Sen (1985, 1992), we claim that capabilities are a manifestation of a 'complex sets of *functionings*'.

The following section thus delves into the 'complexity' of the capabilities approach, using employability as an example of an 'intermediate' category between individual and collective capabilities.

Step 3: Employability as an Example of an Intermediate Category between Individual and Collective Capabilities

The concept of employability, integral to the historical fabric of labour market policies within developed economies, has undergone several refinements (Gazier 2022a, 2022b). Fundamentally, employability has an individual meaning as it revolves around the likelihood of someone obtaining a job within a defined period, thus serving as a metric for measuring his/her own capacity to secure employment. Key policies linked to enhancing individual employability encompass initiatives focused on (re)training, enabling access to prospective employers, and the handling of unemployment benefits. These policies aim to strike a balance, providing replacement income while incentivizing individuals to actively seek and accept paid employment opportunities.

Some narrowly defined individualistic interpretations of employability have unfairly placed blame on job seekers for being unemployed or overly selective: workers should adapt to the market whatever its conditions. We call for a broader perspective of employability taking an intermediate position, such as between an individual and a collective definition of capability. As said, the organizational structure of work, combined with varying skill levels within companies, can lead to vastly different 'transition capacities' for their workers—ranging from nearly non-existent to robust (Korver and Schmid 2012). Beyond the skills-opportunities nexus, some companies actively cultivate the employability of their workforce. Not necessarily belonging to buoyant sectors, these companies prioritize continuous skills updates and autonomy for their employees, embodying what has been termed 'capability-based employability' (Zimmermann 2022). Although such practices are still in the minority, the development of employability may increasingly be regarded as a 'managerial imperative' encompassing the overarching dimensions of workers (Noël and Schmidt 2022).

Accordingly, employability transcends traditional individual-based job-search requirements to increasingly encompass the collective dimension of labour market structures and policies, involving a wide array of stakeholders such as companies, labour unions, public and private employment services, and training services (Gazier 2022b). A noteworthy example of this development is the collaboration between public employment services and companies with a view to assessing and co-constructing present and future skills needs. For example, when a company is faced by a challenge necessitating restructuring and significant innovation for market survival, such as an outdated product portfolio, its workforce may find their employability diminishing, particularly in local contexts where the company is a major employer. An abrupt and poorly managed wave of dismissals can result in severe setbacks for workers who previously felt secure, substantially impacting their employability and self-confidence. Here the role of public players, such as the state through public policies, becomes important. They are able to create a collective public space in which to (re-)establish employment security. At the same time, one may observe a virtuous circle between the quality of the workforce (i.e., skills, cohesion, adaptability) and the policies of investors and managers who may choose a promising location or plant for developing their business. Competent and motivated workers attract investment, potentially fostering employability as a collective capability not only for people through jobs but also for business.

Hence, as the ability to secure employment and earn a living through the labour market, employability may serve as a pivotal link connecting individual resources to individual achievements. At the same time, employability emerges as an interactive notion involving numerous players, thereby resembling a collective dimension. In essence, and in line with Sen's (1980, 2009) main concerns of social justice and equality, employability extends beyond job acquisition to encompass emancipation, self-discovery, on-the-job learning, managing personal and professional careers, along with promoting voice and well-being in the workplace.

Step 4: 'Exit' and 'Voice' as Capability Complements—Recalling TLM

In accordance with traditional segmentation and dualization theories (Emmenegger et al. 2012), workers in the 'primary' segment may likely express themselves by channels of collective 'voice', for example by organizing in labour unions, building coalitions, and possibly by using the weapon of strikes. Conversely, workers in the secondary segment may 'exit' unsatisfactory jobs or tasks and look for alternative opportunities. However, it may also be expected that workers in a precarious segment of the labour market may be able to use 'voice', and that those unable to use either 'voice' or 'exit', due to global competition, may opt for 'loyalty' (see Hirschman 1970).

Both 'voice' and 'exit' can align with state policies, working together to facilitate the development of collective capabilities by implementing new norms, such as minimum wage standards and negotiated working hours. This perspective aligns with a normative and policy-oriented approach of capabilities. It also recalls the argument at the core of the TLM theory (Schmid and Gazier 2002; Schmid 2017) which proposes leveraging collective capabilities (see also ILO 2019; Delautre et al. 2021) for transitions in labour markets by complementing 'voice' and 'exit' with state policies and collective representation in companies.

TLM theory focuses on 'transitions', understood as any step in an individual's personal and professional career. Promoting the idea of a systematic and negotiated management of 'transitions' in and around the labour market, the main tenet of TLM is the idea of 'empowering' workers, including career progress and mobility. Its key motto is not just to 'equip people for the labour market' but also and more importantly to 'equip the labour market for people', which means going beyond simply adapting workers to existing labour market conditions—good or bad—by creating institutions and 'social drawing rights' (Supiot 2001), and through promoting non-profit organizations to exercise control over jobs, work, working hours, pay, etc. Such a perspective combines bottom-up with top-down action. One important aspect here is that TLM integrates unpaid domestic work by conceptualizing work—as this book does—at the continuum of paid and unpaid (see Part I). In so doing, TLM fosters gender equality by providing rich mobility and work options to both men and women, with incentives to equally take parental leave and to equally take on educational tasks in the family. In essence, TLM can be seen as a systematic policy effort to fight segmentation by rebalancing the power divide between workers of different gender and capital in four different ways, resembling the four principles at the core of TLM.

The first principle of TLM is 'empowerment'. It enriches the option sets available to workers and citizens in different life situations through providing them with new entitlements and ensuring effective access and implementation. The second principle is 'solidarity' which means that all groups within the labour market, especially disadvantaged ones, should benefit from good opportunities. In essence, favoured workers should contribute to the financing of the whole mobility and retraining system for less advantaged groups. The third principle is 'efficiency' which means aligning the interests of all stakeholders. For example, all stakeholders within an apprenticeship system, i.e. companies, the state with its vocational educational departments, and the trainees themselves, have an interest in achieving good outcomes, such as having a competent workforce. The fourth and last principle is 'decentralised management by projects' which means that transitions, while collectively organized, should result from bottom-up initiatives.

The concept of collective capabilities cuts across all four principles underpinning TLM. In essence, the four principles of TLM are aimed at creating better collective control over negative competition between workers and employers, and among workers themselves, including different genders, by setting systematic counterweights through establishing 'transitional collective rights', such as the right to temporary paid positions and to empowering support. One example of an empowering support is the British 'Union Learning Reps' (Stuart et al. 2016) system, where union representatives are assigned the role of identifying and reaching out to low-skilled workers, encouraging them to engage into training opportunities while helping them overcome their reluctance to take up (vocational) education and training.

At the same time, those in the self-employed category should be empowered. Wilks (1996: 538) argued that all markets 'are created by governments, ordered by institutions, and sustained by regulation'. In other words, business strategies and operations as the expression of models of capitalism are or should be responsive to government regulation. Within the European market, control of private market governance principles, including target setting and resource allocation, are delegated to different organizations developing regulation in the context of 'competition-oriented' collective bargaining (Schulten 2002). Within this market, we increasingly observe emerging digital platforms that are defining the rules organizing the online labour market (OLM) where the economic exchange between freelancers and clients occurs. This rule setting is done through platforms using digital technology to automate the exchange transactions. While the *raison d'être* of any labour platform is to generate profit, either through charging freelancers for providing them with access to clients (and thus performing the marketing that freelancers would otherwise have to perform themselves) or through charging client companies for access to freelancers, the question of the extent to which it empowers or disempowers freelancers, for example with regard to their bargaining power to autonomously set prices *vis-à-vis* clients, requires critical analysis. Rethinking the conditions for 'fair competition' within a global and increasingly digitally mediated labour market is pivotal to establishing recognition and respect *vis-à-vis* 'real' freelancers. This is an area this book could not explore in any great depth and which surely needs further investigation.

The Politics of Unpaid Labour and Collective Capabilities

The book's core theorization of the politics of unpaid labour offers significant economic and sociological insights reflecting the concept of collective capabilities. It does this by spotlighting the dynamics and processes explaining why workers in diverse contexts experience varying degrees of 'empowerment' or a lack thereof in their job roles and career prospects. It consequently sheds light on the opportunity structures where capabilities within the labour market are created. As the book shows, these structures are class- or segment-based, reflecting hierarchies and power dynamics in labour markets.

In essence, we have illustrated how unpaid labour can serve as a competitive resource for workers, acting as a favourable capability or asset in certain class- or segment-based contexts and circumstances. At the same time, we have shown that unpaid labour can also act as a constraint, exacerbating precarity and leading to more challenging circumstances in other class- and segment-based contexts and circumstances. Hence, we developed an argument under which understanding the conditions fostering the former and/or the latter is key to identifying how individuals and workers can together build collective capabilities. These capabilities offer scope for *agency*, with further research needed to investigate the forms it takes in these and other occupational fields.

What are the benefits of this book? We have mentioned several from a theoretical and empirical perspective. The conclusion by Damian Grimshaw which follow will present a more detailed discussion around policy implications. Here we would like to briefly highlight a very few practical recommendations that emerge from our discussion. This book introduces a concrete pathway for developing policy recommendations to help build collective capabilities. Within care work, for example, this entails recognizing the time and effort involved in care and its management—currently hidden by schedules dictated by the stopwatch—and consequently reflecting this in pay structures. Moreover, it calls for the establishment of generous state provisions, for example for childcare tailored to address the needs of those with atypical work schedules, in our case many dancers and caregivers. Similarly, addressing challenges within platform work involves establishing platforms resembling the traditional model of the non-profit employment agency aimed at bolstering portfolios opportunities for fair competition among freelancers. Furthermore, for professions like dancers, robust state funding and encompassing public-based social security provisions (e.g., unemployment benefits during periods of inactivity) are key. Here, the French *Intermittents du spectacle* (Menger 2011) can be used as an example, as this framework explicitly takes account of rehearsal times and fosters alternative career trajectories for senior dancers, ensuring their overall security even during periods of inactivity.

Conclusion

Damian Grimshaw

A major lesson from the ideas and evidence presented in this book is that unpaid labour is not a residual effect, observable only at the peripheries of economic activities, but is in fact a core feature of the political economy of work in contemporary Europe. Unpaid labour, experienced as wage theft among employees and income theft among self-employed workers, is propping up key segments of our economies by delivering cost-free labour. In a context of poorly organized and underresourced forms of employment, it is too often seen by many workers as a necessary sacrifice as they respond to, and impart, varied norms of the 'ideal worker' (Williams et al. 2013).

Applying a wide, sociological lens of enquiry, informed by Glucksmann's (2005) perspective of 'total social organisation of labour', this book demonstrates in unnerving detail the wider social, cultural, and economic consequences of unpaid labour. Described as stigma or punishments (Tyler 2020) which are embedded in, and amplify, deep structural class inequalities in economic life (Chapter 1), the multiple penalties of unpaid labour impede and undermine multiple facets of workers' lives—their family life, their health, their democratic engagement at work (including rights to own and access information and data), and their freedom from a life of poverty. The retelling of workers' experiences in Chapters 4, 5, and 6 places in rich context the overlapping adversities which require them to lean where possible on the 'scaffolding' of family and class-based (and unequally distributed) economic resources (Beckman and Mazmanian 2020). Additional protections from institutional resources in the form of worker rights, employment protection, and social protection are also patchy and limited in most of the cases examined. Overall, the workers' narratives reveal major flaws and gaps in Europe's policies and practices designed by governments, employers, and trade unions to protect workers and improve their lives. In this concluding chapter, we summarize the major areas of damage experienced by workers who regularly undertake unpaid labour and call for an urgent re-invigoration of worker rights, collective bargaining, social protection, and programmes of

Damian Grimshaw, *Conclusion*. In: *The Politics of Unpaid Labour*, Oxford University Press. © Valeria Pulignano and Markieta Domecka (2025). DOI: 10.1093/oso/9780198888130.003.0009 family support with the objective of reducing the cumulative disadvantage and misery caused by unpaid labour.

The Damage Caused by Unpaid Labour

Unpaid labour puts a massive strain on family life. Many workers talked about how the precarities and income uncertainties associated with their work inhibited or delayed decisions to have children. Online freelancers said they were 'always on stand-by' to protect their algorithmic ratings, severely impairing family relationships. Others relied on family members to share resources, whether income or time, as employers, clients, or algorithms changed their working schedules (and expected income) abruptly. Many workers interviewed for this book were young. How can they plan a life, settle down, raise a family, and enjoy a decent level of security in societies that allow unpaid labour to flourish?

The political economy of unpaid labour also impairs the health of Europe's workforce. Common among all workers' experiences illuminated in this book is the need to continuously strive for perfection and to be permanently available. Dancers said this means training, rehearsing, and performing even when sick or suffering an injury, while the untenable situation of care workers having to work while sick was amply evidenced during the Covid-19 pandemic. The demands of unpaid labour further damage workers' mental health, although further research is required to unpack the likely short- and long-term effects. In a political economy of precarious work and striking inequalities of work status, the feeling that you are replaceable, 'treated like crap' (as one care worker put it in Chapter 5) and that your unpaid working time is not seen or valued is likely to foment a complex raft of insecurities, low self-worth, and unhappiness among workers, particularly those unable to rely on the 'scaffolding' of close social and familial networks (Beckman and Mazmanian 2020). What can be done to mitigate the heightened risks to workers' physical and mental health which overlay the 'corrosion of character' (Sennett 1998) caused by employer-led practices of flexibilization and precarization of work?

A related consequence of unpaid labour and the sacrifices made by workers is the extreme subordination required of workers with zero opportunity to speak up, voice complaints, or contest stupid or unjust decisions at work. This makes for a badly organized economy, poor quality service (affecting care for the elderly and online translation, for example) and undermines the ideals of liberal democracies. Establishing the conditions that enable proactive worker engagement in workplace decisions is just as important as enjoying wider civil and political rights to ensure society functions in the interests of a diverse range of individuals and collectives (Ferreras 2018; ILO 2024). Many workers interviewed for this book felt isolated, experienced fear and intimidation (memorably described by one online freelancer in Chapter 6 as acting as 'cannon fodder'), and sometimes were forced to quit and work elsewhere. Having to continuously scan the labour market for more suitable opportunities is a further drain on an individual's time and a waste of resources. Indeed, we have long known that worker voice and mutual commitment are more effective instruments for a productive society than exit and alienation (Hirschman 1970), yet the political economy of unpaid labour is denying workers their right to exercise judgement at work and to enact positive change through solidarity with each other.

A final interlocking source of damage experienced by workers who routinely submit to unpaid labour is the reality of poverty and the fear that paid work cannot provide a pathway out of it. Workers interviewed for this book were often unable to afford the basic necessities, did not have the time or income to enjoy social and cultural activities, and were drifting further and further away from an ideal of middle-class comfort and stability. The irregularity and seeming informality of work, particularly workers' limited ability to negotiate a suitable volume and schedule for working hours, along with near-absent bargaining power over fees or rates of pay, and limited access to unemployment benefits mean workers lack the instruments to advance their earnings, other than by taking on multiple jobs and registering for work on multiple platforms. Many of the online freelancers interviewed said they were under pressure not to be 'too expensive' and felt they were 'held hostage' by clients. Care workers talked about the moral and economic injustices of the financialized ownership structures that privilege higher rates of profit over decent rates of pay; 'owners just reap in the money, the rest doesn't matter', as Susanne (DE08_Susanne) in Germany put it.

Here the inappropriateness and injustice of new instruments of financial extraction are perhaps most acute (see also Horton 2022; Hoppania et al. 2024). Private equity fund ownership of care homes, condoned by governments around the world, extracts profit from property assets while relying on the mostly female workforce to continue working under deteriorating conditions 'for the sake of others'. What new forms of protection are needed to shift the balance of power and impose limits to financialization? And more generally, what protections can establish workers' capacities to negotiate pay for a decent income and working hours and to escape the damage of living in poverty caused by excessive unpaid labour?

Forging Stronger Protections

Figure 8.1 sets out four key protections required to mitigate the cumulative damage caused by unpaid and precarious labour on workers' family life, their health and engagement in their work, and their capacity to bargain for decent income to avoid poverty (see Figure 8.1).

A first set of protections concern those characteristic of an *egalitarian family policy*. The availability and affordability of childcare has a major impact on workers', particularly women's, ability to take on work requiring variable hours and irregular time scheduling. Excessive childcare costs impose a quasi-tax on workers who decide to take on more work and may confine them to an unsuitable volume of short working hours. Employers may assume their female workforce has access to family support networks, but many are geographically isolated or unable to rely on stable families and suffer high costs. Consequently, the ability to accept last-minute changes to work schedules or a client's request for a quick turnaround of work is severely hampered by the absence of local childcare options that cater to flexible working hours rather than the assumed (and no longer standard) 9–5, Monday–Friday schedule. Limited access, rigid schedules, and the high cost of childcare are therefore major contributors to a gender unequal societal regime (Rubery 2015; Plomien 2019).

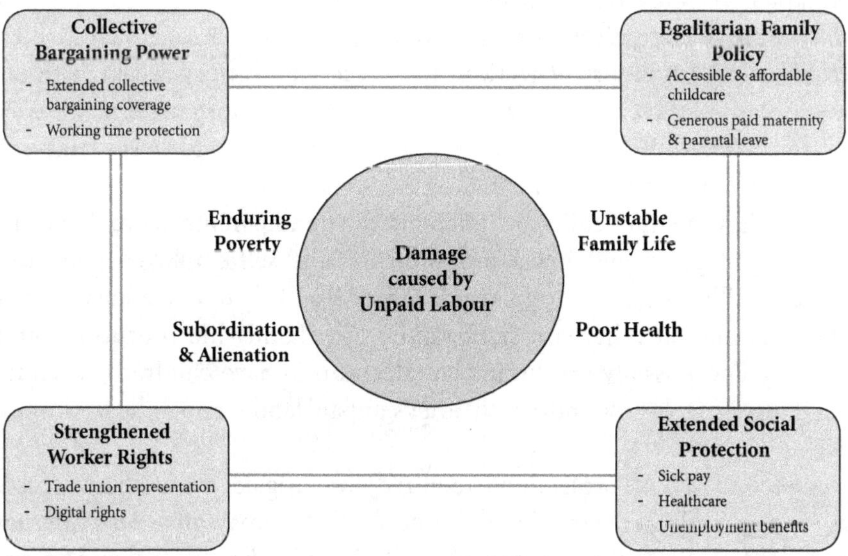

Fig. 8.1 Necessary protections to mitigate the damage caused by unpaid labour
Source: Author's original figure.

An egalitarian family policy also requires a sufficiently generous and accessible maternity and parental leave system to provide protection for all workers, regardless of their type of work contract, during the critical family formation stage of giving birth and caring for newly born infants. While the generosity of maternity and parental leave varies significantly across Europe, so too does the degree of its accessibility to workers with variable hours, those who are poorly paid, and those who have an irregular income, as well as the self-employed (Grimshaw et al. 2016).

One of the least generous and exclusive systems is found in the UK where not only is the level of payment among the lowest but where women must also prove they have had continuous work over the previous twenty-six weeks with the same employer at earnings above a certain threshold, thereby excluding many of those interviewed for this book who are in precarious and low-income work. Self-employed workers can opt in but only to an even less generous system. Moreover, many of the employer schemes, which are very important in the UK context with its low statutory provision, often exclude or disadvantage women with irregular work contracts, including the many care workers with zero-hour contracts and other forms of fixed-term contracts (see, also, Davies et al. 2022). In the case of the care worker, Lynn (UK05_Lynn), for example, her employer had calculated her maternity pay based on the lowest weekly hours she had worked rather than the full volume of her hours, leading to significant underpayment of maternity pay (Chapter 5). More just policies are found in France where self-employed workers have compulsory social insurance, in Denmark where entitlement requires just 120 hours of work in the preceding thirteen weeks with any number of employers, and in Slovenia where the statutory maternity leave is relatively generous, being the equivalent of forty-eight paid weeks (full-time equivalent) (Grimshaw et al. 2016).

Overall, systems of childcare, and maternity and parental leave that insufficiently integrate, and make provision for, the self-employed and other workers with precarious and irregular work are likely to inject tensions and obstacles into an otherwise stable and happy family life (not to mention delaying and possibly precluding any decision to have children), as family members struggle to support each other's unpaid labour and difficult working lives.

A second set of protections required to mitigate the damage caused by unpaid and precarious labour concern those areas of *social protection* dedicated to the adequate provision of sick pay, healthcare, and unemployment benefits (see Figure 8.1). Many of the workers interviewed for this book were not entitled to sick pay or healthcare (or were unaware of their entitlement—see, also, Weinkopf 2014 on the example of mini jobs in Germany) and said they often worked through their illnesses and injuries. This issue came to the fore during the Covid-19 pandemic and highlighted the enormous protection gaps among workers providing essential labour (ILO 2023). For employees, part of the problem is that sick pay and healthcare insurance are often tied to a minimum level of tenure in an organization, which biases against fixed-term and seasonal workers. Self-employed workers, including many of the dancers and online freelance workers interviewed for this book, are not entitled in most of Europe, although Denmark and Sweden are positive outliers with their systems of universal worker coverage (Eichhorst et al. 2013) and supplementary protections for specific occupations. The freelance dancer, Sandra (SE02_Sandra), for example, said that having injury protection via membership of the association Dansalliansen gave her 'a feeling of safety' (Chapter 4).

A major social protection gap affecting the workers represented in this book concerns access to adequate unemployment benefits. Workers suffer when hours, earnings, and job continuity thresholds exclude many work patterns, job types, and forms of employment. Self-employed workers are typically excluded from this important protection, although there are exceptions as we saw in the case of freelance dancers in Sweden who could be members of the insurance fund, Unionens A-kassa. This limited benefit provides some compensation for the many unpaid auditions, photo shoots, grant applications, and training sessions that arise between periods of paid work. Some countries are also better than others at providing unemployment benefits to help workers experiencing intermittent paid work and enabling them to accumulate rights to unemployment benefits rather than excluding them outright for failing to reach a given threshold of hours or income earned (Rubery et al. 2022). There is of course a potential two-way process because some countries require those in receipt of unemployment benefits to seek casual paid work. This can be viewed as encouraging the participation of disadvantaged workers in unpaid and precarious labour, or as providing a positive entry pathway into paid work, or as a means by which employers can seek subsidies in their support of unpaid and precarious labour.

A third set of protections requires the *strengthening of worker rights*, particularly for trade union representation and digital rights for all workers. A major theme in the interviews documented through Chapters 4, 5, and 6 is the real fear workers have about voicing complaints or contesting the status quo. Some dancers felt forced to quit where they experienced conflict. Care workers worried about the risk of harm to patients from a misguided emphasis on 'stopwatch care' or 'Minutenpflege', but in the absence of union representation felt powerless to speak up. And many of the online freelancers talked of being 'silenced' and discouraged from contesting algorithmic decisions for fear of future 'punishment'.

The risk for Europe is that growing segments of work become bastions for one-sided, unitarist models of work organization in which only one set of economic interests drive change. The necessary alternative is to establish workplaces in which a plurality of competing interests and ideas can flourish, and where participative representation is particularly assured for those workers who find themselves in relatively vulnerable and disadvantaged work situations (Grimshaw 2024). Regulations therefore ought to guarantee all workers, including self-employed freelancers (see Heery et al. 2004; Bertolini and Dukes 2021), the right to freedom of association to form and join a union (in line with International Labour Organization (ILO) conventions) and encourage social norms of mutual respect and commitment to dialogue between individual managers, employees, and freelancers, as well as formal channels of social dialogue between the relevant representative collective bodies.

Furthermore, workers reliant on income from digital labour platforms deserve the right to monitor, check, and correct all personal data relevant to systems of algorithmic performance ratings (including the right to share the data with their union representative) and ownership of work portfolios for use on and off any given platform (ILO 2019, 2022; Rani and Singh 2019; Grimshaw 2020). New regulations need to ensure all platform companies have policies on transparency and data protection, including what monitoring of workers is undertaken.

The final set of necessary protections needed to mitigate the damage caused by unpaid labour is the *strengthening of collective bargaining power*. Perhaps more than any other labour institution, encompassing structures for collective bargaining are best positioned to foster and sustain a fair organization of paid labour. Operating at multiple levels (workplace, company, sector, and domestic and global value chains) and inclusive of all forms of work, collective bargaining can even out the bargaining power between capital and labour; distribute the gains from income and productivity growth; give collective voice to the least powerful workers in society; combat discrimination on the grounds of gender, age, disability, race, religion, and sexuality; and guard against corrupt and socially irresponsible employer and client practices (ILO 2022).

The power of collective bargaining in specific country's institutional settings is evident from workers' experiences described in this book. In the Netherlands, trade unions representing salaried and freelance dancers leveraged a recent re-interpretation of competition law to bargain collectively with the employers' organization for minimum rates of pay for freelancers (equivalent to 150% of pay of salaried dancers when working alongside each other) and rules concerning working hours, which mitigate some, albeit not all, of the damage caused by unpaid labour (Chapter 4). In Germany, a sector-wide collective agreement for care workers provides a valuable wage scale that values and rewards skill development and guards against excessively exploitative employment arrangements, such as the zero-hour contracts and abandonment of pay progression structures among care organizations in the UK where collective agreements are scarce (Chapter 5). And, while not illustrated in Chapter 6, collective agreements can provide valuable protections for digital platform labour; examples include the agreement between Hilfr and 3F in Denmark and Foodora and the Transport Workers' Union in Norway (Jesnes et al. 2019).

Progress in extending collective bargaining powers to digital platform labour is subject to complex legal battles (that pitch definitions of worker and 'bogus self-employed' against the restrictions of competition law, see Countouris and De Stefano 2021) but is nevertheless advancing across Europe (Lamannis 2023). This is critical as the huge financing that powers digital platform companies ensures that they enjoy 'tremendous first-mover advantages over would be challengers' including trade unions and government legislators (Rahman and Thelen 2019: 184), threatening a long-term structural imbalance between winners and losers. Extending the protections offered by collective bargaining is the best means of preventing a race to the bottom of working conditions on the many freelance tournament platforms (such as Upwork) where practices of underbidding and undercharging for work are rife as workers struggle to win client tasks (Chapter 6; see, also, Pulignano, Dean, et al. 2023; Pulignano, Grimshaw, et al. 2023).

Collective bargaining is thus an important countervailing power for workers who experience the damage of unpaid labour, but it requires structures and strategies of trade unions and employers' associations to be inclusive of workers with insecure, irregular, and often informal attachments to paid work, such as those narrated in this book. This remains a challenge for many social partners in Europe; a meta-analysis of research found that one in four instances actually reinforced dualism by improving conditions for core workers 'with either no attempt to address precarity for peripheral workers or increased precarity for these workers' (Carver and Doellgast 2021). Inclusive strategies instead require: the extension of collective agreements to cover entire sectors so that all organizations are covered, including those operating on the fringes of the informal economy;

the forging of alliances with grassroots organizations with closer ties to disadvantaged workers, such as the migrant care workers in Germany for example who struggled to have their qualifications recognized (Chapter 5); and proactive challenges against narrow legal conceptualizations of employee so that more diverse forms of employment can be adequately protected by collective bargaining agreements. Despite the difficult terrain, when trade unions are able to develop solidaristic strategies of mobilization and organization, outcomes for labour are more likely to improve and all workers' experiences of exploitation reduced (see, also, Chan et al. 2019; Keizer et al. 2023).

Conclusion

Unpaid and precarious labour is causing real damage across Europe. This book has traced problems related to family instability, gender inequality, ethnic discrimination, poor physical and mental health, alienation, insecurity, and a struggle to keep up with living costs. Read as a whole, the compilation of workers' narratives about their paid and unpaid labour contributes to a growing sense that the pathway of development in many European countries risks being stuck in a phase of low growth, stagnant and falling living standards, a shrinking middle class, and growing problems of poverty among working people (e.g., Wade 2013; Vaughan-Whitehead 2016; Peña-Casas and Ghailani 2020; Franzen and Bahr 2024), potentially destabilizing democratic participation (Marinova 2022).

There is an urgent need therefore for new targeted action by governments in conjunction with employers and their associations, workers and trade unions, community organizations, and other activist groups. It is often said that labour markets have both allocative and distributive functions. However, the evidence from this book suggests that the former is failing, since too many workers are in poorly designed or second-choice jobs, having to work unpaid, and struggling with insufficient hours of paid work and limited opportunities for skill development, while the latter is generating a highly segmented pattern of unpaid labour with risks concentrated on women, those with least education, ethnic minorities, people with disabilities, and migrant workers.

With the goal of improving people's working lives and protecting them from exploitation, it is hoped that the sociological perspective advanced in this book, along with the rich empirical data, contributes to better designed labour protections in Europe. Governments, trade unions and employers should consider more carefully the different ways in which a suite of interlocking protections designed to mitigate the damage caused by unpaid and precarious labour can mutually shape the path of inclusive and sustainable economic development and with it the stability and security of society for all of Europe's citizens.

APPENDIX

Methodology and Epistemology

Exploring Unpaid Labour by 'Interpretative' and 'Grounded Theory' Methodology

We employed an interpretive methodology that examined the world through a critical investigative (i.e., *critical enquiry*) lens. The fundamental concept behind this methodology suggests that the researcher is intrinsic to the research process, interpreting data, and consequently cannot remain entirely impartial or detached from the research (Berger and Luckman 1966). Interpretivists focus on individual contextual settings, acknowledging that both reality and knowledge are not objective but rather shaped by individuals within that specific setting (Gadamer 1975; Bernstein 1983). Prioritizing how individuals perceive and interpret their surroundings, the interpretative approach thus directly relates to individuals' experiences and meanings within a given context, evaluating the many different ways individuals make sense of their experiences and the meanings they attribute to various aspects of life, culture, and social interactions. Interpretivists delve into the intricacies of these individual experiences and meanings in an attempt to comprehend the subjective nature of reality as constructed by individuals within their social and cultural frameworks. This perspective allows us to appreciate the richness and complexity of human experiences and the significance of personal interpretations in shaping our understanding of the world.

Our approach has examined how workers talk about their working lives, what types of meanings they build around them, how they understand the changes in the sphere of work, how they provide links between different aspects of work, how they link work to non-work (their private and family life), and how they distinguish (if at all) between paid and unpaid work activities. By emphasizing how workers understand and interpret these aspects, we assume that subjective experiences of unpaid labour are reflected in people's expectations, dependent on their position within the institutional (regulatory) and social and economic context. The institutional (regulatory) context encompasses the labour market, employment, and welfare (including family policy) regulatory systems, while the social context encompasses gender, ethnicity, age, education, and household composition (and other social networks) on the one hand, and financial factors, such as household income and (self-owned) property, on the other. These contexts shape the possibilities and/or constraints experienced by each individual.

We thus use 'cognitive empathy' (Small and McCrory Calarco 2022) or the degree to which the researcher manages to understand those observed in a way closely resembling the way the latter understand themselves in context. Gaining this kind of understanding—about what people perceive and experience, what it means for them, or what motivates them—was the objective of the qualitative study we have conducted.

We combined biographical narrative interviews (Schütze 2008) with audio work diaries in which respondents recorded their work activities, experiences, and reflections over a period of ten working days, providing our informants with sufficient space and time to share all information and knowledge around work (including the motivations of unpaid labour). Grounded Theory Methodology (GTM) (Glaser and Strauss 1967; Strauss and Corbin 1998), guided the whole qualitative research process, from sampling through data collection to data analysis, and when needed, to additional data collection and analysis. These methods were chosen to allow for a certain degree of theoretical and cognitive openness, while remaining sensitive towards new, unanticipated, and potentially surprising aspects of unpaid labour.

Theoretical Sampling

In line with the principles of theoretical sampling (Glaser and Strauss 1967), we selected informants across all three work areas examined (i.e., dance, residential care, and online platform work) differed in terms of age, gender, nationality, socio-economic and ethnic background, education, family constellation, stage of their career, and area of expertise. To gain access to dancers and care workers, we asked for help from trade unions active in these work areas. In the case of online freelancers, we used platform search engines to identify potential respondents who were then contacted via LinkedIn or Facebook (see Tables A.1, A.2, and A.3 for a detailed list of respondents from the different work areas or sectors).

We selected the work areas or occupational fields in a process of 'light theorisation' (Kessel and Bach 2014: 174) based on our prior knowledge of the major transformations in each area, resulting in the re-organization of paid/unpaid work activities for each of the occupational field we selected. This re-organization intersects with 'contested' values of regulatory regimes, production structures, and gender roles, expressed most (for example when compared to software developers) in care work but also present in the other two work areas. Looking at the three work areas or occupational fields and the prevalence of unpaid labour in them, we bear in mind the differences (described in Chapter 1) between employees and the self-employed, noting that employment relationships dominate in the field of residential care, while service provision relationships (involving project workers or freelancers) dominate in dance and online platform work.

Dance: unpaid work is traditionally conceived as being an entry route to longer term employment in dance, and in creative and cultural industries (CCIs) in general. This work is increasingly uncertain and competitive due to the growing dominance of self-employment, which often comes in the form of project work, and which implies taking responsibility for one's own creativity (Bologna and Fumagalli 1997; Siebert et al. 2013; Lorey 2015). Our analysis of this work area reveals that the majority of dancers are unable to recoup the time and effort invested in pursuing their careers through their chargeable fees. In many cases, their fees, when looked at in relation to the time and effort invested, are lower than the country minimum wage, meaning that they have to draw on other resources to make ends meet.

Residential care work: labour market and welfare reforms in Europe have targeted reducing the cost of care provision and other services through a mix of poorly paid and unpaid jobs in both private and public care providers (profit and not-for-profit). Unpaid work may be: unpaid overtime (Szebehely et al. 2017; McDonald et al. 2018); informally subsidized by minimum income schemes or community-service work supplied by recipients of unemployment benefits (Perlin 2012); the outcome of refamiliarization (Simonazzi 2009). It covers core functions (Baines et al. 2017), with employers expecting workers (predominantly women) to take on unpaid work as an expression of their 'love towards others' (Lewchuk et al. 2015; Duffy 2017; Hayes 2017).

Online platform work: a myriad projects and tasks seek input from unpaid 'citizens' providing digital labour (e.g., to map croplands, to build tech products in marathon coding sessions (hackathons), to upload player-produced modifications for videogames) (Cherry 2016; Ekbia and Nardi 2017). Freelancers have to be available when requested (Berg 2016), the work may involve long hours (Pulignano, Grimshaw, et al. 2023), and it may be unpaid either because platforms' terms of service allow unsatisfied customers to retain a product for free without having to provide an explanation (Aloisi et al. 2017) or because unpaid work is a prerequisite to accessing paid work (D'Cruz and Noronha 2016).

The country-based selection per work area reflects both the cross-country institutional diversity regarding regulatory (including social) settings and the economic relevance of each work area within a particular national economy:

Sweden and the Netherlands for dance, whereby dancers have experienced a drastic reduction in public funding in the latter in comparison to Sweden.

The United Kingdom (UK) and Germany for residential care work, whereby care workers in the former have experienced an increasingly neoliberal path, caused by more extensive privatization than in Germany.

Belgium, France, Italy, the Netherlands, and Poland for online platform work. We specifically selected freelancers with different occupations (information technology (IT), graphic design, translation, copyrighting) from these countries and across four platforms (i.e., Upwork, AddLance, Malt, and Jellow) to pick up similarities and differences across contexts.

Data Collection: Biographical Narrative Interviews

We used biographical narrative interviews to focus on workers' lived experiences of work expectations (i.e., in relation to their overall work and life situation), shedding light on how a worker 'makes sense' of the dimensions of the 'ideal worker' norm governing the conduct of work and life, and on their capacity to order specific events within a medium- to long-term perspective (Riessman 1993). When conducting biographical narrative interviews, we started by asking our informants to tell us about their current and past work experiences against the backdrop of their life histories. Instead of entering the field with preconceived hypotheses and assumptions, we kept the questions open, seeking a deeper understanding of work, both paid and unpaid, and the motivations for performing it. We thus define narratives as being crucial for understanding how people imbue their experiences with meaning (Cinque et al. 2021).

We started each interview with an introduction, explaining that we were interested in both the work and the life experiences of our interviewees. In the narrative part, they were given time to talk about their life-work experiences, while in the semi-structured part they were asked about unpaid labour, their work conditions, and work expectations, and about how they conducted their work. We did not interrupt the narrations of our interviewees with any further questions arising from the encoding asked later (see Vignette A.1).

Vignette A.1 Unveiling life through work: a biographical narrative open interview

Mission: to delve into the intertwining stories of work and life, to understand how individuals navigated the complex terrain of their careers, and to unearth the narratives that shaped their professional journeys.

Format: The interviewer introduced her-/himself, emphasizing the keen interest in both work and life experiences. The opening question was a gateway to their stories: 'Could you tell me about your work experiences within the context of your life history, from when you started working until now?'. The interviewer listened attentively as participants intertwined their life narratives with their careers. From early influences to serendipitous moments, their stories painted rich tapestries of journeys shaped by family, upbringing, and unexpected turns. The interviewer delved into participants' class backgrounds, prior skills, and the alignment of initial expectations with the realities of the job market. Their current livelihoods were evaluated, uncovering joys and challenges alike. The exploration extended to competitive dynamics in diverse work areas and the pressures endured, including the burden of unpaid labour. The interviewer learned of long hours, work-life balance struggles, and relentless pursuit of success. As the interview concluded, the interviewer posed additional questions to deepen understanding. These interviews were not mere data collection but windows into the intricate dance between life and work. Each interview revealed a unique narrative of resilience, ambition, and the complex interplay of life and work.

The open narrative interview format allowed informants to go into details not only about their work experiences, but also about the biographical and social costs they associate with doing unpaid labour, consequently allowing us to view them from a longitudinal and processual perspective (Schütze 2008; Neale 2021). In the pilot phase, we also conducted semi-structured expert interviews with policymakers, trade unionists, and academics in order to expand our understanding of each work field. The knowledge shared with us, together with our own desk research, helped us clarify the sampling criteria for each work area, occupation, and country involved. Data collection followed GTM in the sense that it evolved based on the ongoing analysis (see Vignette A.2).

Vignette A.2 Data collection through GTM

The GTM process was marked by three sequential yet interconnected steps.

First, we engaged in open coding, meticulously dissecting narrative interviews and audio diaries. Each transcript underwent line-by-line analysis, and codes emerged like pieces of a jigsaw puzzle, capturing the essence of participants' experiences.

Second, axial coding entered the stage. We organized these codes into broader categories, creating a structured framework that included 'paid work', 'unpaid work', 'unpaid work in employment', 'unpaid work in self-employment', and more. This step provided a higher level perspective, allowing us to see patterns and relationships within the data.

Third, the final step, was selective coding where we honed in on 'unpaid work' across various sectors and country settings. The evolving analysis and codes influenced our selection of subsequent participants, enriching our exploration. New layers of insight were continuously added to our evolving theoretical framework.

In essence, our data collection and analysis were not separate entities but partners in discovery. As the analysis evolved, so did our understanding, shaping our research journey and enriching the tapestry of our findings.

Data Collection: Work Diaries

The primary method of data collection were biographical narrative interviews, with audio work diaries as the secondary method. Diaries complemented the interviews by validating what had been said and giving further analytical insights (Morse and Niehaus 2009). While the interviews enabled a deeper understanding of work experiences and the meaning-making practices of interviewees, the work diaries allowed us to examine patterns of action within a specific timeframe, offering rich, detailed, and contextualized accounts of a working day (Crozier and Cassell 2016) through which researchers were able to capture real-time activities (Whiting et al. 2018), how many hours were worked, and which tasks were remunerated. Work diaries consisted of the audio recording (on smartphones) of work experiences for ten successive working days, with a focus on working time and pay, job tasks, forms of proximate unpaid labour, as well as the emotions experienced at work. Subsequently sent to one of the researchers via the Belnet secure transfer network, the diaries provided highly detailed meanings and accounts of respondents' day-to-day life. Each work diary started with a broad qualitative question asking respondents to describe their working day (namely, the time they started and finished work, what was done within that period and why, for how long, and for whom). Diaries covered three other topics: respondents' experiences of autonomy (what to do, when to do it, how much, how fast), pay (how much was earned, the form of payment, any non-pay extras), and whether they performed any task 'for free' and providing concrete examples. The audio format for the diaries was chosen as it was easier to handle by respondents than a written diary (Harvey 2011). Moreover, we expected oral accounts to be spontaneous and rich (Crozier and Cassell 2016).

Narrative Interviews and Work Diaries in Numbers

Primary data collection included 129 biographical narrative interviews: twenty-six with dancers (twelve collected in the Netherlands and fourteen in Sweden), thirty-nine interviews with workers in residential elderly care (twenty in Germany and nineteen in the UK), and sixty-four interviews with freelancers working on four different online platforms (fourteen in Belgium, fifteen in France, fourteen in the Netherlands, fourteen in Italy, and seven in Poland). While some respondents (N = 38) consented to both an autobiographical narrative interview and a work diary, others (N = 91), consented solely to an interview. We thus collected thirty-eight audio diaries: eight in dance, seven in residential care, and twenty-three in online platform work (see Tables A.1, A.2, and A.3).

The biographical narrative interviews were conducted in the interviewees' native languages: Dutch, French, German, Swedish, Italian, Polish, and English, as our research team was fluent in these languages. All interviews were professionally transcribed and translated into English (the shared language of the research team). Interviewers wrote detailed summaries in English of each interview, including context and observations, subsequently sharing them within the research team. This improved the understanding of data, with the native speaker providing contextual knowledge and interpretation.

Interviews were conducted partly face to face (with physical distancing) and partly online, via Zoom (with subscription) between April 2020 and January 2021, a period during which Covid-19 pandemic restrictions were in place.

Interviews lasted between ninety minutes and four hours (average two hours). This provided us with 258 hours of exposure, an important precondition for good quality in qualitative fieldwork research (Small and McCrory Calarco 2022: 18–20). Respondents provided information on their demographic profiles, earnings, working hours, household composition, and job characteristics, providing useful socio-demographic background information. Given the established salience of class-based resources in access to work (see Brook et al. 2018), we asked each participant to self-identify in class terms (Reay 1998) and in the types of resources available, as in Savage et al. (2005). Securing and perpetuating access to economic capital (Crompton 1998: 149), resources could be institutional (regulatory settings related to welfare benefits and childcare provisions), financial (income and property), social (socially reproductive labour and networks), or cultural (educational credentials and competencies acquired through the family). We were also able to assess class-based resources through narrative analysis, such as a family's financial support in relation to training, unpaid work, and unemployment; parents' occupation and family lifestyle (place of residence, holidays, and activities); as well as networks of family and friends. This informed our understanding of our interviewees' professional choices and their decisions to stay in or to quit a job.

Data Analysis and Theoretical Coding

Data analysis followed GTM in the sense that the data collection evolved based on the ongoing analysis. It proceeded in three sequential (but not necessarily linear) steps: (1) open coding of

Table A.1 Description of sample in dance

No.	Code and name	Gender	Age	Ethnicity	Class background	Professional category	Diary
1	NL01_Anis	M	30	Non-white German	Lower middle class	Freelance dancer	
2	NL02_Jane	F	38	White Canadian	Middle class	Dancer employed in a state-funded dance company for 15 years	
3	NL03_Lisa	F	36	White	Upper middle class	Freelance dancer who has been working for several companies in France, Israel, Spain	
4	NL04_Sara	F	36	White	Middle class	Freelance dancer	X
5	NL05_Leen	F	28	White	Middle class	Freelance dancer, dance teacher, and photographer	
6	NL06_Alessandro	M	31	White Italian	Middle class	Freelance dancer from an artistic family (mother a painter), studying piano & an engineering graduate	X
7	NL07_Francesco	M	34	White	Working class	Freelance dancer	X
8	NL08_Mia	F	32	White	Lower middle class	Freelance dancer	
9	NL09_Alba	F	41	White	Working class	Freelance dancer	
10	NL10_Dominika	F	32	White	Middle class	Freelance dancer	
11	NL11_Bart	M	40	White	Middle class	Dancer employed in a dance school	
12	NL12_ Jasmin	F	28	Non-white	Middle class	Dancer employed in a dance school	
13	SE02_Sandra	F	32	White	Middle class	Freelance dancer graduated ballet academy in Stockholm, dance pedagogue, and choreographer. Side jobs (i.e., nanny, waitress, shop assistant, model)	
14	SE03_Astrid	F	33	White	Middle class	Dancer employed in a state-funded dance organization	
15	SE04_Jon	M	41	White	Middle class	Dancer employed in a state-funded dance organization	

Continued

Table A.1 *Continued*

No.	Code and name	Gender	Age	Ethnicity	Class background	Professional category	Diary
16	SE06_Arianna	F	28	White Italian	Middle class	Freelance dancer, obtained small public grants	
17	SE07_Iris	F	28	White	Middle class	Dancer employed in a state-funded dance organization	
18	SE08_Nikola	NB	31	White	Middle class	Freelance dancer	X
19	SE10_Isabelle	F	23	White	Middle class	Freelance dancer	X
20	SE11_Fabiano	M	50	White Italian	Working class	Dancer previously employed on annual contracts, but now a freelance dancer following non-renewal of contract due to injury. Previous casual dance contracts in France (plus side jobs). Reliant on social security system (housing benefit)	
21	SE12_Hiroko	F	44	Non-white Japanese origin	Middle class	Dancer previously employed in a state-funded dance organization. Now a freelance dancer and choreographer with her own dance school in the small town where she lives	X
22	SE18_Filip	M	27	Non-white	Middle class	Dancer employed in a state-funded dance organization	
23	SE21_Nadja	F	30	Non-white	Lower middle class	Freelance dancer in musicals, side job as a shop assistant in a clothing chain store	X
24	SE22_Anna	F	39	White	Lower middle class	Freelance dancer finding it difficult to stay in ballet; doing side jobs	
25	SE27_Elias	M	29	White	Middle class	Dancer employed in a state-funded dance organization	
26	SE28_Jaime	M	32	Non-white Philippine origin	Middle class	Freelance dancer, dance teacher, choreographer, worked off-stage as a cameraman and on-stage as a dancer	X

Source: Author's elaboration.

Table A.2 Description of sample in residential care

No.	Code and name	Gender	Age	Ethnicity	Class background	Professional category	Diary
1	DE01_Renata	F	55	White Polish origin	Working class	Care assistant with a private care provider	
2	DE02_Beate	F	61	White	Middle class	Care assistant with a private care provider	X
3	DE03_Doreen	F	28	White	Working class	Care assistant with a private care provider	
4	DE04_Sonja	F	52	White	Lower middle class	Care assistant with a private care provider	
5	DE05_Sarah	F	59	White	Working class	Care assistant with a private care provider	
6	DE06_Zarima	F	41	Roma from the Balkans	Working class	Care assistant with a private care provider	
7	DE07_Julia	F	42	White	Working class	Care assistant in various private care providers for dementia, ranging from large scale to small scale	X
8	DE08_Susanne	F	52	White	Working class	Care assistant in a public care provider	
9	DE09_Rashid	M	29	Non-white Pakistani origin	Working class	Care assistant with a private care provider	
10	DE10_Ruby	F	62	Non-white Philippines origin	Lower middle class	Care assistant with a private care provider	
11	DE11_Sinem	F	39	Non-white Turkish origin	Working class	Care assistant in a public care provider	
12	DE12_Marianne	F	55	White	Working class	Care assistant in a public care provider	
13	DE13_Nele	F	53	White	Working class	Care assistant and nurse with a voluntary care provider	X
14	DE14_Maggie	F	62	White	Working class	Care assistant with a public care provider	
15	DE15_Michaela	F	60	White	Lower middle class	Care assistant with a public care provider	
16	DE16_ Nadja	F	56	White	Working class	Care assistant with a private care provider	X
17	DE17_Özlem	F	45	Non-white Turkish origin	Working class	Care assistant with a private care provider	
18	DE18_Eva	F	53	White	Working class	Care assistant with a private care provider	
19	DE19_Alina	F	34	White	Working class	Care assistant with a private care provider	

Continued

Table A.2 *Continued*

No.	Code and name	Gender	Age	Ethnicity	Class background	Professional category	Diary
20	DE20_Lilly	F	20	White	Middle class	Care assistant with a private care provider	
21	UK01_Sophia	F	38	White	Working class	Carer with a voluntary care provider	
22	UK02_Mary	F	41	White	Working class	Carer with a private care provider	X
23	UK03_Diana	F	33	White	Working class	Carer with a private care provider	X
24	UK04_Mauve	F	25	White	Working class	Carer with a private care provider	
25	UK05_Lynn	F	33	White	Lower middle class	Carer with a private care provider	
26	UK06_Ciara	F	19	White	Working class	Carer with a voluntary care provider	
27	UK07_Marc	M	54	White German origin	Lower middle class	Carer with a voluntary care provider	
28	UK08_Monica	F	52	White	Working class	Carer with a voluntary care provider	
29	UK09_Joan	F	54	White	Middle class	Carer with a private care provider	
30	UK10_Matt	M	53	Non-White Caribbean origin	Working class	Carer with a private care provider	
31	UK11_Marika	F	43	White Latvia origin	Middle class	Carer with a private care provider, experience in NHS	
32	UK12_Nelly	F	58	White	Lower middle class	Carer with a private care provider	
33	UK13_Lina	F	64	White	Working class	Carer with a private care provider	
34	UK14_Marta	F	34	White	Working class	Carer with a private care provider	
35	UK15_Tina	F	64	White	Working class	Carer with a private care provider, previously domiciliary, informal	
36	UK16_Marianne	F	62	White	Lower middle class	Live-in carer	
37	UK17_Tara	F	57	White	Lower middle class	Carer with a private care provider for people with disabilities	X
38	UK18_Edith	F	67	Non-white Caribbean origin	Working class	Carer with a private care provider	
39	UK19_Marija	F	37	White Croatian origin	Lower middle class	Carer with a private care provider	

Source: Author's elaboration.

Table A.3 Description of sample in online freelancers platform work

No.	Code and name	Gender	Age	Professional category	Platform	Class background	Work diary
1	IT07_Ugo	M	40	IT & graphic design	AddLance	Middle class	
2	IT26_Angelo	M	27			Middle class	X
3	IT08_Marta	F	43	Translation & copywriting		Middle class	
4	IT09_Marina	F	39			Middle class	
5	IT16_Carla	F	46			Middle class	
6	IT21_Nadia	F	61			Working class	X
7	IT19_Sabrina	F	45			Middle class	
8	BE05_Jeff	M	40	IT & graphic design	Jellow	Lower middle class	
9	BE12_Ben	M	40			Middle class	
10	BE14_Jasper	M	32			Middle class	X
11	BE01_Claire	F	25			Middle class	
12	NL04_Dirk	M	34			Middle class	
13	NL06_James	M	30			Middle class	X
14	BE44_Gloria	F	38	Translation & copywriting		Working class	X
15	BE10_Jamal	M	66			Working class	
16	BE13_Kaat	F	26			Lower middle class	X
17	BE46_Romi	F				Middle class	
18	NL07_Jamie	F	57			Upper middle class	X
19	NL10_Martine	F	30			Middle class	
20	NL05_Stefanos	M	31	IT & graphic design	Jellow and Upwork	Middle class	
21	NL03_Hendrik	M	26			Middle class	X
22	BE15_Marlies	F	22			Middle class	X
23	FR09_August	M	29		Malt	Middle class	
24	FR13_Pierre	M	22			Middle class	X
25	FR15_Fanny	F	20			Middle class	X
26	FR03_Marisol	F	24	Translation & copywriting		Middle class	
27	FR04_Milena	F	47			Middle class	X
28	FR05_Max	M	47			Lower middle class	
29	FR19_Nunzio	M	35			Middle class	X
30	FR27_Jule	F	40			Lower middle class	X
31	BE02_Mathieu	M	32	IT & graphic design	Upwork	Lower middle class	
32	FR02_Paulo	M	38			Working class	X

Continued

Table A.3 *Continued*

No.	Code and name	Gender	Age	Professional category	Platform	Class background	Work diary
33	FR28_Deepa	F	25			Lower middle class	
34	IT02_Marco	M	38			Lower middle class	
35	IT04_Danilo	M	37			Lower middle class	
36	IT29_Zuzka	F	22			Working class	
37	NL03_Dano	M	30			Lower middle class	X
38	NL02_Camila	F	37			Lower middle class	
39	NL06_James	M	27			Middle class	
40	FL03_Krysztof	M	26			Upper middle class	
41	FL28_Nina	F	27			Lower middle class	
42	BE01_Claire	F	35	translation & copywriting		Middle class	
43	BE02_Laura	F	32			Lower middle class	
44	BE01_Diana	F	33			Middle class	
45	BE41_Sigrid	F	30			Middle class	X
46	FR01_Marc	M	27			Middle class	
47	FR06_Bel	F	40			Middle class	X
48	FR16_Namita	F	30			Lower middle class	X
49	FR17_Oliver	M	30			Lower middle class	
50	FR18_Timothy	M	24			Middle class	X
51	IT01_Mirko	M	40			Middle class	
52	IT03_Jessica	F	26			Lower middle class	X
53	IT25_Ludovica	F	26			Lower middle class	
54	IT27_Viola	M	25			Working class	
55	NL01_Jan	M	43			Middle class	
56	NL02_Marie	F	20			Middle class	
57	NL08_Lorenza	F	32			Middle class	
58	NL09_Sasha	F	28			Middle class	
59	NL08_Alma	F	20			Middle class	X
60	PL02_Matylda	F	38			Working class	
61	PL04_Anita	F	30			Working class	X
62	PL06_Barbara	F	36			Middle class	
63	PL07_Anna	F	31			Lower middle class	
64	PL08_Hanna	F	51			Middle class	

Source: Author's elaboration.

narrative interviews and audio diaries, with each transcript meticulously analysed line by line and labelled with a code; (2) axial coding of both data sources where we grouped the codes into larger categories, such as 'paid work' and 'unpaid work', 'unpaid work in employment', 'unpaid work in self-employment', etc.; (3) selective coding of interviews and work diaries where we focused on 'unpaid work' across all sectors and country settings. In this sense, data collection and data analysis proceeded together, with the ongoing analysis and the developed codes guiding the selection of subsequent participants and adding new data slices to the theorization exercise. During our analysis, we identified the following forms of unpaid or underpaid labour time:

(1) In *creative dance work*: unpaid preparation and training time (e.g., daily training in the case of dancers, intensive rehearsals before premières); unpaid rest time (e.g., after exhausting shows and tours); unpaid travel time to various locations for shootings or shows; unpaid extra tasks (e.g., ranging from installing stage lighting to stage cleaning); time needed for relational work (e.g., networking and maintaining relationships with choreographers, directors, and funders over time); time needed for self-marketing (e.g., keeping one's online profile active; regularly posting samples of work; participation in social events).
(2) In *residential care work*: unpaid extra time (e.g., coming in early and leaving late) and underpaid extra workloads (e.g., a single worker doing the job of two workers); working through normal breaks (e.g., baking cakes and doing shopping for residents during a lunch break); time needed to perform emotional labour (e.g., having a cup of tea with a resident who is upset); time needed for extra tasks (e.g., washing their own uniforms as well as resident's clothes, towels, and bedsheets during Covid-19).
(3) In *online platform work*: unpaid working time in the form of searching and applying for new tasks (jobs); time needed to prepare samples of work (e.g., when applying for jobs); unpaid waiting time between paid tasks; time dedicated to admin work (e.g., invoicing, chasing clients who didn't pay); time needed for relational work (e.g., networking, maintaining relationships with clients over time, regular communication with clients); time devoted to updating one's skills (e.g., studying for new certificates); time needed to deal with extra requests of clients when the initial job was completed (e.g., extra tasks performed for free in the very last moment); time needed for self-marketing (e.g., keeping one's online profile active).

We used thematic coding. This involved developing codes, themes, and theoretical constructs following the process suggested by Auerbach and Silverstein (2003). Accordingly, the initial codebook included two overarching concepts as general reflections on the study. Performed using NVivo12, coding was done independently by each researcher and then systematically discussed to identify nuances and significant meanings in the data. Agreement between the coders was reached through constant interaction and joint coding of some cases (both interview and diary transcripts), though no intercoder reliability checks were performed, such as percent agreement, Chi-Square, Intraclass Correlation Coefficient, or Cohen's Kappa (cf. Olson et al. 2016). This was because the aim was not to quasi-quantify the analysis of qualitative data, but to allow patterns and themes to emerge from the data, given the interpretative qualitative framework (e.g., Braun and Clarke 2006). We worked within an epistemological framework which aimed not to reveal 'universal objective facts but to apply their theoretical expertise to interpret and communicate the diversity of perspectives on a given topic' so that 'researcher reflexivity and active personal engagement with the data were considered as resources' (Yardley 2008 in O'Connor and Joffe 2020: 4).

As reported above, coding consisted of rounds of initial open coding and subsequent axial coding (along the significant concepts) to uncover the key factors possibly explaining the occurrence of the phenomenon (i.e., unpaid labour) in question. In particular, the ongoing analytical movement between the institutional and socio-economic context, with a specific reference to the resources to build resilience, and the workers' lived experiences of the extent of unpaid labour steering precarity helped us understand the relationships between unpaid labour, inequality, and precarious work. Interviews were coded line by line, and open codes were broad. When new codes emerged, they were added to the codebook. The focus was then narrowed down, with the second round of axial coding used to determine the key drivers of different outcomes (e.g., inequality in precarious work). Codes from the first stage were reassembled into overarching categories to theoretically saturate the core (open) and related concepts. The argument is illustrated by quotes taken both from the narrative and the semi-structured parts of interviews. The analysis of the narrative part provided the overall interpretative structure, while the semi-structured parts served for detailing and clarification.

The thematic analysis of the work diaries was undertaken separately for each work area since the qualitative interviews sometimes revealed different forms of unpaid labour in the three areas. With regard to the diaries, percentages were calculated by examining per platform the number of working days in which a form of unpaid labour was mentioned by our respondents, and then dividing this number by the total number of working days (i.e., ten) which each respondent filled out in the diary. Work diaries were fully transcribed and translated to uncover variations across platforms. This was all done via a thematic analysis of the diaries (Braun and Clarke 2006; Essén 2008) developed by moving from each code (i.e., forms of unpaid work) within the data towards revealing any differences over time.

Validity and Reflexivity in Qualitative Research

In qualitative research, validity refers to the credibility, trustworthiness, and accuracy of the findings or conclusions drawn from the research process. Unlike quantitative research where validity often refers to whether an instrument measures what it is intended to measure, qualitative research focuses on the rigour and trustworthiness of the research process itself. Our study relied on several types of test in order to build and ensure validity.

Being aware that generalizability and transferability in qualitative research cannot be assessed by referring to the extent to which the findings can be applied or transferred to other contexts or settings beyond the immediate study (e.g., if two people interview the same person at a different moment in time but using the same list of questions, they will get different answers, see Small and McCrory Calarco 2022: 13), we have used credibility to establish the authenticity and believability of the data collected by accurately representing the experiences and viewpoints of the participants (Patton 2014). This often involves the researcher employing different techniques, such as member checking where participants review and confirm the accuracy of the findings; triangulation by using multiple sources or methods to confirm findings; maintaining an audit trail by documenting the research process thoroughly; and employing reflexivity by reflecting on the researcher's own biases and how they might influence the study (Creswell 1994). In particular, reflexivity focuses on a researcher's objectivity and neutrality, ensuring that the findings are not influenced by his/her biases or preferences but rather are grounded in the data collected (Silverman 2000).

The research presented in this book used reflexivity, in combination with multiple member checking, peer debriefing, and audit trails to guarantee validity. Accordingly, researchers acknowledged the biases, values, and assumptions and critically reflected on how these might have influenced the research process and findings. They did this by keeping a reflexive journal or memo, helping them maintain awareness of potential biases by documenting thoughts and feelings throughout the study. Moreover, this research is the result of the joint effort of young researchers tasked with reviewing and providing feedback on the findings. This helped validate the accuracy and interpretation of the collected data. The lead researcher discussed the research process and findings with the two co-researchers directly involved in data collection and with peers not directly involved in the study. This external perspective offered insights and challenged potential biases. All research decisions, procedures, and interpretations were documented in depth. This audit trail allowed us to retrace the steps and decisions taken during the study, ensuring transparency and reducing bias.

References

Acevedo, Bianca. 2020. 'The Basics of Sensory Processing Sensitivity'. In *The Highly Sensitive Brain, In*, edited by Acevedo, Bianca, 1–15. Cambridge, MA: Academic Press.

Acker, John. 1990. 'Hierarchies, Jobs, Bodies: A Theory of Gendered Organizations'. *Gender & Society* 4(2): 139–58.

Ackroyd, Stephen and Thompson, Paul. 1999. *Organizational Misbehavior*, 2nd edition. London: Sage Academic Books.

Agarwala, Rina. 2013. *Informal Labor, Formal Politics, and Dignified Discontent in India.* Cambridge: Cambridge University Press.

Alberti, Gabriella, Bessa, Ioulia, Hardy, Kathy, Trappmann, Vera, and Umney, Charles. 2018. 'In, against and beyond Precarity: Work in Insecure Times'. *Work, Employment and Society* 32: 447–57.

Alimahomed-Wilson, Jake and Reese, Ellen. 2020. *The Cost of Free Shipping: Amazon in the Global Economy.* London: Pluto Press.

Aloisi, Antonio, De Stefano, Valerio, and Silberman, Maria S. 2017. *A Manifesto to Reform the Gig Economy.* http://www.pagina99.it/2017/05/29/a-manifesto-to-reform-the-gig-economy/ (accessed 20 May 2020).

Antcliff, Valerie, Saundry Richard, and Stuart, Mark. 2007. 'Networks and Social Capital in the UK Television Industry: The Weakness of Weak Ties'. *Human Relations* 60(2): 371–93.

Ashforth, Blake E. and Kreiner, Glen E. 2013. 'Profane or Profound? Finding Meaning in Dirty Work'. In *Purpose and Meaning in the Workplace*, edited by Bryan Dik, J., Byrne Zinta, S., and Steger, Michael F., 127–50. Washington, DC: American Psychological Association.

Auerbach, Carl and Silverstein, Louise B. 2003. *An Introduction to Coding and Analysis.* New York: New York University Press.

Ayala-Hurtado, Elena. 2021. 'Narrative Continuity/Rupture: Projected Professional Futures amid Pervasive Employment Precarity'. *Work and Occupations* 49(1): 45–78.

Bá, Stefano. 2019. 'The Struggle to Reconcile Precarious Work and Parenthood: The Case of Italian "Precarious Parents"'. *Work, Employment and Society* 33(5): 812–28.

Baccaro, Lucio and Howell, Chris. 2017. *Trajectories of Neoliberal Transformation: European Industrial Relations since the 1970s.* Cambridge: Cambridge University Press.

Baines, Donna. 2004. 'Caring for Nothing: Work Organization and Unwaged Labour in Social Services'. *Work, Employment and Society* 18(2): 267–95.

Baines, Donna and Broek, Diane van den. 2017. 'Coercive Care: Control and Coercion in the Restructured Care Workplace.' The British Journal of Social Work 47(1): 125–42.

Banks, Mark. 2006. 'Moral Economy and Cultural Work'. *Sociology* 40(3): 455–72.

Banks, Sarah. 2004. *Ethics, Accountability and the Social Professions.* Basingstoke: Palgrave Macmillan.

Barney, Jay and Felin, Teppo. 2013. 'What Are Microfoundations?'. *The Academy of Management Perspectives* 27(2): 138–55.

Barnett, Michael L. and Grabowski, David C. 2020. 'Nursing Homes Are Ground Zero for COVID-19 Pandemic'. *JAMA Health Forum* 1(3): 1261–9.

Bartelheimer, Peter, Leßmann, Ortrud, and Matiaske, Wenzel. 2012. 'The Capability Approach: A New Perspective for Labor Market and Social Policies?'. *Management Revue* 23(2): 93–7.

Bauder, Harald. 2001. 'Culture in the Labor Market: Segmentation Theory and Perspectives of Place'. *Progress in Human Geography* 25(1): 37–52.

BBC. 2020. https://www.bbc.com/news/uk-england-61227709.

Beckman, Christine M. and Mazmanian, Melissa. 2020. *Dreams of the Overworked: Living, Working, and Parenting in the Digital Age.* Stanford, CA: Stanford University Press.

Been, Wike and Keune, Maarten. 2022. Bringing Labour Market Flexibilization under Control? Marginal Work and Collective Regulation in the Creative Industries in the Netherlands. *European Journal of Industrial Relations.* Advance online publication. https://doi.org/10.1177/09596801221127109.

Bell, David, Henderson, David, and Lemmon, Elisabeth. 2020. 'Deaths in Scottish Care Homes and Covid-19'. *Scottish Centre for Administrative Data Research,* 23 July. https://www.scadr.ac.uk/deaths-scottish-care-homes-andcovid-19.

Bendix, Reinhard and Lipset, Seymour M. 1967. *Class, Status, and Power: Social Stratification in Comparative Perspective.* London: Routledge & Kegan Paul.

Berg, Janine. 2015. *Labour Markets, Institutions and Inequality: Building Just Societies in the 21st Century.* London: Edward Elgar Publishing.

Berg, Janine. 2016. Income Security in the On-Demand Economy: Findings and Policy Lessons from a Survey of Crowdworkers. Geneva: International Labour Office.

Berg, Janine. 2019. 'Protecting Workers in the Digital Age: Technology, Outsourcing and the Growing Precariousness of Work', May 31. Geneva: ILO.

Berger, Peter and Luckmann, Thomas. 1964. *Social Construction of Reality: A Treatise in* the Sociology of Knowledge. New York: Anchor Books.

Berger, Peter and Luckmann, Thomas. 1966. *The Social Construction of Reality A Treatise in the Sociology of Knowledge.* London: Penguins Book.

Bernstein, Richard J. 1983. B*eyond Objectivism and Relativism: Science, Hermeneutics, and Praxis.* Chicago: University of Pennsylvania Press.

Bertolini, Alessio and Dukes, Ruth. 2021. 'Trade Unions and Platform Workers in the UK: Worker Representation in the Shadow of the Law'. *Industrial Law Journal* 50(4): 662–88.

Bessa, I., Joyce, S., Neumann, D., Stuart, M., Trappmann, V., and Umney, C. 2022. 'A Global Analysis of Worker Protest in Digital Labour Platforms'. ILO Working Paper 70, International Labour Organization.

Blair-Loy, Mary. 2003. *Competing Devotions: Career and Family among Women Executives.* Cambridge, MA: Harvard University Press.

Blair-Loy, Mary. 2010. 'Moral Dimensions of the Work-Family Nexus'. In *Handbook of the Sociology of Morality,* edited by Hitlin, Steven and Vaisey, Stephen, 439–53. New York: Springer.

Boeri, Tito, Giupponi, Giulia, Alan B. Krueger, Machin, Stephen. 2020. 'Solo Self-Employment and Alternative Work Arrangements: A Cross-Country Perspective on the Changing Composition of Jobs'. *Journal of Economic Perspectives* 34(1): 170–95.

Bologna, Segio and Fumagalli, Antonio. 1997. *Il lavoro autonomo di seconda generazione,* 2nd edition. Milano: Feltrinelli.

Boltanski, Luc and Chiapello, Eve. 2018. *The New Spirit of Capitalism.* New York: Verso.

Bolton, Sharon C. 2005. *Emotion Management in the Workplace.* London: Palgrave.

Bourdieu, Pierre. 1984. *Distinction.* London: Routledge.

Bourdieu, Pierre. 1986. 'The Forms of Capital'. In *Handbook of Theory and Research for the Sociology of Education,* edited by Richardson, James, 241–58. Westport, CT: Greenwood.

Bourdieu, Pierre. 1989. 'Social Space and Symbolic Power'. *Sociological Theory* 7: 14–25.

Bourdieu, Pierre. 1994. *The Field of Cultural Production.* New York: Columbia University Press.

Bourdieu, Pierre and Wacquant, Löic. 1992. *An Invitation to Reflexive Sociology*. Chicago: Chicago University Press.

Brannen, Julia. 2005. 'Time and the Negotiation of Work-Family Boundaries: Autonomy or Illusion?'. *Time & Society* 14(1): 113–31.

Braun, Virginia and Clarke, Victoria. 2006. 'Using Thematic Analysis in Psychology'. *Qualitative Research in Psychology* 3(2): 77–101.

Brook, Orian, O'Brien, David, and Taylor, Mark. 2018. 'Panic! Social Class, Taste and Inequalities in the Creative Industries'. Report. University of Edinburgh.

Brown, Kenneth and Korczynski, Marek. 2017. 'The Caring Self within a Context of Increasing Rationalisation: The Enduring Importance of Clients for Home Care Aides'. *Sociology* 51(4): 833–49.

Bundesagentur für Arbeit. 2022. https://www.arbeitsagentur.de/ (accessed 27 October 2023).

Butler, Judith. 2012. 'Precarious Life, Vulnerability, and the Ethics of Cohabitation'. *The Journal of Speculative Philosophy* 26(2): 134–51.

Butterick, Mark and Charlwood, Andy. 2021. 'HRM and the COVID-19 Pandemic: How Can We Stop Making a Bad Situation Worse?'. *Human Resource Management Journal* 31(4): 847–56.

Campbell, Peter, O'Brien, Dave, and Mark, Taylor. 2019. 'Cultural Engagement and the Economic Performance of the Cultural and Creative Industries: An Occupational Critique'. *Sociology* 53(2): 347–67.

Carver, Laura and Doellgast, Virginia. 2021. 'Dualism or Solidarity? Conditions for Union Success in Regulating Precarious Work'. *European Journal of Industrial Relations* 27(4): 367–85.

Case, Anne and Deaton, Angus. 2020. *Deaths of Despair and the Future of Capitalism*. Princenton, NJ: Princenton University Press.

CBS. 2020. Ontwikkeling ZZP. Den Haag: CBS.

Chan, Jenny, Nair, Manjusha, and Rhomberg, Chris. 2019. 'Precarization and Labour Resistance: Canada, the USA, India and China'. *Critical Sociology* 45(4–5): 469–83.

Cherry, Miriam. 2016. 'Beyond Misclassification: The Digital Transformation of Work'. *Comparative Labor Law and Policy Journal* 37: 577–604.

Choonara, Joseph. 2020. 'The Precarious Concept of Precarity'. *Review of Radical Political Economics* 52(3): 427–46.

Choonara, Joseph. 2022. 'The Problem with Precarity'. In *Faces of Precarity: Critical Perspectives on Work, Subjectivities and Struggles*, edited by Choonara, Joseph, Carmo Renato, M., and Murgia, Annalisa, 114–29. Bristol: Bristol University Press.

Cini, Lorenzo, Maccarrone, Vincenzo, and Tassinari, Arianna. 2021. 'With or Without U(nions)? Understanding the Diversity of Gig Workers' Organizing Practices in Italy and the UK'. *European Journal of Industrial Relations* 28(3): 341–62.

Cinque, Silvia, Nyberg, Daniel, and Starkey, Ken. 2021. '"Living at the Border of Poverty": How Theatre Actors Maintain Their Calling through Narrative Identity Work'. *Human Relations* 74(11): 1755–80.

Clarke, Stephen and D'Arcy, Conor. 2016. *Low Pay Britain 2016*. London: Resolution Foundation. www.resolutionfoundation.org/app/uploads/2016/10/Low-Pay-Britain-2016.pdf (accessed 22 April 2020).

Clegg, Stewart and Baumeler, Carmen. 2010. 'From Iron Cages to Liquid Modernity in Organizational Analysis'. *Organization Studies* 31(12): 1713–33.

Cohen, Laurie, Duberley, Joanne, and Bustos, Torres Adriana B. 2023. 'Experiencing Gender Regimes: Accounts of Women Professors in Mexico, the UK and Sweden'. *Work, Employment and Society* 37(2): 525–44.

Cole, Mathew, Spencer, David, Hardy, Kathy, and Stuart, Mark. 2022. 'Wage Theft and the Struggle over the Working Day in Hospitality Work: A Typology of Unpaid Labour Time'. *Work, Employment and Society*. https://doi.org/10.1177/09500170221111.

Coleman, James S. 1990. *Foundations of Social Theory*. Cambridge, MA: Harvard University Press.

Collinson, David. 2003. 'Identities and Insecurities: Selves at Work'. *Organization* 10: 527–47.

Countouris, Nicola, Stefano, Valerio De, and Lianos Ioannis. 2021. 'The EU, Competition Law and Workers' Rights'. CLES Research Paper Series, n 2.

Cooper, Melinda. 2017. *Family Values: Between Neoliberalism and the New Social Conservativism*. New York: Zone Books.

Coulson, Susan. 2012. 'Collaborating in a Competitive World: Musicians' Working Lives and Understandings of Entrepreneurship'. *Work, Employment and Society* 26(2): 246–61.

Creswell, John W. 1994. *Research Design: Qualitative & Quantitative Approaches*. London: Sage Publications.

Crompton, Rosemary. 1980. 'Class Mobility in Modern Britain'. *Sociology* 14(1): 117–19.

Crompton, Rosemary. 1989. 'Class Theory and Gender'. *The British Journal of Sociology* 40(4): 565–87.

Crompton, Rosemary. 1998. *Class and Stratification: An Introduction to Current Debates*, 2nd edition. Cambridge: Polity Press.

Crompton, Rosemary. 2006. *Employment and the Family*. Cambridge: Cambridge University Press.

Crompton, Rosemary and Gubbay, Jon. 1976. *Economy and Class Structure*. London: Macmillan.

Crouch, Colin. 1999. *Social Change in Western Europe*. Oxford: Oxford University Press.

Crouch, Colin. 2020. *Post-Democracy after the Crisis*. London: Polity.

Crozier, Sarah E. and Cassell, Catherine M. 2016. 'Methodological Considerations in the Use of Audio Diaries in Work Psychology'. *Journal of Occupational & Organizational Psychology* 89(2): 396–419.

Dardot, Pierre and Christian, Laval. 2013. *The New Way of the World: On Neoliberal Society*. London: Verso.

Davies, Joanna, Brighton, Lisa, Reedy, Florence, and Bajwah, Sabrina. 2022. 'Maternity Provision, Contract Status, and Likelihood of Returning to Work: Evidence from Research Intensive Universities in the UK'. *Gender, Work & Organization* 29(5): 1495–510.

D'Cruz, Premilla and Noronha, Ernesto. 2016. 'Positives Outweighing Negatives: The Experiences of Indian Crowdsourced Workers'. *Work Organisation, Labour & Globalisation* 10(1): 44–63.

Delautre, Guillaume, Gardiner, Drew, and Verick, Sher. 2021. 'Moving towards a Life-Course Perspective to Labor Market Transitions: Approaches and Challenges'. Background Papers 1 ILO. Geneva: ILO.

Devi, Reena, Goodman, Claire, Dalkin, Sonia et al. 2021. 'Attracting, Recruiting and Retaining Nurses and Care Workers Working in Care Homes: The Need for a Nuanced Understanding Informed by Evidence and Theory'. *Age and Ageing* 50(1): 65–7.

Doellgast, Virginia, Lillie, Nathan, and Pulignano, Valeria. 2018. *Reconstructing Solidarity: Labour Unions, Precarious Work, and the Politics of Institutional Change in Europe*. Oxford: Oxford University Press.

Doeringer, Peter B. and Piore, Michael J. 1971. *Internal Labor Markets and Manpower Analysis*. Lexington, MA: Health.

Dolvick, Jon E. and Martin, Andrew. 2015. *European Social Models from Crisis to Crisis: Employment and Inequality in the Era of Monetary Integration*. Oxford: Oxford University Press.

Dörre, Klaus. 2015. 'Test for the Underclass: The Social Effects of Activating Labour Market Policy in Germany'. In *The New Social Division: Making and Unmaking Precariousness*, edited by Della Porta, Donatella, Hannimen, Steve, Siisidinen, Martti, and Silvastri, Tito, 83–100. London: Palgrave MacMillan.

du Gay, Paul. 1996. *Consumption and Identity at Work.* Thousand Oaks, CA: Sage.

Duffy, Brook Erin. 2017. *(Not) Getting Paid to Do What You Love: Gender, Social Media, and Aspirational Work.* New Haven, CT: Yale University Press.

Edwards, Richard. 1979. *Contested Terrain: The Transformation of the Workplace in the Twentieth Century.* London: Heinemann.

Eichhorst, Werner et al. 2013. 'Social Protection Rights of Economically Dependent Self Employed Workers'. Report for DG Internal Policies, European Commission.

Ekbia, Hamid R. and Nardi, Bonnie A. 2017. *Heteromation, and Other Stories of Computing and Capitalism. Cambridge*, MA: MIT Press.

Ellison, Nick, Blomqvist, Paula, and Fleckenstein, Timo. 2022. 'Covid (In)Equalities: Labor Market Protection, Health, and Residential Care in Germany, Sweden, and the UK'. *Policy & Society* 41(2): 247–59.

Emmenegger, Patrick, Häusermann, Silja, Palier, Bruno, and Seeleib-Kaiser, Martin. 2012. *The Age of Dualization: The Changing Face of Inequality in Deindustrializing Societies.* Oxford: Oxford University Press.

Esping-Andersen, Gosta. 1990. *The Three Worlds of Welfare Capitalism.* Cambridge: Polity Press.

Essén, Anna. 2008. 'Variability as a source of Stability: Studying Routines in the Elderly Home Care Setting'. *Human Relations* 61(11): 1617–44.

Evans, Peter E. and Tilly, Chris. 2016. 'The Future of Work: Escaping the Current Dystopian Trajectory and Building Better Alternatives'. In *The Sage Handbook of the Sociology of Work and Employment*, edited by Stephen, Edgell, Heidi, Gottfried, and Granter, Edward, 651–70. London: Sage.

Eviringham, Christine. 2002. 'Engendering Time Gender Equity and Discourses of Workplace Flexibility'. *Time & Society* 11: 335–51.

Farris, Sara R. and Marchetti, Sabrina. 2017. 'From the Commodification to the Corporatization of Care: European Perspectives and Debates'. *Social Politics: International Studies in Gender, State & Society* 24(2): 109–31.

Federici, Silvia. 1975. *Wages against Housework.* London and Bristol: Power of Women Collective and Falling Wall Press.

Federici, Silvia. 2012. *Revolution at Point Zero: Housework, Reproduction, and Feminist Struggle.* Brooklyn, NY: London: PM Press.

Ferreras, Isabelle. 2018. 'Should Labor Rights Count as Civil and Political Rights? Reflections on Worker Participation in the Government of Firms'. *Revue de droit comparé du travail et de la sécurité sociale* 4: 78–85.

Finch, J. 1989. *Family Obligations and Social Change.* Oxford: Polity Press.

Fischer, Thomas. 2022. 'Home Care in Germany during the COVID-19 Pandemic: A Neglected Population?'. *Journal of Nursing Scholarship*, DOI: 10.1111/jnu.12851.

Fleckenstein, Timo and Seeleib-Kaiser, Martin. 2011. 'Business, Skills and the Welfare State: The Political Economy of Employment-Oriented Family Policy in Britain and Germany'. *Journal of European Social Policy* 21(2): 136–49.

Fleming, Peter. 2014. 'Review Article: When "Life Itself" Goes to Work: Reviewing Shifts in Organizational Life through the Lens of Biopower'. *Human Relations* 67(7): 875–901.

Flisbäck, M. and Lund, A. 2015. 'Artists' Autonomy and Professionalization in a New Cultural Policy Landscape'. Professions and Professionalism 5(2): 1–16.

Folbre, Nancy. 2012. 'Should Women Care Less? Intrinsic Motivation and Gender Inequality'. *Journal of Industrial Relations* 50(4): 597–619.

Foucault, Michel. 1979. *Discipline and Punish: The Birth of the Prison*. New York: Vintage.

Foucault, Michel. 1988. *Madness and Civilization: The Birth of the Asylum*. New York: Vintage.

Foucault, Michel. 2010. *The Birth of Biopolitics: Lectures at the Collège de France, 1978–1979*. New York: Palgrave.

Frankl, Viktor E. 1996. *Der Wille zum Sinn* [*The Will to Meaning*]. Bern: Huber.

Franzen, Axel and Bahr, Sebastian. 2024. 'Poverty in Europe: How long-term poverty developed following the financial crisis and what drives it'. *International Journal of Social Welfare* 33(2): 482–94.

Fraser, Nancy. 1994. 'After the Family Wage: Gender Equality and the Welfare State'. *Political Theory* 22(4): 591–618.

Fraser, Nancy. 2016. 'Contradictions of Capital and Care'. *New Left Review*, July/August.

Freeman, Richard B. and Medoff, James L. 1984. *What Do Unions Do?* New York: Basic Books.

Friedland, Roger and Alford, Robert. 1991. 'Bringing Society Back In: Symbols, Practices and Institutional Contradictions." In *The New Institutionalism in Organisational Analysis*, edited by Powell, Walter W. and DiMaggio, Paul J., 232–66. Chicago: University of Chicago Press.

Gadamer, Hans-Georg. 1975. 'Hermeneutics and Social Science'. *Philosophy and Social Criticism* 2(4): 307–16.

Gallie, Duncan. 2017. 'The Quality of Work in a Changing Labour Market'. *Social Policy Administration* 51(2): 226–43.

Gazier, Bernard. 2022a. 'Employability and Public Policy: A Century-Long Process and Unfinished Process'. In *Employability and Industrial Mutations: Between Individual Trajectories and Organizational Strategic Planning*, edited by Noël, Florent and Schmidt, Géraldine, 7–18. London: Wiley.

Gazier, Bernard. 2022b. 'Towards a General Theory of Employability'. In *Employability and Industrial Mutations: Between Individual Trajectories and Organizational Strategic Planning*, edited by Noël, Florent and Schmidt, Géraldine, 3–6. London: Wiley.

Gazier, Bernard and Petit Héloïse. 2007. 'French Labour Market Segmentation and French Labour Market Policies since the Seventies: Connecting Changes'. *Economie et Sociétés, Socio-Économie du Travail* 41(28): 1027–56.

Girardi, Silvia, Pulignano, Valeria, and Maas, Roland. 2020. 'Activated and Included? The Social Inclusion of Social Assistance Beneficiaries Engaged in "Public Works"'. *International Journal of Sociology and Social Policy* 39(9–10): 738–51.

Glaser, Barney and Strauss, Anselm. 1967. *The Discovery of Grounded Theory: Strategies for Qualitative Research*. Mill Valley, CA: Sociology Press.

Glaser, Barney and Strauss, Anselm. 2012. *The Discovery of Grounded Theory: Strategies for Qualitative Research*. New Brunswick: Aldine Transaction.

Glucksmann, Miriam. 1995. 'Why "Work"? Gender and the "Total Social Organisation of Labour"'. *Gender, Work & Organisation* 2(2): 63–75.

Glucksmann, Miriam. 2005. 'Shifting Boundaries and Interconnections: Extending the "Total Social Organization of Labour"'. In *A New Sociology of Work*, edited by Lynne, Pettinger, Jane, Parry, Rebecca, Taylor, and Miriam, Glucksmann, 19–36. Oxford: Blackwell.

Glucksmann, M. 2009. *Women on the Line*. London: Routledge.

Goffman, Erving. 1963. *Stigma: Notes on the Management of Spoiled Identity*. London: Penguin Books.Gomberg, Paul. 2018. 'Work'. In *The Oxford Handbook of Distributive Justice*, edited by Olsaretti, Serena, 559–78. Oxford: Oxford University Press.

Gough, Ian. 1972. 'Marx's Theory of Productive and Unproductive Labour'. *New Left Review* I (76): 47–72.

Greer, Ian and Doellgast, Virginia. 2017. 'Marketization, Inequality, and Institutional Change'. *Journal of Industrial Relations* 59(2): 192–208.

Greer, Ian and Umney, Charles. 2022. *Marketization*. London: Bloomsbury Academic.

Greer Ian, Breidahl Karen, Knuth Matthias, and Larsen Flemming. 2018. *The Marketization of Employment Services and the Dilemmas of Europe's Work-First Welfare States*. Oxford: Oxford University Press.

Greer, Ian, Samaluk, Barbara, and Umney, Charles. 2019. 'Toward a Precarious Projectariat? Project Dynamics in Slovenian and French Social Services'. *Organization Studies* 40(12): 1873–95.

Grimshaw, Damian. 2020. 'International Organisations and the Future of Work: How New Technologies and Inequality Shaped the Narratives in 2019'. *Journal of Industrial Relations* 62(3): 477–507.

Grimshaw, Damian. 2024. 'Social Dialogue and the Challenges of Delivering Sustainable Economic Development and Social Progress for All'. *ILO Working Paper*. Geneva: ILO (International Labour Organization) (forthcoming).

Grimshaw, Damian, Johnson, Mat, Rubery, Jill and Keizer, Arjan. 2016. 'Reducing Precarious Work: Protective Gaps and the Role of Social Dialogue in Europe'. Report for the European Commission. https://documents.manchester.ac.uk/display.aspx?DocID=48966.

Gruber, Eva Maria, Zeiser, Silvana, Schröder, Dorit, and Büscher, Andreas (2021). 'Workforce Issues in Home- and Community-Based Long-Term Care in Germany'. *Health and Social Care in the Community* 29:746–55.

Habermas, Jürgen. 1981/1984. *Theory of Communicative Action*, Vol. One: *Reason and the Rationalization of Society*, translated by Thomas A. McCarthy. Boston, MA: Beacon.

Hall, Peter A. and Lamont, Michèle. 2009. *Successful Societies: How Institutions and Culture Affect Health*. Cambridge University Press.

Hall, Peter A. and Lamont, Michèle. 2013. *Social Resilience in the Neoliberal Era*. Cambridge: Cambridge University Press.

Harvey, Laura. 2011. 'Intimate Reflections: Private Diaries in Qualitative Research'. *Qualitative Research* 11(6): 664–82.

Häusermann, Silja and Palier, Bruno. 2008. 'The Politics of Employment-Friendly Welfare Reforms in Post-Industrial Economies'. *Socio-Economic Review* 6: 559–86.

Hay, Colin and Wincott, Daniel. 2012. *The Political Economy of European Welfare Capitalism*. London: Palgrave Macmillan.

Hayes, Lydia. 2017. *Stories of Care, a Labour of Law*. Basingstoke: Palgrave Macmillan.

Health Foundation. 2021. 'Social Care Funding Gap'. https://www.health.org.uk/news-and-comment/charts-and-infographics/REAL-social-care-funding-gap (accessed 29 March 2023).

Hebson, Gail, Rubery, Jill, and Grimshaw, Damian. 2015. 'Rethinking Job Satisfaction in Care Work: Looking beyond the Care Debates'. *Work, Employment & Society* 29(2): 314–30.

Heery, Ed, Conley, Heather, Delbridge, Rick, and Stewart, Paul. 2004. 'Beyond the Enterprise: Trade Union Representation of Freelances in the UK'. *Human Resource Management Journal* 14(2): 20–35.

Hemerijck, Anton. 2013. *Changing Welfare States*. Oxford: Oxford University Press.

Hermann, Christoph and Flecker, Jörg. 2012. *Privatization of Public Services Impacts for Employment, Working Conditions, and Service Quality in Europe*. London: Routledge.

Hesmondhalgh, David. 2007. *The Cultural Industries*. London: Sage.

Hesmondhalgh, David and Baker, Sarah. 2011. *Creative Labour: Media Work in Three Cultural Industries*. London: Routledge.

Hilgers, Mathieu and Mangez, Eric. 2015. *Bourdieu's Theory of Social Fields: Concepts and Applications*, edited by Hilgers, Mathieu and Mangez, Eric. London: Routledge.

Hirschman, Albert. 1970. *Exit, Voice and Loyalty: Responses to Decline in Firms, Organizations, and States*. Cambridge, MA: Harvard University Press.

Hochschild, Ruth. 1983. *The Managed Heart Commercialization of Human Feeling*. Berkeley, CA: University of California Press.

Hoppania, Hanna-Kaisa, Karsio, Olli, Näre, Lena, Vaittinen, Tiina, and Zechner, Minna. 2024. 'Financialization of Eldercare in a Nordic Welfare State'. *Journal of Social Policy* 53(1): 26–44.

Honneth, Axel. 2014. *Freedom's Right. The Social Foundations of Democratic Life*, translated by Joseph Ganahl. New York: Columbia University Press.

Horton, Amy. 2022. 'Financialization and Non-Disposable Women: Real Estate, Debt and Labour in UK Care Homes'. *Environment and Planning A: Economy and Space* 54(1): 144–59.

House of Commons. 2022. 'Adult Social Care Workforce in England'. https://researchbriefings.files.parliament.uk/documents/CBP-9615/CBP-9615.pdf (accessed 27 March 2023).

House of Commons. 2023. 'Adult Social Care Funding'. https://commonslibrary.parliament.uk/research-briefings/cbp-7903/#:~:text=How%20social%20care%20is%20funded,22%20was%20%C2%A319%20billion (accessed 27 March 2023).

Howell, Chris. 2021. 'Rethinking the Role of the State in Employment Relations for a Neoliberal Era'. *Industrial and Labor Relations Review* 74(3): 739–72.

ILO (International Labour Organization). 2019. *Global Commission on the Future of Work: Work for a Brighter Future*. Geneva: ILO.

ILO (International Labour Organization). 2022. *Social Dialogue Report: Collective Bargaining for an Inclusive, Sustainable and Resilient Recovery*. Geneva: ILO.

ILO (International Labour Organization). 2023. *The Value of Essential Work: World Employment and Social Outlook 2023*. Geneva: ILO.

ILO (International Labour Organization). 2024. *Social Dialogue Report: The Role of Social Dialogue in Promoting Economic Development and Social Progress*. Geneva: ILO (forthcoming).

Jamal, Amal and Lavie, Noa. 2021. 'Self-Categorization, Intersectionality and Creative Freedom in the Cultural Industries: Palestinian Women Filmmakers in Israel'. *Ethnic and Racial Studies* 44(6): 1030–50.

Jesnes, Kristin, Ilsøe, Anna, and Hotvedt, Marianne. 2019. 'Collective Agreements for Platform Workers? Examples from the Nordic Countries'. Nordic Future of Work, Brief 3. FAFO.

Johnson, Mathew and Pulignano, Valeria. 2021. 'Editorial: Transforming Care Work within an Era of Changing Priorities of Care Policy'. *Transfer: European Review of Labour and Research* 27(3): 1–3.

Jones, Edward, Farina, Amerigo, Hastorf, Albert, Marbus, H., Mitler, David T., Scott, Richard, and French, Rita. 1984. *Social Stigma: The Psychology of Marked Relationships*. New York: Freeman.

Joyce, Simon, Stuart, Mark, and Forde, Chris. 2023. 'Theorising Labour Unrest and Trade Unionism in the Platform Economy'. *New Technology, Work and Employment* 38(1): 21–40.

Joyce, Simon, Stuart, Mark, Forde, Chris, and Valizade, Danat. 2020. 'Work and Social Protection in the Platform Economy in Europe'. *Industrial and Labor Relations* 25: 153–84.

Judge, Lindsay and Cominetti, Nye. 2019. *From Rights to Reality: Enforcing Labour Market Laws in the UK*. London: Resolution Foundation. www.resolutionfoundation.org/app/uploads/2019/09/Enforcement-spotlight-1.pdf (accessed 22 April 2020).

Kalleberg, Arne L. 2009. 'Precarious Work, Insecure Workers: Employment Relations in Transition'. *American Sociological Review* 74: 1–22.

Kalleberg, Arne L. 2018. *Precarious Lives: Job Insecurity and Well-Being in Rich Democracies*. London: Polity Press.

Kalleberg, Arne L. and Hewison, Kevin. 2013. 'Precarious Work and the Challenge for Asia'. *American Behavioral Scientist* 57(3): 271–88.

Kalleberg, Arne L. and Vallas, Steven P. 2018. *Precarious Work.* Bingley: Emerald Publishing.

Kanter, Rosabeth Moss. 1977. *Men and Women of the Corporation.* New York: Basic Books.

Keizer, Arjan, Johnson, Mat, Larsen, Trine, Refslund, Bjarke, and Grimshaw, Damian. 2023. 'Unions and Precarious Work: How Power Resources Shape Diverse Strategies and Outcomes'. *European Journal of Industrial Relations*: 09596801231162517.

Kelly, Erin L. and Moen, Phyllis. 2020. *Overload: How Good Jobs Went Bad and What We Can Do About It.* Princeton, NJ: Princeton University Press.

Kessel, Ian and Bach, Stephen. 2014. 'Comparing Cases'. In *Studying Organisations Using Critical Realism*, edited by Edwards, Paul, O'Mahoney, Jon, and Vincent, Steven, 168–84. Oxford: Oxford University Press.

Kessler, Sarah. 2018. *Gigged: The End of the Job and the Future of Work.* New York: St Martin's Press.

Khlystova, Olena, Kalyuzhnova, Yelena, and Belitski, Maksim. 2022. 'The Impact of the COVID-19 Pandemic on the Creative Industries: A Literature Review and Future Research Agenda'. *Journal of Business Research* 139: 1192–210

King, David and LeGales, Patrick. 2017. *Reconfiguring European States in Crisis.* Oxford: Oxford University Press.

Knaebel, Rachel. 2022. 'The Invisible Workers Caring for the German Elderly'. ETUI Special Report, Spring/Summer. https://www.etui.org/sites/default/files/ez_import/Hesamag_11_EN_26-29.pdf (accessed 24 April 2023).

Koellinger, Philipp, Mell, Julija, Pohl, Irene, Roessler, Christian, and Treffers, Theresa. 2012. 'Self-Employed but Looking: A Labor Market Experiment'. ERIM Report Series Reference No. ERS-2012-022-ORG.

Konstnärsnamnden. 2016. *Konstnärernas demografi, inkomster och sociala villkor.* Stockholm: Konstnärsnamnden.

Korver, Ton and Schmid, Gűnther. 2012. 'Enhancing Transition Capacities and Sustainable Transitions'. In *Renewing Democratic Deliberation in Europe: The Challenge of Social and Civil Dialogue*, edited by De Munck, Jean, 23–55. Brussels: Peter Lang.

Kunst, Bojana. 2015. *Artist at Work: Proximity of Art and Capitalism.* Winchester: Zero Books.

Laaser, Knut and Karlsson, Jan Ch. 2022. 'Towards a Sociology of Meaningful Work'. *Work, Employment and Society* 36(5): 798–815.

Laaser, Knut and Karlsson, Jan Ch. 2023. *The Politics of Working Life and Meaningful Waged Work.* Cambridge: Cambridge University Press.

Lahaut, D. 2019. *Kunst als gunst. Beloning van ZZP'ers in de sector kunst.* Amsterdam: Bureau Lahaut.

Lamannis, Mariagrazia. 2023. 'Collective Bargaining in the Platform Economy: A Mapping Exercise of Existing Initiatives'. ETUI Research Paper-Report No. 2.

Lamont, Michèle. 1992. *Money, Morals, and Manners: The Culture of the French and the American Upper-Middle Class.* Chicago: Chicago University Press.

Lamont, Michèle. 2018. 'Addressing Recognition Gaps: Destigmatization and the Reduction of Inequality'. *American Sociological Review* 83(3): 419–44.

Lamont, Michèle. 2019. 'From "Having" to "Being": Self-Worth and the Current Crisis of American Society'. *The British Journal of Sociology* 70(3): 660–707.

Lamont, Michèle. 2000. *The Dignity of Working Men: Morality and the Boundaries of Race, Class, and Immigration.* New York: Russell Sage Foundation.

Lamont, Michèle. 2023. *Seeing Others: How to Redefine Worth in a Divided World.* Dublin: Allen Lane Penguin.

Lamont, Michèle and Molnár, Virág. 2002. 'The Study of Boundaries in the Social Sciences'. *Annual Review of Sociology* 28: 167–95.

Lamont, Michele and Hall, Peter A. 2009. Successful Societies: How Institutions and Culture Affect Health. Cambridge, UK and New York: Cambridge University Press.

Lamont, Michèle, Stefan, Beljean, and Matthew, Clair. 2014. 'What Is Missing? Cultural Processes and Causal Pathways to Inequality'. *Socio-Economic Review* 12: 573–608.

Land, Hilary. 1980. 'The Family Wage'. *Feminist Review* 6: 55–77.

Land, Hilary and Himmelweit, Susan. 2010. *Who Cares: Who Pays? A Report on Personalisation in Social Care.* London: Unison.

Lee, Byoung-Hoon, Swider, Sarah, and Tilly, Chris. 2020. 'Informality in Action: A Relational Look at Informal Work'. *International Journal of Comparative Sociology* 61(2–3): 91–100.

Lee, David. 2015. 'Internships, Workfare, and the Cultural Industries: A British Perspective'. *Triple C* 13: 459–70.

Lefebvre, Henry. 1974/1991. *The Production of Space.* Oxford: Blackwell Publisher.

Leiulfsrud, Håkon and Woodward, Alison. 1987. 'Women at Class Crossroads: Repudiating Conventional Theories of Family Class'. *Sociology* 21(3): 393–412.

Lewandowski,P. and Magda, I. 2018. The labor market in Poland, 2000–2016. IZA World of Labor.

Lewchuk Wayne, Lafleche Michelynn, and Procyk Stephanie. 2015. 'The Precarity Penalty: The Impact of Employment Precarity on Individuals, Households and Communities—and What to Do about It'. https://pepso.ca/documents/precarity-penalty.pdf (accessed 8 July 2021).

Link, Bruce G. and Phelan, Jo C. 2001. 'Conceptualizing Stigma'. *Annual Review of Sociology* 27(1): 363–85.

Link, Bruce G. and Phelan, Jo C. 2014. 'Stigma Power'. *Social Science & Medicine* 103: 24–32

Lomax, Richard. 2017. 'Self-Employment: A View from the Inside'. *Transfer: European Review of Labour and Research* 23(3) 367–69.

Longo, Julieta and Massi, Mariana F. 2023. 'Autonomy, Subordination and Dependence: A Study on High-Skilled Solo Self-Employment'. *Rassegna Italiana di Sociologia* 2: 287–316.

Lorey, Isabelle. 2015. *State of Insecurity: Government of the Precarious.* London: Verso.

Low Pay Commission. 2021. Low pay Commission Report 2021. London.

Lunt, I. 2008. 'Ethical Issues in Professional Life.' In *Exploring professionalism*, Cunningham, B., 73–98. London: Bedford Way Papers.

MacKenzie, Ewan and McKinlay, Alan. 2020. 'Hope Labour and the Psychic Life of Cultural Work'. *Human Relations* 61(4): 515–37.

Mann, Michael. 1993. *The Sources of Social Power*, Vol. II: *The Rise of Classes and Nation-States, 1760–1914.* Cambridge: Cambridge University Press.

Mara', Claudia, Pulignano, Valeria, and Stewart, Paul. 2023. 'Dynamics of Unionism in the Platform Economy: The Case of the Food Delivery Sector in Bologna (Italy)'. *The Economic and Labour Relations Review* 34(3): 395–412.

Marinova, Dani. 2022. 'Working Poverty, Nonstandard Employment and Political Inclusion'. *West European Politics* 45(2): 381–402.

Marsden, David. 1999. *A Theory of Employment Systems: Micro-Foundations of Societal Diversity.* Oxford: Oxford University Press.

Martin, Bill. 1994. 'Segmentation in the Labour Market: An Empirical Study of Earnings Determination in Australia'. *Work, Employment and Society* 8(3): 357–85.

Martindale, Nicholas and Vili, Lehdonvirta. 2023. 'Labour Market Digitalization and Social Class: Evidence of Mobility and Reproduction from a European Survey of Online Platform Workers'. *Socio-Economic Review* 21(4): 1945–65.

Marx, Karl. 1939/1973. The Grundrisse. New York: Penguin

BooksMarx, Kar. 1976. *Capital: A Critique of Political Economy*, vol. I. Harmondsworth: Penguin.

Mas, Alexander and Pallais, Amanda. 2017. 'Valuing Alternative Work Arrangements'. *American Economic Review* 107(12): 3722–59.

May, Rollo. 1991. *Cry for Myth*. New York: Norton.

Mazzucato, Marianna. 2017. 'Mission-Oriented Innovation Policy: Challenges and Opportunities'. UCL Institute for Innovation and Public Purpose Working Paper No. 2017-1, UCL.

McDonald, Fiona, Bentham, Eleonora, and Malone, Jenny. 2018. 'Wage Theft, Underpayment and Unpaid Work in Marketised Social Care'. *The Economic and Labour Relations Review* 29(3): 80–96.

McDonald, Paula, Price, Robin, and Bailey, Janis. 2013. 'Knowledge Is Not Power, but It's a Start: What Young People Know about Their Rights and Obligations in Employment'. *Youth Studies Australia* 32(2): 49–58.

McIntosh, Mary. 1978. 'The State and the Oppression of Women'. In *Feminism and Materialism*, edited by Annette, Kuhn and Anne Marie, Wolpe, 254–90. London: Routledge and Kegan Paul.

McKinlay, Alan and Smith, Chris. 2009. *Creative Labour: Working in the Creative Industries*. London: Palgrave.

McNay, Lois. 2009. 'Self as Enterprise'. Theory, Culture and Society 26(6): 55–77.

Meiksins, Ellen W. 1981. 'The Separation of the Economic and the Political in Capitalism'. *New Left Review* I (127): 66–95.

Menger, Pierre M. 2011, *Les intermittents du spectacle. Sociologie du travail flexible*. Paris: Editions de l'EHESS.

Mijs, Jonathan Jan B. 2018. 'Visualizing Belief in Meritocracy, 1930–2010'. *Socius* 4(1): 1–2.

Millar, Kathleen M. 2014. 'The Precarious Present: Wageless Labor and Disrupted Life in Rio de Janeiro, Brazil'. *Cultural Anthropology* 29(1): 32–53.

Mills, Wright C. 1959. *Sociological Imagination*. New York: Oxford University Press.

Mitchell, Juliet. 1975. *Psychoanalysis and Feminism*. Harmondsworth: Penguin.

Ministry of Welfare, Public Health and Culture. 1999. Culture as Confrontation, Not a Culture 2001–2004. Den Haag.

Molyneux, Maxime. 1979. 'Beyond the Domestic Labour Debate'. *New Left Review* 116: 3–27.

Moore, Sean and Hayes, Lydia J. B. 2017. 'Taking Worker Productivity to a New Level? Electronic Monitoring in Homecare: The (Re)Production of Unpaid Labour'. *New Technology, Work and Employment* 32(2): 101–14.

Moore, Sian and Newsome, Kirsty. 2018. 'Paying for Free Delivery: Dependent Self-Employment as a Measure of Precarity in Parcel Delivery'. *Work, Employment and Society* 32(3): 475–92.

Morozov, Evgeny. 2015. Socialize the Data Centres! https://onwork.edu.au/bibitem/2015-Morozov,Evgeny-Socialize+the+Data+Centres+/ (accessed 20 January 2016).

Morse, Janice M. and Niehaus, Linda. 2009. *Mixed Method Design*. Walnut Creek, CA: Left Coast Press.

Mosoetsa, Sarah, Stillerman, Joel, and Tilly, Chris. 2016. 'Precarious Labor, South and North: An Introduction'. *International Labor and Working-Class History* 89: 5–19.

Mullen, Brian, Salas, Edoardo, and Driskell, James E. 1989. 'Salience, Motivation, and Artifact as Contributions to the Relation between Participation Rate and Leadership'. *Journal of Experimental Social Psychology* 25: 545–59.

Myndigheten för Kulturanalys. 2017. Dramatiska villkor: Länsteatrarnas ekonomiska handlingsutrymme 1980–2015. Stockholm: Myndigheten för Kulturanalys.

Neale, Bren. 2021. *The Craft of Qualitative Longitudinal Research: The Craft of Researching Lives through Time*. London: Sage.

Neff, Gina. 2012. *Venture Labor: Work and the Burden of Risk*. Cambridge, MA: Massachusetts Institute of Technology Press.

Neff, Gina, Wissinger, Elizabeth, and Sharon, Zukin. 2005. 'Entrepreneurial Labor among Cultural Producers: "Cool" Jobs in "Hot" Industries'. *Social Semiotics* 5(3): 307–34.

Noël, Florent and Schmidt, Géraldine. 2022. *Employability and Industrial Mutations: Between Individual Trajectories and Organizational Strategic Planning*. London: Wiley.

Nussbaum, Martha. 2003. 'Capabilities as Fundamental Entitlements: Sen and Social Justice'. *Feminist Economics* 9(2–3): 33–59.

Nussbaum, Martha. 2011. *Creating Capabilities: The Human Development Approach*. Cambridge, MA: Harvard University Press.

O'Connor, Cliodhna and Joffe, Helene. 2020. 'Intercoder Reliability in Qualitative Research: Debates and Practical Guidelines'. *International Journal of Qualitative Methods* 19: 1–13.

Oesch, Daniel. 2006. *Redrawing the Class Map: Stratification and Institutions in Britain, Germany, Sweden and Switzerland*. London: Palgrave.

Olson, Joel D., McAllister, Chad, Grinnell, Lynn D., Walters, Kimberly G., and Appunn, Frank. 2016. 'Applying Constant Comparative Method with Multiple Investigators and Inter-Coder Reliability'. *The Qualitative Report* 21(1): 26–42.

O'Neill, Oliver. 2002. *A Question of Trust*. Cambridge: Cambridge University Press.

O'Neill, Oliver. 2014. 'Trust, Trustworthiness and Accountability'. In *Capital Failure: Rebuilding Trust in Financial Services*, edited by Morris, Nicholas and Vines, David, 172–89. Oxford: Oxford University Press.

Pachucki, Mark, Pendergrass, Sabrina, and Lamont, Michèle. 2007. 'Boundary Processes: Recent Theoretical Developments and New Contributions'. *Poetics* 35: 331–51.

Palmer, Elyane and Eveline, Joan. 2012. 'Sustaining Low Pay in Aged Care Work'. *Gender, Work & Organization* 19(3), 254–75.

Parry, Jane. 2005. 'Care in the Community? Gender and the Reconfiguration of Community Work in a Post-Mining Neighborhood'. *Sociological Review* 53: 149–66.

Paton, Kirsteen. 2018. 'Beyond Legacy: Backstage Stigmatisation and "Trickle-Up" Politics of Urban Regeneration'. *Sociological Review* 66(4): 919–34.

Patton, Michael Quinn. 2014. *Qualitative Research and Evaluation Methods*, 4th edition. Thousand Oaks, CA: Sage.

Peña-Casas, Ramon and Ghailani, Dalila. 2020. 'A European Minimum Wage Framework: The Solution to the Ongoing Increase in In-Work Poverty in Europe'. In *Social Policy in the European Union: State of Play*, edited by Vanhercke, Bart, Spasova, Slavina, and Fronteddu, Boris, 133–53. Brussels: ETUI.

Perlin, Ross. 2012. *Intern Nation: How to Earn Nothing and Learn Little in the Brave New Economy*. London: Verso.

Pettinger, Lynne, Parry, Jane, Taylor, Rebecca, and Glucksmann, Miriam. 2005. *A New Sociology of Work*. Oxford: Blackwell.

Picot, Georg. 2023. 'Minimum Wages: By Collective Bargaining and by Law'. In *Handbook of Labour Market Policy in Advanced Democracies*, edited by Clegg, Daniel and Durazzi, Nicolo, 234–48. London: Edward Elgar.

Plomien, Ania. 2019. 'Gender Inequality by Design: Does Successful Implementation of Childcare Policy Deliver Gender-Just Outcomes?'. *Policy and Society* 38(4): 643–62.

Polanyi, Karl. 1944/2001. *The Great Transformation: The Political and Economic Origins of Our Time*. New York and Boston, MA: Farrar & Rinehart and Beacon Press.

Pots, R. 2000. Cultuur, koningen en democraten: Overheid & cultuur in Nederland. Nijmegen: Uitgeverij SUN.

Pugh, Alison J. 2015. *The Tumbleweed Society*. Oxford: Oxford University Press.

Pulignano, Valeria. 2018. 'Precarious Work, Regime of Competition and the Case of Europe'. In *Precarious Work*, edited by Kalleberg, Arne L. and Vallas, Steven, 33–60. Bingley: Emerald Publishing.

Pulignano, Valeria and Doerflinger, Nadja. 2018. 'Labour Markets, Solidarity and Precarious Work: Comparing Local Unions' Responses to Management Flexibility Strategies in the German and Belgian Metalworking and Chemical Industries." In *Reconstructing Solidarity: Labour Unions, Precarious Work, and the Politics of Institutional Change in Europe*, edited by Doellgast, Virginia, Lillie, Nathan, and Pulignano, Valeria, 104–23. Oxford: Oxford University Press.

Pulignano, Valeria and Morgan, Glenn. 2022. 'The Social Foundations of Precarious Work: The Role of Unpaid Labour in the Family'. In *Faces of Precarity: Critical Perspectives on Work, Subjectivities and Struggles*, edited by Choonara, Joseph, Carmo, Renato M., and Murgia, Annalisa, 114–29. Bristol: Bristol University Press.

Pulignano, Valeria and Morgan, Glenn. 2023. 'The "Grey Zone" at the Interface of Work and Home: Theorizing Adaptations Required by Precarious Work'. *Work, Employment and Society* 37(1): 257–73.

Pulignano, Valeria, Domecka, Markieta, Muszyński, Karol, Vermeerbergen, Lander, and Riemann, Me-Linh. 2021. 'Creative Labour in the Era of Covid: The Case of Freelancers'. ETUI Working Paper Series, Brussels, February.

Pulignano, Valeria, Thompson, Paul, and Doerflinger, Nadja. 2022. 'When Accumulation Pressures Meet Regulatory Institutions: A Comparison in Logistics'. *European Journal of Industrial Relations* 28(3) 273–94.

Pulignano, Valeria, Grimshaw, Damian, Domecka, Markieta, and Vermeerbergen, Lander. 2023. 'Why Does Unpaid Labour Vary among Digital Labour Platforms? Exploring Socio-Technical Platform Regimes of Worker Autonomy'. *Human Relations* 77(9): 1243–71.

Pulignano, Valeria, Dean, Deborah, Domecka, Markieta, and Vermeerbergen, Lander. 2023. 'How state influence on project work organization both drives and mitigates gendered precarity in cultural and creative industries'. *British Journal of Industrial Relations* 61(2): 313–35.

Pulignano, Valeria, Marino, Stefania, Johnson, Mathew, Domecka, Markieta, and Riemann, Me-Linh. 2024. '"Digital Tournaments": The Colonization of Freelancers' "Free" Time and Unpaid Labour in the Online Platform Economy'. *Cambridge Journal of Economics* 48(1): 133–50.

Pulignano V., Muszyński K., Tapia M. (2024). Variations of Freelancers' 'Effort-Bargain' Experiences in Platform Work. The Role of Skills. *Industrial and Labor Relations Review* 77(5): 742–69.

Pulignano, Valeria, Riemann, Me-Linh, Stephenson, Carol, and Domecka, Markieta. 2024. 'Emotion Management within Residential Care Work in the United Kingdom and Germany: COVID-19 as a "Breaching Experiment"'. *Research in the Sociology of Work* 36: 57–79.

Rahman, Hatim A. 2020. 'Understanding Ratings Inflation in Online Labor Markets'. Paper presented at the 39th International Conference on Information Systems, San Francisco.

Rahman, K. Sabeel and Thelen, Kathleen. 2019. 'The Rise of the Platform Business Model and the Transformation of Twenty-First-Century Capitalism'. *Politics & Society* 47(2): 177–204.

Rani, Uma and Singh, Parminder. 2019. 'Digital Platforms, Data, and Development: Implications for Workers in Developing Economies'. *Comparative Labor Law and Policy Journal* 41(1): 263–88.

Reay, Diane. 1998. *Class Work: Mothers' Involvement in Their Children's Primary Schooling.* Oxford: Taylor & Francis.

Riessman, Catherine K. 1993. *Narrative Analysis.* Newbury Park, CA: Sage.

Rijksoverheid. 2020. *Kunst-en cultuurbeleid.* Amsterdam: Rijksoverheid.

Rosa, Hartmut. 2015. 'Capitalism as a Spiral of Dynamisation: Sociology as Social Critique'. In *Sociology, Capitalism, Critique*, edited by Dörre, Klaus, Lessenich, Stephan, and Rosa, Hartmut, 67–97. London: Verso Books.

Rosa, Hartmut and Henning, Christoph. 2018. *The Good Life beyond Growth: New Perspectives.* London: Routledge.

Rose, Nikolas. 1989. *Governing the Soul: The Shaping of the Private Self.* London: Routledge.

Rose, Nikolas and Miller, Peter. 1992. 'Political Power beyond the State: Problematics of Government'. *British Journal of Sociology* 43(2): 173–205.

Rubery, Jill. 2015. 'Regulating for Gender Equality: A Policy Framework to Support the Universal Caregiver Vision'. *Social Politics: International Studies in Gender, State & Society* 22(4): 513–38.

Rubery, Jill and Wilkinson, Frank. 1981. *The Dynamics of Labour Market Segmentation.* Cambridge, MA: Academic Press.

Rubery, Jill and Urwin, Peter. 2011. 'Bringing the Employer back in: Why social care Needs a standard Employment Relationship.' *Human Resource Management Journal* 21(2): 122–37.

Rubery, Jill, Grimshaw, Damian, and Hebson, Gail. 2015. '"It's All About Time": Time as Contested Terrain in the Management and Experience of Domiciliary Care Work in England'. *Human Resource Management* 54(5): 753–72.

Rubery, Jill, Grimshaw, Damian, and Keizer, Arjan. 2018. 'Challenges and Contradictions in the "Normalising" of Precarious Work'. *Work, Employment and Society* 32(3): 509–27.

Rubery, Jill, Grimshaw, Damian, Méhaut, Philippe, and Weinkopf, Claudia. 2022. 'Dualisation and Part-Time Work in France, Germany and the UK: Accounting for within and between Country Differences in Precarious Work'. *European Journal of Industrial Relations*: 1–19. 09596801221120468.

Sanchez, Mari, Lamont, Michèle, and Zilberstein, Shira. 2022. 'How American College Students Understand Social Resilience and Navigate towards the Future during COVID and the Movement for Racial Justice'. *Social Science & Medicine* 301: 1–10. doi: 10.1016/j.socscimed.2022.114890.

Savage, Mike, Warde, Alan, and Devine, Fiona. 2005. 'Capitals, Assets and Resources: Some Critical Issues'. *British Journal of Sociology* 56(1): 31–47.

Sayer, Andrew. 2005a. 'Class, Moral Worth and Recognition'. *Sociology* 39(5): 947–63.

Sayer, Andrew. 2005b. *The Moral Significance of Class.* Cambridge: Cambridge University Press.

Scambler, G. 2006. 'Sociology, Social Structure and Health-Related Stigma'.*Psychology, Health & Medicine* 11(3): 288–95. https://doi.org/10.1080/13548500600595103.

Schmid, Günther. 2017. 'Transitional Labour Markets'. In *The Palgrave Dictionary of Economics*, edited by Polinski, Andrew M., 1–15. London: Palgrave.

Schmid, Günther and Gazier, Bernard. 2002. *The Dynamics of Full Employment. Social Integration through Transitional Labour Markets.* London: Edward Elgar.

Schneider, Kirk J. 2008. *Existential-Integrative Psychotherapy.* New York: Routledge.

Schnell, Tatiana. 2008. 'Existential Indifference: Attributes of a New Category of Meaning in Life'. *International Journal of Psychology* 43: 695.

Schnell, Tatiana. 2009. 'The Sources of Meaning and Meaning in Life Questionnaire (SoMe): Relations to Demographics and Well-Being'. *Journal of Positive Psychology* 4: 483–99.

Schor, Juliet. 2020. *After the Gig: How the Sharing Economy Got Hijacked and How to Win It Back.* California: University of California Press.

Schulten, Thorsten. 2002. 'A European Solidaristic Wage Policy?'. *European Journal of Industrial Relations* 8(2): 173–96.

Schulten, Torsten, Bispinck, Reinhard, and Schafer, Claus. 2006. *Minimum Wages in Europe.* Brussels: ETUI.

Schütze, Frederic. 2008. *Biography Analysis on the Empirical Base of Autobiographical Narratives: How to Analyze Autobiographical Narrative Interviews.* Part I and II. http://www.uni-magdeburg.de/zsm/projekt/biographical/1/B2.1.pdf and http://www.uni-magdeburg.de/zsm/projekt/biographical/1/B2.2.pdf.

Seccombe, Wally. 1993. *Weathering the Storm: Working-Class Families from the Industrial Revolution to the Fertility Decline.* London: Verso.

Sen, Amartya. 1980. 'Equality of What?'. *Tanner Lectures on Human Values*, 197–220. Cambridge: Cambridge University Press.

Sen, Amartya. 1985. *Commodities and Capabilities.* Oxford: Oxford University Press.

Sen, Amartya. 1992. *Inequality Reexamined.* Oxford: Clarendon Press.

Sen, Amartya. 1993. 'Capability and Well-Being'. In *The Quality of Life*, edited by Nussbaum, Martha and Sen, Amartya, 30–53. Oxford: Oxford University Press.

Sen, Amartya. 2009. *The Idea of Justice.* London: Penguin Books.

Sennett, Richard. 1998. The Corrosion of Character: The Personal Consequences of Work in the New Capitalism. New York: W.W. Norton & Company.

Sherman, Rachel. 2018. '"A Very Expensive Ordinary Life": Consumption, Symbolic Boundaries, and Moral Legitimacy among New York Elites'. *Socio-Economic Review* 16(2): 411–33.

Shutes, Isabel and Walsh, Kieran. 2012. 'Negotiating User Preferences, Discrimination, and Demand for Migrant Labour in Long-Term Care'. *Social Politics: International Studies in Gender, State & Society* 19(1): 78–104.

Siebert, Sabina and Wilson, Fiona. 2013. 'All Work and No Pay: Consequences of Unpaid Work Experience in the Creative Industries'. *Work, Employment and Society* 27: 711–21.

Silverman, David. 2000. *Doing Qualitative Research: A Practical Handbook.* Thousand Oaks, CA: Sage.

Simonazzi, Annamaria. 2009. 'Care Regimes and National Employment Models'. *Cambridge Journal of Economics* 33(2): 211–32.

Skeggs, Beverly. 1997. *Formations of Class and Gender: Becoming Respectable.* London: Sage.

Skeggs, Beverley. 2004. *Class, Self, Culture.* London: Routledge.

Skills for Care. 2021. 'The State of the Adult Social Care Sector and Workforce in England'. https://www.skillsforcare.org.uk/Adult-Social-Care-Workforce-Data/Workforce-intelligence/publications/Data-and-publications.aspx (accessed 28 April 2022).

Skills for Care. 2022. 'The State of the Adult Social Care Sector and Workforce in England'. https://www.skillsforcare.org.uk/adult-social-care-workforce-data/Workforce intelligence/publications/national-information/The-state-of-the-adult-social-care-sector-and-workforce-in-England.aspx (accessed 27 March 2023).

Skinner, Quentin. 2011. *Families and States in Western Europe.* Cambridge: Cambridge University Press.

Small, Mario L. and Calarco, Jessica McCrory. 2022. *Qualitative Literacy: A Guide to Evaluating Ethnographic and Interview Research.* California: University of California Press.

Smith, Andrew and McBride, Jo. 2021. '"Working to Live, Not Living to Work": Low-Paid Multiple Employment and Work-Life Articulation'. *Work, Employment and Society* 35(2): 256–76.

Smith, Paul. 1996. 'Unified Capital and the Subject of Value'. In *Mapping Multi-Culturalism*, edited by Gordon, Avery F., and Newfield, Christopher, 646–62. Minneapolis: University of Minnesota Press.

Smith, Vicky. 2010. 'Enhancing Employability: Human, Cultural, and Social Capital in an Era of Turbulent Unpredictability'. *Human Relations* 63(2): 279–300.

Solow, Robert M. 1991. *The Labour Market as a Social Institution*. Oxford: Blackwell.

SOU. 2009. Betänkande av Kulturutredningen: Grundanalys. Statens Offentliga Utredningar. Stockholm: SOU.

Stacey, Claire Louise. 2011. *The Caring Self: The Work Experiences of Home Care Aides*. New York: Cornell University Press.

Spasova, S., Baeten, R., Coster, S., Ghailani, D., Peña-Casas, R., and Vanhercke, B. 2018. *Challenges in long-term care in Europe. A study of national policies, European Social Policy Network (ESPN)*. Brussels: European Commission.

Standing, Guy. 2011. *The Precariat: The New Dangerous Class*. London: Bloomsbury Academic.

Statistisches Bundesamt. 2018. 'Pflegestatistik 2017: Pflege im Rahmen der Pflegeversicherung Deutschlandergebnisse'. https://www.destatis.de/DE/Themen/Gesellschaft-Umwelt/Gesundheit/Pflege/Publikationen/Downloads-Pflege/pflege-deutschlandergebnisse-5224001179004.pdf?__blob=publicationFile (accessed 28 March 2023).

Statistiska Centralbyrån. 2021. Studenter och examina i högskoleutbildning på grundnivå och avancerad nivå. Stockholm: Statistiska Centralbyrån.

Stephens, Thomas C. 2023. 'The Quality of Work (QoW): Towards a Capability Theory'. *Journal of Human Development and Capabilities* 24(3): 309–35.

Strauss, Anselm and Corbin, Juliet. 1998. *Basics of Qualitative Research: Techniques and Procedures for Developing Grounded Theory*. Thousand Oaks, CA: Sage Publications.

Strauss, Kendra. 2012. 'Coerced, Forced and Unfree Labour: Geographies of Exploitation in Contemporary Labour Markets'. *Geography Compass* 6(3): 137–48.

Streeck, Wolfgang. 2009. *Re-Forming Capitalism: Institutional Change in the German Political Economy*. Oxford: Oxford University Press.

Streeck, Wolfgang. 2016. *How Will Capitalism End? Essays on a Failing System*. London: Verso.Stuart, Mark. 2016. 'Evaluation of the Union Learning Fund, Rounds 15–16, and Support Role of Unionlearn'. Final Report, University of Leeds.

Supiot, Alain. 2001. *Beyond Employment*. Oxford: Oxford University Press.

Sydow, Jörg and Staber, Ugo. 2002. 'The Institutional Embeddedness of Project Networks: The Case of Content Production in German Television'. *Regional Studies* 36: 215–27.

Szebehely, Marta, Strantz, Arnold, and Strandell, Rebeka. 2017. *Who Will Work in Elderly Care in the Future?* Stockholm: Stockholm University Press.

Taylor, Rebecca. 2004. 'Extending Conceptual Boundaries: Work, Voluntary Work and Employment'. *Work, Employment and Society* 18(1): 29–49.

Taylor, Rebecca. 2005. 'Rethinking Voluntary Work'. In *A New Sociology of Work*, edited by Pettinger, Lynne, Parry, Jane, Taylor, Rebecca, and Glucksmann, Miriam, 119–35. Oxford: Blackwell.

Terranova, Tiziana. 2000. 'Free Labor: Producing Culture for the Digital Economy'. *Project Muse* 18(2): 33–58.

Thompson, Neil. 2018. *Social Problems and Social Justice*. London: Bloomsbury.

Thompson, P. and Vincent, S. 2010. 'Labour Process Theory and Critical Realism'. In *Working Life: Renewing Labour Process Analysis*, edited by Thompson, P. and Smith, C. 47–69. London: Palgrave Macmillan.

Tillväxtverket. 2018. Kreametern – analysrapport #1: Den kulturella och kreativa sektorns ekonomiska utveckling 2010–2016. Stockholm: Tillväxtverket.

Tilly, Charles. 1998. *Durable Inequality*. California: University of California Press.

Tilly, Chris and Tilly, Charles. 1994. 'Capitalist Work and Labor Markets'. In: *The Handbook of Economic Sociology*, edited by Neil, Smelser and Richard, Swedberg, 283–312. Princeton, NJ, and New York: Princeton University Press and Russell Sage Foundation Press.

Trappmann, Vera, Umney, Charles, McLachlan, Christopher J., Seehaus, Alexandra, and Cartwright, Laura. 2023. 'How Do Young Workers Perceive Job Insecurity? Legitimising Frames for Precarious Work in England and Germany'. *Work, Employment and Society.* https://doi.org/10.1177/09500170231187.

Tronto, Joan. 1993. *Moral Boundaries. A Political Argument for an Ethic of Care.* New York: Routledge.

Tronto, Joan. 2013. *Caring Democracy: Markets, Equality, and Justice.* New York: New York University Press.

Tyler, Imogen. 2020. *Stigma: The Machinery of Inequality.* London: Zed.

Tyler, Imogen and Slater, Tom. 2018. 'Rethinking the Sociology of Stigma'. *The Sociological Review* 66(4): 721–43.

Umney, C. and Kretsos, L. 2015. '"That's the Experience": Passion, Work Precarity, and Life Transitions among London Jazz Musicians'. *Work and Occupations* 42(3): 313–34.

Ungerson, Claire. 1997. 'Social Politics and the Commodification of Care'. *Social Politics: International Studies in Gender, State & Society* 4(3): 362–81.

Vallas, Steven P. and Cummins, Emily R. 2015. 'Personal Branding and Identity Norms in the Popular Business Press: Enterprise Culture in an Age of Precarity'. *Organization Studies* 36: 293–319.

Van Andel, W. and Loots, E. 2022. 'Measures for the Betterment of the Labor Market Position of Non-standard Working Regimes in the Cultural and Creative Sector in the Netherlands.' *International Journal of Cultural Policy* 28(4): 431–45.

Vaughan-Whitehead, Daniel (ed.) 2016. *Europe's Disappearing Middle Class?* Geneva: International Labour Organization.

Verdi. 2020. 'Care Premium: 1,500 Euros More with the July Salary: Working in Times of Corona'. https://www.verdi.de/themen/corona/++co++e21b0650-780b-11ea-b703-525400b665de (accessed 28 March 2023).

Vidal, Matt. 2022. *Management Divided.* Oxford: Oxford University Press.

Virno, Paolo. 2004. A Grammar of the Multitude. *For an Analysis of Contemporary Forms of Life.* Cambridge, Massachusetts: MIT Press Bookstore.

Vitellone, Nicole. 2002. '"I Think It More of a White Persons Sort of Awareness": Condoms and the Making of a White Nation in Media Representations of Safer (Hetero)Sex'. *Feminist Media Studies* 2(1): 19–36.

Voss E., Schoneberg K., and Rodriguez Contreras, R. 2015. *Collective* Bargaining in Europe in the 21st Century. Dublin: Eurofound.

Wacquant, Loïc. 1991. 'Making Class: The Middle Class(es) in Social Theory and Social Structure'. In *Bringing Class Back In*, edited by McNall Scott, Gray, Levine, Ronda, and Fantasia, Rick, 39–64. Boulder, CO: Westview.

Wade, Robert. 2013. 'How High Inequality Plus Neoliberal Governance Weakens Democracy'. *Challenge* 56(6): 5–37.

Walker, Robert. 2014. *The Shame of Poverty.* Oxford: Oxford University Press.

Warikoo, Natasha K. 2016. *The Diversity Bargain: And Other Dilemmas of Race, Admissions, and Meritocracy at Elite Universities.* Chicago: University of Chicago Press.

Weber, Max. 1922/1964. *Economy and Society: An Outline of Interpretive Sociology.* New York: Bedminster Press.

Weeks, Kathi. 2011. *The Problem with Work. Feminism, Marxism, Antiwork Politics, and Postwork Imaginaries.* Durham, NC: Duke University Press.

Weil, David. 2014. *The Fissured Workplaces.* Cambridge, MA: Harvard University Press.

Weinkopf, Claudia. 2014. 'Women's Employment in Germany. Robust in Crisis but Vulnerable in Job Quality'. Revue de l'OFCE, *Presses de Sciences-Po* 0(2): 189–214.

Wheeler, Kathryn and Glucksmann, Miriam. 2015. *Household Recycling and Consumption Work: Social and Moral Economies*. New York: Springer.

Whiting, Rebecca and Symon, Gillian. 2020. 'Digi-Housekeeping: The Invisible Work of Flexibility Work'. *Work, Employment and Society* 34(6): 1079–96.

Wichterich, Christa. 2019. 'Care Extractivism and Care Struggles in the Reconfiguration of Social Reproduction'. *Urdhva Mula* 11(1): 12–34.

Wilks, Stephen. 1996. 'Regulatory Compliance and Capitalist Diversity in Europe'. *Journal of European Public Policy* 3(4): 536–59.

Williams, Joan C., Blair-Loy, Mary, and Berdahl, Jennifer L. 2013. 'Cultural Schemas, Social Class, and the Flexibility Stigma'. *Journal of Social Issues* 69(2): 209–34.

Witteveen, Dirk. 2018. 'Precarious Early Careers: Instability and Timing within Labor Market Entry'. In *Precarious Work: Causes, Characteristics, and Consequences: Research in the Sociology of Work*, vol. 31, *In*, edited by Kalleberg, Arne L. and Vallas, Steven P., 363–96. Bingley: Emerald.

Wood, Alex. 2020. *Despotism on Demand*. Ithaca, NY: Cornell University Press and ILR Press.

Wood, Alex, Graham, Mark, Lehdonvirta Vili, and Hjorth, Isis. 2019. 'Networked but Commodified: The (Dis) Embeddedness of Digital Labour in the Gig Economy'. *Sociology* 53(5): 931–50.

Woodcock, Jamie and Graham, Mark. 2020. *The Gig Economy: A Critical Introduction*. Cambridge: Polity Press.

Whiting, R., Roby, H., Symon G, et al. 2018. 'Participant-led Video Diaries'. In *Unconventional Methodology in Organization and Management Research*, Bryman, A., and Buchanan, D.A., 190–211. Oxford: Oxford University Press.

Wright, Erik O. 1989. 'Women in the Class Structure'. *Politics and Society* 17(1): 35–66.

Wright, Erik O. 1997. *Class Counts: Comparative Studies in Class Analysis*. Cambridge: Cambridge University Press.

Wulff, Helena. 2014. 'Ballet Culture and the Market: A transnational Perspective.' In Dancing cultures, edited by Kringelbach, N. H. and Skinner, J., 46–59. London: Berghahn Books.

Yeoman, Ruth. 2014. *Meaningful Work and Workplace Democracy: A Philosophy of Work and a Politics of Meaningfulness*. London: Palgrave.

Zimmermann, Bènèdicte. 2022. 'The Five Features of a Capability Enhancing Organization: Bridging Organizational and Workers' Capabilities'. *Management Revue: Socio-Economic Studies* 197–212.

Zimmermann, Bènèdicte. 2024. Transforming Work towards Social-Ecological Sustainability: A Capability Perspective.

Index

For the benefit of digital users, indexed terms that span two pages (e.g., 52–53) may, on occasion, appear on only one of those pages.